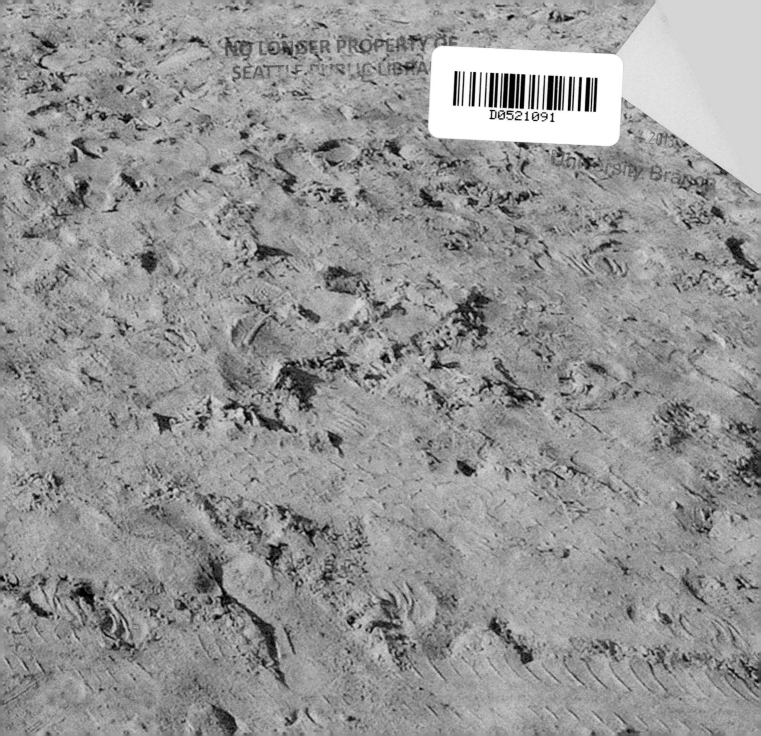

Design

Building Change from the Ground Up

Like You Give a Damn [2]

Design Like You Give a Damn [2]

Building Change from the Ground Up

Abrams, New York

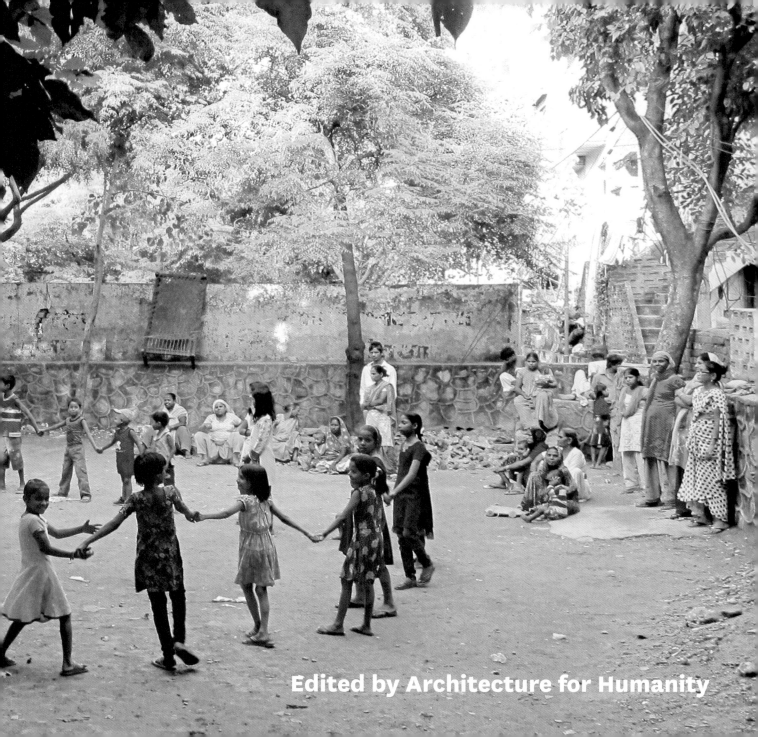

EDITOR: Deborah Aaronson
DESIGNER: Pure+Applied | [pureandapplied.com]
PRODUCTION MANAGER: Jules Thomson

Cataloging-in-Publication Data has been applied for
and may be obtained from the Library of Congress.

ISBN: 978-0-8109-9702-8

Printed and bound in China
10 9 8 7 6 5 4 3 2

Abrams books are available at special discounts
when purchased in quantity for premiums and
promotions as well as fundraising or educational
use. Special editions can also be created to
specification. For details, contact specialsales@
abramsbooks.com or the address below.

THE ART OF BOOKS SINCE 1949
115 West 18th Street
New York, NY 10011
www.abramsbooks.com

PREVIOUS
Children in New Delhi, India,
participate in a game led by Magic
Bus, an organization that will develop
sports infrastructure with Architecture
for Humanity and funding from Nike
Gamechangers to promote physical
fitness, community integration and
welfare for marginalized youth.
Photo: alix ogilvie/Architecture for Humanity

This book is dedicated to our clients:
the passionate, the dogged and determined,
the openhearted and the survivors.

DISASTER RECONSTRUCTION

Architecture for Humanity Design
Fellow Greg Elsner stands with
community members and students of
Mahiga, Kenya, in front of the Mahiga
Hope High School Rainwater Court
(pp. 222–225), which collects rainwater
for the high school. The building was
designed by Dick Clark Architecture
with Architecture for Humanity Design
Fellow Greg Elsner.
Photo: George Abrahams/Nobelity Project

HOUSING

COMMUNITY

GATHERING SPACES

EDUCATION

Community members of San Pedro
Apóstol in Oaxaca, Mexico, help
construct a bamboo shade structure
for the Rural Sports Center designed
by CaeiroCapurso.
Photo: Joao Caeiro/CaeiroCapurso

Introduction
Lessons learned...
Cameron Sinclair

"The land we bought was literally 'the site from hell.' Architecture for Humanity's design fellow managed to design classrooms that we will be able to replicate on any site. I really think it could be the best built school in rural Uganda."

Carol Auld, Kutamba AIDS Orphans School, Bikongozo, Uganda

Architecture for Humanity began with a very simple idea: to provide professional design services to communities in need. Mass global urbanization, coupled with a lack of schools, medical clinics, low-cost housing and blighted public space present a tremendous opportunity for building professionals to not only "give back," but to become active partners in the development process.

Rather than assume we were experts, Co-founder Kate Stohr and I deliberately set small goals and took each project in steps, learning from one to the next. It took us nearly six years to complete a dozen structures. Then, in early 2005, we began to grow faster. As of 2011, when this book was written, more than 2 million people live, learn, heal or work in the 2250 buildings built by our design and construction professionals. Nowadays we are involved in design, development, construction management, construction financing, and implementation of small-scale urban planning projects.

As the organization developed, we learned a lot about what it takes to implement this work and adapted our model as we've grown. In 2012, we plan to build in over 25 countries, tackling issues related to poverty alleviation,

LEFT
The Homeless World Cup Legacy Center in Santa Cruz, Rio de Janeiro, Brazil opened in 2010 as part of the 2010 Homeless World Cup and is now operated by Instituto Bola Pra Frente. It is one of many projects designed and developed by Architecture for Humanity with funding from Nike.
Photo: Daniel Feldman/
Architecture for Humanity

ABOVE
The Nadukupam Vangala Women's Center in Tamil Nadu opened in April 2008 for three women's self-help groups. Today social enterprises are run from these one-room centers.
Photo: Purnima McCutcheon/
Architecture for Humanity

YEARS
that the
office was
open

NUMBER
of people
in the
office

GALLONS
of coffee
consumed
per day

2 | .3

1999–2004
NEW YORK CITY

climate change, conflict resolution and long-term disaster reconstruction efforts in Haiti and Japan. We have had great successes and some failures, but most importantly we learned what it takes to get the job done. What follows is a brief account of the past decade: how things changed and the challenges we faced. While we can't cover every project, we want to thank our army of dedicated building professionals for coming on this journey with us.

Lesson 1:
Unless You Build It, It Doesn't Matter.

Sounds harsh, but it's true. In the eyes of a community, be it recovering from disaster, living in systemic poverty or ravaged by blight and neglect, visions and designs for a project are simply a dream. A well-rendered set of images, an exquisitely built model or a prototype structure is a great start, but it isn't the solution. Communities want results. When you live and work alongside the end user of your structure, they demand it.

The most important thing we learned from the 2004 South East Asia tsunami was the need to work simultaneously on local and virtual levels. This was the birth of the Architecture for Humanity Design Fellowship Program, a "tour of duty" with a small living allowance for professionals to work alongside local architects and engineers.

Our work primarily focused in India and Sri Lanka, and while dozens of designers were involved, the programs were anchored by three talented design professionals: Purnima McCutcheon, Susi Platt and Samir Shah. It began with Samir. On the day of the tsunami he happened to be living in Sri Lanka on a Fulbright scholarship to study the vernacular building of the island.

On December 26, 2004, a powerful magnitude 9.2 earthquake ruptured the seabed, triggering a tsunami that devastated the region. Like many of the architects in our network, Samir contacted me to see if he could get involved. As he had been working alongside a number of Sri Lankan architects and had nine months in country, he was the perfect candidate to spend a few months figuring out how and where we could support the recovery effort.

continued text on page 13

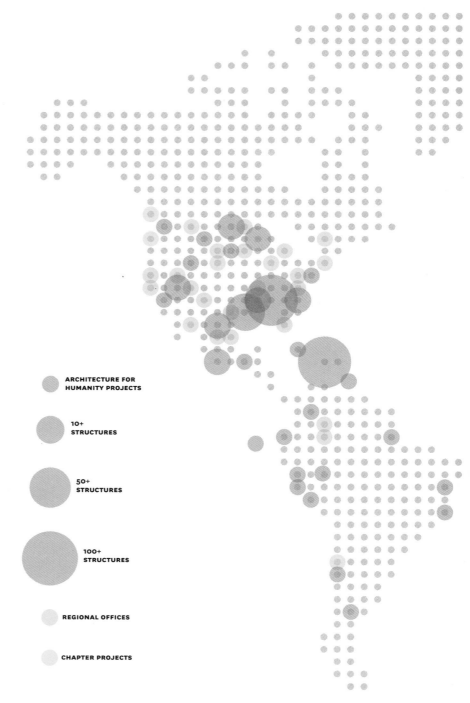

ARCHITECTURE FOR
HUMANITY PROJECTS

10+
STRUCTURES

50+
STRUCTURES

100+
STRUCTURES

REGIONAL OFFICES

CHAPTER PROJECTS

12

A 2011 map of Architecture for Humanity offices and building sites around the world. More than 2 million individuals live, learn, heal or work in structures built or funded by us. In 12 years we have worked in 44 countries and opened four regional offices.
Image: Architecture for Humanity

East Asia Tsunami Reconstruction

LOCATION Ampara, Appirampattu, Hambantota, Sri Lanka; Banda Aceh, Indonesia; Tamil Nadu, India

DATE 2005–07

IMPLEMENTING AGENCY
Architecture for Humanity

PROJECT PARTNERS
League for Education and Development, Relief International, United Nations Human Settlements Programme

CLIENTS Appirampattu Panchayat, Palmyra, PBRC, Pinsara Federation of Community Development Councils, Prajnopaya Foundation

DESIGN TEAMS Jason Andersen, ARUP Associates, Rebecca Celis, Travis Eby, Lauren Farquher, Harvard University Graduate School of Design, Malea Jochim, Kirinda UDA Team, Massachusetts Institute of Technology

DESIGN FELLOWS Purnima McCutcheon, Susi Platt, Samir Shah

FUNDERS American Institute of Architects, Apartments Illustrated Inc., Artech Design Group Inc., Avatech Solutions Inc. The Boston Society of Architects, BPB Ltd., Butler Rogers Baskett Architects, The Caltech Y, Center for Universal Truth, Community Foundation of Greater Chattanooga, Do Something, EDAW Inc., Emerson Waldorf School, The Environments Group, Freshfields Bruckhaus Deringer, Harry Abrams, Inc., HOK Inc., International Interior Design Association, The Ken and Judith Joy Foundations, Kimura–Harrison, Konawaena Middle School, LEF Foundation, Network for Good, Northwood School, Pace Academy, Inc., Parallax, Pei Cobb Freed and Partners, Quaker Service Australia, Smith Group, United States Indonesia Society (USINDO), Wert & Company, Zyscovich Architects, and individual donors

COST $643 044 USD

BUILDINGS CONSTRUCTED 122

NUMBER OF BENEFICIARIES 12 534

BUILDINGS REPLICATED 89

FEATURED PROJECT
Yodakandiya Community Complex

LOCATION Hambantota, Tissamaharama, Uddakandara, Sri Lanka

CLIENT Pinsara Federation of Community Development Councils

PARTNER United Nations Human Settlements Programme

DESIGN AGENCY Architecture for Humanity

DESIGN FELLOW Susi Platt

COST $104 000 USD

BENEFICIARIES 1490

TOP LEFT
A child plays with the decorative steel window treatments in the nursery. The design is based on drawings by children of animals in a nearby preserve.
Photo: Susi Platt/Architecture for Humanity

TOP RIGHT
The library was constructed from local materials and features locally inspired detailing.
Photo: Eresh Weerasuriya/
Aga Kahn Award for Architecture

BOTTOM
Perspective drawing of the Yodakandiya Community Complex.
Image: Susi Platt/Architecture for Humanity

TOP
**The main Community Hall at the
Yodakandiya Community Complex.**
Photo: Eresh Weerasuriya/
Aga Khan Award for Architecture

BOTTOM LEFT
**Hand-carved wooden doors adorn the
entry to the Community Hall.**
Photo: Susi Platt/Architecture for Humanity

BOTTOM RIGHT
**The first game on the new
cricket pitch brought together
local community groups.**
Photo: Susi Platt/
Architecture for Humanity

On the virtual side of things Worldchanging Co-founder Alex Steffen and I spoke about trying to build one small, sustainable project in a huge tragedy—a civic or public building in a community overlooked by traditional non-governmental organizations. Our aim was to raise $10 000 USD in one month. Thirty-six hours after posting a small piece on Worldchanging.com, we surpassed that number and my inbox was filled with hundreds of requests for help and offers of support. By the end of our appeal we would raise over $70 000 USD. Between donations from family foundations, individual checks, local fundraisers and online giving we managed to raise close to $400 000. It was a huge sum to us, though it would have been a tiny amount to an established non-governmental organization.

From the beginning, our philosophy has been to partner with like-minded groups—the scrappy tugboat organizations as opposed to the lumbering oil tankers of development. Our first partner was Relief International, who we had supported in the rebuilding of Bam, Iran the prior year to the tsunami. With our ground team set up in Sri Lanka, we began a series of successful transitional schools on the eastern coast near the seaside village of Pottuvil.

Our Design Fellow Samir also partnered with a group of Sri Lankan architects in the planning of Kirinda, a small fishing community near Yala National Park. As we put our trust in this team, we soon saw the dark side of international assistance. By engaging the community, dealing with shifting government policies and involving important local religious institutions, we set up a strategic planning process for a five-year reconstruction. It wasn't highbrow architecture, but it was solid grassroots development. A few months into the project all our hard work was negated as a private western real estate company bulldozed its way into the village with different ideas for rebuilding. Unbeknownst to their foreign architect, who had been flown in for a weekend, the community rebuilding process was well underway and we were dealing with a bevy of issues including land negotiations, access to water, power and sanitation, and new economic corridors.

The for-profit group decided that to "make a difference" they would build 50 homes right in the center of the new town development and, ideally,

Hurricane Katrina Reconstruction Program

LOCATIONS Biloxi, Jackson, Waveland, Mississippi, USA; New Orleans, Louisiana, USA

DATE 2005–08

CLIENTS 500 individual homeowners, Calhoun McCormick Studio, City of Biloxi, Greater Little Zion Baptist Church Field School, Guardians Institute, Willie Mae's Scotch House

DESIGN AGENCY Architecture for Humanity

PROJECT PARTNERS AIA New Orleans, Enterprise Corporation of the Delta, Gulf Coast Community Design Studio of Mississippi State University School of Architecture, Art + Design, Hands On Gulf Coast, HandsOn New Orleans, Hope Community Development Agency, Heritage Conservation Network, Neighborhood Empowerment Network Association, Preservation Trades Network, Tulane City Center, Warnke Community Consultants

PROGRAM MANAGEMENT Sherry–Lea Bloodworth, Marvin Cabrera, Laura Cole, Joyce Engebresten, John Dwyer, Michael Grote, Kelsey Ochs, Kimberley O'Dowd, Stacy Sabraw

DESIGN FELLOWS Thomas Calhoun, Eric Cesal, Melanie De Cola. Ben Gauslin, Nicole Joslin, Nadene Mairesse, Matt Miller, Brandon Milling, Sola Morrisey, Tracy Nelson, Maureen Ness, Nicole Nowak, Shana Payne, Elish Warlop (hundreds of volunteers)

DESIGN FIRMS Brett Zamore Design, CPD Workshop, Huff & Gooden Architects, Loci Architecture, Marlon Blackwell Architect, MC2 Architects, Rockwell Group, Studio Gang

CONTRACTORS George Boatner, Cox & Carr Construction, Express Constructors, John Holbrook, Herbie Holder, Walter Hopkins, House Calls Construction, Southern Steel Buildings

CONSULTANTS Arup USA, Black Rock Engineering, CSF–PE Service Consulting Engineers, Forensic Engineering Solutions, Paul Hendershot Design, Hudson & Smith, Quality Engineering Services, Reno & Cavanaugh, Tatum Smith Engineering, Williams Engineering

FUNDERS American Red Cross; Autodesk; Blinds.com; Boston Society of Architects; Ceasarstone; Chris Madden Inc.; Daltile; Duo–Gard; IBM; Isle of Capri Casinos; Gulf Coast Community Foundation; JamesHardie; Kohler; LEF Foundation; McCormick Tribune Foundation; MortarNet USA; Myrtle L. Atkinson Foundation; New York Foundation for Architecture; Nourison; Oprah's Angel Network; Polshek Partnership; Senox Corp.; The Planning Center; The Salvation Army; State of Mississippi, University of Arkansas; and many other donors

COST $4.4 million USD (includes $3 million USD revolving loan fund)

BUILDINGS CONSTRUCTED 85

BUILDINGS REHABILITATED 787

NUMBER OF BENEFICIARIES 3137

BUILDINGS REPLICATED 81

TOP
In 2005 severe flooding lasted for days after Hurricane Katrina caused widespread damage to buildings, leading to mold, rot and structural damage.
Photo: Jocelyn Augustino/
Federal Emergency Management Agency

BOTTOM LEFT
After the hurricane, houses were inspected, the markings cataloguing the number of deaths remained for more than a year, in some cases.
Photo: Cameron Sinclair/
Architecture for Humanity

BOTTOM RIGHT
Many people were forced to abandon their homes in New Orleans, Louisiana.
Photo: Cameron Sinclair/
Architecture for Humanity

TOP
Willie Mae's Scotch House, a historic restaurant in New Orleans' Seventh Ward, experienced severe damage. Architecture for Humanity made a $10 000 USD grant to the Heritage Conservation Network to restore the building and provide an economic boost to the neighborhood.
Photo: Jason Perlow/
www.offthebroiler.wordpress.com

BOTTOM LEFT
The restaurant's interior was stripped by volunteers before being renovated.
Photo: Pableaux Johnson/
Architecture for Humanity

BOTTOM RIGHT
Willie Mae's Scotch House reopened in May of 2007 and remains a beloved landmark to many loyal customers.
Photo: Jason Perlow/
www.offthebroiler.wordpress.com

only for one ethnic group. Soon the team was under political pressure. I received a very aggressive call from one of the company's executives telling me our "piss-ant do-gooder organization better clear out, or else." I realized they would build whether we, or the community, liked it or not. There was no compromise and the project collapsed. Our team licked their wounds and simply relocated support north of the town to start work on another project. We learned that doing good and doing the right thing does not always align, and that the world of rebuilding is fraught with vested interests and duplicitous work.

At the time we thought we were missing something, but many years later we found that an independent group had documented this story and published its findings in a book entitled *Tsunami Box*. The book described an effort that excluded the community and left a trail of economic disinvestment which forced families to leave their town. Quite often these stories never make the light of day.

By the end of Samir's tour of duty we had started a number of schools, built 50 homes and received non-governmental organization status in the country. He was followed by Design Fellow Susi Platt. Given our experience in Kirinda, we decided to change our way of working. Rather than commute to project sites while working out of major cities, we felt that to expedite projects, our architects would need to live in the community in which they would work. Not in a nearby hotel, but in a rented room in the heart of the town, spending 24/7 with our clients and becoming part of the community themselves. This physical presence rapidly accelerated our pace, allowing us to take on more ambitious requests.

Perhaps our greatest impact happened in partnership with United Nations Human Settlements Programme (UN-HABITAT) and the village of Yodakandiya, where 218 families had been relocated from the sea to a small inland lake. UN-HABITAT had planned and was building all the homes, but there was no central gathering space, school or medical clinic. Susi and I met with community leaders in their tiny one-room tin roof center. We worked hand-in-hand with the community to design and develop a complex that included central community space, medical clinic,

FAR LEFT
Audrey Robinson and her son Andre celebrate being chosen to participate in the Biloxi Model Home Program, 2006.
Photo: Sherry-Lea Bloodworth/ Architecture for Humanity

LEFT
Karen Parker at the dedication of her home, designed by Brett Zamore Design, in East Biloxi, Mississippi, 2008.
Photo: Sun Herald

ABOVE
The Biloxi Model Home Fair gave families a chance to learn about 12 home designs and talk to the architects before selecting a design team.
Photo: Tracy Nelson/ Architecture for Humanity

OPPOSITE TOP
The Tyler Residence in East Biloxi, Mississippi uses metal siding and operable shutters to improve its resilience.
Photo: Marlon Blackwell Architect

OPPOSITE BOTTOM
The Tran Home by MC2 Architects includes a wraparound porch.
Photo: Leslie Schwartz/ Architecture for Humanity

For more information on the Biloxi Model Home Program, including full project details, see page 108.

library, computer room, organic gardens, kindergarten and cricket pitch. All on a budget of less than $100 000 USD.

Susi lived and breathed this facility, pouring a year of her life into building the complex. During the process she worked alongside local engineers and contractors, brought construction training into the community, hired dozens of villagers, involved local elephant migration experts, helped start small businesses, empowered the local community federation and integrated rainwater catchment systems and new building methodologies. In a bold move, she brought together nearby Sinhalese, Tamil and Muslim villagers, combatants in the country's recent civil war, to play cricket on the newly built field. She got quite a colorful nickname by the community after kicking down a newly constructed wall that was poorly built by one of the sub-contractors. To the outside world, she was building a few structures, but for the village, she was building its heart. The complex, funded in part from hot chocolate sales by high school students, would go on to be the only tsunami project shortlisted for the prestigious 2010 Aga Khan Award for Architecture. Seven years later, it is still active and used for anything from after-school programs to weddings.

Not all our projects worked, we also failed in unexpected ways. For Susi and I, our biggest regret was the Pottuvil Women's' Cooperative Bakery. After building transitional schools in the area, we were approached by a number of mothers who had lost their husbands. Widowed, and with children to raise, they were selling "shorties" (afternoon snacks) as a means of income. As we held weekly meetings under a mango tree, the idea blossomed of creating a baking cooperative and allowing the women to start a business to stabilize their incomes.

While Susi worked on a design she organized site visits to other bakeries, began sourcing equipment and found a small storefront to set up. This took months of planning and development. Then something strange happened. A couple of the women received threats and were warned against starting this business. First the threats were insinuated, then as the project progressed, they became very pointed. Within weeks the entire project collapsed. The women lost confidence, and, to our shock, our local partners walked away.

What we came to find out was that we ignored the obvious. The other bakeries in town were run by one person. Despite the need to create jobs, this was encroaching on his turf. This project was the anomaly in our work. While the thanks of hundreds of beneficiaries fades in your memory, you never ever forget the disappointment of a failed project.

5 | 2.5

2005-06
BOZEMAN

We also did work in India with Design Fellow Purnima McCutcheon. After completing a number of community centers with the League of Education and Development and the Pitchandikulam Bio Resource Center, an off-grid, solar-powered, eco-training center, we began building a series of weaving cooperatives. These small one-room structures were built from stabilized soil block and cost between $3000 and $6000 USD each. They were built to house small women-owned businesses. At one facility the members of a women's group noted the lily pads that adorned a nearby lake. The designers positioned the women's center to overlook the lake and integrated the flowers into metal windows. Thoughtful design details won't transform a community, but they do bring joy. Visiting several years later, it was immensely satisfying to see women teaching each other to read in one of our buildings, the only formal structure in sight.

During this period Kate and I relocated to Bozeman, Montana as I was teaching at a university there. In our office above the Cateye Cafe, we had assembled half a dozen volunteers to help with fundraising, program management and drawing up projects. Since it was difficult to turn around drawings on the ground we in-sourced the CAD work to Montana, letting the teams on-site focus on community engagement and development.

In total, in response to the 2005 South Asia tsunami, we built eight transitional schools, two kindergartens, four community centers, six women's cooperatives, 50 homes and an inspiring community complex that became the heart of a new village. We advised on housing and a teacher-training center in Banda Aceh, Indonesia, and gave seed funding to a couple of small projects in the region. We learned that a grassroots approach to design and construction, working directly with the beneficiaries and hiring them to be a part of the process, created social cohesion and incredible trust between all the stakeholders.

As architects we are given an incredible opportunity to work in partnership with clients to transform a family, a community and sometimes a city. Given this opportunity, it is then our responsibility to work as hard as possible to see the concept through. The best way to do that is to be present. By working on the ground, design fellows can develop and refine construction documents, create real-time budgets and timelines, garner necessary approvals, help select contractors, oversee the construction process, garner a certificate of occupation and make sure all the stakeholders have been actively involved.

In July of 2005 I was in Arugam Bay, Sri Lanka to review our programs. I woke at 5 am and walked along the shoreline where I met a man sitting by the water's edge. I sat down beside him and, in broken English, he described losing 17 family members, six months of endless paperwork, land issues and burials. He was sure his daughter was the only one left—until his mother-in-law showed up. He looked at me with a straight face and exclaimed, "I didn't like her before the tsunami and now I have to live with her!" We laughed. We sat together sketching out a "granny flat" in the sand. A simple house with a separate structure for an extended family member. Dawn broke. He gave me a long hug and went on his way. It was a poignant reminder that despite tragedy we are all dealing with the same basic issues, whether it's finding a way to live with your mother-in-law or starting your own business with your friends. Design is a tool that helps us do more than just survive, it helps us live.

Lesson 2:
Innovation Is Only Valuable If It Is Shared.
By late 2005 we had become a ragtag global network of pragmatic architects, designers and builders. With a number of projects finished, one of the biggest headaches we had to manage was multiple projects on multiple sites, with various stakeholders and differing reporting requirements. Administrative work was run out of our headquarters, and it quickly became a logistical nightmare. On a weekly basis we would get burlap sacks stuffed with drawings, poorly faxed contracts and hundreds of construction photos emailed to us. A team would work for weeks to come up with a solution that had already been designed in a prior disaster. To make matters worse, we were

continued on page 25

Football for Hope Program

CURRENT LOCATIONS 20 locations in Africa

DATE 2008–present

PROJECT SPONSOR FIFA

IMPLEMENTING AGENCY streetfootballworld

DESIGN AGENCY Architecture for Humanity

COMMUNITY PARTNERS Association des Jeunes Sportifs de Kigali Espérance, Association Malienne pour la Promotion de la Jeune Fille et de la Femme, Delta Cultura Cabo Verde, Grassroot Soccer, Grupo Desportivo de Manica, Iringa Development for Youth, Disabled and Children Care, Kick 4 Life, LoveLife, Mathare Youth Sports Association, Play Soccer, South African Red Cross, South East District Youth Empowerment League, Special Olympics Namibia, United Action for Children, Whizzkids United

DESIGN FIRMS ARG Design, Architectural Engineering Services, Bartsch Architects, Bureau d'Etudes Quarc, Constructs LLC, DCAD, John Edgar, Emerging Services, Jose Forgaz, Andrew Gremley, Lakes Consortium, Nina Maritz, MMA Architects, M. Youseff Berthe, Pharos Architects, Phinduze Architects, Studio 610, Wasserfall Munting Architects

PROGRAM MANAGEMENT Marvin Cabrera, Eugene da Silva, Joyce Engebretsen, Kevin Gannon, Satu Jackson, Gretchen Mokry, Kelsey Ochs, Kimberley O'Dowd, Kate Stohr, Jonathan Thompson, Gaurav Vashist

DESIGN FELLOWS Jhono Bennett, Thomas Calhoun, Alma Rosalio Ruiz Delgado, Killian Doherty, Ifeoma Ebo, Elisa Engel, Paulo Fernandez, Michael Heublein, Alina Jeronimo, Nathan Jones, George Kinuthia, Christine Lara, Delphine Luboz, Thembe Mekwa, Luvuyo Mfungula, Unathi Mkonto, Isaac Mugumbule, David Pound, Ana Reis, Oana Stanescu, Axel Stelter, Mark Warren

ENGINEERING Baeletsi ty Ltd., BerteCo, Eyethu Engineers, Mike Gumbi, Henry Fagan and Partners, Richard Ngenahayo, Peter Wanjau, ZMCK Consulting Engineers

CONTRACTORS Alpages, Drucon Building and Roofing, EFS Construction, E-Marks Construction, Enterprise Bengaly, Gravity Contractors, Lesotho Steel, Samwilco Construction

CONSULTANTS
AECOM, AKT Consultants, Sierra Banbridge, Barker & Barton, Ben Behm, Kobus Carstens, Francis Hillman, Moutanbou Michael Fru, Green Architecture Ltd., Gumbi & Associates, JSmart, Lesotho Quantity Surveyors, Mapsurveys (K) Ltd, Froudouard Ngayaboshya, Richard Ngendahayo, Dr. Alfred Omenya, Gerd Scheuerpflug, Bamba Souleyman, SVP Quantity Surveyors, Technisol

IN-KIND AMOD China, GreenFields, Mosaic Works, Yingli Solar

COST ESTIMATORS
Barker & Barton Kenya, Davis Langdon, LDM, Lesotho Quantity Surveyors

PROJECT TYPE
A community center and a youth football pitch

AREA 170–300 sq m/1830–3229 sq ft

CONSTRUCTION COST PER CENTER
$115 000–$266 000 USD

CONSTRUCTION PROGRAM

COST $1.3 million USD (as of Dec. 2011)

NUMBER OF BENEFICIARIES 38 192

TOP
The opening of the first Football for Hope Centre in Khayelitsha, in 2009. The center was designed by ARG Design, with Design Fellows Oana Stanescu and Christine Lara.
Photo: Kate Stohr/Architecture for Humanity

BOTTOM
Children meet Lucas Radebe, former captain of Bafana Bafana, the South African national football team, at the Khayelitsha Football for Hope Centre.
Photo: Kate Stohr/Architecture for Humanity

LEFT
**A map showing the 16
completed or in-construction
Football for Hope Centres
in Africa.**
Image: Architecture for Humanity

LOCATION Khayelitsha, South Africa
PARTNER Grassroot Soccer
PHASE Opened December 2009
Photo: Kimberley O'Dowd/
Architecture for Humanity

LOCATION Baguineda, Mali
PARTNER Association Malienne
pour la Promotion de la
Jeune Fille et de la Femme
PHASE Opened October 2010
Photo: Mike Heublein/
Architecture for Humanity

LOCATION Katutura, Namibia
PARTNER Special Olympics Namibia
PHASE Opened September 2010
Photo: Marcus Weiss/Studio One Photography

LOCATION Mathare, Kenya
PARTNER Mathare Youth
Sports Association
PHASE Opened October 2010
Photo: Patricia Menadier/
Architecture for Humanity

LOCATION Maseru, Lesotho
PARTNER Kick4Life
PHASE Opened May 2011
Photo: Kick4Life

LOCATION Kimisagara, Rwanda
PARTNER Association des Jeunes
Sportifs de Kigali Espérance
PHASE Opened December 2011
Photo: Killian Doherty/
Architecture for Humanity

LOCATION Oguaa, Ghana
PARTNER PLAY SOCCER Ghana
PHASE Opened December 2011
Photo: David Pound/
Architecture for Humanity

LOCATION QwaQwa, South Africa
PARTNER LoveLife
PHASE In tender
Image: George Kinuthia/
Architecture for Humanity

LOCATION Edendale Hospital,
South Africa
PARTNER Whizzkids United
PHASE In tender
Image: Luvuyo Mfungula/
Architecture for Humanity

LOCATION Alexandra,
Johannesburg, South Africa
PARTNER Grassroots Soccer
PHASE In development
Image: Unathi Mkonto/
Architecture for Humanity

TOP
A soccer match at the Katatura Football for Hope Centre in Namibia, which was built in memory of Eunice Kennedy Shriver, founder of the Special Olympics. The architects of record were Nina Maritz and Wasserfall Munting Architects, assisted by Architecture for Humanity Design Fellows Jhono Bennet and Thomas Calhoun.
Photo: Marcus Weiss/Studio One Photography

BOTTOM LEFT AND BOTTOM RIGHT
The Oguaa Football for Hope Centre in Cape Coast, Ghana, was built in 2011. It is run by the nonprofit PLAY SOCCER Ghana, an organization promoting health and leadership through sports. The center was designed by Joe Addo of Constructs LLC, and Architecture for Humanity Design Fellow David Pound oversaw construction.
Photo: David Pound/ Architecture for Humanity

doubling in staff every six months and had begun responding to the 2005 Kashmir Earthquake and Hurricane Katrina, as well as running a construction program in South Africa. Growth was creating unwanted bureaucracy. Trying to stay on top of versioning issues and program management was more than a full-time job. Then one day it all changed.

I was returning to Montana from Sri Lanka and on the drive back to Colombo I turned on my mobile phone, which had gone off a number of times. We were driving through Ratnapura when it rang yet again. I picked up the phone to hear a very polite English voice. "Hi, this is Chris Anderson. I'm calling because you've won the TED prize." My first response was "Who's Ted?" Chris corrected me. "The conference. The TED Conference. We are doing an event in a few weeks in New York, please come out and meet the other winners. We will be in touch about your wish."

The TED prize confers a unique opportunity. Prize winners are granted one wish to change the world. The TED community helps make it happen. By the time we got back home I knew what to wish for: to create an open-source, collaborative project management website that would empower building professionals with design solutions to improve life.

On return to our office, Kate and I spent the next few months developing our idea for the Open Architecture Network. Coming from an online background, Kate was an incredible asset. We had first met when she worked at Pathfinder, Time Inc.'s first venture into the Internet, where she was a Web producer. In the following months we assembled a team of practitioners, tech professionals and community organizations.

Similar to our methodology of working with communities, we listened and learned about the needs of other groups, the things that mattered and the roadblocks faced in building in remote, austere environments.

Fascinated by the free culture movement being developed by Lawrence Lessig and Creative Commons (CC), we wondered if you could put a Creative Commons license on a building. So we did. This allowed architects to retain their intellectual assets and decide who could use their design. This meant that you could do a pro bono home design for a family displaced by Hurricane Katrina and, with a CC license, share that design with other nonprofits for free. At the same time, if a commercial company wanted to replicate the design, the designer could get paid a fee for each structure built. This would be the key to encouraging professionals, who would otherwise not share their intellectual property, to participate on the website.

We knew our TED wish was going to be incredibly complex and nerdy. Chances were it would be received with a thud. Our best decision was to create a wish that enhanced our mission and made it easier to do the work we were already doing rather than starting something new. It was vital for the survival and growth of Architecture for Humanity.

At the 2006 TED conference in Monterey, California, I presented our vision for an Open Architecture Network. Like a great party, you soon find that the folks who become your strongest allies are the same ones who end up in the kitchen long after the music has stopped. Almost all the support offered came from the San Francisco Bay Area, and thanks to an office space donation from Dr. Dean Ornish, we relocated to Sausalito, California. Hot Studio, Sun Microsystems, Cisco, Autodesk, Amazon, Creative Commons, and others, donated services and support to develop and refine the system.

continued text on page 31

BELOW
Architect Peter Rich gives a lecture at the Kimisagara Football for Hope Centre, in Rwanda. The center is run by Association des Jeunes Sportifs de Kigali Espérance, an organization working to bridge ethnic divides in Rwanda. Architecture for Humanity Design Fellow Killian Doherty designed the building and oversaw its construction. The center hosts events at night.
Photo: Killian Doherty/ Architecture for Humanity

7 · 4
2006–07
SAUSALITO

ARCHITECTURE FOR HUMANITY

Through a global network of building professionals, Architecture for Humanity brings design, construction and development services to communities in need.

WE ARE A GROWING GRASSROOTS MOVEMENT

Together we help solve local issues through design

21 Counties
62 Chapters
208 Chapter Members
40 000 Professional Network

1 Communities send us their requests
[school, clinic, soccer field, library]

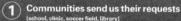

2 We evaluate each request to make sure the project meets our mission and the partnership is a good fit

3 We work with the community to design the structure THEY need and want

4 Sometimes, we even ship our design fellows to the work site

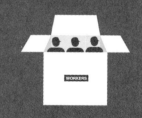

5 And work with local builders

To evaluate the grounds
Assess risk management
Employ green practices
And lots of other complicated stuff

6 A community gets a new resource

I love my new school!

What Do We Care About?

Povery Alleviation
Post-conflict Community Building
Design for At-risk Populations
Disaster Mitigation and Reconstruction
Addressing Climate Change

What Kinds of Things Do We Build?

Shelters in Disaster Areas
Neutral Spaces for Dialogue in Conflict Zones
Accessibility Modifications for Those with Disabilities
Environmenatlly Friendly Buildings

What Else Do We Do?

Design Competitions
Publications
Exhibitions
Conferences
Workshops

Designed By **elefint designs** elefintdesigns.com

There is no such thing as a typical architect. However, over the years we have noticed a few recurring patterns in our designers.

They embody one or more of the following traits:

1. THE GLOBAL NOMAD
A wandering free spirit who connects deeply on a local level. They tend to be highly sensitive to needs of the building end user, the community as a whole, and the impact of the project on a regional level. Most likely to be found relaxing at Burning Man or living in a treehouse on an island in the Pacific.

2. THE LONE WOLF EMBED
Works solo. Fights for the client and doesn't leave until it is done. Occasionally goes AWOL.

3. THE ZEN DESIGNER
Nothing fazes them, cool exterior and a design purist. Every joint, detail and material selection has been thought through. They don't say much but when they do, it changes everything.

4. THE GRASSROOTS LEADER
A humble galvanizing force. Empowers the community to take ownership of every stage of the project. Makes sure the building is a catalyst to job creation on a local level. A selfless mentor to students and work colleagues.

5. THE COMMITTED DIASPORA
When working in a particular country, we receive a huge amount of résumés from its diaspora. Someone with cultural understanding and deep ties to the area is an incredible asset to the team.

6. THE APPROPRIATE TECHNOLOGY GURU
A designer with very specific expertise. From bamboo, to adobe construction, to understanding the impact of different types of sanitation systems. Most likely to be found in a bar talking about composting toilets.

7. THE PHD MACGYVER
Exceptionally sharp, has incredible street smarts and able to find solutions in the most unlikely places. Hand them a pack of chewing gum, 10 feet of steel wire, recycled cocoa sacks and some pliers. In 24 hours, you'll have a operational medical clinic.

OPPOSITE
A graphic description of how Architecture for Humanity works, donated by Elefint Designs.
Image: Elefint Designs

ABOVE
Design Fellows Mike Hueblein (L) and Isaac Mugumbule (R) share a laugh at the Cape Town, South Africa office of project partner streetfootballworld, in 2010.
Photo: Kimberley O'Dowd/
Architecture for Humanity

GameChangers Grant Program

PROGRAM NAME GameChangers

LOCATION Capao Redondo, Sao Paulo, Brazil; Ganhaizi, China; Guatemala City, Guatemala; Jharkhand, India; Kabul, Afghanistan; Mahiga, Kenya; Moreno, Buenos Aires, Argentina; New Delhi, India; New Orleans, USA; New York City, USA; San Pedro Apóstol, Oaxaca, Mexico; Santa Cruz, Rio de Janeiro, Brazil; Sao Paulo, Brazil

DATE 2009–12

PROGRAM SPONSOR
Nike, Inc., Nike Sustainable Business and Innovation

DESIGN AGENCY Architecture for Humanity

PROJECT PARTNERS
Associação de Moradores da Cohab Adventista 1, Ayuntamiento Municipal Constitucional de San Pedro Apostól, Bola Pra Frente, Corredores do Parque Santo Dias, Futbol para el Desarrollo (FUDE), George Washington Carver High School, Guatemala City, Habitat for Humanity China, Homeless World Cup, Liga FOS, Magic Bus, Municipio de San Pedro Apóstol, The Nobelity Project, NYC Department of Parks and Recreation, Organização Civil de Ação Social, Steve Rodriguez, St. Joseph Mahiga Hope Schools, Skateistan, Yuwa India

DESIGN FIRMS blaanc borderless architecture, Buró de Intervenciones Públicas, CaeiroCapurso, Casa Tierra, Convic Designs, Es como vivir afuera, Eskes Consultoria, Fábrica de Projetos, GRUBA arquitectura y diseño, Holm Architecture Office, Lompreta Nolte Arquitetos, Multiplex Systems, Steve Rodriguez, Juan Jose Santibañez, SITE Design Group, Urban Recycle Architecture Studio, VM Design Studio

PROGRAM MANAGEMENT
Marvin Cabrera, Joyce Engebretsen, Michael Jones, Gretchen Mokry, Kelsey Ochs, alix ogilvie, Cameron Sinclair, Elaine Uang

DESIGN FELLOWS Andrew Burdick, Greg Elsner, Daniel Feldman, Gabriel Kaprielian, Keshav Kumar, Carla dal Mas, alix ogilvie, Preeti Sodhi

CONTRACTORS Boslika Building Contractors, California Skateparks, Jermo Engenheria, GreenFields, and many other building consultants

PROGRAM COST $2.1 million USD

NUMBER OF GRANTS 12

GRANT AMOUNT $5000–$300 000 USD

NUMBER OF BENEFICIARIES 7786

TOP
A concept rendering of the Homeless World Cup Legacy Center in Santa Cruz, Rio de Janeiro, Brazil, designed by Lompreta Nolte Arquitetos and Nanda Eskes Arquitetura.
Image: Daniel Feldman/
Architecture for Humanity

BOTTOM
Since the 2010 opening of the Homeless World Cup, the local nonprofit Bola Pra Frente runs the center. Architecture for Humanity Design Fellow Daniel Feldman oversaw construction.
Photo: Daniel Feldman/
Architecture for Humanity

Skateistan
LOCATION Kabul, Afghanistan
PARTNER Skateistan
PHASE Opened October 2009
Photo: Jacob Simkin/Skateistan

Mahiga Rainwater Court
LOCATION Mahiga, Kenya
PARTNER St. Joseph Mahiga Primary and Secondary School
PHASE Opened October 2010
Image: Michael Jones/
Architecture for Humanity

ABOVE
A map of GameChangers sites around the world.
Image: Architecture for Humanity

My Game Is Beautiful
LOCATION Ruka Village, Jharkhaud, India
PARTNER Yuwa India
PHASE In construction
Image: Greg Elsner, Michael Jones/
Architecture for Humanity

Creation of Sports Infrastructure
LOCATION New Delhi, India
PARTNER Magic Bus
PHASE In design
Photo: alix ogilvie/
Architecture for Humanity

Ooya Green Sports Park
LOCATION Kesennuma, Japan
PARTNER Ooya Junior High School
PHASE In construction
Image: Tomoro Aida/Aida Atelier

Una Cancha Muchas Canchas
LOCATION
Guatemala City, Guatemala
PARTNER
Buro de Intervenciones Publicas
PHASE Opened in October 2011
Image: Buró de Intervenciones Públicas

Manhattan Bridge Skatepark
LOCATION New York City, USA
PARTNER Steve Rodriguez
PHASE In design
Photo: Preeti Sodhi/
Architecture for Humanity

Community Center for Youth and Sports
LOCATION Moreno, Argentina
PARTNER Liga FOS
PHASE In design
Image: Urban Recycle Architecture Studio

Rural Sports Center
LOCATION
San Pedro Apóstol, Mexico
PARTNER Ayuntamiento Municipal Constitucional de San Pedro Apóstol
PHASE In construction
Photo: Joao Caeiro/CaeiroCapurso

Games in Lost Heavens
LOCATION Gan Hai Zi Village, China
PARTNER Habitat for Humanity
PHASE In construction
Photo: Stef Chu/Habitat for Humanity

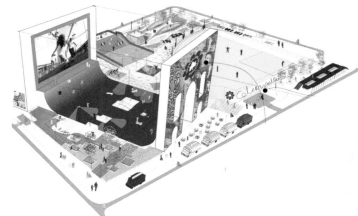

ABOVE LEFT
Project partner and New York City skate legend Steve Rodriguez, bottom right, talks to local kids about redoing the Manhattan Bridge Skatepark in New York City.
Photo: Preeti Sodhi/Architecture for Humanity

ABOVE RIGHT
A conceptual rendering of the Manhattan Bridge Skatepark's renovation imagines the park as a vibrant public space used by many different neighborhood groups.
Image: Jens Holm/Holm Architecture Office

BELOW
The San Pedro Apóstol Rural Sports Center will be built using various forms of adobe construction, such as mud bricks and rammed earth. Local villagers will learn the techniques by helping to build the Center.
Image: Maarten de Cock/CaeiroCapurso

FAR LEFT
Workers constructing the rammed earth walls of the Sports Center in October of 2011.
Photo: Joao Caeiro/CaeiroCapurso

LEFT
The first portion of the Rural Sports Center, a bamboo shade structure for meetings and lessons, was completed in October 2011.
Photo: Joao Caeiro/CaeiroCapurso

ABOVE LEFT
Barrio La Limonada, in the center of Guatemala City, is home to the Una Cancha Muchas Cancha street pitch. The building density of the informal settlement made it difficult to identify a site for a new sports facility.
Photo: Buró de Intervenciones Públicas

ABOVE RIGHT
The project Una Cancha Muchas Cancha converts low-traffic streets into futsala, or impromptu football pitches through painted roads, movable goal post, traffic signs and speed bumps.
Image: Buró de Intervenciones Públicas, GeoEye

ABOVE
A finished futsala street pitch, the first of two, opened in October 2011.
Photo: Buró de Intervenciones Públicas

It turned out that Architecture for Humanity was the perfect guinea pig. We learned that remote design fellows had a hard time uploading files, teams needed to see CAD files online, we needed levels of privacy for projects in development, and early Web 2.0 technologies were buggy and fraught with continual updates.

We also wanted to address the needs of other aid and development groups. Like many industries, non-governmental organizations had become very specialized. One group would provide school construction, another, safe sanitation, and a third, access to water. The community is left to negotiate coordination between donor groups or, as is often the case, duplicitous work is created and therefore a waste of donor funds.

We needed to think about how multiple groups, partners or organizations could have a central node to share information and distribute updates to the numerous coordination entities that have sprung up to tackle this problem. We added in geodata for mapping projects and finding "response" deserts, places where no projects are taking place.

Additionally, securing funding proved incredibly hard. Foundations were interested in bricks and mortar over management and efficiency. We persevered, and with a motley crew of coders and developers were able to tweak the system to work.

In 2012, more than 7000 projects are shared by some 35 000 members on the network. We have hosted over a dozen international design competitions, created request for bid systems, built a mobile app, and even used the system to write this book. In 2011, we acquired Worldchanging. We are now merging the two sites under the Worldchanging brand and are working to expand the scope of the site beyond just buildings and to build a more robust system of

28 | 10
2008–present
SAN FRANCISCO

Classroom Upgrade Competition: 2009–2010

LOCATION 342 entries from 65 different countries

DATES 2009–present

END USERS Students and teachers around the world

BENEFICIARIES 6857

CHALLENGE LEAD Architecture for Humanity

CHALLENGE PARTNER Orient Global

CHALLENGE SPONSORS 50x15, Bezos Family Foundation, Google SketchUp, Graham Foundation for Advanced Studies in the Fine Arts, Irvin Stern Family Foundation, National Endowment for the Arts

EDUCATION PARTNERS Curriki, Global Nomads Group

SCHOOL BUILDING PARTNERS Blazer Industries, Building Tomorrow, Modular Building Institute, Rumi Schools of Excellence

CHALLENGE PARTNERS The Aspen Institute, Autodesk, The Collaborative for High Performance Schools, Council of Educational Facility Planners International, DoSomething.org, Dwell, Ethos, Global Green USA, Indian Architect and Builder, Nova Scotia College of Art and Design Design Lab, U.S. Green Building Council, The Third Teacher, SMART Technologies

TOP
A proposal for the Corporacion Educativa y Social Waldorf in Bogota, Colombia.
Photo: Wolfgang Timmer, Fabiola Uribe, T. Luke Young/Arquitectura Justa

BOTTOM
A Google map of the competitions sites. Out of the competition came many projects and partnerships.
Image: Architecture for Humanity/Google Maps

project tracking, monitoring and evaluation. Expect big changes ahead.

Lesson 3:
Be the Last Responders.

In late 2005 Architecture for Humanity would be faced with its biggest challenge to date, a domestic disaster of biblical proportions. On August 29, Hurricane Katrina moved off the Gulf of Mexico and slammed into the coastal shoreline of Louisiana and Mississippi. Before we could decide whether to respond, hundreds of individuals began donating, dozens of local architects reached out either for help or to offer help. We began to mobilize. Learning from prior disasters we were very specific about our role, focusing on long-term reconstruction.

Architects working in post-disaster reconstruction are not needed just in the first four weeks, but for the following three to five years. We are the last responders. Hurricane Katrina was no different. Everyone rushed in. We also saw the results of the Anderson Cooper effect. Wherever the news media reported was where relief organizations would help. If primetime TV cameras didn't show up in your community, chances are you were not going to get assistance anytime soon. So we decided to go where no one was going. At the time, we were experimenting with various models of construction management —embedding building professionals with our design fellowship program; giving grants to local architects; creating rebuilding manuals to promote safe building; supporting long-term design studios in the heart of impacted communities. The latter would turn out to be the most effective in our arsenal for empowering communities to rebuild.

This was not a new concept. The 1960s and 1970s saw the birth of community design centers across the United States. However, they were located in blighted communities, and we aimed to create a center that would serve a disaster zone for four or five years during the height of reconstruction. Think of these rebuilding centers as temporary operating theaters where professionals with a range of skills are in the trenches, supporting the local industry, to repair the urban fabric.

TOP
Architecture for Humanity managed the reconstruction of Ceverine School for Save the Children. The school, located outside Maissade, Haiti, opened in March 2011.
Photo: Tommy Stewart/
Architecture for Humanity

BOTTOM LEFT
The Bottle School, in Laguna, Philippines, modified a design from the Open Architecture Network.
Photo: Kristel Gonzalez/My Shelter Project

MIDDLE RIGHT AND BOTTOM RIGHT
Recycled bottles were used as infill and provide natural light.
Photos: Illac Diaz/My Shelter Project

FEATURED PROJECTS
Maria Auxiliadora School
LOCATION Calderones, Ica, Peru
DATES 2010–11
PROGRAM SPONSOR Happy Hearts Fund
and ING School Reconstruction Program
DESIGN AGENCY Architecture for Humanity
PROJECT COORDINATOR
Ofelia Harten (ING)
DESIGN TEAM Diego Collazos
(Architecture for Humanity);
Arturo Novelli
(Edificaciones America)
AREA 500 sq m/5382 sq ft
COST $112 000 USD
BENEFICIARIES
78 primary school students

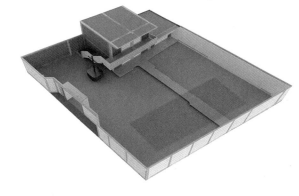

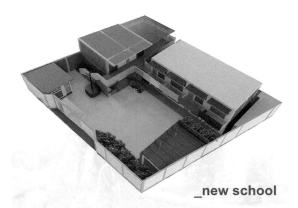

_new school

TOP
The completed Maria Auxiliadora School in Calderones, Ica, Peru consists of a renovated older building and a newly built classroom block.
Photo: Diego Collazos/
Architecture for Humanity

BOTTOM
Before (TOP) and after (BOTTOM) renderings of the proposed addition for the Maria Auxiliadora School.
Image: Diego Collazos/
Architecture for Humanity

FEATURED PROJECT
Francisco Perez Anampa School
LOCATION Tate, Ica, Peru
DATE 2010–11
PROGRAM SPONSOR Happy Hearts Fund and ING
School Reconstruction Program
DESIGN AGENCY Architecture for Humanity
PROJECT COORDINATOR Ofelia Harten (ING)
DESIGN TEAM Diego Collazos
(Architecture for Humanity);
Arturo Novelli (Edificaciones America)
AREA 557 sq m/5995 sq ft
COST $193 000 USD
BENEFICIARIES 160 primary school students

TOP
**The Francisco Perez Anampa School
was damaged in the 2007
Ica, Peru earthquake.**
Photo: Diego Collazos/
Architecture for Humanity

MIDDLE
**Children play in the new schoolyard
of the Francisco Perez Anampa School,
completed in 2011.**
Photo: Diego Collazos/
Architecture for Humanity

BOTTOM
A parent helps rebuild the school.
Photo: Diego Collazos/
Architecture for Humanity

We couldn't do it alone and we partnered with a local councilman, Bill Stallworth, who had started the East Biloxi Rebuilding Center (today the Hope Community Development Agency) in a local church. Inside this center, we funded and partnered with what would become the Gulf Coast Community Design Studio run by David Perkes and Mississippi State University. The design studio allowed for a wide range of services to be available to a broader constituency at a fixed cost. It supported micro-planning and volunteer participation in construction. Together with the Hope coordination center and its partners, we rebuilt more than 35 percent of East Biloxi in the three years after the storm.

Architecture for Humanity's anchor project was the Biloxi Model Home Program. A series of seven homes designed by regional architects selected by the families that would live in each. The program explored new construction methods that improve structural integrity, sustainability, and cost-efficiency, while working with homeowners to determine what is and isn't affordable. We created a revolving loan fund to support the model homes and home repairs. The solutions devised through this process have directly influenced the design and construction of other new homes in the region and the work of the Gulf Coast Community Design Studio. From adopting driven wood piles as a standard foundation system to leveraging innovative financing instruments.

In the aftermath of Hurricane Katrina, government agencies, private non-governmental organizations and funders struggled to distribute funds to families in need. The primary obstacle was the lack of a local fiduciary agent. It took more than nine months to develop a forgivable loan program to jumpstart construction in East Biloxi. The revolving loan fund, developed by Architecture for Humanity with Warnke Community Consultants, recaptured between 20 and 90 percent of the cost of constructing new homes, freeing funding to assist more families and seeding a long-term economic development agency that we hope will serve East Biloxi for years to come. More telling still, the model of pairing community members with professional designers—and the strategy of locating a community design studio within a housing recovery center—was replicated across

Post-Conflict Reconstruction

PROJECT NAME
Gaza Alternative Repair Strategies
LOCATION Gaza, Palestinian Territory
DATE 2010
END USER Nonprofit groups working in Gaza
IMPLEMENTING AGENCIES
American Friends Service Committee,
Unitarian Universalist Service Committee
DESIGN AGENCY Architecture for Humanity
PROJECT TEAM Gretchen Alther, Mohammed Eila,
Joyce Engebretsen, Nicholas Escalante, Danna
Masad, Gretchen Mokry, Amal Sabawi, Ayman
Saidam, Ahmed Saleh, Anand Sheth
NUMBER OF BENEFICIARIES 1405 Gaza residents

Priority		# of Homes
1	Basic Needs	40
2	Life Safety	97
3	Improved Conditions	98
4	Cosmetic	98
	Totals	**333**

Building Type

Most of these families are living in a building with a concrete roof.
Around 7 percent are living under a roof made of asbestos or metal sheets.

	Frequency	Percent	Valid Percent	Cumulative Percent
1.0	15	11.4	71.4	71.4
2.0	6	4.5	28.6	100
Total	21	15.9	100	
Missing System	111	84.1		
Total	132	100		

Suggested Domestic Water Repair Strategies

If available, water supplies have biological and mineral contaminants, forcing many to purchase bottled water.
Some households do have an available water source, but many storage tanks, supply lines and fixtures are damaged beyond use.

System	Benefits	Materials & Methods	Cost
Rainwater Harvesting	Greater self-sufficiency, reduces potential for flooding or drainage system overload in dense areas	Sheet metal for gutters and storage tanks locally available	$400 USD per 150 sq m
Solar Hot Water	Reduces fuel demands for water heating		Varies
Supply Lines, Fixtures, Sinks	Repairs and upgrades to ensure water efficiency	Low-flow fixtures such as faucet aerators	$100 USD
Well Water Filter	Many different types, from simple to complex	Whole house filters can be installed anywhere on main line; point-of-use filters installed on supply side of a fixture	
Reverse Osmosis Filter	Has the greatest range of contaminant removal, but should be paired with an ultraviolet system and/or a water softener and iron filter	Commonly available in local markets	$400 USD per unit; requires annual maintenance

the Gulf Coast.

While we were involved in the repair and building of 60 homes in New Orleans, together with our partners we managed 10 times that amount in Biloxi, Mississippi. If you want to be the last responder, you also need to bring your own capital to the table.

Lesson 4:
It Is More Fun to Partner.

Since our inception we've worked with youth sports groups and looked at how physical space can produce social change. Early on we distributed footballs to engage communities. We donated several balls to Balkan Sunflowers in Kosovo, in 2000, then again two years later in Kenya through a program called Who's Got Balls?

After hosting a competition to develop mobile health clinics for sub-Saharan Africa, we held a two-week workshop at the Africa Center for Health and Population Studies in Somkhele, South Africa. During that event we investigated how to dock clinics in the community, and the idea arose to use youth football (soccer) fields as anchor points. So in 2004 we launched Siyathemba, a design competition to develop a soccer facility for girls.

The competition was a great success with hundreds of entries, but implementation turned out to be a lesson in perseverance. The selected design by Swee Hong Ng was refined with East Coast Architects and we spent much time trying to sort out land rights, building use, and commitment from the client. When we won the INDEX: Award in 2005 we directed half of the prize money to the project. Unfortunately our original local partner organization went through an internal upheaval. Land surveys revealed shallow graves, including those of young children, on the site where we hoped to build a field. Then, the tribal chief who had originally offered the land passed away. After years

OPPOSITE PAGE
Excerpts from the Gaza Repair Strategy Manual aimed to support non-governmental organizations and community agencies seeking sustainable approaches to rebuilding.
Image: Architecture for Humanity

TOP
A boy stands next to a damaged wall in his home in Gaza City, on the Gaza Strip. Many residences were damaged during the 2008/2009 conflict between Israel and the Palestinian Authority.
Photo: American Friends Service Committee

BOTTOM LEFT
A residential building in Gaza City is marked with shells. Scarce building supplies means damages often go unrepaired.
Photo: Dr. Mohammed Eila/
Ministry of Environmental Affairs Gaza Strip

BOTTOM RIGHT
A man walks through the debris in a home that was destroyed in Gaza City.
Photo: Dr. Mohammed Eila/
Ministry of Environmental Affairs Gaza Strip

12 2
2008–present
CAPE TOWN

Poverty Alleviation

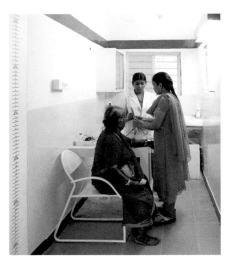

FEATURED PROJECT Razi Clinics
LOCATION Hyderabad, Andhra Pradesh, India
CLIENT Razi Healthcare Design Studio
DESIGN FIRM (re)DO Hyderabad, India
DESIGN AGENCY Architecture for Humanity
PROGRAM MANAGEMENT
Joyce Engebretsen, Satu Jackson
DESIGN FELLOW Sandhya Naidu Janardhan
COST PER CLINIC $5000–$6000 USD
NUMBER OF CLINICS 40+

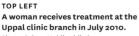

TOP LEFT
A woman receives treatment at the Uppal clinic branch in July 2010.
Photo: Salone Habibuddin/ Architecture for Humanity

TOP RIGHT
The formal development of the Nallakunta clinic elevation sets it apart from the neighboring informal economic activities.
Photo: Sandhya Naidu Janardhan/ Architecture for Humanity

BOTTOM LEFT AND RIGHT
The rehabilitation of the doctor's offices included new furniture, sanitary improvements and bright colors to give it a more professional appearance and feel.
Photo: Sanhya Naidu Janardhan/ Architecture for Humanity

of raising funds we had no land, no partner and no contracts in place. Then, in 2007, the original director of the Africa Center, Dr. Michael Bennish, offered an alternative option to partner with a local school less than 10 minutes away. His organization Mpilonhle would use the sports field to dock their mobile medical facilities. After years of development, the idea had come full circle.

With funds from INDEX and The Woolworths Trust we built phase 1 of the project at Silthukukhanya High School. With little funding for a typical on-the-ground design fellow we placed our trust in Dr. Bennish and East Coast Architects to see the project through. The site analysis showed the school had no water source. Together we made the decision to use half of the funds to dig a well, nixing the changing room structure but leaving enough for the field and solar lighting. By the spring of 2008, despite all the hurdles and heartache, the Silthukukhanya High School field opened, complete with a mobile medical station. The project showed the importance of sticking to a tight schedule. A small investment in a design fellow on site, saves much more by keeping the project on track. We thought that was it. Fours years of hard work for a simple field. Boy, were we wrong.

Midway through the project we got two phone calls, one from streetfootballworld, and the other from Nike. The former asked if we were interested in partnering on facilities with specific community-based groups throughout Africa. This project would also be a partnership with the FIFA World Cup. The second call, from Ziba Cramner at Nike, was about building innovative social programs around sports.

In a short time we became deeply involved in the sports for social change movement. With FIFA and streetfootballworld we established a regional office in Cape Town to design, develop and build a series of non-governmental organization-led youth football facilities. This multi-year, multi-site, multi-client program gave a platform for dozens of architects to engage in community building. Out of this program came a range of diverse structures called Football for Hope Centres. There were centres in South Africa, with Grassroots Soccer; Namibia, with the Special Olympics; Rwanda, with Esperance; and Ghana, with PLAY SOCCER Nonprofit International.

We launched the Football for Hope Program with our partners in 2008. Communication was a challenge. We triangulated conference calls on three continents. Miscommunications led to unnecessary delays. We decided to share an office with streetfootballworld in Cape Town. Having our partners a desk away made problem solving and collaboration much more efficient. Likewise, we had problems maintaining design standards between projects. Originally, our design fellows went straight to the job site, and designs often went through several revisions before all parties were happy. We decided it was more effective for new recruits to spend a few months in Cape Town getting immediate feedback, while arranging site visits and client meetings as needed to ensure local input. Then, they moved on-site as construction began. The project has shown how close collaboration can foster replicable, scalable change.

Likewise, partnering with Nike's Sustainable Business and Innovation team we set up a $1.1 million USD construction fund that would focus on supporting grassroots organizations. Unlike the highly-defined program for the Football for Hope Centres, this program was all about finding innovation in the least likely places. Over the years we've helped build skateboarding, basketball and football facilities all over the world, from Afghanistan to Guatemala. Nike has also supported rebuilding access to sports in post-disaster areas, and we are completing projects in Brazil, Chile, Haiti and Japan.

By committing to help other groups with shared goals, a simple project has become a robust practice for our organization. While creativity can lead to a single idea, innovation is adaptable and constantly learned. To date, more than 500 000 children currently use these facilities, and by 2014 that number will be closer to 1 million.

Lesson 5:
Design Is an Economic Tool.

Another area that has become an emerging part of our work is our relationship with social enterprises and businesses. Too often non-governmental organizations fail to engage and support the local business sector, instead building only homes, schools and clinics. To rebuild holistically after a disaster it is imperative to have a series of strong economic anchors in the community. Quite often, these small business are the heart of the community. Without them you are putting the community at-risk to become a future slum beset by unemployment, violence and social ills. The number one request we get from clients is a job, often before housing. No one is looking for a handout.

We first learned this lesson in India. We were very preemptive in making sure social enterprises were using the buildings and creating revenue for the long-term maintenance of the structures. In the post-occupancy analysis of the Ambedgar Nagar Community Complex we found the library space was being used to store materials used by a women's cooperative. Without a regular source of income, reading came second. We then began building a series of standalone women's cooperatives that became hubs of microeconomic development. Designing even small spaces in a village that cater to commercial activity can change the face of the whole community. We had been working on economic development in post-disaster contexts, without really realizing it. It's now become a core practice area.

Recent examples are the Hikado Marketplace in Motoyoshi, Japan (after the 2011 Tohoku Earthquake) and Willie Mae's Scotch House in New Orleans, Louisiana, which was restored by the Heritage Conservation Network with a grant from us (after Hurricane Katrina). Both eating establishments had been community nodes prior to the disaster; both have charismatic business leaders and dedicated clients. These were healthy businesses that needed support. The Hikado Marketplace was a $7500 USD investment that salvaged materials from homes set for demolition. The construction team consisted of local traditional carpenters and out of work fishermen. Instead of spending funds on community meetings or needs assessment surveys, we built an impromptu gathering space and a business.

During a post-opening lunch at the marketplace a group of fishermen and our design team realized they could create a small microenterprise by building hammocks using the same technique that is used to make fishing nets. Word of mouth and social networking yielded 750

Disaster Reconstruction

PROJECT NAME Centre de Reconstruction

LOCATION Port-au-Prince, Ouest, Haiti

DATES 2010–present

END USERS community members in Haiti

BENEFICIARIES 49 150 Haitians

SPONSOR ORGANIZATION
Architecture for Humanity

SPONSORS
Autodesk, Bezos Family Foundation,
Clinton Bush Haiti Fund, Curriki,
Global Nomads Group, Heath Ceramics,
Innergey Power, Johnsonite,
Nvidia Foundation, Students Rebuild

PROGRAM COORDINATORS
Eric Cesal, Sandhya Naidu Janardhan,
Martine Theodore, Frederika Zipp

DESIGN FELLOWS Stephane Cherduville,
Kate Evarts, Darren Gill, Dave Hampton,
Carl Harrigan, Schendy Kernizan,
Jean Rene Lafontant, Lyndia Mesidor

VOLUNTEERS 70 and counting

STRUCTURAL ENGINEER Rick Ehlert

CONSTRUCTION MANAGERS
Stanley Joseph, Marie Elizabeth Nicolas,
Jacques Nixon, Ulrick Pierre

ADDITIONAL SUPPORTERS
Rolande Augustin, Sergine Francoeur,
Yves Francois, Nicole Jeanty

PROGRAM COST $720 000 USD per year

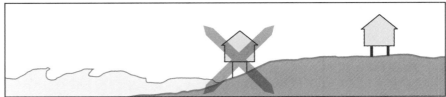

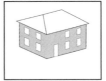
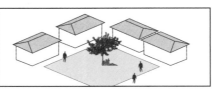

TOP
A damaged building in Haiti after the 2010 earthquake.
Photo: Eric Cesal/Architecture for Humanity

BOTTOM
The Rebuilding 101 Manual laid out simple building techniques to ensure that new buildings were safely constructed.
Image: Architecture for Humanity–Haiti

orders within three months. A month later we awarded construction funding to build a small workshop for the company creating 12 jobs.

In Haiti the issue was even more extreme. Families living in tents, most working in the informal economy, watched and waited as the international community struggled to rebuild homes. Meanwhile, once active commercial areas were atrophying. Our team, which had a mandate to rebuild schools (an equally important need in Haiti), realized that if we did not rebuild businesses there would be no jobs for the next generation of students. Taking all the lessons learned from our previous work, we established a rebuilding studio that from the beginning set as its goal the economic revitalization of the metro Port–au–Prince area. It would be "the bank." Connecting small and medium sized businesses, street vendors and entrepreneurs with construction capital. Rather than competing with local architecture and construction firms, we would create opportunities for local firms to fully participate in the reconstruction effort and use our leverage as funders to ensure safe construction standards.

Lesson 6:
Unleash Local Talent.

Every two years we host an international design competition around a particular global theme. In 2007, it was access to technology. In 2009, we focused on improving education facilities. In 2011, we called on designers to re-envision abandoned and closed military sites. Previously we had invited designers to develop a solution for a specific site. In the 2009 challenge, because everyone has a school in need of upgrading, we decided to change the rules. This time we invited entrants to design for a site in their own community. Sure, it would be harder to jury. But, we said, they have a reason to enter.

Hundreds of teams developed thoughtful and innovative solutions. Better yet, entrants continued to work on their projects, whether they placed or not. One of the honorable mentions to the 2009 challenge served as inspiration to a school being built in the Philippines. In Uganda, we were busy constructing one of the finalist designs, when we learned during our annual forum, that another architect had downloaded the

TOP
The Haiti Partners' Children's Academy in Bawosya was developed through an office fellowship with BAR Architects.
Image: BAR Architects

TOP MIDDLE
Ecole Baptist Bon Berger serves 2000 students near the slum of Cite Soleil. The reconstruction includes new athletic facilities.
Image: Alison McCabe/Architecture for Humanity

BOTTOM MIDDLE
The École Elie Dubois School, all-girls vocational program, is located in down-town Port-au-Prince. The courtyard includes space for an outdoor market.
Image: Dorothy Miller, TJ Olson, Jeremy Warms/ Architecture for Humanity-Haiti

BOTTOM
The Rebuilding Center in Port-au-Prince.
Photo: Karl Johnson/ Architecture for Humanity

37 | 7.5'
2010-present
PORT-AU-PRINCE

FEATURED PROJECT
Hikado Marketplace
LOCATION Kesennuma–shi,
Motoyoshi–cho, Miyagi, Japan
DATE 2011
CLIENT Atsushi Hatakeyama, market owner
DESIGN AGENCY Architecture for Humanity
DESIGN FELLOWS
Autumn Ness Taira, Yuji Taira
COST $7500 USD
OCCUPANCY 40
BENEFICIARIES
450 displaced families

TOP
The renovated Hikado Marketplace,
completed in June 2011, is the only
place for lunch for the people living in
nearby relief camps.
Photo: Autumn Ness Taira/
Architecture for Humanity

BOTTOM LEFT
A local carpenter's toolbox. The
marketplace was rebuilt using
traditional Edo carpentry.
Photo: Autumn Ness Taira/
Architecture for Humanity

BOTTOM RIGHT
Timbers salvaged after the tsunami
were joined together without nails by
local master carpenters.
Photo: Autumn Ness Taira/
Architecture for Humanity

Save to My Places

Pakistan Flood Rebuilding Grant - Heritage Foundation

In the summer of 2010, many provinces in Pakistan were affected by the death of enormous flooding conditions. The floods caused the death of 1,600 people and some 20 million citizens were displaced by this natural disaster. These devastating floods have had a serious impact on an already vulnerable population. It is estimated that, at one point, one fifth of the country's total land area was underwater. Much of the farming land, housing and infrastructures were completely destroyed, leaving millions of people living in precarious, sub-standard conditions. The population has since struggled with severe food shortages, lack of sanitation and access to clean, drinking water.

Public : 484 views
Created on Aug 20 By Updated Aug 21
Rate this map Write a comment KML

GKG No. 1 - Demo Unit
Pakistan Flood Rebuilding Grant Program - The Heritage Foundation/Green KaravanGhar bamboo relief housing and homeless training in construction techniques

GKG Nos. 2 & 3
Pakistan Flood Rebuilding Grant Program - The Heritage Foundation/Green KaravanGhar bamboo relief housing and community training in construction techniques

GKG No. 4
Pakistan Flood Rebuilding Grant Program - The Heritage Foundation/Green KaravanGhar bamboo relief housing and

Pakistan Flood Rebuilding Grant Program - The Heritage Foundation
Green KaravanGhar bamboo relief housing and community training in construction techniques

Directions Search nearby Save to map more ▾

PROGRAM NAME
Pakistan Flood Rebuilding Grant Program
LOCATIONS
Khairpur, Nodo Bara, Goth Angario Jati, in Sindh Province, Pakistan
PROGRAM PARTNERS
Architecture for Humanity-Karachi, The Heritage Foundation (Pakistan), Karachi Relief Trust
PROJECT COORDINATORS
Mahboob Kahn, Mariyam Nazir, Frederika Zipp
COST $60 000 USD for three villages
NUMBER OF BENEFICIARIES 800

TOP
One of 29 housing units built in the village of Swaleh Satho Goth Angario, in the Province of Sindh, Pakistan, after the 2010 Pakistan Floods. New housing was built by Architecture for Humanity-Karachi chapter and Karachi Relief Trust.
Photo: Architecture for Humanity-Karachi

BOTTOM
The Google Map displays the locations of the Green KaravanGhar bamboo relief houses constructed by the Heritage Foundation. GPS data allows individual donors to see their funds being used well.
Image: The Heritage Foundation/Google Maps

solution and had already built the design in nearby Kenya. The same design, slightly adapted, was being used to educate hundreds of children in two countries. The secret to a design competition's success is not who wins or what is the first thing to be built. Every month we hear of a design team that finally saw their scheme come to life, or a town or city that has used our model to run a similar program. Going forward all of our competitions will allow architects to address an issue affecting the built environment in their own community.

Lesson 7:
Let Scale Happen.

We never dreamed that the organization would scale. Our biggest success happened partly due to an off-the-cuff joke. When Architecture for Humanity consisted of a laptop and a cellphone I would receive emails and calls from around the world about setting up a branch of the organization. Explaining that our limited resources couldn't allow us to do it, I'd often joke they should organize some like-minded individuals at a coffee shop or bar and start an informal "drinking for humanity" group. Whether it was the name or the permission for self-organizing, the idea took off, and before long architects and community leaders stopped chatting over beers and started developing their own potential projects.

In the last six years we saw huge growth at this local level. Our independent chapters expanded to over 100 locations and hundreds of pro bono projects have been developed and implemented. In most cases, projects exemplified the ideals that we were trying to achieve, from sustainable classrooms in Dhaka, Bangladesh; equipment lending libraries in Sioux Falls, South Dakota; homeless shelters in London; to developing disaster preparedness plans for New York City. It has been amazing to arrive in a city like Pittsburgh, Pennsylvania or Auckland, New Zealand to meet dozens of design professionals deeply engaged in the shaping of their cities and responding to the needs of overlooked communities.

Occasionally we ran into hurdles with chapters that were either stepping outside of our mission or, in some cases, competing with another chapter in the same location. As a result we began to formalize these associations. This allowed us to strengthen

Economic Development

PROJECT NAME
Commercial Corridors
LOCATION Port-au-Prince, Haiti
START DATE 2011
IMPLEMENTING AGENCY
Architecture for Humanity
PROJECT MANAGEMENT
Eric Cesal, Henri Dupont,
Sandhya Naidu Janardhan,
Kate Stohr, Martine Theodore,
Gaurav Vashist
DESIGN FELLOWS
Kate Evarts, Darren Gill,
Stacey McMahan
DESIGN TEAM Abbey Kurlinkus,
James Lutz, Amanda Pederson,
Kaitlin Schalow, Cody Stadler,
Emerson Stepp, Brent Suski
CONSULTANT
ShoreBank International
LOAN FUND $1 million USD
BENEFICIARIES
30 small business owners
in Port-au-Prince and the
communities they serve

ABOVE
**The markets of Haiti continue
to do business in the shadow of
damaged buildings.**
Photo: Abby Kurlinkus/
University of Minnesota

BELOW AND OPPOSITE BOTTOM
**A diagrammed street map provides
detailed information about traffic,
street congestion, and the use and
condition of each building along one of
Port-au-Prince's earthquake-damaged
economic corridors.**
Image: Brent Suski/University of Minnesota

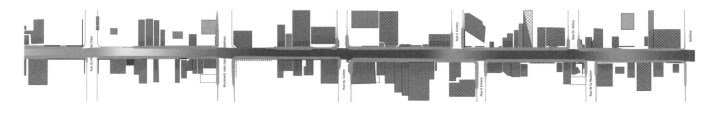

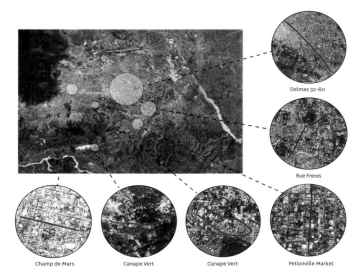

Delmas 32-60

Rue Freres

Champ de Mars   Canape Vert   Canape Vert   Petionville Market

ABOVE TOP
Aerial view of series of economic corridors surveyed to identify targeted areas for small-business reconstruction.
Image: Eric Cesal/
Architecture for Humanity–Haiti

ABOVE MIDDLE
The North Pole proposal seeks to develop a new mixed-use district north of Port-au-Prince to relieve congestion in the city.
Image: Architecture for Humanity–Haiti

our relationship with chapter members, further develop an online network and host an annual forum, Design Like You Give a Damn: LIVE!

While this saw a dip in our numbers, it helped us reorganize and develop a stronger network for chapters to communicate, collaborate and run programs. In 2011, we began a chapter grants program, distributing small funds for local projects. In years to come we will probably find that the true legacy of the organization will be the hundreds of projects completed by our chapters.

Lesson 8:
There Is No Such Thing As a Typical Architect.

I wrote earlier about our design fellowship program, but it's important to note the value and quality of our design work comes down to our people. Take a highly skilled, motivated and talented professional, partner them with a strong and dedicated community leader, fund them to live and work on the ground, allow them to challenge each other and watch a true partnership grow. It is really that easy . . . and complicated. Our clients select an architect or designer off a shortlist in our network, and, depending on the scope of work, we then partner them with locally licensed professionals. A tour of duty can range from 6 to 18 months and is usually tied to a specific building or community group.

Each designer brings a particular aesthetic and approach to the work while working under the guidelines set out in our design fellow manual. After a brief training program at our headquarters, they head out into the field. Partnering them with the right client is the key to a successful project. A prime example is Eric Cesal, a PhD MacGyver–Grassroots Leader hybrid (see design fellow personality types on page 27). After a couple of tours of duty with us on the Gulf Coast, he established and now runs our office in Haiti. His on-the-ground experience with long-term reconstruction was vital, making him a perfect candidate for running a rebuilding center.

Lesson 9:
Have a Sense of Humor.

When someone introduces their project earnestly and philosophically, I can sense they haven't really connected with the community. Chances are the community didn't really connect with the project either. For all the blood, sweat and tears shed over the course of a project, the one thing that prevails is laughter. I could write books on the small, comical things that happen on a daily basis on the ground. Communities shattered by natural or man-made disasters are unbelievably resilient, and are filled with hope and love for one another and those working alongside them.

We tend to take ourselves way too seriously, and that becomes an unnecessary hurdle when working on the ground. There is nothing more amazing than sitting around a table, breaking bread together and telling stories of mishaps, misfortunes and the downright comical. If working in this environment is challenging, then getting to discover what makes us unique is incredibly rewarding.

Our Growth + Impact

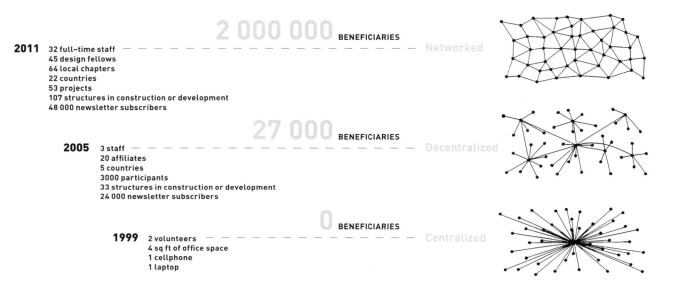

2 000 000 BENEFICIARIES

2011 32 full-time staff — — — — — — — — — — — — — — — —   Networked
45 design fellows
64 local chapters
22 countries
53 projects
107 structures in construction or development
48 000 newsletter subscribers

27 000 BENEFICIARIES

2005 3 staff — — — — — — — — — — — — — — — —   Decentralized
20 affiliates
5 countries
3000 participants
33 structures in construction or development
24 000 newsletter subscribers

0 BENEFICIARIES

1999 2 volunteers — — — — — — — — — — — — — — — —   Centralized
4 sq ft of office space
1 cellphone
1 laptop

On Distributed Communications by Paul Baran, Rand Corp., 1962.

Lesson 10:
Design Yourself Out Of a Job.

Part of our goal in building a sustainable model for our long-term rebuilding centers is to eventually transform them into local economic development corporations. Staffed and run locally, these centers are proof that our services have a lifespan and that we need to constantly look for ways to make ourselves redundant. Often when a building opens, we know it has been successful given the size of the party, the number of speeches and, more importantly, the local community directing their thanks to one another rather than us. This is a very humbling moment for the architect on a project. Perhaps the most emotional is the moment that you have to say goodbye. And for the success of the project you do.

Our philosophy for the organization is no different. Having worked on the idea of Architecture for Humanity for the past 15 years, I've had the honor of watching an idea grow to a living organism with over 100 dedicated staff members and design fellows; from enlisting a handful of building professionals to creating a network of thousands; from building a couple of structures, to transforming communities and truly building change from the ground up. If we believe in creating sustainable models, then the organization should reflect that in its growth.

As founders, Kate and I continue to strive to develop internal procedures and mechanisms that can run and evolve without the original creators at the helm. We know it is soon time for us to go. So, over the next several years, we will work ourselves

out of a job. This will allow Architecture for Humanity to be transferred to those who have worked so hard to shape it into the organization it has become: our staff.

As I write, hundreds of people are building on four continents, technology teams are refining our project management and evaluation tools on Worldchanging, and architects are working together with communities to build new holistic towns and civic structures. We are excited by the upcoming challenges, new projects, and the continued growth of local chapters (especially the renegade ones).

**We look forward to working with you.
Thank you.**

Your Project Here

Your Project Here

Your Project Here

Your Project Here

TOP LEFT
The Alternative Masonry Unit project, designed by Architecture for Humanity volunteers, in Oakland, California tests methods for making sundried bricks.
Photo: Nathaniel Corum/
Architecture for Humanity–San Francisco

BOTTOM LEFT
The Crisis at Christmas project, designed by Architecture for Humanity–London, provides a gathering space for the homeless in London.
Photo: Katherine McNeil/
Architecture for Humanity–London

We have left the "Your Project Here" spaces intentionally blank to allow our chapters, which are too numerous to list, to highlight their work. We encourage them to showcase their projects on this page.

MIDDLE
Children play outside a two-story, bamboo-steel frame prefabricated, retractable classroom in Dhaka, Bangladesh, designed by Architecture for Humanity–Dhaka.
Photo: Imrul Kayes/
Architecture for Humanity–Dhaka

TOP RIGHT
Children play outside a youth center in Shanghai, China, constructed of shipping containers. Design by Architecture for Humanity–Shanghai.
Photo: Architecture for Humanity–Shanghai

BOTTOM RIGHT
Homeless lockers at the nonprofit Voices of Change in Minneapolis, USA. Design by Architecture for Humanity–Minnesota.
Photo: Andrea Rugg/
Architecture for Humanity–Minnesota

Financing Sustainable Community Development

Kate Stohr

In 1889, steel magnate Andrew Carnegie penned a number of articles on the subject of wealth, and specifically on the disposal of "surplus" wealth. At the time, Carnegie wrote that this lack of regulation in a free market economy had created the rise of "robber barons," whose great fortunes multiplied in their sleep as income disparity between the rich and the poor was growing sharply. Socialism was on the rise—and the country was young.

The population density was 20 persons per square mile, according to Carnegie, compared to 15 times that in Britain. America was in the midst of a building boom. A steady flow of immigrants crowded its cities. Development pushed ever westward. Perhaps more importantly, Carnegie himself was just embarking on what would become one of America's most interesting and lasting legacies—the construction of more than 2509 "free" libraries throughout the country, and beyond.

Carnegie was a builder. As an immigrant working in Allegheny, Pennsylvania, a local businessman permitted workers to borrow books from his own personal library on Saturday nights. It left a lasting impression. "And it was when reveling in the treasures which he opened to us that I resolved, if ever wealth came to me, that it should be used to establish free libraries, that other poor boys might receive opportunities similar to those for which we were indebted to that noble man," Carnegie later wrote.

RIGHT
The Seattle Central Library was funded by the "Libraries for All" bond measure, as well as a $20 million USD donation by Bill Gates. It was designed by OMA and opened in 2004.
Photo: Noah Collins

OPPOSITE
The Ballard Library in Seattle, designed by Henderson Ryan, was partially funded with a $15 000 USD grant from Andrew Carnegie and opened in 1904.
Photo: Noah Collins

"No millionaire will go far wrong in his
search for one of the best forms
for the use of his surplus who chooses
to establish a free library in any
community that is willing to maintain
and develop it."

Andrew Carnegie, *The Best Fields of Philanthropy*, 1889

"Yet though the people are very proud of
[the library], many a man said to me,
'We'd rather they hadn't cut our wages and
let us spend the money for ourselves.
What use has a man who works 12 hours
a day for a library, anyway?'"

Margaret Frances Byington, Assistant Secretary,
Charity Organization Department, Russell Sage Foundation,
Homestead: The Households of a Mill Town,
Russell Sage Foundation Publications, 1910

In thinking about the disposal of his own "surplus" wealth, Carnegie developed a framework. He felt strongly that it should be given to projects of lasting value during his lifetime. (As his wealth accumulated this would become a surprisingly daunting—and ultimately impossible—goal.)

All but the first few library grants Carnegie gave in accordance with what became known as the "Carnegie Formula." Any town wishing a library would receive a grant for its construction provided that the town was willing to supply the land and contribute 10 percent of the cost of construction annually to support its operations. There was one condition: the library remain open and free to the public in perpetuity. Construction grants were made by a board of trustees who served life terms. The construction grant amount was determined by two factors: the population which was to pay the tax to maintain the library, and a specified minimum revenue from the tax.

Cities issued bonds to cover their share of the costs, asking taxpayers to pay about 19 cents on every $1000 USD of assessed property annually. Interestingly, many cities were legally barred from issuing bonds for the purposes of building a library. To accept Carnegie's offer, many had to put new legislation in place. Women's groups across America caught wind and stepped in to raise local shares of the library costs, establish library committees and lobby their fellow citizens to vote in support of the new library tax. "Shall pennies outweigh brains? Let the workingman's vote answer," urged the Bingham Citizens Library Committee in one pamphlet.

Once a city had raised the necessary funds to accept Carnegie's offer, the design and construction of the building was left largely to them. Grants were disbursed in draws based on progress. A "Daily Register of Donations" recorded as many as 10 to 20 transactions each day.

However, as time went on, there were many instances of construction overruns, and Carnegie's secretary James Bertram, who managed the program, responded by developing guidelines. Towns were to receive a "circular" that included recommended building plans and gave notes on "modesty in design." As one architect said, the buildings were designed to "tell the same story, but each in different words." In New York City, where Carnegie funded 67 branch libraries, library trustees hired three firms and requested they work together—forming a committee that approved each other's designs and shared standards and lessons learned.

Carnegie libraries promoted innovations in library design, most significantly open stacks. Previously, it was more common for readers to ask clerks to fetch books from closed stacks. In Carnegie's libraries they were invited to browse themselves. Central circulation desks offered sightlines of the well-lit open-plan reading room, which usually remained open evenings to cater to the workingman. A typical library might also include a children's room and an assembly hall in the basement for lectures and concerts. To encourage walk-in traffic, the reading room was placed on the ground floor with large arched windows facing the street. Many libraries were located near immigrant or working-class neighborhoods to support acculturation. Whether built in the Beaux-Arts or Spanish Mission style, they were often the most prominent building in town. Today, many are listed in historic registries.

Carnegie built 2811 free libraries in all. Of these, 1946 were located in the United States (in every state except Rhode Island). There were 660 in Britain and Ireland and 156 in Canada. A handful of libraries were also scattered in New Zealand, the West Indies and Fiji. When the last grant was made in 1919, there were a total of 3500 libraries in the United States, nearly half of them built with construction grants paid by Carnegie. Perhaps more significantly, he caused cities around the world to invest many multiples more into their operation. It was a marriage of philanthropy, civic engagement and municipal financing—what today we call public-private partnership, leaving behind a legacy of landmark buildings.

Yet even during his lifetime, some called into question Carnegie's priorities. In 1910, 12 years after he funded the construction of a library in the Carnegie Steel Company mill town of Homestead, Pennsylvania, Margaret Frances Byington conducted a research study of mill worker living conditions there. "Yet though the people are very proud of [the library], many a man said to me, 'We'd rather they hadn't cut our wages and let us spend the money for ourselves. What use has a man who works 12 hours a day for a library, anyway?'" she wrote.

Byington's research uncovered that though the mill and most of the Carnegie Steel Company holdings were located in Munhall, the workers generally lived in Homestead, a different borough. Tax dollars that improved the living conditions and paid for sanitation, clean water and other improvements in Munhill stopped at the borough line. Homestead's workers, whose taxable income and property holdings were far less—and whose wages were cut in the years following deadly labor union conflicts—could not collectively fund improvements needed to provide clean water and sanitation to their own crowded community.

Hindsight is imperfect. However, it's interesting to wonder what impact could Carnegie's philanthropy have had in the many communities in which he bestowed his generosity, if he had also focused his attention on helping to make systemic changes to improve the immediate living conditions of workers as well as their minds.

It's a conversation that is as relevant today as it was a century ago. Community development is unique. Investing in the improvement of a place as opposed to a person or people includes investments in infrastructure (water, sanitation, energy, telecom, roads) as well as investments in parks and open space, cultural amenities, education, health care and job creation. The investments are generally long-term, one-time capital outlays, yet they impact generations. With the rise of the city, mobile workforces, climate change, and shifting populations, sustainable community development increasingly involves complex trade-offs. And, just as in Carnegie's own time, questions of how and when to use public funds versus private capital, land use and community empowerment are at the heart of the work.

Financing for community development is not just a question of priorities. How projects are financed weighs heavily on their planning and design—and ultimately their success. Clearly, we no longer live in a world where communities can wait for the largesse of wealthy patrons to improve their living conditions. The constraints faced by community development professionals, particularly architects and urban planners, in meeting the needs of communities can often only be addressed through equally thoughtful financing.

A major barrier to finding solutions for both urban crises in emerging economies, and sustainable maintenance of existing cities and small

HOUSING

Location Randburg, South Africa

Cost

1 million Rand/$149 543 USD

Area 147 sq m/1582 sq ft

Photo: Letitia Botha/Remax

Location San Bruno, California, USA

Cost

$399 750 USD

Area 137 sq m/1470 sq ft

Photo: Bo Wongkalasin

Location Nontaburi, Bangkok, Thailand

Construction Cost

$53 000 USD

Area 135 sq m/1453 sq ft

Photo: Bo Wongkalasin

Location Karlskrona, Sweden

Cost

3 million Kron/$316 465 USD

Area 145 sq m/1561 sq ft

Photo: Andreas Svensson

SCHOOLS

Maosi Ecological Demonstration Primary School

Location Xifeng City, Gansu Providence, PR China

Design Firm Edward Ng and Jun Mu

Cost

70 000 EU/$99 656 USD

Area 1005 sq m/10 818 sq ft

Photo: Jun Mu/Edward Ng

El Porvenir Kindergarten

Location Bogota, Colombia

Design Firm Giancarlo Mazzanti Arquitectos

Cost

1.8 billion COP/$967 742 USD

Area 2100 sq m/22 604 sq ft

Photo: Rodrigo Davilo/Giancarlo Mazzanti Arquitectos

Dano Secondary School

Location Dano, Burkina Faso

Design Firm Kéré Architecture

Cost

70 000 EU/$99 656 USD

Area 318 sq m/3 423 sq ft

Photo: Kéré Architecture

Marin Montessori School

Location Corte Madera, California, USA

Design Firm Pfau Long Architecture

Cost

$4.5 million USD

Area 1 115 sq m/12 000 sq ft

Photo: Pfau Long Architecture

towns, is the disconnect between financing and place. Broadly speaking, this is largely due to three main hurdles.

The first is the more obvious issue of sector-based funding. Take for example a project to build a basketball court and storage facility on land adjacent to a school. Typically, funds for school construction and maintenance (often handled at the county or provincial level) are separated from funds for school operations (handled at the local level) and further separated from funds for parks and recreation (handled by a different local agency). As a result, developing recreational opportunities on school grounds can require threading funding from three or more sources. At the international level, bilateral and multilateral aid delivery is focused on housing, health, education, etc. As a result, funds earmarked for health care delivery cannot be used to support an investment in sanitation infrastructure in tandem—despite the obvious correlation between improved sanitation and improved health.

The second obstacle is the issue of "restrictions," be they eligibility requirements or exceptions. Restrictions on funding are usually put in place to create incentives for certain perceived positive development attributes (walkability, owner-occupied home ownership, savings requirements) or to cure perceived or real market deficiencies. For example, following the devastating earthquake and tsunami that struck Japan in 2011, the Japanese government announced that any school that accepted private donations for reconstruction would not be eligible for government funds. The intent was likely to prevent schools from double-dipping, but the result was a slowdown in school reconstruction. Schools declined private donations for fear of losing larger sums of government funds that took much longer to disperse.

The third and most subtle hurdle relates to timing. For those of us who are community development practitioners, this may be the most critical. In most parts of the world construction financing is unavailable to homeowners, small businesses and most critically community groups. As a result, facilities are built incrementally at much greater cost to their users.

The timing issue is felt most acutely after disaster. It took nearly two years for funds that had been earmarked for Hurricane Katrina reconstruction to reach the ground. The same is also true in Haiti, where families displaced after the 2010 earthquake lived in tents for more than two years awaiting international pledges from donor nations to be fulfilled and disbursed.

If public financing is slow and restrictive, and private financing is risk averse, the result is a delay in capital that can significantly increase the costs of managing and implementing community development projects. The cost of that delay is typically born by community development agencies.

Finally, financing schemes, because of their high cost to implement, are still often modeled on macroeconomic data at the national level. This data is interpreted to create regional or national programs that are then carried out at the local municipal level. The issue, of course, is that needs and demographics differ at the local level. Any program designed in this way will by default work better in communities that more closely reflect the population makeup and economic trends of the norm. If that's 2 percent growth, then the program will be designed to support and manage that growth through housing production or infrastructure investment. What to do about the community that differs from the norm, either because its main job generator requires seasonal labor (therefore rental housing is at a premium) or because it has a shrinking population due to competition from nearby regional centers with greater international ties?

Many people have tried to solve this problem and connect finance and place through calls for better coordination or community engagement. The United Nations Cluster approach is an example of this. Depending on how these meetings are run they can be effective or waste the energy and time for the participating agencies. There have also been various online aid reporting tools like www.oneresponse.org, which we suspect will evolve and become increasingly effective. However, again, coordination comes at the expense of the agencies and citizens participating—oftentimes with hidden costs—and is rarely funded.

More successful are programs that offer flexible grants to communities, provided the funded activities tie to an overall development plan. For example, in the United States, cities can apply to the US Department of Housing and Urban Development for Community Block Development Grants to fund affordable housing, anti-poverty programs, and infrastructure development. Use of the funds is left largely to the discretion of the state and local municipality.

By far, municipal financing continues to represent the bulk of financial support for infrastructure development and services in most communities, whether urban or rural. Increasingly, however, public-private partnerships are combined with innovative planning approaches that offer broader access to capital for infrastructure and community development—from small-scale projects such as facade upgrades, to school construction, to community-wide slum upgrading.

In our experience, the most effective solution seems to be the creation of community development corporations or economic development authorities. They solve the timing issue (by offering liquidity and access to credit) and have the ability to bundle or thread funding from a number of different sources— including private investment and government funding. They are flexible containers in the way that municipal agencies are generally not. And more importantly, they can be accountable for meeting broader development goals over a long period using monitoring and evaluation tools from the onset to measure their impact. One example of this kind of quasi-public agency is the Empresa de Desarrollo Urbano de Medellín (see pages 318-21).

Understanding the intersection between urban planning and finance is of critical importance to the future of cities. In 2007, and for the first time in human history, the world's urban population exceeded its rural population. The shift impacts both historically large cities like London and Tokyo, and secondary cities as disparate as Memphis, Tennessee in the United States, and Changzhou, China. More dramatic still are the number of emerging cities such as Kigali, Rwanda, where today cranes building high-rise office towers stud the skyline.

HOSPITALS

Beit-Cure Hospital

Location Blantyre, Malawi

Design Firm MOD Chartered Architects

Cost

$1.3 million USD

Area 3082 sq m/33 174 sq ft

Photo: Mod Chartered Architects

Evelina Children's Hospital

Location London, United Kingdom

Design Firm Hopkins Architects Partnership LLP

Cost

£41.5 million GBP/$67 million USD

Area 16 500 sq m/177 605 sq ft

Photo: Glitzy queenoo/Wikipedia

Providence Newberg Medical Center

Location Newberg, Oregon, USA

Design Firm Mahlum

Construction Cost

$42 million USD

Area 16 782 sq m/180 636 sq ft

Photo: Benjamin Benschneider/Mahlum

The Royal Women's Hospital

Location Parkville, Melbourne, Australia

Design Firm
Woodhead International and Design, Inc

Cost

$246 million AUD/$264 million USD

Area 73 000 sq m/785 765 sq ft

Photo: Royal Women's Health Partnership

COMMUNITY CENTERS

Quincho Gorro Capucha

Location Pinohuacho, Villarrica, Chile

Design Firm GrupoTalca

Cost

$6000 USD

Area 106 sq m/1 141 sq ft

Photo: Rodrigo Sheward/GrupoTalca

East Community Center

Location Pierrefonds, Montreal, Quebec, Canada

Design Firm Les Architectes FABG

Cost

$3.5 million CAD/ $3.5 million USD

Area 1208 sq m/13 000 sq ft

Photo: Louis Rachiele/City of Montreal

Surry Hills Library and Community Center

Location Sydney, Australia

Design Firm Frances-Jones Morehen Thorp

Cost

$16 million AUD/$17 million USD

Area 2 000 sq m/21 528 sq ft

Photo: John Gollinas/City of Sydney Council

Spikkerelle Cultural Centre

Location Avelgem, Belgium

Design Firm Dierendonckblancke Architects

Cost

3.6 million EU/$5 million USD

Area 2370 sq m/25 510 sq ft

Photo: Dierendonckblancke Architects

The world's poor—those earning less than $2 USD a day—make up the majority of people migrating to cities. In 2003, nearly one-sixth of the world's population lived in slums, according to the United Nations Agency for Human Settlements. Demographic researchers forecast that 1.9 billion people will migrate to urban centers by 2030, drawn by the promise of opportunity, education and jobs. The future of the world's emerging cities lies in their ability to convert the tremendous potential of urban migration into economic prosperity. The challenge for these cities is formalizing their informal settlements.

At the same time, for every city that is growing there are others that are shrinking. These include former Rust Belt hub Detroit, Michigan, in the United States, and cities such as Leipzig, East Germany, which saw a dramatic population decline after the fall of the Berlin Wall. Research shows that the number of shrinking cities has increased faster than the number of boomtowns. Between 1950 and 2000, the number of cities with significant, ongoing population loss has grown by 330 percent. Meanwhile, the number of cities with more than 100 000 residents has increased 240 percent. In the last 50 years, about 370 cities with more than 100 000 residents have temporarily or lastingly shrank in population by more than 10 percent. In extreme cases, the rate of loss reached peaks of up to 90 percent (Âbâdân, Iran).

Moreover, population indicators show that many regions of the world are entering into an era of overall population decline, though fear of a population explosion is pervasive in some parts of the world. Globally, birthrates have declined by more than half since 1979, according to the documentary film *The New Economic Reality: Demographic Winter* (2011). This decline in fertility, primarily in developing countries, means that many nations will be coping with aging populations and shrinking economic bases. There are now 59 nations—comprising close to half of the world's population—with below-replacement fertility rates.

In her 1991 book, *The Global City: New York, London, Tokyo*, Saskia Sassen writes of urban "winners" and "losers." The winners are cities that offer a wide range of financial and specialized services in one place—command centers in the global economy—and the losers being those with outdated infrastructure and economies. Similarly, economist Richard Florida points to the importance of the "creative class" and the need for cities to attract talent from a mobile workforce in order to thrive. In the end, cities will need to watch and anticipate these demographic shifts in the same way that corporations already do.

Today, few cities put adequate resources into analyzing their own market viability. Increasingly, however, it is possible to very cheaply gather data at the local level. Rather than relying on national census results, communities can track their own data sets. The rise of user-generated data mapping tools such as Ushahidi, FrontlineSMS, and OpenStreetMap (see our section on Crowd-Sourced Planning on pages 294–95) are one of the most exciting changes brought by the digital revolution. Now it is up to cities to use that kind of data to create short- and long-term development priorities and a case for investment.

So what do these global trends mean for cities?

Place matters. Just as we need to invest in people, we must also invest in place—and like car racing, every square meter counts. Cities that turn a blind eye to pockets of blight and violence not only put community members at risk, but also put themselves at greater risk for the flight of capital and jobs. This, combined with the leveling of populations in many areas, and projected population declines in others, means that cities cannot count on urbanization and rising birthrates to fuel economic development. Companies can and do go "city shopping," looking for "creative" places that are safe and desirable. Cities that breed cultural diversity as well as opportunity—where the walk to and from work offers spontaneity and chance inspiration—will thrive. Others will shrink, creating a different but equally challenging kind of opportunity to reinvest in open space and renew the natural environment.

Food security, clean water access and natural resources will force communities to find far more responsive models for managing the balance between the built and natural environment in response to shifting populations.

Professionals charged with stewarding the built environment—architects, planners, builders, real estate developers, city managers—must also shift their focus. More holistic investments in place require an understanding of how cities and natural eco-systems function. Urban planners with business degrees will be offering comprehensive urban management models along with master plans. As stewards of an increasingly competitive landscape, these models will use demographic modeling, return on investment analysis on tax investments, land-use inventories, data tracking and impact measurements to target design and planning interventions.

A typical large-scale development today will use any and all of the tools available to it and often in combination. As a result, community development financing has become a complex and often opaque field dominated by specialists. Ultimately, however, there are four basic considerations that any financing structure for community development must take into account: 1) how are funds to be raised, 2) what kind of entity will hold and disperse the funds, 3) what is the legal structure binding the parties, 4) how is land acquired and who will ultimately own it.

The following chart offers a (simplified) view of some common tools available to communities and their use. It is organized into three sections: Municipal Finance, Public-Private Finance and Private Finance. While not exhaustive, it is intended to serve as a primer for community groups, architects, and others seeking to finance their initiatives.

It is not intended to be an exhaustive survey of financial models and their risks, but rather a reference guide to the types of financial approaches and instruments—both public and private—that have been used historically and are in use today to fund the design and construction of civic infrastructure such as schools, hospitals, urban streetscapes, parks and museums, among others. In short, the kinds of projects, large and small, that community designers take up each day.

PARKS & URBAN LANDSCAPES

Centro Abierto de Actividades Ciudadanas

Location Cordoba, Spain

Design Firm Paredes Pino Architects

Construction Cost

3.3 million EU/ $4.6 million USD

Area 11 920 sq m/128 306 sq ft

Photo: Parades Pino Architects

Miami Beach Soundscape

Location Miami, Florida, USA

Design Firm West 8

Construction Cost

$13 million USD

Area 10 117 sq m/108 900 sq ft

Photo: John Loewy/New World Symphony

Paddington Reservoir Gardens

Location Sydney, Australia

Design Firm Tonkin Zulaikha Greer, JMD Design

Construction Cost

$8.7 million AUD/ $9.3 million USD

Area 3600 sq m/38 750 sq ft

Photo: Eric Sierens/City of Sydney Council

Namba Parks

Location Osaka, Japan

Design Firm Jerde Partnership

Construction Cost

$520 million USD

Area 130 064 sq m/1.4 million sq ft

Photo: Jerde Partnership

MUNICIPAL FINANCE	Source of Funds	Holding/Collection Entity
CENTRAL GOVERNMENT TRANSFERS		
Redistribution of tax revenues collected centrally, either nationally or on a regional level. A main source of revenue to local municipalities. Used to bridge the gap between the revenue-raising capacity of municipalities and mandatory local expenditures	Central taxes on income, capital gains, corporate revenue, sales, etc.	National and/or regional tax authorities
PROPERTY TAX		
Levied on the assessed market value of the property and paid by the property owner. More than one jurisdiction can tax the same property owner. Often the main source of local municipal revenue because it can be geographically defined	Paid by property owners within a defined geographic jurisdiction	Municipal, provincial/state, central government tax authorities
LAND TRANSFER TAX		
Levied at the time of sale or transfer of real property	Paid by buyer (more common), seller or both	Municipal tax authorities
LOCAL TAX ON ECONOMIC ACTIVITIES		
Includes local sales tax, local business tax, "hotel" tax, etc.	Paid by business (usually passed on to the consumer through higher prices)	Municipal tax authorities
TAX CREDITS		
Can be offset against a tax liability. Several income tax systems provide income subsidies to influence public sector activities or to assist lower income households by way of credit	Refunded to taxpayers who qualify through credits or rebates	Central and municipal tax authorities
USER FEES		
User fees, tolls or other types of assessments charged in exchange for particular goods, services, use of property, or specific rights. Not considered taxes, as long as they are levied as payment for a direct benefit to the payee	Paid by households and businesses (e.g. utility fees, road tolls, parking meter fees, etc.)	Responsible government agency, utility or other agent on behalf of municipal government
MUNICIPAL BONDS		
Long-term loans issued by banks and credit agencies to local municipalities. The two basic types of municipal bonds are: · **General obligation bonds: Secured by the issuer's credit and supported by the issuer's taxing power** · **Revenue bonds: Secured by revenues derived from tolls, charges or rents from the facility built with the proceeds of the bond issue. Municipal bonds are assessed by credit rating agencies and the issuer's credit may be downgraded if at risk of default.**	· Direct borrowing by central government and on-lending to subnational tiers · Through a public intermediary, a state-owned financial institution · Direct borrowing from capital markets (private investors)	Municipal bonds may be issued by cities, countries, line ministries and redevelopment agencies, special-purpose districts, pubic utilities, publicly owned airports and seaports, provided that the bond is secured by government. In many cases, the issuer must get voter approval through a bond measure
TAX INCREMENT FINANCING		
Municipal bonds issued, based on future tax revenues, to pay for current projects within a specific area. Once a project is completed, nearby properties values are expected to increase, generating an increase in property tax revenues, which repays the original bond. Often the bond is issued on a percentage of the anticipated future tax revenues	Bonds that will be repaid through future tax revenue generated by, and within, a Tax Increment Financing District	Municipal or government entity

Legal Structure	Implementing Agency	Typical Use	Limitations
Grant	State/provincial and/or municipal governing body	Recurrent expenditures (municipal salaries, water, sanitation, roads, policing, public education, etc.)	Limits local independence. Reliance on central government transfers can result in deferred maintenance and lack of infrastructure investment
Tax	Municipal governing body	Typically used to support services and infrastructure construction and maintenance at the local level	Requires regular property revaluations, often with public resistance. In areas where renters outnumber owners can result in inequity
Tax, assessed at the time the deed or title is recorded	Municipal governing body	Supplemental tax often used for infrastructure upgrades	Unreliable returns and subject to market volatility. Slim tax base
Tax	Municipal governing body	Funds typically support recurring expenses	Can make local market less competitive with other markets
Tax refund	Municipal or central tax authority	Provide incentives to act such as mortgage tax credits for homeownership or historic preservation	To be effective, the individual or business must have the cash on hand to make the investment. Often too complex for lower income families, many of whom do not pay taxes or may participate in informal economies
Fee based on usage	Government agency, utility or other agent. Utilities typically regulated by municipal government agency	Common fees include water, power or sanitation or other utility service charges; road tolls, parking meter fees, vehicle registration and license fees.	Revenues are typically returned to support the utility or service (e.g. park rental fees support upkeep of the park). Those charged a fee may unfairly bear the burden of a service enjoyed by the broader public (e.g. congestion charges paid only by vehicle drivers but which support public transportation used by all citizens)
Government-backed security. Typically issued in denominations of $5000 USD or greater	Funds are managed by a government or quasi-government entity that may undertake the work itself or may contract private parties to undertake the work	Examples of public projects financed by municipal bonds include toll roads, bridges, airports, water and sewage treatment facilities, hospitals, and subsidized housing	Municipal bonds are highly regulated and often require voter approval. As a result they are appropriate for large-scale, multi-year projects. Equally, the ability for local governments to issue debt obligations independently of, and in addition to, central governments can mask total debt obligations of a municipality and lead to a lack of transparency and increased risk for investors. Once considered safe investments, after the 2009 housing crisis many municipalities defaulted on their debt causing credit agencies and investors to reassess the risk
State enabling legislation gives local governments the authority to designate tax increment financing districts, which usually last 20 years	Municipal agency or governing body	Often used as a subsidy for development and community improvement projects in areas where they might not otherwise occur, such as low-income neighborhoods	As investment occurs in a neighborhood, the original residents can sometimes be pushed out due to rising costs and gentrification. The increase in development requires an increase in municipal services. Since the increased tax revenue must repay the original bond, there may not be enough revenue to meet the demand for services

MUNICIPAL FINANCE

	Source of Funds	Holding/Collection Entity
BETTERMENT TAX OR SPECIAL ASSESSMENT A betterment tax is a levy on private property owners whose lands have gained value due to public property improvements outside of the owner's control such as a change in zoning or infrastructure investments. The tax recaptures part of the unearned increment in real estate values resulting from public investment.	Compulsory one-time property assessments paid by property owners whose land stands to increase in value from the proposed public improvements. Payments typically spaced out over a number of years to lessen burden	Municipal tax authority
IN-LIEU-FEES A type of development exaction, this is an agreement between a regulatory agency (state, federal, or local) and a public or nonprofit sponsor. Entities pay fees to the sponsoring organization in lieu of meeting regulatory requirements. Used for small-scale projects in lieu of the developer making the investments as mandated by a traditional development exaction	Fees based on regulatory requirements and are paid to the sponsoring agency. Payment is usually triggered by a permit application or sale of property	Government regulatory agency
DEVELOPMENT EXACTION A provision in the approval process for a development that requires a developer to give or provide something to a local government. Intended to shift the burden of shared costs for new development from existing taxpayers to new residents. ("Growth should pay its own way.") They can take several forms including impact fees levied on developers (see below), funding for infrastructure improvements, and land donations. Revenue can be tapped at lower political cost than other sources. Used as a tool for managing growth in areas experiencing high market demand.	Paid by the developer and typically passed on to the end user. Methods of payment and timing vary by type of exaction. If a developer is paying a fee, it is usually paid when the building permit is issued. For commercial exactions, the costs may be paid over a period of several years, allowing the developer to use income from the development's operations rather than having to make the payment before the development is built. If a jurisdiction is providing subsidy to a new development, exactions may offset the costs of the subsidy	Local planning or public works agency
IMPACT FEE A type of development exaction. Impact fees are a charge a developer is required to pay to local government in order to offset costs for necessary capital improvements to roads, libraries and other services located outside (or off-site) of the proposed development	Developers pay fees based on use and siting of proposed project. Cost is passed on to end user	Local planning or public works agency
LINKAGE FEES Another type of development exaction, linkage fees typically apply to commercial development as opposed to residential development. Linkage fees tie new economic development to the construction and maintenance of affordable housing or other community needs. Fees can be assessed on commercial areas and applied to impacted residential areas. Unlike Impact Fees or Development Exactions, Linkage Fees can be applied regionally.	Developers of new commercial properties pay fees (usually a one-time fee assessed per square foot of development) to support community needs. Some programs allow developers to provide the needed community benefit directly	Local planning or public works agency

Legal Structure	Implementing Agency	Typical Use	Limitations
One-time tax assessment. Property lien filed with property registrar by municipality.	Typically a municipal development authority. Funds may be earmarked toward specific municipal budget line items within specific municipal agencies.	Rezoning of agricultural land for residential use. Introduction of transit in a neighborhood. Sometimes used as a disincentive to speculation	"Betterment" is a subjective concept. Use of the tax frequently raises questions of governmental rights. If the government can charge a "betterment" tax, should it not offer a "worsening" subsidy for those affected by infrastructure with negative impacts? Others cite that use of the tax can also lead to higher level of investments in areas better able to afford the levy at the expense of poorer areas
Established by legislation or ordinance and levied at the time of permitting. Legal agreement between the regulatory agency and the sponsor (often include performance criteria and long-term requirements)	A sponsor may be a housing agency, environmental agency or nonprofit group	Funds low-income housing as part of inclusionary housing regulation; funds specific environmental mitigation or remediation to meet environmental regulations.	Use of funds often limited to specific mitigation project or area. Funds cannot be collected in advance of the impact.
Localities can establish the legal basis for levying exactions by passing an ordinance requiring adequate public facilities. Such laws require necessary infrastructure and services before any new development can be approved. For example, a law may mandate a specific number of acres of parkland per 1000 inhabitants. In exchange for compliance, developers receive their building permits	Improvements may be made by the developer (on site or off site) or by government agencies	Fees are used to fund new schools and parks; construction or maintenance of public infrastructure such as roads, utilities, police and emergency services, directly connected to the new development. Can include the expansion, upgrade or new construction of off-site improvements and services provided they serve the new development as well as the wider community. In addition, exactions can serve to discourage new development on "greenfield" (open space) sites by charging higher rates for extending public infrastructure to those areas. In this usage, exactions can create incentives for infill development because development costs are lower where infrastructure and services already exist	Inappropriate for areas with shrinking population or which face heavy regional competition for investment. Can have the adverse effects of making housing less affordable; and encouraging development outside municipal boundaries, resulting in sprawl and/or disinvestment within urban cores. Can lead to a negative cycle of lower investment necessitating the need for increased development fees. (In the United States before the 1960s only 10 percent of localities charged exactions. By the mid-1980s that figure jumped to 90 percent, according to Policy Link)
Established by legislation or ordinance and levied at the time of permitting	Government agency responsible for specific improvements (e.g. public works, transportation, sanitation, etc.)	Typically used to fund the incremental addition of emergency services and expansion or new construction of roads, water, power, etc.	Often the need for services is only indirectly attributed to a specific development, giving rise to developer objections to funding general improvements
Established by legislation or ordinance and levied at the time of permitting	Improvements made by the developer, by a government agency or by a nonprofit in lieu of the developer	In metropolitan areas experiencing growth, commercial development (usually office or retail space) can outpace housing production. This can create an imbalance. Linkage fees are most often used to restore the balance of affordable housing relative to new commercial development. Also used for jobs training, transit, or other benefit.	Can be a disincentive to economic development or new commercial investment in markets where there is strong competition from other areas.

MUNICIPAL FINANCE

	Source of Funds	Holding/Collection Entity
GOVERNMENT HOUSING SUBSIDY **A subsidy offered directly to targeted groups of people, typically those earning below median income levels, to provide access to affordable housing. Can be used to support affordable rental housing or home ownership**	Funded by taxpayers, either locally or nationally	Ministry of housing or local housing authority
PROVIDENT FUND HOUSING PLANS **Combines nationalized pension savings plan with subsidized mortgage rates and discounts to provide a mechanism for an employee to eventually buy a home. Savings plans may be compulsory or voluntary. Savings may also sometimes be used for health care**	Funded by workers and subsidized by tax revenue	Government-sponsored pension fund
EMINENT DOMAIN **The right of a government or its agent to expropriate private property for public use. Also referred to as compulsory purchase or declaration of public utility. In most countries the private property holder is entitled to compensation, the land must be condemned in accordance with a legal process that recognizes the rights of the property owner, and may only be taken for the benefit of the public and not specific individuals or entities. In some cases the government may first be required to negotiate a purchase with property owners**	Compensation to landowners typically funded by tax revenues. Where no compensation is made, the burden falls on private landholders	Eminent domain is declared by central government or municipal agency. In some cases the land is delegated to a third party who will use it for public benefit
GOVERNMENT LAND GRANT **A government grant of public land to a private entity or corporation. Commonly for education and health care facilities. In emerging markets land grants may be used to subsidize private investment for special economic zones or commercial development**	Typically land is removed from the public domain; cost is born by the public at large	Central government or municipal agency deeds a parcel of land in perpetuity to a third party
GOVERNMENT LAND LEASE **Lease of government land to private entities. Lease terms vary. May or may not include building improvements or utilities. Often land is leased at a nominal or symbolic rate and used to serve needs of the community not met by the market**	Tenant, based on lease terms	Government or municipal agency maintains ownership of land and collects leasing fees, if any
GOVERNMENT LAND TRUSTS **Public purchase of land. Land is typically held in perpetuity and maintained by a government ministry such as a national parks service. In some cases government may purchase land using a trust for public housing, utilities or other purposes**	Tax dollars or private land donation to government agency	Municipal or government entity
MUNICIPAL LAND BANKING **A tool for assembling land for either conservation or redevelopment. Government purchases the property. However, unlike a land trust, a land bank does not hold property in perpetuity. Properties can be resold or exchanged for more valuable or contiguous properties to allow for efficient land use**	Properties are purchased using tax revenues or bonds, through eminent domain, or through tax foreclosure	Municipal agency or governing body Established by municipal charter, ordinance or state legislation.

Legal Structure	Implementing Agency	Typical Use	Limitations
Can take many forms including a grant, below-market interest rates on loans or direct provision of housing	Nonprofit housing agencies or private developers on behalf of local authorities	Typically used to offset the costs of new housing production or increase access to affordable housing for low-income households	Can create a disincentive to private housing developers to increase supply. Doesn't usually offer relief to middle-income families; Can result in sprawl
Pension savings plan. Housing purchases often restricted to the purchase of government-owned housing units	Administered by provident fund managers on behalf of the government and in conjunction with the ministry of housing or other housing agency	Typically used as a tool to privatize state-owned housing. Seen in China and Singapore where pension fund contributions are mandatory but where robust private mortgage markets do not yet exist	There is no incentive necessarily for participants to purchase their homes if rental rates (often subsidized) remain low or if other market conditions do not support homeownership. Participants may prefer to wait or not to purchase their unit at all, leaving the government with both the cost of maintaining the unit and the cost of subsidies
Land is taken through a legal proceeding or condemnation. Typically involves a public process and public notice. Property owners typically are allowed opportunities for redress	Land is transferred through the legal system. The transfer is recorded by the land registrar or title agency. The land title is then transferred to government agencies that may delegate the land to third parties	Most commonly used for public utilities, roads, railways, low-income housing and other public uses. In some cases land is expropriated for economic development, such as the development of a public port or convention center	Often controversial, disputed cases can be time consuming and costly. Due process disputes can lead to title uncertainty. Land taken by eminent domain presents an opportunity cost as it is no longer available for development that may generate tax revenue. If the market perceives a risk to private property, there can be negative economic consequences
Land grants sometimes require a public vote, but are more commonly made by a municipal agency	Land title is transferred to a nonprofit organization or corporation that then makes improvements to the property	Typically support the founding of educational institutions, hospitals or community centers. Also a politically expedient tool to meet bilateral or multilateral requirements for government cost-sharing	When land in the public domain is less desirable, the cost of improvements (e.g. grading or providing transit) can outweigh the benefits of receiving the land grant. Often bypasses public comment, resulting in redundant development or social and environmental harms
Leasing agreement between government agency and private entity	Lessors include private individuals, nonprofit agencies, corporations and other government agencies.	Private individuals or corporations may lease government land for agriculture and livestock production, mining and development of other natural resources. Non-profits may enter a long-term lease to develop amenities such as community and recreation centers	Lease terms govern the utility to government and private sector alike. In some cases (such as stadium development) research shows the cost to government exceeds the economic returns to the public. In other cases the lease terms may exceed market value if land values decrease. For longer term leases, the duration of the lease may prevent more valuable use of the land
Established by municipal charter, ordinance or state legislation	Land is owned by a government or municipal agency. May be leased or managed by private entities	A tool for preservation or conservation. Often government leases certain rights to the property such as grazing, agricultural or mineral rights, while maintaining control of the property	Land put aside in a public trust is often removed from the private sector in perpetuity. One exception is "Municipal Land Banking" (below). This may make land that might otherwise support economic activities off limits to private development
Property is held in a land trust with covenants governing its purchase, use and resale	Some local governments manage their land banks directly, while other land banks are managed by a nonprofit entity or private land trust	Land banks are created to control future development, support environmental preservation, or turn over abandoned or tax-delinquent properties to nonprofits or private entities for development	Can lead to speculation and drive up property values if not carefully managed

MUNICIPAL FINANCE

	Source of Funds	Holding/Collection Entity
MITIGATION BANKING		
The restoration, creation, enhancement, or preservation of a wetland, stream, or habitat conservation area. Conservation offer offsets to expected adverse impacts to similar nearby ecosystems. The goal is to replace the function and value of the specific wetland habitats that would be adversely affected by a proposed project.	Developers typically purchase credits from a "mitigation bank" which then purchases conservation land equal in environmental value to the land adversely impacted by development	Government environmental or wildlife protection agency
STATE LOTTERY		
When "lots" are drawn, the owner of the winning ticket wins money or prizes. Tickets are sold to raise money for administration and prize costs; a percentage of the sales then goes to the supporting institution for their use, such as to a state for schools	Lottery ticket buyers	Regional or national government

PUBLIC-PRIVATE FINANCE

	Source of Funds	Holding/Collection Entity
PUBLICLY OWNED ENTERPRISES		
Local governments can establish independent income-generating enterprises to enhance their overall revenue-generation capability or mitigate against risk. Equity in the company is held in whole or in part by the government, which may also regulate its operations	Seed funds procured by tax revenue or more typically by a bond	Typically owned and operated by a parastatal (a company or agency owned or controlled wholly or partly by the government)
PRIVATIZATION		
Transferring state-owned business, infrastructure or enterprise to private sector, or to nonprofit agencies. It can also refer to the outsourcing or contracting of specific state functions, such as sanitation or policing	Private firms purchase state-owned assets or bid for contracts	Private firms
BUILD-OPERATE-TRANSFER		
The private partner receives a concession from the public partner to finance, design, build and operate a facility. The public partner owns the facility but the private partner operates it until the concession period is over, at which time the private partner transfers operations to the public partner. At this time, the public partner can assume operations, retain the private partner for operations, or contract a new operations provider. The private partner assumes a greater portion of the risk, including financing, technical and construction risks	The private partner supplies most of the original funds, therefore the contract must allow the private partner to realize a satisfactory rate of return. The public partner will sometimes supply land or other incentives such as tax credits	Wholly owned by the public partner (usually a government agency)

Legal Structure	Implementing Agency	Typical Use	Limitations
Required by environmental legislation. Mitigation banks place a perpetual conservation easement on the land, with a trust to fund its stewardship	Government environmental agency or third-party environmental organization on its behalf	An outgrowth of government legislation requiring mitigation for the disturbance or destruction of wetland, stream, or endangered wildlife habitat. Typically used to offset the environmental impacts of public works such as highways, sanitation facilities, etc. Offers alternatives to on-site mitigation and often used to consolidate conservation parcels to make management and monitoring easier for resource-strained wildlife protection agencies	Limited to off-site conservation; potentially causing a disincentive for on-site mitigation of environmental impacts. Expensive to manage and includes risk of failure if upfront fees do not cover costs of managing conservation land
Not all countries or states allow lotteries and they are often strictly regulated, though ticket sales can usually be bought without limitations, except for age; are subject to tax laws	A government agency or private entity that is contracted and regulated by a government agency	Government-supported lotteries have become a significant source of funding for schools and other community assets	Like most forms of gambling, lotteries are controversial
Corporation	Corporation	Supports the development of community-owned utilities such as power, sanitation and water as a way to control costs or offset market risks. Also used to support the development of ports, airports, convention centers, stadiums where private operators manage the development but some share of the profits is returned to the public	The advantage of using an income-generating enterprise is that its activities can be accounted for independently of general tax-borne activities. Success is limited by appropriate incentives in place and ability of the private operator to effectively manage the entity and maximize returns. In cases where the chosen operator cannot be replaced, the barrier to entry is high, or there is a lack of competition, the use of this tool can lead to a de facto monopoly
Legislation or contracts	Private firms, usually governed by regulation	Used to provide services such as water, power and sanitation, public safety. Can be used to privatize government-owned industries (mining, defense, etc.)	Privatization is controversial. Proponents assert that free-market policies, specifically competition, drive up efficiency, performance and accountability. It is often opposed on the grounds that it fails to benefit lower-income communities
Contract between public and private partners	The public partner initiates the process and selects the private partner, which is in charge of financing and building the project	Often used for the development of infrastructure such as mass transit, railways and power generation	Additional costs are incurred to pay the private partner for its time and expertise and to enable it to recoup a profit; the public partner is tied to work with a single provider, creating potential disadvantages and preventing the public partner from switching to lower cost or more effective partners

PUBLIC-PRIVATE FINANCE

	Source of Funds	Holding/Collection Entity
BUILD-OWN-OPERATE-TRANSFER **Though similar to Build-Operate-Transfer financing, in this case the private entity owns the facility during its concession period**	The private partner supplies most of the original funds, therefore the contract must allow the private partner to realize a satisfactory rate of return. The public partner will sometimes supply land or other incentives such as tax credits	The private partner owns the facility during its concession period, after which ownership is transferred to the public partner
GOVERNMENT LOAN GUARANTEE **Use of government funds to back private loans to spur economic development, construction of affordable housing or other private investment**	Funded by taxpayers	Government or municipal agency repays the loan in the event of a default
PENSION/PROVIDENT FUND GUARANTEES **Programs that allow private companies or individuals to borrow from banks, using pension plan or government-backed provident fund savings as cash collateral. In the event of default, the loan is paid from the pension or government-backed provident fund.**	Funded by pension plan/provident fund participants	Funds are lent by private lending institutions with guarantees made by the pension/provident fund
NEW MARKET TAX CREDITS **A term specific to a United States program established in 2000 and administered by the Department of the Treasury to attract investment to low-income areas. Tax relief (the credit) is given in exchange for equity investment in certified Community Development Entities (currently up to 39 percent of investment allocated over seven years)**	Lending and investment institutions, high-net-worth individuals	Community Development Entities are allocated capital from a national fund administered by the United States Department of the Treasury
MORTGAGE SUBSIDY **Financing whereby homebuilder permits the purchaser of a new home to occupy the home for a period of time without making monthly payments. The money saved goes toward down payments, and acts as a reserve to help make monthly payments once the financing is in place.**	Governments, and sometimes non-profits	Lending institutions
RENTAL SUBSIDY **Subsidies given to landlords as incentive to rent to tenants that meet certain qualifying criteria, such as income level**	Funded by taxpayers	Private housing provider
VOUCHER PROGRAMS **Help subsidize housing or other social services by providing subsidies to market-based providers. Eligible clients receive a voucher for services in the market. The provider redeems the voucher and is reimbursed by government agencies for the cost. Like other housing subsidies, vouchers offer choice, but often through a limited pool of providers**	Funded through tax revenues or bonds	National, state and municipal governments, such as ministry of housing

Legal Structure	Implementing Agency	Typical Use	Limitations
Contract between public and private partners	The public partner initiates the process and selects the private partner, which is in charge of financing and building the project	Often used for the development of infrastructure such as mass transit, railways and power generation	The disadvantages of this model are the same as the previous model, with the added limitation that the public partner may be forced to buy or own a facility that is out-of-date or otherwise uncompetitive at the end of the contract term
Legislation allowing specific types of guarantees	Private lending institutions	Often used to spur private investment in a region or reduce the risk for lenders backing private companies undertaking large-scale, long-term capital projects	If private lending institutions are unwilling to lend, it may be a sign that the project is too risky and likely to fail. If these risks are not adequately understood, government guarantees can be costly for taxpayers
Legislations or pension plan regulations that permit funds to be used for this purpose, typically to a specified limit	Private institutions use the guarantees to reduce the risk of lending	Can be used as a tool to provide guarantees for community or economic development projects. More typically used to support homeownership by allowing plan participants that would otherwise not have adequate cash collateral to access the private mortgage market	Can put pension or provident fund plans at risk if managed poorly
Private equity	Funds are raised and managed by Community Development Entities certified by the United States Department of the Treasury, which then on lend in the community	Used to encourage investment in underserved, low-income communities through investment in housing and small businesses	The Internal Revenue Service must certify Community Development Entities, which is a barrier. There is a national cap to the amount of New Market Tax Credits issued in a given year ($3.5 billion USD in 2011). Acceptance into the program is not guaranteed; too complex and costly to implement on a small-scale
Mortgage note	The borrower	Lessens the cost of a mortgage by providing a portion of the down payment or interest payments, helping low-income individuals receive mortgages when they might not otherwise qualify	Some limitations can come with receiving private mortgage subsidies; the beneficiary may be limited in their mortgage type options, or be limited in which properties they can choose. There might also be restrictions on when the mortgage holder can resell their home
Contract between government housing agency and private housing provider	Small-scale landlords, privately owned housing corporations, real estate developers, nonprofits and community development agencies	Often targeted to aid low- and very low-income households (50–80 percent of Area Median Income), or to specific disadvantaged groups (e.g. disabled persons, recovering substance abusers, homeless persons)	The quality of housing provided can be very low, leading to a loss of equity for nearby properties. Caps on subsidies and inability of tenants to pay market rate can lead to disincentives to maintain the property
Established by governmental agencies	Typically implemented by housing authority or nonprofit agency	Typically used to create a market for affordable housing by subsidizing the difference between the cost of market-based housing and what low-income families can pay. Also used to speed reconstruction after disaster	Subject to market conditions (low supply of affordable housing from which to choose or reluctance from the market to participate) limiting government's ability to target a specific population. Can lead to poorly built or maintained housing when the voucher does not fully subsidize the cost

PUBLIC-PRIVATE FINANCE

	Source of Funds	Holding/Collection Entity
BUSINESS IMPROVEMENT DISTRICT		
Formed by a group of property/business owners in a specific area or neighborhood, each agreeing to pay extra taxes that are used for specific maintenance or improvement projects within the district	Property and/or business owners pay extra taxes or fees to the local government, which then uses the funds for maintenance or improvements	Community-based organization, such as a neighborhood business association. Contract between public and private partners
SPECIAL ECONOMIC ZONES		
A geographic area where a country's economic and trade laws are modified or changed to encourage a specific economic activity, usually global in nature, such as trading or exporting	Combination of government credits and incentives, such as lower import tariffs, and private investment	In the past, special economic zones were developed and operated by government, but public-private partnerships are becoming more common, and some are wholly developed and operated by private interests
HISTORIC PRESERVATION INCENTIVES		
A number of communities provide financial incentives in the form of tax credits, grants and loans for the rehabilitation of historic properties	Properties identified through a historic zoning or landmark designation are made eligible by local ordinances	Private property owners apply for grants or tax credits

PRIVATE FINANCE

SAVINGS		
Savings are a key component of community development as they allow private investment and stimulate bank lending for housing, commercial activity and economic development	Deposits	Bank
PROPERTY MORTGAGE		
A loan secured by real property	Bank or private lending institution	Bank or private lending institution
BRIDGE LOAN		
Short-term loan (two weeks to three years) taken out to provide capital until long-term financing can be obtained	Bank or private lender	Bank or private lender
CONSTRUCTION LOAN		
A type of loan used to fund construction, with added risk analysis, payment requirements (known as draws) and building inspections to minimize the risk of financing construction	Bank or private lender	Bank or private lender

Legal Structure	Implementing Agency	Typical Use	Limitations
Property owners initiate the process, but municipal authorities must enact legislation allowing the Business Improvement District	Quasi-public entity or nonprofit led by property owners, governed by a board of directors	Often used to revitalize underperforming commercial districts and finance increased maintenance and capital improvements, such as street cleaning and new landscaping	Business Improvement Districts can lead to increased rental rates that push out smaller business owners; public space can become more privatized; activities are not subject to voter or governmental approval
An independent governing entity administers the zone; it is crucial that the entity does not own, develop or operate entities with interests in the zone	Development authority or quasi-public agency	Purpose is to stimulate foreign investment and economic activity by lowering the cost of doing business and reducing risk. Often established in developing countries to attract employers, reduce unemployment and increase economic activity	Special Economic Zones are often criticized for favoring multinational corporations at the expense of local companies. Nations can become involved in "bidding wars" to attract investors by offering incentives such as tax breaks. Corporations will sometimes move between zones to continue receiving favorable treatment and incentives. Working and living conditions, as well as social and environmental protections, can be poor
Zoning or municipal ordinance regulates the identification of historic properties and permitting review of proposed development or rehabilitation	Private property owner or nonprofit entity	Typically used to preserve the historic character of a specific neighborhood or a landmark property. May be used in conjunction with land trust or other tools	While preservation of historic properties has been shown to increase property values and generate economic activity, strict historic preservation ordinances or burdensome review processes can act as a disincentive to develop offsetting any gains from tax incentives or grants
Savings account, often regulated. In some countries deposits are insured	Individual or private entity	Housing purchase, retirement, health care and seed capital for businesses	Savings globally have been declining as credit has become more available; the countries in which most of the urban growth will take place in the next 20 years have very low rates of domestic savings
Mortgage note secured by a lien recorded on the property title	Individual or private entity	Purchase of real estate	Requires a down payment and formal credit history, which makes this form of financing inaccessible to many
Loan note; sometimes secured by collateral	Individual or private entity	Often used in real estate development to fund pre-development costs such as designs and permitting	Interest rates are above conventional financing and may be capped at a lower loan-to-value ratio
Loan note; typically funds are released per a construction budget in installments (or draws) that reflect progress	Individual or private entity	Used to finance the construction phase of a project. Banks manage these loans differently, recognizing that if construction is not completed on time and on budget then the borrower's ability to repay will be impacted	Higher interest rate than conventional loans. The loan-to-value ratio may be lower than what would be allowed on a completed project, recognizing that the property may need to be sold prior to completion. Code inspections may be required

PRIVATE FINANCE

	Source of Funds	Holding/Collection Entity
TITLE INSURANCE		
Protects property owners or lenders against issues or defects in property title that would otherwise prevent them from recovering their investment	Paid by owner and often required by lenders at the time of purchase	Insurance company
PROPERTY INSURANCE		
Insures property owners against common risks to property such as fire, theft and some weather damage	Paid by owner and often required by lenders at the time of purchase	Insurance company
PRIVATE EQUITY REAL ESTATE FUND		
Debt and equity investments in real estate, typically made by institutional or high-net-worth investors over a long time	Paid by investors; funds are recouped through sale of interest in real property	Typically channeled through a fund or special purpose entity that pools funds from investors
REAL ESTATE INVESTMENT TRUST (REIT)		
A structure similar to a mutual fund, through which investors can invest specifically in real estate. Unlike investing in a Real Estate Fund or directly purchasing property, shares can be exchanged and sold and are more liquid	Paid by investors; funds are recouped through sale of interest in property; shares are sold and exchanged	Corporation, trust or special-purpose entity jointly owned by shareholders
FOREIGN DIRECT INVESTMENT		
Used to denote a direct investment in the construction of a building, factory or enterprise. The net inflow of investment to acquire a lasting management interest (10 percent) in an entity that does not operate in the same country as the investor. It is a measure of ownership in productive assets and can be used as a measure of globalization.	Individuals, corporations, banks and governments	Corporations and businesses
LOW-INTEREST LOANS/ NO-INTEREST LOANS		
A loan that does not charge interest, or charges interest below the market rate	Bank or private lender	Bank or private lender
LOAN GUARANTEES (PRIVATE)		
A promise by a third party to assume the debt obligations of a borrower to a lender should the borrower default	Private entities, typically high-net-worth individuals, corporations or institutional investors	Funds are held by the guarantor to be claimed by the lender in the event of default (in some cases funds are held in escrow)
MICROFINANCE		
A small loan given to a low-income individual who would otherwise be unable to access credit	Donations by individuals and foundations, government programs	Banks, community development funds and individuals

Legal Structure	Implementing Agency	Typical Use	Limitations
Insurance policy	Individual or private entity	Typical in United States where title transfers are the responsibility of parties involved rather than the government. Most other countries use land registration systems in which government determines title and is responsible for errors made	Adds costs but mitigates against title risk. Useful in places where government land registration systems are unavailable or unreliable
Insurance policy	Individual or private entity	Typically used to protect against damage to buildings when a third-party lender is at risk	Policies often exclude natural disasters or damages caused by war. Policies are complicated and can be hard for owners to understand. Insurance may not cover the full cost of reconstruction
Typically investments are legally codified through limited partnership agreements	Projects are selected and funds are stewarded by a fund manager	Used to invest in a portfolio of properties, usually in a specific region or of a specific type, such as distressed or foreclosed properties	Funds are locked for a period of 10 to 15 years and the risk to investors is comparatively high. Most funds require a minimum investment of $1 million USD or more
The corporation, trust or special-purpose entity sells "shares" in its investments similar to a corporation	Like companies, REITs may be private or publicly held and traded	Created to allow investors to invest small amounts of money in real estate	The 2009 crash in the real estate market showed REITs are exposed to speculative investing that can undermine the broader market. Few funds currently set social or environmental performance requirements
Investment agreement between investor and foreign firm	Foreign firm	Provides foreign funds and capital that can result in increased job opportunities, technology and skills for the recipient country through the construction, or investment in commercial activity	Multinational corporations can wield an undue amount of influence in smaller, weaker economies, driving out local competition and forcing dependence on foreign capital
Loan note	Individual or private entity	Often used to fund commercial invest-ments that would otherwise be too costly or risky to undertake, such as lending to small businesses or construction of affordable housing	Low-interest loans can be hard to qualify for, and they are usually given when the borrower does not have collateral
Guarantors are usually signatories on the loan note who enter into a separate legal agreement with the lender and/or borrower	The lender manages repayment from both the borrower and the guarantor	Used when the borrower does not have either the cash or collateral to receive a loan. Housing agencies and nonprofits will often turn to a guarantor when seeking development financing	In cases where the borrower is relieved of risk, guarantees can create a disincentive to repay. Used on a larger scale, such as to spur investment in affordable housing or small businesses, this can result in market distortion
Similar to conventional banking and lending operations, but on a much smaller scale	Commercial banks, cooperatives, nonprofit groups	Used to foster social and business development; beneficiaries are low-income individuals and entrepreneurs	Profits may or may not circulate in the local economy. Returns on microfinance activities may not recover management costs; use of funds is at the individual's discretion and may or may not result in increased long-term prosperity for participants

PRIVATE FINANCE

	Source of Funds	Holding/Collection Entity
HOUSING ALLOWANCE		
Private programs that provide grants, subsidies or payroll credits to individuals to defray the costs of market-based housing. Sometimes part of an employment package	Funded by employers, nonprofit agencies, or other institutions on behalf of eligible participants	Employers, nonprofit agencies and other private entities
COMMUNITY DEVELOPMENT BANK OR CREDIT UNION		
Established to provide capital for rebuilding, strengthening and improving low-income communities through targeted lending and investments	Deposits (often reinvested in the community at below market returns) from individuals; nominal membership fees	Bank
COOPERATIVES		
Also known as a co-op, it is an organization that is wholly owned and operated by individual members	Capital raised from the members; part of the capital is often common property of the cooperative	The cooperative and its members
COMMUNITY BENEFITS PACKAGE		
A legally binding agreement between a developer and a community-based organization. The developer agrees to provide specific benefits in return for the community's support (or non-opposition) of the developer's project(s)	Developer	The benefits are often routed through a nonprofit or community organization
COMMUNITY LAND TRUST		
The acquisition and management of land by a nonprofit corporation on behalf of the residents in order to preserve affordability and prevent foreclosures. Land purchased can be a single tract, scattered throughout a target area or encompass an entire community	Paid for by commercial mortgages, construction loans, national, state and municipal grants and credits, private donations, etc.	Nonprofit agencies
CONSERVATION EASEMENTS		
A voluntary agreement that allows a landowner to limit the type or amount of development on their property in perpetuity while retaining private ownership of the land. A property owner may choose to reserve some development rights. In some instances, no further development is allowed on the land. In other circumstances some additional development is allowed, but the amount and type of development is less than would otherwise be allowed	Landowner	Conservation entity
CARBON TRADING		
A market-based approach to controlling climate change through economic incentives for reducing the emission of carbon that is monitored by as central authority. A company must buy permits to continue to produce emissions above their allowance, while a seller is rewarded for producing less emissions	Companies provide the capital needed to pay for the carbon permits. Regulatory agencies are funded by governments	Regulatory agencies

Legal Structure	Implementing Agency	Typical Use	Limitations
Privately managed	Employers, nonprofit agencies and other private entities	Often used to attract workers to relocate to underserved communities, such as teachers to rural areas. Given to eligible groups such as low-income households, government workers, or overseas personnel to help defray the cost of housing. Allows the recipient to choose where they live	Typically subject to a means test, which determines how much a tenant can afford to pay. Abuse can occur if regular income checks are not conducted. Landlords are not required to accept a housing allowance
Normal banking regulations apply	For-profit, nonprofit, foundation, or cooperative	Provides mortgage financing, business loans and consumer banking services typically in low-income communities	Banks and credit unions take on a greater risk by catering to clients with lower credit ratings and collateral. They are limited in size and scope, having fewer locations and resources to provide large loans
There are four general types of cooperatives: worker, producer, consumer and multi-stakeholder. Most act as a limited liability corporation	Initiated by the members of the cooperative. Subsequent membership is by application	Earnings are shared with members as dividends. They are usually formed on the basis of providing a service, such as housing, or to work toward a goal, such as organic farming	Since cooperatives are democratically controlled, decision making can be slow. Keeping members informed can take up a lot of time and effort
Contract between a community-based organization or developer; does not have to be project specific	Can be initiated by either party	Used to encourage or fund local hiring and living wage jobs; affordable housing; can fund traffic mitigation/traffic calming measures; job training programs, etc.	Community benefits may be contingent on the success of the development; what is offered can fall short of a community's needs and expectations; the community loses its leverage to renegotiate once the development is complete
Independent, nonprofit organization	A community-run nonprofit with open membership and an elected board of trustees	Generally established by community members to address a specific need. They will sometimes act as developers of specific projects, such as low-income housing; focus on long-term issues of affordability, or open space preservation	Assessment expenses may be charged or exceed revenues. The most apparent limitations are restrictions to resale, occupancy and development. The dual-ownership model has been criticized for limiting the equity the homeowner receives. The homeowner can be accountable for taxes on the property they do not actually own
Legal agreement that creates a binding encumbrance on the property. The encumbrance is recorded in the land registry or title and is typically enforced in perpetuity	As the recipient of the easement, the conservation entity is responsible for enforcing and maintaining development restrictions	Typically used to allow private landholders to protect their property from unwanted future development and/or to protect valuable natural resources and wildlife	Can decrease the value of the property to future purchasers
There are several trading systems, most notably the Kyoto Protocol and the European Union Emission Trading Scheme	United Nations Framework Convention on Climate Change, an international environmental treaty, and its enforcement treaty, the Kyoto Protocol	Carbon trading aims to financially disincentivize carbon emissions by assigning a dollar amount to an externality, which is an activity of one entity that affects others outside in a way that is outside the purview of the market	Carbon is offset and only "additionality" (emissions above or below standard consumption) can be traded. To achieve significant additionality, projects must be large in scale or aggregated in order to cover the costs of recouping the credit. Critics charge that carbon markets do not address the root causes of climate change, can be a disincentive to developing viable alternative energy sources and lack enforcement.

PRIVATE FINANCE

	Source of Funds	Holding/Collection Entity
CORPORATE SOCIAL RESPONSIBILITY FUNDS **Funding sources created by companies (usually larger corporations) as a way to give back to communities and organizations in need. The funding is usually by application only, and given in the form of grants to organizations that fit a specific mission or theme, such as historic preservation. It can also take the form of job training programs, education or trading commitments with local partners**	Corporations	Corporations
PROGRAM RELATED INVESTMENTS **Investments made by foundations to support charitable activities that involve the return of capital. They use similar methods as traditional banks, such as loan guarantees and equity investments, but are targeted toward charities or business ventures with a charitable purpose**	Foundations and private individuals	Foundations and private individuals hold the debt obligation
CHARITABLE DONATION **A gift made by an individual or an organization to a nonprofit, charity or private foundation. Charitable donations are commonly in the form of cash, but can also be gifts of real estate, vehicles, appreciated securities, clothing and other assets or services**	Individual, corporation or foundation	Nonprofit or foundation
IN-KIND CONTRIBUTIONS **A non-cash contribution or donation that has a monetary value (e.g. construction materials, environmental consulting services, etc.)**	Individuals, companies, professional service providers	Donated materials or services are provided to a nonprofit or community group
SWEAT EQUITY **In the nonprofit or community development field, sweat equity refers to a type of in-kind contribution whereby labor is provided by volunteers or by the recipient of a project in lieu of cash or as a requirement for funding.**	Individual beneficiary, volunteer, employee or vendor	Labor is provided to a nonprofit, community-based entity or corporation
RAFFLES AND AUCTIONS **A common form of charitable fundraising through the auction or raffle of items that are usually donated**	Individuals	Charities such as nonprofits and religious institutions

Researched by Kate Stohr, Sandhya Naidu Janardhan and Nick Brown

Legal Structure	Implementing Agency	Typical Use	Limitations
Corporations are not required to make any charitable donations, but all appropriate tax laws and limitations apply	Organizations usually must apply for funds	Benefits include better reputation, employee satisfaction and brand differentiation. Can also improve the long-term health of a corporation by cultivating lasting relationships with suppliers and employees, as well as generating goodwill with governments and regulatory agencies	Corporate social responsibility programs can result in giving based on factors other than need
Appropriate loan and investment contracts	Nonprofit agency or community-based organization	Foundations use PRIs to supplement existing grant programs when the request suggests an alternative form of financing, such as when the borrower has the potential for generating income to repay a loan	Program Related Investments are not a common form of grant-making or investment, and relatively few foundations run a formal PRI program. They are often distributed through community-based financial institutions
Donations of a sizable amount are usually governed by a grant agreement. Often charitable donations are tax deductible	Nonprofit or foundation	Typically used to support the activities of nonprofit organizations meeting needs in the community that would not otherwise be met	Many grants specifically prohibit the use of funds for capital investments, including the construction of offices or housing. Grants may be restricted to specific activities, making it challenging for nonprofits to fund indirect or overhead expenses. Tax regulations and other factors often influence the amount and timing of donations, making them an often unpredictable source of revenue
In-kind contributions are subject to tax and business law restrictions, which vary by jurisdiction	Donor	A way for nonprofits to receive free or reduced prices on needed materials or professional services. The donor receives a tax deduction for materials donated	Can result in donations that do not match the need. Material donations in particular can be costly to ship or store
The contribution of labor may be informal (volunteers) or formal, which is typically governed by an agreement and measured by hours worked or value of service given	Work is performed by the individual or vendor and managed or overseen by the nonprofit or employer	In the community development field, sweat equity is a means of ensuring that beneficiaries contribute to and have a stake in the success of a project	The skills and training of the individual or group providing the labor may limit the value of the contribution by requiring additional oversight. As a means of creating a sense of ownership, the effect is often limited as people often value time less than they would a cash contribution
Revenue raised is subject to normal tax restrictions	Charities such as nonprofits and religious institutions	Often used to fund capital campaigns for construction projects	Both forms of fundraising may not be as successful as anticipated, depending on participant interest and/or desirability of goods up for auction. Auctions especially require a fair amount of organization and coordination to ensure a return on the time invested

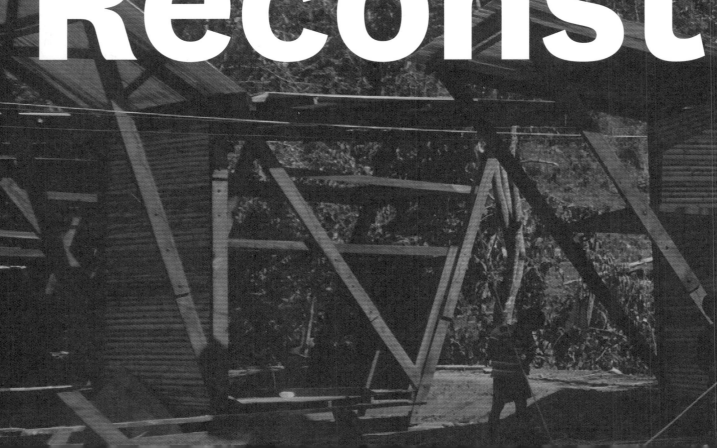

Disaster
Reconsti

Bamboo Shelter

PROJECT LOCATION
Ramsar, Mazandaran, Iran
DATE 2008–9
END USER Latifi family
CLIENT Manouchehr Mirdamad
DESIGN TEAM Javad Abbasi,
Kaveh Akef, Milad Haghnejad,
Pouya Khazaeli Parsa
CONTRACTOR Javad Abbasi
FUNDER Manouchehr Mirdamad
COST $1200 USD (prototype)
AREA 40 sq m/430 sq ft
OCCUPANCY 4 people

Milad Haghnejad, from the design team, stands inside a completed bamboo shelter. Bundles of rice stems are tied to bamboo stalks on the exterior for climate control.
Photo: Pouya Khazaeli Parsa

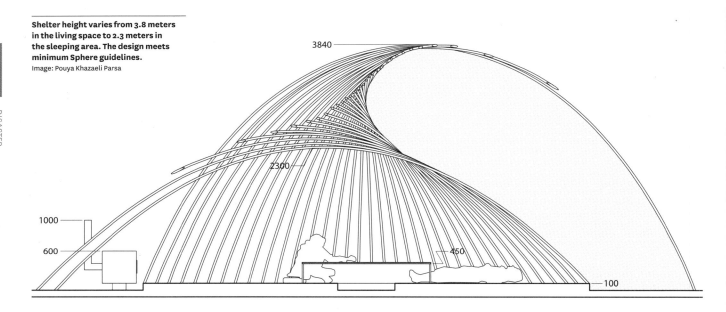

3840

2300

1000

600

450

100

"It is a wonderful method of sheltering—far more interesting than a conventional dome—beautiful and very simple."

Pouya Khazaeli Parsa, architect

In the fall of 2008, Iranian Architect Pouya Khazaeli Parsa wanted his students at Azad University of Tehran to research shelter alternatives for post-disaster situations. The assignment was inspired by late architect Nader Khalili's innovative earthen dome design at The California Institute of Earthen Art and Architecture, which Parsa learned of in the first *Design Like You Give a Damn* book.

One of Parsa's students, Javad Abbasi, took his inspiration from Iran's iconic Sultania Dome, but during the course of building a project model, discovered the strips of foam he was spiraling to form it were too thick. Abbasi realized his error about one-third of the way through model construction and considered it a failure. However, Parsa urged his student on, seeing potential in the

form developing from the flawed dome design. The result was simple and beautiful.

They set out to create a bamboo prototype of the structure of the unique, dome-like form. Bamboo is an abundant and affordable natural resource in the region. The frame was constructed by overlapping half circles formed by joining two strips of bamboo. Gas pipes acquired from the local market were arranged to make a foundation for the bamboo strips. The finished frame was covered with rice stems gathered from nearby fields after harvest. They were bundled together, then placed in layers to create a climatic regulating membrane that expands when wet and shrinks when dry, regulating airflow as seasons change. There are no windows and the thick layer of rice stems on the exterior blocks out daylight.

Candles or lanterns are needed to brighten the interior.

After construction of the bamboo shelter prototype, which took five days total to refine, the owner of the land on which it was built allowed his gardener's family to inhabit it for three months. Parsa hopes to continue improving on the spiral dome design. He's considering incorporating windows and having it produced on a mass scale as a cost-effective, viable shelter.

Architecture for Humanity dedicates this page to our colleague Nader Khalili, who died before he could know how many he inspired.

ABOVE
Gardener Ibrahim Latifi and
family reside in the bamboo shelter
prototype in Ramsar, Iran.
Photo: Pouya Khazaeli Parsa

TOP
Shelter frame made
from 35 bamboo poles
Photo: Majid Zamani

MIDDLE
Bamboo poles twist in over-
lapping half circles to form
the dome-like shelter.
Photo: Majid Zamani

BOTTOM
Rice stems are an abundant
agricultural waste material
in the region.
Photo: Majid Zamani

Soe Ker Tie Hias (Butterfly Houses)

LOCATION Noh Bo, Tak province, Thailand

DATE 2008–9

END USER 60–70 Karen refugee orphans

CLIENT Ole Jørgen Edna

DESIGN FIRM TYIN Tegnestue

CONTRACTOR TYIN Tegnestue, local workers

FUNDER 60 Norwegian companies

TOTAL PROJECT COST $12 300 USD

AREA 10 sq m/107 sq ft (per unit)

OCCUPANCY 4 or 5 people

The siding of the *Soe Ker Tie Hias* (Butterfly Houses) features a local technique of weaving bamboo.

Photo: Pasi Aalto/TYIN Tegnestue

Years of conflict have forced many of the Karen tribal people living along the Burma–Thai border to seek refuge in Thailand. As a result of the mass displacement, there are many homeless Karen orphans in northern Thailand. In 2008, Norwegian architecture firm TYIN Tegnestue was moved to assist in providing Karen children and teens with shelter, hygienic facilities, formal education, and a sense of home. "Building a place helped them build an identity and connect them to that place," says architect Andreas Gjertsen.

From fall of 2008 to May of 2009, the architects completed four related projects in Thailand with this goal. Each project incorporates traditional Karen materials and building methods. The projects included Old Market Library in the Thai capital Bangkok; Safe Haven Library, and Safe Haven Bath house, both in Ban Tha Song Yang, Thailand. Of these projects, perhaps the most innovative was *Soe Ker Tie Hias* (Butterfly Houses) in the small village of Noh Bo, Thailand, a design for sheltering orphans.

> "Working with children is not only enjoyable, it is an extremely efficient and foolproof way to tap into potentials in the community that normally are hidden to practitioners like ourselves."
>
> Pasi Aalto, architectural photographer

Children play on swings made of rope and bamboo hanging from the extended roof of the transitional shelter, which was designed for that purpose.
Photo: Pasi Aalto/TYIN Tegnestue

It was after visiting an existing orphanage and interacting with locals that the design team decided not to build a new proposed orphanage in the conventional block dormitory style. Instead, they pursued the Butterfly Houses design featured here. These cozier dwellings house Karens ranging in age from 2 to 16 years old and feature designated play spaces and swings. "The children we met in Noh Bo have had the worst imaginable start of their lives," Gjertsen says. "There is little doubt that the lack of parents, a home, and an identity makes life hard for them far beyond the actual abuse they have experienced."

Using locally harvested bamboo, the Butterfly Houses consist of six structures, each accommodating six children. "Small, sheltered spaces are easier to 'make your own' and large spaces are good for meetings and social life," Gjertsen says. "We imagined that the children would enjoy and benefit from a range of different spaces." The irregularly arranged buildings create outdoor areas, like those found in Karen villages, where youth can play and relax. Interior spaces double as playrooms, lofted sleeping areas become jungle gyms, and floor space is open for games or impromptu lessons. Siblings are allowed to bunk together in the Butterfly Houses, offering them added peace.

"All of a sudden our clients had to cope with three times the amount of people to shelter and feed," Gjertsen says. The second floor of the library became a sleeping area for close to 50 Karen refugees and the bathhouse had increased the sanitary capacity a lot. Gjertsen recalls the crisis bringing deeper meaning to the work for the design team.

Experts say play therapy helps children cope with trauma. Child protection advocates use it to help Karen orphans. "Play materials and space to play are extremely important in the relief phase, when refugees are in shelters," explains Carol Raynor, a clinical therapist in youth services from Marshall, Missouri. "Children are still reliving the terrors internally, and they need opportunities to play out the trauma with toys and art materials."

TOP
Local workers raise the wooden frame of the first Butterfly House.
Photo: Andreas Gjertsen/TYIN Tegnestue

MIDDLE
Workers installing metal roofing on the house.
Photo: Pasi Aalto/TYIN Tegnestue

BOTTOM
A rendering of a Butterfly House displays its multiple uses.
Image: TYIN Tegnestue

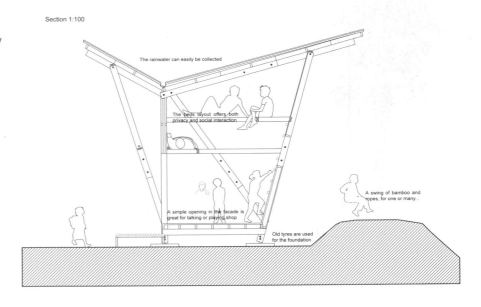

Section 1:100

The rainwater can easily be collected

The beds layout offers both privacy and social interaction

A simple opening in the facade is great for talking or playing, shop

A swing of bamboo and ropes, for one or many...

Old tyres are used for the foundation

Transitional
to What?

LOCATION Port-au-Prince;
Leogane; Papette, Haiti

DATE 2010

END USER 1.1 million internally displaced
refugees following the January 2010 earthquake

PROJECT PARTNER Habitat for Humanity

DESIGN AGENCY Architecture for Humanity

DESIGN TEAM Heidi Arnold, Eric Cesal,
Adam Saltzman, Schendy Kernizan,
Cara Speziale, Megan Roy

FUNDER Individual donations

UNIT COST $700–$6000 USD

RECOMMENDED UPGRADES
$675–$1620 USD/unit

WEB RESOURCE
www.openarchitecturenetwork.org/projects/
transitional_to_what

Temporary or transitional shelters were
deployed en masse to Haiti following the
magnitude 7.0 earthquake that rattled Port-au-
Prince on January 12, 2010. Designs varied from ad
hoc wood and plastic sheeting construction to
sturdier structures secured with hurricane ties
(metal straps that reinforce structural
connections) and built on foundation piers.
Costs ranged between $700 and $6000 USD.
With hurricane season looming, many non-
governmental organizations were concerned
about the safety of families living in flimsy shelters
and called on Architecture for Humanity for help.

People displaced by natural disasters will often
live in transition for several years succeeding the
event in structures intended to be temporary. This
indefinite time frame in Haiti was due to the large
number of people displaced by the earthquake and
the unclear land tenure archive, according to Eric
Cesal, regional program manager for Architecture
for Humanity. To assist relief organizations
building temporary structures, Cesal and a team
of architects evaluated the most common
structures in Haiti and provided a report with
recommendations on how to make them last
longer and withstand the fast-approaching
hurricane season.

The effort resulted in the Transitional-to-
Permanent Housing Evaluation Report, a 51-page
document released in fall 2010 that examined and
compared 10 emergency shelter types in common
use throughout Haiti. The team assessed shelters

TOP
**An aerial view of the damage in
Port-au-Prince, Haiti, after the
January 12, 2010, earthquake.**
Photo: International Organization for Migration

BOTTOM
**Plastic buckets filled with cement
were used to anchor temporary
structures; however, the study found
that they would likely not withstand
hurricane-force winds.**
Photo: Adam Saltzman/
Architecture for Humanity

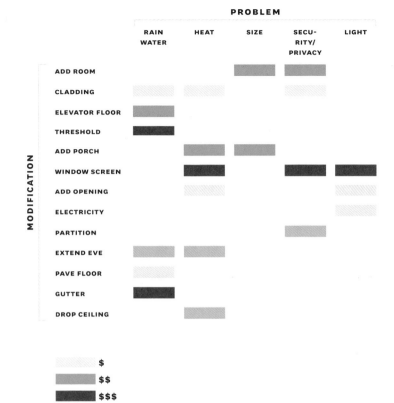

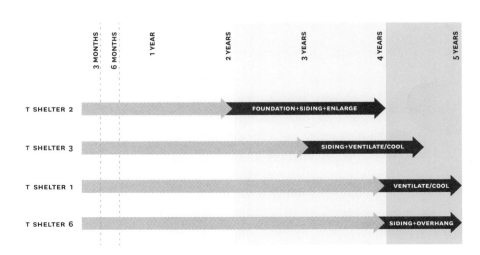

built by various organizations including ADRA, Center for Haitian Studies, the International Organization for Migration, Habitat for Humanity, Samaritan's Purse, the Spanish Red Cross and World Concern. The report evaluated the structures but also provided design solutions and outlined cost predictions and steps to improve safety or extend a given shelter's lifespan.

The study proposes simple, low-cost modifications to transitional shelters—in many cases changes that promise to extend the lifespan by 2 to 3 years. One of the options is a priority upgrade package that includes a floor/ foundation upgrade and the addition of hurricane strapping and siding. A second tier of upgrades covers structural additions such as corrugated steel roofing, block foundations and cladding such pressure-treated wood siding. Finally, the report recommends infrastructure and interior upgrades, adding a latrine, providing water collection, pouring a floor slab or adding interior finishes.

"How can you make a better shelter and not increase the cost?" volunteer Heidi Arnold recalls wondering. "Some of them only cost $700 but some of them cost $3000 and were obviously a better shelter. Then again, some companies were making a better shelter just by using resources more appropriately, using local labor, saving on time."

MOD500-01
SANITATION
FACILITY

Detached pit latrine & shower
stall w/plywood enclosure

Size 4' X 6'

$$

MOD500-02
WATER CATCHMENT
GUTTER

50 gallon
storage barrel

12' horizontal run

$

MOD500-03
POWER CONTROL
BOX

2 surface mount
light fixtures

2 duplex outlets

$

MOD300-02
METAL LATH &
STUCCO

$$$

MOD300-03
MASONRY
FACING

Permanent locations

$$$

MOD300-04
WATTLE &
DAUB &
PLASTER

$$

TOP ROW
**Sanitation facilities, water catchment
and storage, and adequate light
fixtures were critical modifications
recommended by the report to make
temporary shelters more livable.**
Image: Transitional to What?/
Architecture for Humanity

BOTTOM ROW
**Several enclosure and cladding
options were presented to extend
the lifespan of the shelters.**
Image: Transitional to What?/
Architecture for Humanity

The team identified other areas for improvement. "A lot of the residents had really similar issues or problems that needed to be addressed," Arnold says. "Ventilation was a major problem. [Residents] would have to close the shutters at night for security. So people would add ventilation high up on the walls where others could not break in as easily." Although these ad hoc changes did not necessarily compromise the structural integrity of the shelters, their inhabitants often were compelled to add their own customizations. "Typically the shelters were really hot during the day, so a lot of people were building additional shade areas and outside kitchens," Arnold recalls.

In the case of shelters made from plastic sheeting, many people would seek out scrap material as siding to provide a measure of security. Others cut out back doors themselves. "It's really important to have an emergency exit in the back," Arnold says. An additional door provides a critical second exit, particularly in light of the rise in crime following the earthquake.

The team was careful to present its findings in a constructive way. Although the report did not establish correlations or mention any shelter organization by name, the findings were shared with each of the organizations whose structures were evaluated. The report was also shared at the Inter-Agency Standing Committee Haiti Shelter Cluster, a panel of major organizations that met monthly during relief efforts.

CHF International, which was among the agencies whose shelters were evaluated, used the third-party findings to lobby for—and secure—a 15 percent increase in funding to make improvements to its existing shelter model. "[The study gave] us the clout to go back to our donors and say we really need to move away from the plastic sheeting, we need to focus more on hurricane straps as well as plywood, because of the security issue," says Ann Lee, CHF International's emergency program director. "And we actually used the study to go back to our donors and get funding for the remainder of our shelters. Out of 2000 shelters, we had between 500 and 1000 shelters left to construct, and we were able to change the plastic sheeting into plywood. It was great for us to be able to justify that."

To ensure that the findings were made widely available, the report was published on the Open Architecture Network and the Inter-Agency Standing Committee websites and can be downloaded at no cost.

T-SHELTER 2	TRANSITIONAL	SEMI-PERMANENT	PERMANENT
FOUNDATION	concrete footing	tie porch footings	continuous footing around outside
FLOOR	none		pour concrete slab 16' x 12'
STRUCTURE	PT wood 2' x 4'		
ENCLOSURE	nailed tarp		exterior stone/cmu wall
OPENINGS	1 door, 3 windows + clearstory	rear window into door	
ROOF			tarp moved to ceiling for air gap
SIZE	16' x 8' + 16' x 4' porch		optional 2nd 8' x 8' room

TOP
An example of proposed modifications for one type of shelter. The study proposed specific modifications to each shelter to make it semi-permanent and permanent.
Image: Transitional to What?/
Architecture for Humanity

BOTTOM
Renderings of T-Shelter 2 show the modifications (pictured above).
Image: Adam Saltzman/
Architecture for Humanity

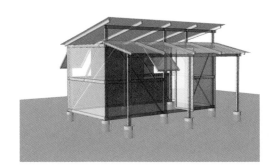

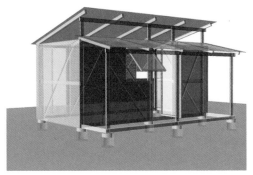

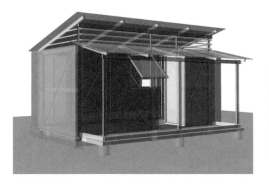

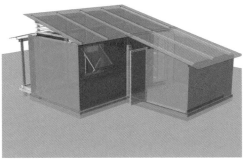

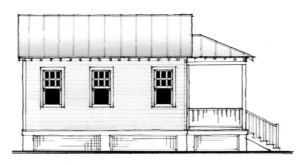

PORCH
8'-0" X 12'-6"

BED
7'-0" X 13'-0"

LIVING
13'-11" X 8'-8"

LEFT
The original Katrina Cottage was designed at the 2005 Mississippi Renewal Forum, a design charrette organized by the Governor's Commission on Recovery, Rebuilding and Renewal.
Image: Marianne Cusato

Katrina Cottage

LOCATION Ocean Springs, Mississippi, USA
DATE 2005–present
END USER Hurricane Katrina survivors
AGENCY State of Mississippi Governor's Commission on Recovery, Rebuilding and Renewal
DESIGNER Marianne Cusato
ADVISERS Michael Barranco, Andrés Duany
ADDITIONAL CONTRIBUTORS Ben Brown, Jodie Cook, Diane Dorney, Susan Henderson, Cheryl Lewis, Connie Moran, Eric Moser, Steve Mouzon, National Association of Home Builders, Craig Savage, Bruce Tolar, Irina Woelfle
CONTRACTOR Andy Mills, Jason Spellings
FUNDERS State of Mississippi Governor's Commission on Recovery, Rebuilding and Renewal; James Hardie Building Products
PROTOTYPE COST $55 000 USD
PROTOTYPE AREA 28 sq m/308 sq ft
MANUFACTURED COST PER UNIT
$33 000–$77 500 USD
SITE BUILT COST PER UNIT $112 084–$152 494 USD
UNIT TYPES 1 bdrm, 2 bdrm, 3 bdrm
AREA PER UNIT 56 sq m–167 sq m/
600 sq ft–1800 sq ft
NUMBER OF UNITS 2666 (Mississippi);
479 (Louisiana)
PROGRAM COST $281.3 million USD (Mississippi);
$74.5 million USD (Louisiana)

A brightly colored cottage, 300 square feet in size, was dwarfed by the huge model homes at the 2006 International Builders Show in Orlando, Florida. It was the original Katrina Cottage, a permanent alternative to the ubiquitous Federal Emergency Management Agency (FEMA) trailers that had cropped up around the Gulf Coast region. Marianne Cusato designed the cottage during a design charrette after Hurricane Katrina, facilitated by the planning firm Duany Plater–Zyberg and hosted by the Governor's commission on rebuilding. The small home met international building codes and was viable for long–term use, unlike the trailers, which were falling under scrutiny for health concerns.

Federal disaster relief statutes prevented FEMA from supplying permanent housing to hurricane survivors immediately after Katrina. So, in 2006, Congress appropriated $400 million for the Alternative Housing Pilot Program to fund testing of new approaches in four states affected by Hurricane Katrina. Much of this funding went to efforts in Louisiana and Mississipi, which deployed designs inspired by the original Katrina Cottage that was developed during the Mississippi Renewal Forum.

The Mississippi Alternative Housing Program was awarded $281.3 million for 2666 prefabricated cottages, at about $105 000 per unit on average including hard and soft costs. Hard construction costs are about $33 000 for one–bedroom cottages, $38 000 to $40 000 for two–bedroom cottages, and $48 000 to $50 000 for three–bedroom cottages, according to Jason Spellings, former housing policy adviser to Mississippi Governor Haley Barbour. (It is interesting to note the Make It Right housing program and Biloxi Model Home programs built permanent, traditionally constructed homes with hard costs as low as $80 000.)

Tennessee firm Looney Ricks Kiss Architects designed the Mississippi Cottage. They were delivered to the site on trailers and could be built on permanent foundations. Many communities rejected the cottages because, though up to code, they were perceived as temporary.

"We built the cottages to the US Department of Housing and Urban Development Manufactured Housing Standards so that we would not need to modify them to every small town zoning ordinance," Spellings says. "When towns saw this, they thought 'mobile home,' and banned them, sometimes without ever seeing them."

There were other factors that dissuaded people from embracing the cottages. Zoning regulations in Mississippi often stipulate a minimum home

**The Katrina Cottage was built
on a tractor and could be wheeled
onto site.**
Photo: Jeffrey K. Bounds

square footage, a reflection of the drive of the real estate industry toward larger houses, according to Bruce Tolar, architect and developer of the Cottage Square neighborhood in Ocean Springs, Mississippi. Additionally, residents risked losing their warranty on additions and renovations so they chose not to build them on permanent foundations.

The Katrina Cottage was also piloted in Louisiana. Cypress Realty Group drafted Louisiana's proposal for stick-frame construction cottages. Due to increased costs, the state received $74.5 million to build 479 cottages, at about $112 084 to $152 494 per unit including soft and hard costs. Hard construction costs averaged $77 500 for these units.

No houses had been built four years after Katrina. The Louisiana Legislative Auditor published a review in March of 2009 that detailed the delays and chronicled 14 months of program

development by the Louisiana Housing Finance Agency before Governor Bobby Jindal transferred the program to the Louisiana Recovery Authority, which spent five months renegotiating the original contract with the government and Cypress Realty Group. As of April 2011, 336 cottages were completed, and 143 more were planned that year, according to the association's Housing Policy Director Wil Jacobs.

Quality control was a challenge when it came to applying the architectural standards of Katrina Cottages to manufactured housing. "We had to fight to preserve roof pitches, ceiling heights, window configurations and other details. That's because, in manufactured housing, what fit existing machines and satisfied current industry price points often trumped the design and materials quality we were after," says Ben Brown, a principal at PlaceMakers planning. For three months in the fall of of 2010, he lived and worked

in the original Katrina Cottage. "It was designed for a family of four, so I slept in a bunk bed for the first time since I was a kid," Brown says, adding that the cottage's small size made it impossible to hide any design defects and poor workmanship more visible. The Katrina Cottages are an improvement on government-supplied trailers but the deployment has been slower than anticipated and it is unclear where the units will go next. Though designed with the vision of being reused in another disaster, no real plans have been made, says architect David Perkes, founding director of the Gulf Coast Community Design Center, who helped address some of the issues associated with distributing the cottages.

Ma'erkang Steel Frame Housing

LOCATION Yang Liu Village,
Sichuan Province, China
DATE 2008–9
END USER 400 earthquake survivors
in Yang Liu Village
CLIENT Chinese government
DESIGN FIRM Rural Architecture Studio
DESIGN TEAM Mei Fan, Tsing Hua,
Jiang Jiaije, Liang Jin, Ma Maolin,
Huang Yabin, Hsieh Ying-Chun
ENGINEERING Hsieh Ying-Chun,
Autodesk-China
CONTRACTOR Autodesk-China,
local villagers, Hsieh Ying-Chun
MANUFACTURER Rural Architecture Studio
CONSULTANTS Luo Jiade
(Tsinghua University sociology department)
FUNDERS Autodesk; Beijing Red Cross
Foundation; Narada Foundation;
Hsieh Ying-Chun
COST PER UNIT 90 000 Chinese yuan/
$14 000 USD
AREA 108 sq m/1162 sq ft
NUMBER OF UNITS 56

Roofs are built from corrugated steel and walls from cement. Insulation consists of local materials such as bamboo, wood, stone, straw, and earth, which minimized construction and transportation costs.
Photo: Rural Architecture Studio

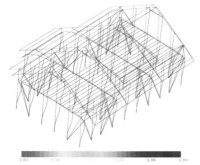

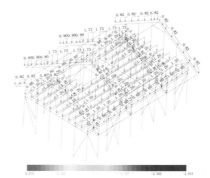

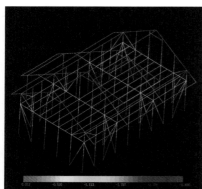

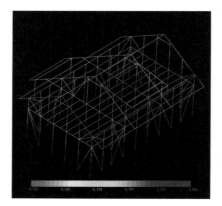

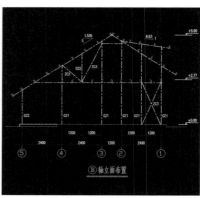

China and Taiwan are in a region with complex tectonic geography and seismic activity. In the fall of 1999, a 7.6-magnitude earthquake struck Taiwan, destroying the stacked brick and stone buildings common to the country's rural areas. Thousands of people died and many were displaced. The widespread devastation created an immediate need for housing.

Among the first to respond was Taiwanese architect Hsieh Ying-Chun. He realized the need for quick, resilient housing that could be erected by people who did not have specific training—a departure from the traditional *chuan-dou* wood frame construction used for over 5000 years. Ying-Chun turned to preformed steel beams as a solution. "Lightweight steel helps to create the openness for my building system and can be applied to different sorts of houses," Ying-Chun says.

When an equally catastrophic earthquake hit China's Sichuan province in 2008, the software company Autodesk teamed with Tsinghua University and Ying-Chun to create the Ma'erkang Project. Using 3-D design and engineering rendering technologies and Ying-Chun's steel frame design, the team created a disaster response plan focused on providing a blueprint for permanent, sustainable, replicable rebuilding on a large scale.

In order to ensure maximum stability and earthquake resistance, the Autodesk research and development team in Shanghai, China, ran Ying-Chun's design through rigorous structural simulations, according to Autodesk spokeswoman Roohi Saeed. In addition, analysis visualization modeling of sun, shade and wind conditions showed the thermal activity of the house through all seasons. "Using Autodesk Revit Architecture software, the team analyzed energy savings and ultimately designed a 50 percent energy-efficient building that performs well in summer and winter in different climatic conditions," Saeed said.

Detailed reports of materials and construction costs were calculated to reduce waste. The team also did data output on the carbon emissions of product production and construction to understand and reduce their carbon footprint for the project. Within nine months, a team of designers had produced five standardized home designs that could be configured in multiple ways.

ABOVE
The Autodesk Research and Development team in Shanghai ran a load analysis on the steel frame design through structural simulations to help ensure maximum stability and earthquake resistance.
Image: Autodesk

ABOVE
An earthquake survivor surveys the reconstruction efforts in Yang Liu, China. Steel beams can be bolted together into easily configured forms.
Photo: Rural Architecture Studio

RIGHT
Architect Hsieh Ying–Chun continues to help with disaster reconstruction. Since the Ma'erkang Project, his firm Rural Architecture Studio has helped organize labor and financing so that the steel frame design can be built independently.
Photo: Autodesk

Flooding in New Orleans, Louisiana, after Hurricane Katrina struck on August 28, 2005.
Photo: Jocelyn Augustino/ Federal Emergency Management Agency

40 million people were at risk from coastal flooding from rivers and oceans in 2007. By 2075, that number is expected to climb to

150 million

Organisation for Economic Co-operation and Development, Cities and Climate Change, 2010.

In 2010 **89%** of the world's natural disaster victims were from Asia.

China alone represented **67%** of those reported victims.

North and South America combined with Europe accounted for only **6%** of the worldwide victims.

"Annual Disaster Statistical Review 2010," The International Disaster Database www.emdat.be/

Worldwide, the total number of natural disasters reported each year has been rising steadily in recent decades, from

78 in 1970

to

348 in 2004

The International Disaster Database www.emdat.be/

LIFT House

PROJECT TYPE Prototype
LOCATION Dhaka, Bangladesh
DATE 2009–10
END USER Mia family
DESIGNER Prithula Prosun
ENGINEER ABC Associated Builders Ltd.
CONTRACTOR/MANUFACTURER
ABC Associated Builders Ltd.
ADDITIONAL CONSULTANTS
Bangladesh Housing and Building Research
Institute, Buoyant Foundation Project,
Elizabeth C. English, University of Waterloo
School of Architecture
FUNDER International Development
Research Centre ECOPOLIS
Graduate Research and Design Award
COST $5000 USD per unit
AREA 37 sq m/400 sq ft per unit
UNIT OCCUPANCY 5 people

In January 2010, Prithula Prosun worked with ABC Associated Builders Ltd. to design and build the first Low Income Flood-proof Technology (LIFT) house in Dhaka, Bangladesh. A result of Prosun's master's thesis in architecture from Canada's University of Waterloo, the house is designed to float two connected residential units upwards with rising floodwaters and allows them to return to ground level as the water recedes.

"Bangladesh is known for two things: poverty and floods," Prosun says. Dhaka, the capital city, struggles to provide adequate housing and basic services for its urban poor, which comprises 37 percent of the city's population. People who live in the flood-stricken slums and squatter settlements of the city have a shortage of clean drinking water and many health problems due to inadequate shelter. The LIFT concept aims to create a cost-effective solution to these issues.

The team broke ground on the house in November 2009 inside the Bangladesh Housing and Building Research Institute and now uses it to give demonstrations for the public. Prosun describes the foundation as "8000 used water bottles, thickly stacked and covered with a waterproof membrane." A brick and reinforced concrete service spine provides vertical guidance and stability to the house, allowing it to rise and fall with changing water levels. For the pilot project, this house is built on two large holding tanks, 3 feet (91 cm) in depth, to demonstrate the floating mechanism.

The amphibious houses are built from bamboo and outfitted with solar panels, natural ventilation, rainwater harvesting, and composting toilets. Water is collected and filtered through a rainwater harvesting system, and a portion of the used water is recycled through bio-sand filters so residents can use it throughout the year. Electricity is derived from two 60-watt solar panels providing enough power to illuminate 10 light fixtures and two fans, as well as power cell phone chargers and small appliances. The shared double pit latrine system composts human waste by diverting urine away from the building through an underground pipe that deposits it under the garden as a nutrient source for plants.

Its economic and eco-friendly design makes the two-unit house habitable for two families at once,

ABOVE LEFT
Laal Mia (not pictured) and his family occupy one LIFT house unit. The other is reserved for demonstrations.
Photo: Prithula Prosun

ABOVE RIGHT
Photo diagram of the mostly bamboo LIFT house, which slides along guiderails on exterior brick walls.
Image: Prithula Prosun

providing sufficient water, electricity and plumbing. "The LIFT house has had a very positive reception," says Srabanti Datta, head of operations for ABC Associated Builders Ltd., the company that helped engineer and build it. "In fact, there were many inquiries of families who wanted to live in the completed LIFT house and only the [one] family was chosen." Laal Mia and his wife and children occupy one of the units while the other is used for community demonstrations.

Datta says there is hope in the community that the government will move quickly to provide land grants and arrange for microcredits to build clusters of LIFT house neighborhoods in the low-income, low-lying slums of Dhaka. This is a way for urban people to coexist with the natural flooding process that occurs in the area. "Floods are a fact of life," Prosun says. She hopes her LIFT house design will become a symbol of the country's reaction to population growth that is quickly overtaking the buildable land. "Where the rise in sea levels is not seen as a threat, but a circumstance to which we can adapt," Prosun says.

ABOVE
A hollow ferrocement foundation (pictured) serves as a mechanism for one house to float. A bamboo frame foundation filled with plastic water bottles is used for buoyancy in the other house.
Photo: Prithula Prosun

BELOW
Photo diagrams of simulated flood conditions to show how the LIFT house rises with water levels.
Image: Prithula Prosun

Alluvial Sponge Comb

PROJECT TYPE Concept
LOCATION New Orleans, Louisiana, USA;
Venice, Italy
DATE 2005–present
END USER Flood-prone neighborhoods
DESIGN FIRM Anderson Anderson Architecture
DESIGN TEAM Mark Anderson, Peter Anderson
MANUFACTURERS Bay Rubber Company,
New World Manufacturing, Seattle Tarp Company
FUNDER Anderson Anderson Architecture;
US Department of State
COST PER UNIT $3200 USD
VOLUME 8300 liters per sponge
LENGTH 12 m/39 ft
DIAMETER 2.4 m/8 ft

What if a levee could expand and contract, swelling and receding with the water's flow? What if a floodwall could help retain soil along fast-eroding shorelines? What if a floodwall wasn't a wall at all?

These are the questions Hurricane Katrina raised for brothers Mark and Peter Anderson, of San Francisco's Anderson Anderson Architecture, when they entered a design contest organized to find solutions for a 160-unit housing complex in New Orleans, Louisiana. The brothers' entry in the High Density on the High Ground competition focused on a corner in the city's Marigny District, along the Mississippi River. It sought to prevent floods and riverbank erosion with the Alluvial Sponge Comb, a configuration of polyvinyl chloride (PVC) bladders filled with super-absorbent polymers like those used in diapers.

These bladders, capable of absorbing 1000 times their weight, create fingers that are placed perpendicular to the waterfront in a comb formation. Spacing between the fingers allows people and wildlife to move between land and water during appropriate conditions. The comb's "teeth" dangle in the water, slowing flow to minimize erosion. Floodwaters rise until reaching the absorbent section and the polymers expand to create a larger barrier. Once the floodwaters recede, retained water evaporates and they revert to their original form.

The opportunity to build and display a prototype of this design concept came in 2006 at the Venice Biennial. At half the size of the New Orleans design, the Alluvial Sponge Comb model playfully greeted visitors to the US Pavilion. "People love them," architect Peter Anderson says. "They love to touch them, to get up close to them, to sit on them; it is important that they are approachable."

The brothers would like to collaborate with polymer manufacturers and hope their development efforts will attract interest in Alluvial Sponge Combs as a viable flood control option, potentially in markets where traditional flood control measures are cost-prohibitive. Currently production costs $2000 USD per finger; however, they are willing to license the product royalty free to nonprofit organizations that want to test them out. The Alluvial Sponge Comb has been exhibited around the world, but as a small company Anderson Anderson Architecture has not had the resources to distribute it.

BELOW
Once the combs expand with absorbed water they create an 8-foot barrier wall.
Image: Anderson Anderson Architecture

OPPOSITE TOP
People lounging on the combs at the 2006 Venice Biennal, where the idea was exhibited.
Photo: Anderson Anderson Architecture

OPPOSITE BOTTOM
Visualization of proposed deployment. The fingers of each comb are portable and can be rearranged. For example, a low-lying riverbank or estuary could be changed by environmental conditions.
Image: Anderson Anderson Architecture

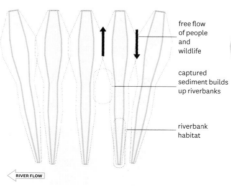

free flow of people and wildlife

captured sediment builds up riverbanks

riverbank habitat

RIVER FLOW

TYPICAL PREPAREDNESS MODE

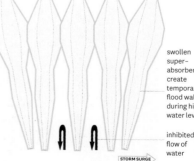

swollen super-absorbents create temporary flood wall during high water level

inhibited flow of water

STORM SURGE

FLOOD BARRIER MODE

Make It Right

LOCATION Lower Ninth Ward, New Orleans, Louisiana, USA
DATE 2007–present
END USER 75 Lower Ninth Ward households
DESIGNERS Adjaye Associates; Atelier Hitoshi Abe; Bild Design; Billes Partners; BNIM; buildingstudio architects; Concordia Architecture & Planning; ELEMENTAL; Eskew+Dumez+Ripple; Gehry Partners; GRAFT; KieranTimberlake; Morphosis Architects; MVDRV; Pugh+Scarpa Architecture; Shigeru Ban Architects; Trahan Architects; Waggoner & Ball Architects; William McDonough + Partners
ARCHITECT OF RECORD John C. Williams
STRUCTURAL ENGINEERS Steve Cali, Frank Fromherz
ELECTRICAL/MECHANICAL ENGINEER Moses Engineers
CONTRACTOR Local contractors in the New Orleans area
SUSTAINABILITY CONSULTANT William McDonough + Partners

FUNDERS Community Development Block Grant (CDBG) program; corporate sponsorships; individual donors; homeowner insurance (as applicable); homeowner cash contributions; mortgage income; in-kind contributions of goods and services; New Market Tax Credits; Road Home Grant Program of the United States Housing and Urban Development (HUD)
PROGRAM FUNDING $40.3 million USD (per audited financials)
AVERAGE COST $340 000 USD (pilot homes); $150 000 USD (subsequent homes)
COST BY AREA $300 USD per sq ft (pilot projects); $150 USD per sq ft (subsequent homes)
TYPE OF UNITS 2–3 bedroom single-family residences
NUMBER OF COMPLETED UNITS 75 (as of August 2011)
NUMBER OF UNITS PLANNED 150

Since Hurricane Katrina struck New Orleans in 2005, the city has been struggling to recover. The rebuilding effort has been marked by population and demographic shifts, the diaspora of many longtime New Orleans residents, and heated political debate and economic challenges.

Among the neighborhoods hardest hit when the levees failed was the city's Lower Ninth Ward, where the average annual income was $27 000 and 25 percent of families lived at or below the federal poverty level. At the same time, the neighborhood had an above average rate of home ownership, as families tended to pass their traditional shotgun-style houses from generation to generation. The Lower Ninth Ward became a touchstone in a debate about the wisdom of rebuilding in areas that are vulnerable to natural disaster. The Make It Right Foundation sided with the residents who wished to stay and rebuild.

Special NO 9 House designed by
architecture firm KieranTimberlake.
Photo Credit: Rafael Longoria

FEATURED PROJECT Special NO 9 House
LOCATION New Orleans, Louisiana, USA
DATE 2009
CONCEPT ARCHITECT KieranTimberlake
ARCHITECT OF RECORD John C. Williams
STRUCTURAL ENGINEERS
Cali & LaPlace Engineers, LLC (execution);
CVM Engineers (design)
ELECTRICAL/MECHANICAL ENGINEERS
Bruce E. Brooks and Associates (design);
Moses Engineers Incorporated (execution)
CONTRACTOR
C&G Construction of Louisiana, Inc.
COST Approximately $462 000 USD (pilot
home); $192 508 USD (subsequent homes)
AREA 141 sq m/1520 sq ft

Founded by actor Brad Pitt with design firm GRAFT and sustainability expert Bill McDonough, Make It Right raised $32 million and made a commitment to build 150 homes. As of fall 2011, the organization has completed 75 LEED Platinum homes, halfway to their goal. Tom Darden, executive director of the Make It Right Foundation, talks with Kate Stohr, co-founder of Architecture for Humanity, about how the program got started, lessons learned, and the foundation's mission to help one community come home after disaster.

KS: You started working to rebuild the Lower Ninth Ward about five years ago. Talk about how the program got started. I know it's been a journey . . .

TD: It has taken a lot longer than we thought and has been a lot more complicated than we anticipated. We started out with a goal of building 150 sustainable houses. That was loosely defined at the beginning. It was houses that were based on these sustainability principles that we believed in –cradle to cradle, which is a philosophy that has been espoused by William McDonough and Michael Braungart in their book *Cradle to Cradle*.

KS: How did the program get started and how did you become involved?

TD: We got started more than a year after the storm. Pitt was concerned about the slowness of the reconstruction effort. He started working with McDonough to bring on board architects to develop concept designs. (We are working with 21 architects, which is a huge number.) My background is real estate development. I signed up to do three weeks worth of research, and eventually came on board to help resolve the property issues, how financing was going to work, and how to get resources for the families.

Pitt funded the initial start-up effort, and then we did a big fundraiser in December 2007 and that is where we raised the initial capital.

It was really gutsy. When we launched, Pitt had the idea to put hot pink fabric around life-size house shaped scaffolding in this Christo-esque public art installation. The hot pink houses represented where we were going to be building the real houses. The idea was to draw attention to the fact that the Lower Ninth

Ward and a lot of areas in New Orleans were still completely abandoned two years after the storm.

KS: What is your process of community engagement?

TD: We literally knocked on the doors of FEMA trailers and asked, "What are your plans for rebuilding?" At first there was a lot of concern in the community, about people coming in and buying up property. We built trust and worked with the state and the Road Home program to acquire the lots people were not returning to. Once a property is transferred to us, we build a house for a family. The qualifying criteria for getting a house is that you, or an immediate family member, lived in the Lower Ninth Ward before the storm.

We started by working with community leaders and the goals came from their feedback. We asked them what they needed. They told us, "Houses. We need schools and grocery stores and all this stuff too, but we're living in FEMA trailers. The first thing we need to do is get out of these trailers and into permanent houses." So that is

what we took on. In addition, the community also told us they wanted to be self-sustainable in the long-term. So when we structured the program financially, we didn't want to continually fund the community. We wanted it to be self-supporting and self-sustainable.

REBUILDING CRADLE-TO-CRADLE

KS: Can you briefly explain the Cradle-to-Cradle principle?

TD: The basic principle is to change the way we design things to be more in line with natural systems, where there really is no such thing as waste. McDonough describes our current manufacturing strategy as Cradle-to-Grave; basically, everything we use is designed to be thrown away. Cradle-to-Cradle products are

ABOVE
Pink Project, an art installation of 150 pink fabric houses in 2007.
Photo: Make It Right Foundation

designed with recycling and reuse in mind from the very start. Not only is the product redesigned, but the entire manufacturing process changed so that pre-consumer waste is used to generate energy. For example, a carpet is made of materials that can be endlessly recycled or a flooring company operates their own recycling facilities.

We wanted all of our building materials to be Cradle-to-Cradle, so that nothing we produced could end up in a landfill. In doing that, all of a sudden, we were getting phone calls from the United States Green Building Council who were saying, "What is going on down there? You guys are submitting more applications for our highest certification level than anyone else."

KS: LEED certification can be expensive. Any resources you spend on certification means that that much less goes toward rebuilding for families. Why did you think that was an important step to take?
TD: We never set out to build LEED Platinum houses, and we were having these similar conversations about whether we should spend

money on certification. The debate was: these houses are green, but how green are they? We needed an elevator speech answer to that and the easiest answer is to certify them. I think it also builds equity for the families who own the houses. If they ever sell these houses, they will have an easy answer to that question too.

KS: Was it hard to build sustainably at a price point that makes sense? In Architecture for Humanity's work we often find there is that learning curve for contractors. The first time they use a new material or building method they price at a higher rate because they are in unfamiliar territory . . .
TD: We work with local contractors and often they are working with a new product. Since they have never used it before they will quote us twice as much to install it. Then, the second time around, they quote it accurately and the cost drops by about 50 percent. Right now we are at about $150 a square foot, which is getting close to market rate construction. So we're spending close to what you would spend on traditional construction for LEED Platinum houses.

At one point, I was riding around the Lower Ninth Ward, and there were so many building materials we use in Make It Right houses, being used in non–Make It Right houses, that I was worried people were stealing them. I thought, "Do we have a theft problem?" No, they were just looking at what we were doing and copying it. It was things like the Green Guard House wrap, the Blue Wood lumber.

Every once in a while there is a product that we don't like, but that we don't have an alternative, or affordable alternative, to use, so we flag that. We are constantly looking for better alternatives. We are tracking all the materials, and evaluating how they help us get to our goal of achieving a Cradle-to-Cradle house.

KS: The pilot houses cost an average of $340 000 for a 1200-square-foot house, on average. Today you are building the same size home for under $200 000. Where did you find cost savings and how have the designs evolved?
TD: We do costing for the roof, the flooring—all the systems—for every phase. We look at it and

TOP LEFT
The first phase of Make It Right houses had over-engineered and unnecessarily costly foundation columns.
Photo: Make It Right Foundation

TOP MIDDLE LEFT
In the second phase, the number of foundation columns were reduced and cantilevers added. This helped drop costs of Make It Right homes.
Photo: Make It Right Foundation

BOTTOM MIDDLE LEFT
The first phase also used custom-fabricated metal brackets to attach the houses to their foundations.
Photo: Make It Right Foundation

BOTTOM LEFT
By using a construction detail that only required off-the-shelf brackets, Make It Right was able to further reduce the costs of the foundation.
Photo: Make It Right Foundation

say, "We spent this amount on the foundations, how can we maintain structural integrity and reduce costs?" We study each aspect of the house.

The first houses had a lot of features we have been able to adjust. For example, the first set of houses had over-engineered foundations. As we got more data on the soil conditions, we reduced the number of house-elevating columns by 50 percent. We were using custom metal brackets that were very expensive; now we're using an off-the-shelf bracket. We have developed wall sections that use 30 percent fewer materials but are five times stronger than what is required by code. We've changed from all carpet to recycled/reclaimed wood flooring options. We've had to have these conversations with the families, and say, "You may not have that really fancy countertop but you will have windows that will help you save on your energy bill."

One of the homes in the first set of homes had a roof that was designed at a 33-degree slope, the perfect angle for solar gain at this latitude. We looked at the cost of building the roof at a strange angle, which is very complicated from a framing perspective, and then we realized that we could just add one more panel at a cost of $300 and achieve the same gain, in terms of solar production.

Another example is the rooftop porch on the house designed by KieranTimberlake. As part of the design specifications we required that architects design for access onto the roof. Because so many people died in their attics in the storm, we didn't want that to happen ever again. Some of the architects developed that idea further in allowing usable space, which I think was really amazing, for a couple reasons. One reason is the view. You had families that were living below the levees, just looking up at these levees, because their houses were slab on grade, below sea level. So the rooftop access has given people a totally new perspective on their community.

At the same time, when we talked to the residents we learned that some of them don't ever use those rooftop porches. The first

A less expensive adaptation of the Special NO 9 House prototype features a simple wood and metal wire balcony.
Photo: Jordan Pollard/Make It Right Foundation

KieranTimberlake house has a very large roof deck, but the owner doesn't use all of it. So we've reduced the size of that space. That's a savings, obviously. We'll take that savings, and one place we might spend it, for example, is in solar panels.

KS: How do you track all of these modifications?

TD: In the specs for each of the designs. Originally we wanted to make sure it got done the way we wanted, so we just did it ourselves. The general contractors got a flat fee. Everything was open book for all the costing, the roof, the flooring, etc. We'd look at the books and say, "We spent this amount on the foundations, how can we reduce costs while maintaining the structural integrity?" We'd study each aspect of the house—by phase and by design.

For the next phase, we are allowing the general contractors to bid using their own sub-contractors. Before, we micromanaged the entire process. We ordered the materials. We negotiated the prices. We got an email from a guy in the Netherlands saying, "We're trying to get our contractors to use these Cradle-to-Cradle materials but they won't actually do it. We specify them, but then they just order their own materials." We were worried about that as well, which is why we took that extra step.

KS: Sounds like a lot of Excel spreadsheets.
TD: It was, but the data is all there and you don't necessarily need an Excel spreadsheet because it is all very blatant, very obvious. You're looking at it saying, "We spent way too much on this one aspect, let's dive into that area." The biggest systems, the ones where we spend the most money, offered the biggest opportunity for savings. So we targeted those specifically. Over time, we're honing in on smaller systems.

KS: How did you determine the elevation of the homes? That can be a major cost-driver...
TD: The feedback that we were getting from the community charrettes was varied. Some people said, "I want my house elevated to minimize flood risk," others said "I want it as high as possible," and still others said, "I want to be able to sit on my front porch without going down the stairs." We wanted to offer two options of five or eight feet above the ground, which are based on flood standards.

KS: Has all this work paid off in terms of the performance of the houses? How much energy are the residents saving?
TD: Energy efficiency shouldn't just be for rich people; working families benefit even more, on a direct, day-to-day basis. New Orleans home-owners in conventional homes on average spend $2075 annually on their utility bill, while Make It Right homeowners spend an average of $1068. For families that have very little disposable income, a few hundred dollars in energy savings a month makes a huge impact. We track the savings but not as well as I would like. I've been trying to get every appliance monitored. That would be ideal, because usage habits come into play heavily.

One of our homeowners came in and asked, "My energy bill just went up, is there something wrong with the solar panels?" Turned out the solar panels were working fine so we knew it was usage. That family has eight teenage grandchildren that live in the house, and play a lot of video games. Another family had a high bill and we found out they work on cars, and were charging the car batteries off of solar.

KS: I know you've gotten some criticism about the designs not being in-keeping with the New Orleans vernacular. How do you respond to that? And more importantly, do the homeowners like the houses?
TD: In terms of the design selection, not everyone loves all of the designs, but they always love one of the designs, right? Something else to note is that we are not—and I think we get criticized for this all the time—master planning this neighborhood. We are not saying, "This house should only go next to this house." The residents make those decisions. They choose the colors. They choose which house goes next to which house. Those are decisions that are being made by the residents who are living in the community, and I think that is empowering.

KS: So if a house looks a little wacky, your view on it is that somebody likes it.
TD: Yeah. At the end of the day, we won't build any houses unless they are chosen. So someone liked that house for it to be built.

KS: That's a market-based process . . .
TD: Exactly, and the architects knew that on the front end. If they wanted their house to be built, then they had to think about what the families they met through the community charrettes would want in a house. The goal was to design a house that met their needs and would be marketable. The way you test that is to see if it gets chosen.

The one exception is the FLOAT House [by Morphosis]. The reason we did not allow it to be selected as part of the catalog is because we didn't know whether we could get it permitted. So we built that one speculatively, and one of the residents in our program fell in love with it and moved in.

KS: Where did the initial funding for the program come from?
TD: We launched the program in December of 2007, which is when we raised the initial capital of $5 million. This was after a year of research and our initial seed money for that was $200 000. The first year we were operating with just a couple interns.

We were constantly thinking, we had X amount of capital and it changed all the time, even with the initial launch. We'd get pledges, but the pledges sometimes took years to come in. So while it looks like these funds are available on our IRS forms, you can't always tap them.

KS: Tell me more about some of the financing issues that needed to be worked through before starting construction.
TD: We had to develop new financing structures from scratch; we couldn't just take your standard affordable housing template. For example, the Lower Ninth Ward had the highest percentage of homeownership in New Orleans. Families had owned their lots for generations, but with no paperwork. So we had title issues.

We worked with families on the loan programs. We would go to community meetings a couple times a week with PowerPoints with bar charts showing how financing structures work. We work with each family to determine what they can afford. We use basic principles. No family pays more than 30 percent of annual income for their total housing costs, including taxes and insurance. That means we customize each loan to fit those requirements. Whenever they can qualify for grants; we'll help them do that. We ask them to pay as much as they can toward the home, and whatever the gap is, between what they can afford and what the sales price of the home is, we use a soft second forgivable loan to fill it. The loans are forgivable over 15 years, so if a person lives there for 15 years it is forgiven.

KS: Architecture for Humanity used a similar forgivable loan structure in Biloxi, Mississippi. What was really frustrating for us was when we had a family that we knew was eligible for other grants and did everything right, and yet they

wouldn't qualify on a technicality. One of our homeowners had inherited the house the day before the hurricane, so there was no paperwork. She didn't qualify, and she was a single mom with six kids.

TD: We had a lot of similar situations. We had families whose credit was destroyed from being displaced by the storm. They were getting dinged on their credit for not paying their utility bill on a house that was no longer there. These families did not qualify for a traditional mortgage, so for families where that happened we set up our own bank and we financed those first mortgages. One woman had got some Road Home money, paid a contractor, and the contractor stole it. But we didn't tell her, "I'm sorry, now we can't work with you." We worked with her to figure out what she could afford, and we structured a loan for her.

KS: What about the Road Home program [a government grant program for homeowners]? Has that worked to bring people back?

TD: The Road Home program is incentivizing people to come back. If you moved somewhere else, they offer a certain amount for your lot. If you stayed within the state you got a larger amount, but you got the biggest grant if you came back and rebuilt.

But, it's complicated. We had one family who got some Road Home money, I think they had $5000, and we had one family that had $150 000, which is the most you could qualify for. Why? I don't know; how do you plan around a government program that is that random?

KS: Was there homeowner insurance money that you could tap into?

TD: Some families had insurance and some didn't; some families had insurance and couldn't get the insurance companies to pay. Our flood elevation requirements are stricter than they need to be for homeowners to qualify for the National Flood Program [national flood insurance program]. Their requirements were three feet of elevation for base flood, and we were saying we would do two feet above base flood as a minimum, and we would go as high as five feet above base flood.

KS: Have you received government funding or support?

TD: The first check from the government that we got was just a month ago [in August 2011]. We've got a grant now from the city that, we hope, will replace the streets in a way that will capture stormwater using pervious concrete and manage traffic with traffic-calming features. Basically, what we are doing is fronting the money to rebuild, and hoping we can replace most of it through public funding once it gets freed up. The city is proposing a soft second mortgage program that will cut our program fundraising needs in half, if it goes through, and they have been working on it for six years. It is Community Block Redevelopment Grant funding that went to the city of New Orleans and has been sitting there untapped.

NEIGHBORHOOD DEVELOPMENT

KS: Some have questioned whether you should be rebuilding in the Lower Ninth Ward given how vulnerable it is to flooding. How do you respond to that?

TD: We are looking at safety, flood risk—intentionally designing like we give a damn—rebuilding above sea level will minimize flood risk as much as possible.

We are also looking at the macro-level protections. For example, rebuilt levees: they completely replaced them and it is a new design. The largest flood gate, I think in the world, was just installed at the mouth of the Mississippi River to block storm surges. You factor in wetlands restoration work and we hope that we will continue to increase the level of protection over time. We've got to continue to advocate for wetland protection because it is not currently happening at the scale it should.

So that is the risk factor. But the biggest factor, in our decision to rebuild, was that it was happening anyway. While everybody was sitting around talking about whether or not to rebuild in this area, people were rebuilding anyway. What they were building was the same quality, and in some cases a lower quality than what was there before, because they were building whatever they could afford. Often that was with limited

resources and resulted in substandard, more vulnerable housing.

KS: Are you building in the whole Lower Ninth Ward district, or a smaller area within it?

TD: It is a 16-block area, expanded from 12 blocks, but we won't expand it again.

KS: The population of New Orleans had been shrinking even before Hurricane Katrina. I am curious as to whether or not there will be a market for these houses.

TD: All of these houses are pre-sold, so we won't build a set of houses unless they are already sold. So on the small scale of our project, we know there is a market. We don't know whether the Lower Ninth Ward will ever have the 5000 houses that it lost but we were pretty sure 150 of them would be built. The number of 150 is what we came up with because we thought if no one else builds anything else in the area, 150 homes was enough to function as a neighborhood.

KS: So basically Make It Right came up with the lowest number of houses that you felt could function as a viable neighborhood, and you set that as your target, and you are working to create density?

TD: Yes, by limiting it to this one area.

KS: So there was a strategy to it?

TD: You're surprised about that?

KS: Well, it was a big question. New Orleans had a shrinking tax base, so if people rebuilt haphazardly, then the city would continue to have to support a large service area, but with half its former population. It was a huge issue.

TD: And it still is, especially in terms of maintaining infrastructure. I think that what will happen in the future is that certain areas will be much more rural in feel, and in terms of the services that they offer, such as road maintenance. I think that is really what will happen, but the city has said, from a policy perspective, it will support these areas, and is encouraging scattered redevelopments, with no attempts at density or concentration. And it is a problem. From my perspective, we were solving that issue by maintaining our focus on this one very small area.

Children get off a school bus in New Orleans' Lower Ninth Ward. At the program's halfway point, Make It Right has completed about 75 homes (pictured in background).
Photo: TA Smith/Make It Right Foundation

KS: Are you working on trying to address the vacant lots? New Orleans had one of the highest rates of vacant lots in the country.
TD: Yes, it is a big deal. We received a grant to take care of those lots; some of the lots are being maintained, some of them are not. Right now, we are allowing the grass to grow, because we want to see who is maintaining their lot and who is not. It is a visual way to see which property owners we need to [reach out to in order to find out what their plans are for their lot].

KS: Who is buying the houses, is it the people who owned the land previously?
TD: No, not all the time, but they are all former Lower Ninth Ward residents. In some cases it is an immediate family member, like a son or daughter, of someone who owned the lot. We like that, because it is bringing back a younger generation. We have a lot of young families, and we have a lot of older people, so it is a good mix.

KS: Where are you now in the life of the program?
TD: We are halfway to our original goal of 150 houses, but the goal is really more than 150 homes. We have had a catalytic effect; people have taken what we've learned and incorporated it. It is a vibrant neighborhood with streets and streetscapes that are functional in their management of storm water and traffic flow. What is really interesting is that we have stopped seeing new problems. You know you're making progress when you just see the same problems, or at least, not just new problems all the time. So the engine is built, it's running, and we're fine-tuning it.

KS: So, when you think about this community in thirty years time, what do you see?
TD: It is a neighborhood that is diverse, mixed income, with children playing in safe areas. We are getting to that point where we can start turning our attention to making sure there are

some supportive services in place. We have got 75 houses now plus some influx of foot traffic, which is enough of a critical mass. People bicycle down to the Lower Ninth Ward from the French Quarter. Can they stop and buy a cup of coffee and spend some money to help sustain the community? I think the answer is yes, over time.

In 30 years, I think the Lower Ninth Ward will be a functioning neighborhood, and we will have proven that the risks that we took around questions of urban planning, building sustainably, building storm-resistant houses, will have worked.

My favorite part of my day is coming over the Claiborne Avenue Bridge, which connects the Lower Ninth Ward to the rest of the city. It is really high, and you're looking down on the neighborhood, which was nothing, then hot pink houses, then nothing again, and now it is these crazy roof lines, with solar panels. You just see solar everywhere.

Biloxi Model Home Program

LOCATION Biloxi, Mississippi, USA
DATE 2005–8
END USER 7 families
COMMUNITY DEVELOPMENT AGENCY
Hope Coordination Center (now the Hope Community Development Agency)
IMPLEMENTING PARTNER
Architecture for Humanity
PROGRAM PARTNERS
Enterprise Corporation of the Delta,
The Gulf Coast Community Design Studio of Mississippi State University
School of Architecture, Art + Design,
Hands On Gulf Coast,
Warnke Community Consulting
DESIGN FIRMS Brett Zamore Design;
CPDWorkshop; Gulf Coast Community Design Studio of Mississippi State University School of Architecture, Art + Design;
Huff & Gooden Architects; Marlon Blackwell Architect; MC2 Architects; Studio Gang

STRUCTURAL ENGINEER Black Rock
CONTRACTORS More than 300 volunteer groups and construction firms
FUNDERS Autodesk; Blinds.com;
Caesarstone; Chris Madden Inc.;
Daltile; Duo–Gard; IBM; Isle of Capri Casino;
JamesHardie; Kohler; McCormick
Tribune Foundation; Nourison;
Oprah's Angel Network;
Senox, University of Arkansas
NUMBER OF UNITS
7 pilot homes (Model Home Program):
100 new construction; 787 rehabbed homes
UNIT TYPES
2–4 bedroom single–family residences
AREA 18–130 sq m/200–1400 sq ft
CONSTRUCTION COST PER UNIT
$145 000 USD (new construction);
$20 000–$60 000 USD (damage rehab)
PROGRAM COST $5 million USD
(including $3.3 million USD revolving loan fund)

This is an excerpt from *Rebuilding After Disaster: The Biloxi Model Home Program*, a book published by Architecture for Humanity detailing the program's success. To purchase, visit www.architectureforhumanity.org.

The Biloxi Model Home Program was created to assist residents of Biloxi, Mississippi, in meeting the challenges of rebuilding their community after Hurricane Katrina.

East Biloxi, an ethnically diverse community with a large Vietnamese immigrant population, was one of the hardest hit areas of the Gulf Coast. More than 90 percent of the neighborhood's housing stock was damaged or destroyed. Even before the devastation of Hurricane Katrina, the community suffered from poverty, drug activity and disinvestment. Nearly one in four East Biloxi residents earned incomes less than 150 percent of the federal poverty line, and most made less than $26 000 per year. In short, like in many other areas along the Gulf Coast, the effects of Hurricane

Katrina in East Biloxi exacerbated preexisting
social and economic problems.

Rumors spread among those displaced by the
storm. The community feared that new building
elevation requirements would dramatically
increase the cost of rebuilding their homes,
making it impossible for them to return home.
In addition, regional and citywide planning
initiatives raised the threat that some residents
might lose their properties altogether by
recommending that the city reclaim more
vulnerable, low-lying areas through eminent
domain.

There was no single source for reliable, accurate
information. Few agencies were able to answer
homeowners' most basic and pressing questions:
Is it safe to rebuild on my lot? How will the new
building codes and flood elevations affect me?
If I rebuild, what can I afford?

The goal of the Biloxi Model Home Program,
which launched in 2006, was not only to help
answer these questions for homeowners, but

perhaps more importantly, to provide a one-stop-shop for residents seeking assistance in the aftermath of the hurricane, from architectural and construction services to legal and financial aid. The program was groundbreaking because it brought design and construction services, case management and an innovative financing structure together under one roof.

The program lasted more than three years and enlisted a wide array of organizations and agencies. It was led by the Hope Coordination Center (then the East Biloxi Coordination, Relief and Redevelopment Agency). Architecture for Humanity secured $3 million in funding from Oprah's Angel Network and provided a seed grant to the Mississippi State University School of Architecture to relocate its studio from Jackson to Biloxi. Warnke Community Consulting and Enterprise Corporation of the Delta worked to structure a loan fund, which was administered by the Hope Coordination Center and Architecture for Humanity. Support also came from design and construction firms, local community-based organizations and the city of Biloxi itself, which expedited permitting and helped resolve zoning issues. Hands On Gulf Coast provided volunteer housing, and some 300 volunteer organizations participated in mold removal, repairs and reconstruction.

Early on, the center established a grid system of East Biloxi's neighborhoods, assigning a target area on the map to each of the many relief organizations that arrived to help. This was a critical early step. It allowed the relief groups to work quickly with a minimum of confusion and overlap. The grid system was also a huge help to the center's caseworkers because they knew exactly where to refer families based on where they lived.

Next, assessments and a survey conducted by volunteer groups identified owners, including those displaced, and helped prioritize immediate needs. The house-by-house survey gathered key data, such as whether a property was rented or owner occupied, whether the structure was more than 50 percent damaged (and therefore likely to be condemned), the homeowner's interest in selling or rebuilding, as well as income and demographic information.

TOP
A local church after Hurricane Katrina.
Photo: David Perkes/Gulf Coast Community Design Studio

MIDDLE
Architecture for Humanity Program Manager Mike Grote teaches Mike's Construction Fun Time.
Photo: Architecture for Humanity

BOTTOM
The Parker family inside their home
Photo: Leslie Schwartz

The center established a case management system using the Coordinated Assistance Network (www.can.org) platform. In addition to tracking residents' needs, this shared database supported threaded financing from a wide variety of private, state, and local funding sources.

As volunteer groups ramped up, Architecture for Humanity established a Building 101 training program in their off-hours to train volunteer leaders to oversee crews and prevent unsafe construction. Led by Program Manager Mike Grote, and jokingly referred to as Mike's Construction Fun Time, the class covered the basics of housing construction, mechanical, electrical and plumbing systems.

The program was also a chance to set high standards for new construction in the area and establish a set of best practices that could be used going forward. Architecture for Humanity invited (a competition would have taken too long) 12 architects from the region to design sustainable, hurricane-resistant, affordable homes that met new construction standards and height elevations required by the city. Of these, families selected six firms to help them rebuild their homes at a House Fair held in the summer of 2006.

Families worked one-on-one with architects and design professionals. The program approached rebuilding through standardizing design processes, methods, and partnership strategies—as opposed to standardizing a single design. Much effort and time was devoted to creating program materials, from developing family selection guidelines, to assisting families applying for financial aid. The aim was to enable partners, and others, to adopt and adapt the program in the future.

The single biggest hurdle to rebuilding East Biloxi, however, was money. A significant proportion of homeowners in Biloxi were underinsured or uninsured against what insurers called "water-driven" (versus "wind-driven") damage. Mortgage companies require homeowners in flood-prone areas to carry flood insurance, but many families in East Biloxi had inherited their homes and owned them outright. Federal and state financial assistance came slowly and erratically. Complicated rules and restrictions meant that a significant portion of homeowners in Biloxi did not qualify for any kind of assistance at all. Despite billions of dollars of private and public financial assistance flowing into the area,

> **"Through this collaboration we have helped so many people. We've been able to find the resources to bring families back home from one end of Biloxi to the other. It's like a city reborn."**
>
> Bill Stallworth, Hope Coordination Center

families faced a gap between what they could afford and the cost of construction.

To further complicate matters, what assistance was available came in the form of material grants, not cash, or was restricted to filling "unmet needs." Families first needed to receive assistance before they could qualify for these funds. It was a catch-22.

The solution was a revolving community loan fund. Here's how it worked: Families received a loan; however, there was no interest charged on the loan and families were not required to make loan payments. Instead, a lien was placed on the property. If homeowners sold their home within five years, the loan would be recaptured at the time of the sale. Alternatively, each year that homeowners remained in the house a portion of the loan would be forgiven. If they stayed in the home for 10 years or more the debt would be completely forgiven.

These forgivable loans (also called recoverable grants) advanced the entire cost of construction. The loans allowed families to begin rebuilding, while they applied for financial assistance from other sources. Because the funding was structured as a loan instead of a grant, families were still eligible for other types of assistance. Later, as money was released to families from private and federal assistance programs, the lien triggered notices to the Hope Coordination Center, which recovered the funds and recaptured the loan.

The program was not without hurdles. Persuading families that the "loan" was more like a grant took some thought. Case managers stopped calling it a "forgivable loan," and called it a "no-pay" loan instead. As volunteered labor dwindled, experienced construction crews were hard to find, causing delays and additional costs. While the fund was able to recapture 20 to 90 percent of the cost of constructing new homes,

it took several years. Funds from federal financial aid programs administered by the Mississippi Development Authority (MDA), which were a key source of financial assistance, took up to two years and in some cases longer to make their way to families.

Despite these hurdles, by August 2008, three years after the storm struck, this unique collaboration had repaired approximately 75 percent of East Biloxi's 2200 damaged homes and constructed more than 100 new homes (including the pilot Biloxi Model Homes featured here). The Hope Coordination Center and Gulf Coast Community Design Studio continue to serve East Biloxi. It changed its name again and is now the Hope Community Development Corporation.

More telling still, the model of pairing community members with professional designers—and the strategy of locating a community design studio within a housing recovery center—has since been replicated across the Gulf Coast and in other disaster areas.

TOP
Jeanette Desporte (middle) with her daughter and granddaughter on the deck of their wheelchair accessible house.
Photo: Leslie Schwartz

MIDDLE
The Parker kids play outside their house.
Photo: Leslie Schwartz

BOTTOM
Louise Odom with her great-nephew Dajntae in their front screened-in porch
Photo: Leslie Schwartz

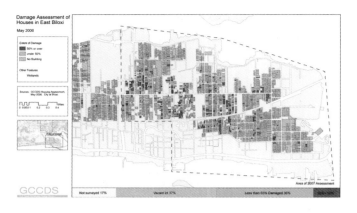

A survey of East Biloxi's building stock.
Image: Gulf Coast Community Design Studio

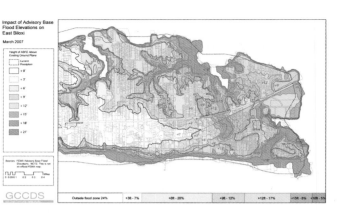

A map of mandated building elevations
Image: Gulf Coast Community Design Studio

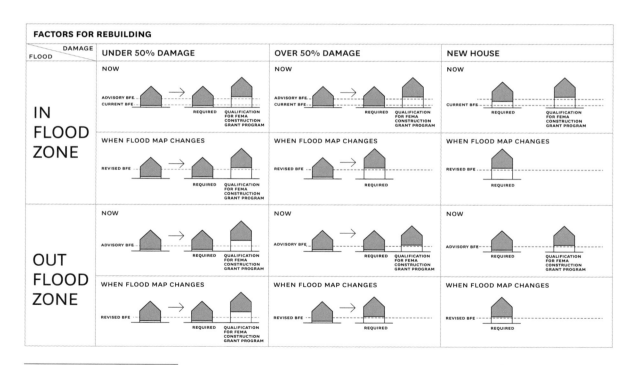

FACTORS FOR REBUILDING

	UNDER 50% DAMAGE	OVER 50% DAMAGE	NEW HOUSE
IN FLOOD ZONE	NOW	NOW	NOW
	WHEN FLOOD MAP CHANGES	WHEN FLOOD MAP CHANGES	WHEN FLOOD MAP CHANGES
OUT FLOOD ZONE	NOW	NOW	NOW
	WHEN FLOOD MAP CHANGES	WHEN FLOOD MAP CHANGES	WHEN FLOOD MAP CHANGES

A diagram of how the new Federal Emergency Management Agency regulations affected efforts to rebuild homes.
Image: Sarah Rowden/Redrawn from Gulf Coast Community Design Studio

Comparing Approaches to Community Design

Architects employed different work models in a number of Gulf Coast communities after Hurricane Katrina. We compared these approaches to rebuilding. By far the most effective approach was the establishment of a community design studio within a local recovery organization. Local firms were quickly overwhelmed with commercial projects. Remote services did not allow for critical construction oversight. Both were difficult to scale. The design studio allowed for a wide range of services to be available to a broader constituency at a fixed cost. It supported micro-planning, volunteer participation and integrated case management. We estimate the cost of design services per household between the three approaches as follows:

Community design studios can be based within a firm, community group or university (but only if allowed to depart from academic calendars and curriculum requirements), and should partner with organizations providing case management.

Energy Efficiency and Carbon Offsetting

We also explored the possibility of funding the construction of more homes through carbon offsets. We applied an energy to CO_2 conversion of 1.413 pounds of CO_2 per kilowatt-hour (the average conversion for the state). New home appliances result in an energy savings of 2.5 tons of CO_2 per year, which over the lifespan of a home (50 years) adds up to a savings of 120 tons of CO_2. Across 100 homes this would equate to 250 tons of CO_2 per year. With market prices for carbon offsets ranging from $4 per ton to $25 per ton. Selling credits for 100 Biloxi Model Homes would earn revenue of between $1000 dollars and $6250 per year. Even selling 10 years worth of credits would yield relatively small savings considering the costs associated with verifying and registering these credits with an official carbon offset market.

Cost Per Household	Percent of Construction	Design Services Model
$1,500	2%	Design Studio (Design professionals only)
$4,800	7%	Design Studio (Design professionals, students and volunteers)
$5,000	3%	Remote/Single Firm (Pro-bono; travel and out-of pocket expenses only)
$10,000	7%	Hybrid (Design studio, individual firms, and volunteers)
$10,400	10%	Design Studio (Including volunteer coordination, case management, construction management)

Please note: All costs are approximate and are based on annualized costs, averaged construction values and beneficiary information provided to Architecture for Humanity in grant reports from partners we funded over the course of three years.

Appliance	Biloxi Model Homes	Typical New Homes
Microwave	98	98
Range with self-cleaning oven	145	145
Color TV	78	78
Stereo with CD player	124	124
Personal computer	208	208
Lightbulbs (compact fluorescent in Biloxi homes, incandescent in typical homes)	500	1090
Refrigerator (Energy Star certified in Biloxi homes)	828	1638
Electric oven	62	73
Dishwasher (Energy Star certified in Biloxi homes)	320	450
Clothes washer	79	90
Clothes dryer	520	570
Hot-water heater	2587	2587
Electric furnace	2427	3467
Electric central air conditioning	1803	2576
Total kilowatt hours per year	**9779**	**13,194**

ABOVE
Chart of the cost per household for various building approaches.
Image: Gulf Coast Community Design Studio

RIGHT
Comparison chart of appliance energy usage in kilowatt-hours per year for Biloxi Model Homes versus typical new homes.
Image: Gulf Coast Community Design Studio

The program explored a range of building methodologies and approaches.

ODOM HOME

DESIGN FIRMS Gulf Coast Community Design Studio; Studio Gang Architects
DESIGN TEAM Kara Boyd, Jeanne Gang, David Gwinn, David Perkes, Mark Schendel, Price Taggart
ENGINEER Roger Roepke, PE, Black Rock Engineering
CONTRACTOR Cox & Carr Construction
LANDSCAPE ARCHITECT Paul Hendershot Design
SIZE 3 Bedroom, 2 Bath, 130 sq m/1400 sq ft
ADVISORY BASE FLOOD ELEVATION 6 m/20 feet (4 m/13 ft above grade)
FOUNDATION Treated wood driven pile
STRUCTURE 2-by-4 wood framing, prefabricated wood trusses
MATERIALS HardiePlank siding, Energy Star windows, soy-based spray foam insulation, engineered wood flooring
ZONING RS-5 single family residential
LOT DIMENSIONS 15 m/50 ft frontage x 38 m/124 ft deep
STANDARDIZED CONSTRUCTION COST $145 175 USD; $89 USD per sq ft
STANDARDIZED COST Hard cost (labor and materials) $128 460 USD; Material donations $37 430 USD;Construction total: $165 890 USD, $118 per sq ft
NOTABLE FOR Pinecone inspiration, connection between indoors and out, passive cooling using breezeways, screened porches and windows for cross ventilation

ROBINSON HOME

DESIGN FIRM Huff & Gooden Architects
DESIGN TEAM Jaime Abel, Ray Huff, Connie J. Kaplan
ENGINEER 4SE, Inc.
CONTRACTORS George Boatner, Cox & Carr Construction
LANDSCAPE ARCHITECT Paul Hendershot Design
SIZE 3 Bedroom, 2 Bath, 149 sq m/1600 sq ft
ADVISORY BASE FLOOD ELEVATION 5 m/18 ft (1.5 m/5 ft above grade)
FOUNDATION Treated wood driven pile
STRUCTURE 2-by-6 wood framing
MATERIALS HardiePlank siding, clerestory polycarbonate windows, soy-based spray foam insulation, aluminum windows, bamboo flooring, Galvalume metal roof & siding
ZONING RS-5 single family residential
LOT DIMENSIONS 20 m/67 ft frontage x 41 m/135 ft deep
ACTUAL COSTS Hard cost (labor and materials): $148 690 USD; Material donations: $40 050 USD; Construction total: $188 740 USD; $118 USD per sq ft
STANDARDIZED CONSTRUCTION COST $159 500 USD; $98 USD per sq ft
NOTABLE FOR Hurricane-resistant clerestory windows that allow ample daylighting to main living areas; the home also has a driven pile foundation with 2-by-6 wood stud framing and a shallow sloped metal roof

NGUYEN HOME

DESIGN FIRM MC2 Architects
DESIGN TEAM Joe Kellner, Jason Logan, Chung Nguyen, Chuong Nguyen
ENGINEER CSF Consulting LP
CONTRACTORS House Calls Construction Co.
LANDSCAPE ARCHITECT Paul Hendershot Design
SIZE 4 Bedroom, 3 Bath, 190 sq m/2046 sq ft
ADVISORY BASE FLOOD ELEVATION 6 m/19 ft (3 m /10 ft above grade)
FOUNDATION Concrete pier on spread footing with wood columns
STRUCTURE 2-by-6 wood framing, 2-by-6 tongue-and-groove decking and finish floor diagonally laid, roof trusses
MATERIALS HardiePlank siding, 2-by-6 tongue and groove finish floor, aluminum windows, 30-year architectural shingles
ZONING RS-5 single family residential
LOT DIMENSIONS 30 m/100 ft frontage x 64 m/210 ft deep
ACTUAL COST Hard cost (labor and materials): $145 940 USD; Material donations: $35 670 USD; Construction total: $181 610 USD; $89 USD per sq ft
STANDARDIZED CONSTRUCTION COST $155 500 USD; $76 USD per sq ft
NOTABLE FOR Design focused upon existing oak tree canopy as a social gathering space and an outdoor kitchen

PARKER HOME

ARCHITECT Brett Zamore Design
ENGINEER CSF Consulting LP
CONTRACTORS Volunteer labor
LANDSCAPE DESIGNER Brett Zamore Design
SIZE 4 Bedroom, 2 Bath, 131 sq m/1415 sq ft
ADVISORY BASE FLOOD ELEVATION
5 m/18 ft (2 m/7 ft above grade)
FOUNDATION Treated wood columns on concrete piers on continuous footing
STRUCTURE 2-by-6 wood infill framing between columns, roof trusses
MATERIALS HardiePlank siding, bamboo flooring, Galvalume panel roof
ZONING RS-5 single family residential
LOT DIMENSIONS
32 m/105 ft frontage x 30 m/100 ft deep
ACTUAL COSTS Hard cost (labor and materials):
$124 685 USD; Material donations: $52 350 USD;
Construction total: $177 035 USD; $125 USD per sq ft
STANDARDIZED CONSTRUCTION COST
$145 000 USD; $102 USD per sq ft
NOTABLE FOR Adaptable, modular system, potential for in-law

TYLER HOME

DESIGN FIRM Marlon Blackwell Architect
ENGINEER Black Rock Engineering,
Tatum Smith Engineering, Inc.
CONTRACTORS Cox & Carr Construction
LANDSCAPE ARCHITECT Paul Hendershot Design
Size 3 Bedroom, 2 Bath, 139 sq m/1500 sq ft
ADVISORY BASE FLOOD ELEVATION
6 m/19 ft (3 m/10 ft above grade)
FOUNDATION
Steel frame on concrete foundation
STRUCTURE Wood framing on steel frame, wood floor trusses
MATERIALS Galvalume metal siding,
Energy Star windows, soy-based spray foam insulation, bamboo flooring, metal hurricane shutter system, steel frame
ZONING RS-5 single family residential
LOT DIMENSIONS
17 m/57 ft frontage x14 m/ 45 ft deep
ACTUAL COSTS Hard cost (labor and materials):
$250 600 USD; Material donations: $50 350 USD;
Construction total: $300 950 USD; $200 per sq ft
STANDARDIZED CONSTRUCTION COST
$197 000 USD; $132 USD per sq ft
NOTABLE FOR Porch concept flexibility, steel frame construction and steel siding, shutter design, two-story living area

DESPORTE HOME

DESIGN FIRMS CP+D Workshop, Gulf Coast Community Design Studio
DESIGN TEAM Maurice Cox,
Giovanna Gaifione-Cox, David Perkes, Joey Rader
ENGINEER Roger Roepke
(Black Rock Engineering)
CONTRACTORS Cox & Carr Construction
LANDSCAPE ARCHITECT Paul Hendershot Design
SIZE 3 Bedroom, 2 Bath, 130 sq m/1400 sq ft
ADVISORY BASE FLOOD ELEVATION
6 m/19 ft (3 m/ 10 ft above grade)
FOUNDATION Driven pile
STRUCTURE 2-by-6 wood framing, engineered wood floor system
MATERIALS HardiePlank siding,
Energy Star windows, bamboo flooring, soy-based spray foam insulation, Galvalume panel roof
ZONING RS-5 single family residential
LOT DIMENSIONS
15 m/50 ft frontage x 34 m/112 ft m deep
ACTUAL COSTS Hard cost (labor and materials):
$153 580 USD; Material donations: $21 770 USD;
Construction total: $175 350 USD; $125 USD per sq ft
STANDARDIZED CONSTRUCTION COST
$149 200 USD; $107 USD per sq ft
NOTABLE FOR Creative integration of wheelchair accessibility throughout, including a ramp system, passive cooling, rainwater harvesting, integration of house and landscape

39571 Project

LOCATION DeLisle, Mississippi, USA

DATE 2006

END USER Communities of Pass Christian and DeLisle, Mississippi

CLIENT Mississippi Katrina Fund

DESIGN FIRM SHoP Architects; Parsons Design Workshop, Parsons The New School for Design

DESIGN TEAM Reese Campbell, Kimberly Holden, Federico Negro, Mark Ours, Gregg Pasquarelli, Christopher Sharples, Coren Sharples, William Sharples

ENGINEER Buro Happold

CONTRACTOR Culbertson Contractors, Parsons Design Workshop, Parsons The New School For Design

LIGHTING DESIGNER Focus Lighting

COST $250 000 USD

AREA 1068 sq m/11 500 sq ft

Some of the Gulf Coast's first reconstruction efforts after Hurricane Katrina took place in the hard-hit town of DeLisle, Mississippi. Addressing emergency and long-term needs of the community, the 39571 Project delivered a community center and vital 24-hour laundromat for the area. SHoP Architects volunteered their services and helped lead a group of design/build workshop students from Parsons The New School for Design, in New York.

"It was like getting pitched into the Stone Age, there was no way to communicate—the phone lines were gone, the cell towers were down, the mail wasn't restored for over a year," local resident Martha Murphy says. She knew the firm from her role as a board member with Tulane University and asked them to come to DeLisle. The firm arrived to help four days later—before the Red Cross.

Once on the ground, SHoP organized government and nonprofit stakeholders to clear debris and set up points of aid. The first structure erected was a tent with wooden floors to store and organize supplies. All of DeLisle's public buildings and 80 percent of its homes were destroyed. "A community isn't in its buildings, but you need the geographic gravity that the buildings provide," Murphy says, adding that it felt as though there

TOP
The InfoWash seen through the community center's dog-trot.
Photo: Ivan Chabra/
Parsons The New School for Design

BOTTOM
The porch has become a gathering place for the community of DeLisle.
Photo: Ivan Chabra/
Parsons The New School for Design

InfoWash

LOCATION DeLisle, Mississippi, USA
DATE 2006
END USER Communities of Pass Christian and DeLisle, Mississippi
DESIGN CENTER Parsons Design Workshop, Parsons The New School for Design
DESIGN/BUILD TEAM Huy Bui, Ivan Chabra, Sarah Coffin, Terry Erickson, Christian Eusebio, Dominique Gonfard, Kailin Gregga, Dominic Griffin, Kip Katich, Parker B. Lee, David J. Lewis, Laura Lyon, Nora Meehan, Shana Sandberg, Joel Stoehr, Emily Wetherbee
STRUCTURAL ENGINEER Compton Engineering
MECHANICAL ENGINEER Hargrove and Associates
CONTRACTOR T&K Trucking, Culbertson Contractors, Omega Construction,
FUNDERS Mississippi Katrina Fund; Martha Murphy
COST $90 000 USD
AREA 185 sq m/2000 sq ft
OCCUPANCY 120 people

TOP
The InfoWash was built by the Parsons Design Workshop, a student design/ build program.
Photo: Ivan Chabra/Parsons The New School for Design

BOTTOM
Site plan shows the InfoWash and Community Center bisected by the loading/access road.
Image: The Design Workshop, Parsons The New School for Design

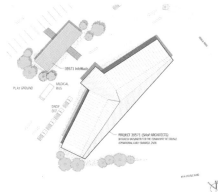

was no place to "be together" in the hurricane-ravaged town.

Reese Campbell and Federico Negro, project managers at SHoP, moved to DeLisle and spent the first three months assisting in relief efforts. The community center was built over the following nine months. In late 2005, Negro, a recent Parsons graduate, contacted the Parsons Design Workshop to contribute a project. Professor David Lewis guided 13 students through the process of designing a small complementary building, the InfoWash, and over the summer they went down to help construct it.

The center consists of two buildings: a community center designed by SHoP Architects that houses nonprofit office space, a business incubator and a cafe. The smaller building, designed by Parsons Design Workshop, features a laundromat and additional offices. The utilitarian

function of the space made seeking help there less intimidating. "The architect's role isn't just to respond and give exactly what is asked of them," Lewis says. "We think it is the architect's role to challenge, to raise other questions, and to see new possibilities."

It was a quick and easy build but procuring materials in Mississippi was a challenge. "Materials were scarce and going to casinos and hotels. Things that had insurance money to rebuild right away," Parsons student Ivan Chabra says. The students fabricated all of the interior furniture in New York and shipped it to the site.

SHoP prefabricated connection pieces and beams for the building's undulating roof in New York. The assembly was speedy and made good use of precious time and materials. Though some criticized the building for not replicating the historic architecture of the region, Murphy never

thought it should. "I couldn't stand the thought of trying to replicate our old vernacular architecture—it was a completely new era for us," she says.

In the years following the storm the center served as a vital meeting spot for residents and reconstruction agencies alike. They gathered at its informal cafe and held sometimes crucial meetings in the outdoor seating area.

Today the 39571 Project continues its efforts to help people affected by Hurricane Katrina regain their lives. "We didn't know that the human need would last this long. We had people owing mortgages on a house and a business they didn't have anymore, with no income to pay it," Murphy says. As such, the InfoWash continues to supply residents with assistance and information. Many people are still working toward rebuilding their lives and homes in the wake of an economic recession and 2010 BP oil spill.

The community center now functions as an economic incubator where locals can start to reestablish their businesses. Some of them, such as a framing shop, have moved on to permanent locations in the downtown area, making room for new businesses to slide in behind them. "The community will once again redefine itself and decide what it needs, and the building will address whatever need that is," Murphy says.

Rector Street Bridge

PROJECT TYPE Temporary bridge
LOCATION Lower Manhattan, New York City, USA
DATE Opened August 2002
IN USE 2002–present
CLIENT New York State Department of Transportation, Battery Park City Authority
DESIGN FIRM SHoP Architects
ENGINEERS Buro Happold (structural), LiRo Group (foundations)
CONTRACTOR/MANUFACTURER LiRo Group, Tully
FUNDER Federal Emergency Management Agency (FEMA)
COST $3.5 million USD
LENGTH 67 m/220 ft

The Rector Street Pedestrian Bridge was one of the first infrastructural elements built near the former World Trade Center after the events of September 11, 2001. Funded by the Federal Emergency Management Agency, the bridge was proposed by traffic engineer Sam Schwartz and the Battery Park City Authority. It was implemented to temporarily reconnect the residents and businesses of New York City's Battery Park neighborhood to the rest of Lower Manhattan but is still in use today.

A six-lane highway served as a crucial access route for emergency and construction vehicles to Ground Zero and was therefore closed to pedestrian and through traffic. The Rector Street Bridge restored pedestrian access while allowing clean-up and construction efforts to continue. "For the first two or three weeks of the project we didn't think about what the bridge would look like, instead we focused on the major implications of the bridge," SHoP Architects principal Bill Sharples says. Construction sequence and design were established in collaboration with several local and federal agencies.

The bridge's superstructure, a prefabricated galvanized steel box truss system, was constructed in eight months to avoid disrupting round-the-clock cleanup efforts on the West Side Highway. A steel roof truss system was then mounted on top, selectively cladding the exterior wall surfaces. Neighbors were concerned that the bridge would become a viewing platform for Ground Zero so the design team organized the cladding on different elevations to create selected apertures that let sunlight into the bridge. At night, light emanates from the light "planks" in the floor.

The bridge was originally expected to remain in use for two and a half years; however, the north span of the bridge remains in use awaiting a more permanent structure.

ABOVE
The temporary Rector Street Bridge at night. The bridge was still in use years after 9/11.
Photo: Seong Kwon / SHoP Architects

RIGHT
Section diagram of the Rector Street Bridge.
Image: SHoP Architects

What If
New York City...

PROJECT TYPE
Design Competition for
Post-Disaster Provisional Housing
PROJECT PHASE Planning
LOCATION
New York City metropolitan area, USA
DATE 2008–present
COMPETITION SPONSOR
New York City Office of
Emergency Management
COMPETITION PARTNER
Architecture for Humanity–New York
FUNDER The Rockefeller Foundation
COST $100 000 USD
WEB RESOURCE www.whatifnyc.net

How do you plan to recover from a disaster that hasn't happened yet? Who leads the reconstruction process and makes the crucial decisions of when, where and how to rebuild? Where does funding come from, and how long will it take? In search of answers, in 2008, the New York City Office of Emergency Management organized the What If New York City...Design Competition for Post-Disaster Provisional Housing. Prompted by the Ready New York emergency preparedness campaign, the competition called on designers to submit an innovative disaster housing recovery plan for a fictitious neighborhood in the event of a catastrophic hurricane. The winning project would be incorporated into an actual plan adopted by the New York City metropolitan area.

Participants were asked to design housing that provided a higher quality of living than the temporary single-family trailers and other prefabricated, short-term living spaces that are often deployed during emergencies. A set of planning premises served as guiding principles, requiring the designers to consider various factors such as New York City's population density and interest in placing residents in their former neighborhoods. Judging was based on 11 criteria from rapid deployment to sustainability.

The entries were directed by a detailed hurricane scenario for the imaginary "Prospect Shore" neighborhood. The scenario tracked 200 days of changing conditions after a destructive storm on three scales: the city, neighborhood, and several households. A pre-hurricane demographic profile listed numbers for families, children, elderly residents, unemployment, housing units

and the type of housing, as well as commuting preferences. Detailed maps showed roads, buildings, parks, vacant lots and a shoreline.

The jury, headed by David J. Burney, commissioner of the city's Department of Design and Construction, selected 10 winners. A technical advisory committee comprised of city officials and industry experts reviewed the chosen projects and gave recommendations on feasibility and practicality. The winners were then awarded a grant of $10 000 to further develop their ideas over three months. The refined entries are featured on the competition websites. Some winning submissions were added to the catalog of housing strategies in New York City's Housing Recovery Plan.

Since then, the Office of Emergency Management has developed a performance specification for urban interim housing with the Department of Design and Construction. It enables the city to leverage the capacity of the private sector in deploying housing as well as guide housing manufacturers and those planning urban temporary communities. It created the Urban Design Playbook for Post-Disaster Interim Neighborhoods with the Department of City Planning and, finally, it plans to create an urban interim housing prototype.

The competition also became a starting point for the Regional Catastrophic Planning Team for the New York metropolitan area, which was established in 2008 by the Department of Homeland Security to encourage collaborative emergency planning. "What if we have thousands of people who are displaced?" says Cynthia Barton, the Disaster Housing Recovery Plan manager. "How are we going to house them in a way that keeps them close to home, and makes it possible to keep their jobs and rebuild their lives?"

The plan is structured like a how-to guide so that emergency managers know where resources are, who has authority over them, and how they can be quickly implemented in a way that does not hamper other rebuilding efforts. The team hopes this coordination will help New York City plan for implementing a housing recovery strategy if the kind of catastrophic disaster scenario contemplated by the competition ever happened.

"Catastrophic events require a new kind of planning."

Joseph Bruno, New York City Office of Emergency Management Commissioner

OPPOSITE
Map of the New York City metropolitan area emergency jurisdictions.
Image: Regional Catastrophic Preparedness Grant Program/New York City Office of Emergency Management

ABOVE
A rendering depicts the Living Modular project entry submitted by PHOAM Architecture.
Image: Morton Fassov, Carsten Laursen/ PHOAM Architecture

BOTTOM LEFT
S.C.A.L.E. Project was designed to be delivered on tractor trailers.
Image: David Mans, Otto Ruano, Robert Wrazen/ Epochcore Design Studio

BOTTOM RIGHT
The winning Threading Water project suggests building dwellings on barges.
Image: Megan Casanega, Laura Garofalo, David Hill, Henry Newell, Nelson Tang

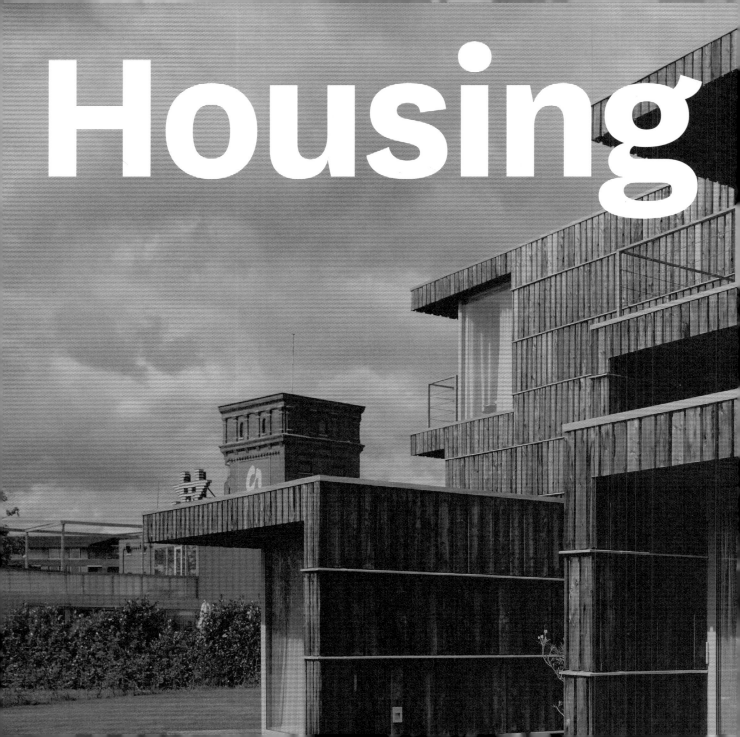

Housing

Sustainability Facts

Average Annual Residential Energy Consumption per Capita   **300.4**
Kilograms of Oil Equivalent (KGOE)*

Asia	208.8
Central America	180.9
Europe	642.1
North America	916.1
South America	140,6

*Source: Internation Energy Agency (IEA) Statistics Division. 2007.
Energy Balances of OECD Countries (2008 Edition) and
Energy Balances of Non-OECD Countries (2007 Edition)

***Design concept by Michelle Kaufman

A woman in front of her home,
a typical one-room house in
KwaZulu-Natal, South Africa.
Photo: Asia Wright/Architecture for Humanity

Green Rating System

Green means many things to many people. In this chapter we survey a few of the initiatives underway that propose solutions for housing the world's population sustainably—from retrofitting existing housing stock, to developing solutions for the world's emerging and rapidly growing urban centers, to balancing housing development with the need to conserve open space. Loosely, we organized the projects from "light green" to "dark green." Taken together they represent just a sampling of the spectrum of design solutions needed to provide sustainable shelter.

NUMBER OF CERTIFIED PROJECTS

0   1 million

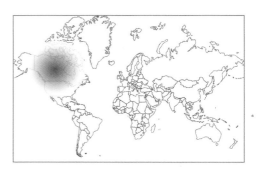

ENERGY STAR – 1 MILLION CERTIFIED PROJECTS
Canada, United States
Note: Does not include product ratings

LEED – 35 000 CERTIFIED PROJECTS
Argentina, Brazil, Canada, Chile, Colombia, India, Italy, Mexico, Norway, Poland, Russia, South Korea, Spain, Sweden, United States

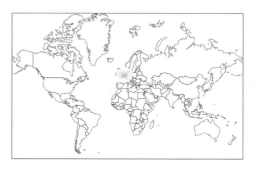

PASSIVHAUS – 25 000 CERTIFIED PROJECTS
Germany, United Kingdom

GREEN STAR – 400 CERTIFIED PROJECTS
Australia

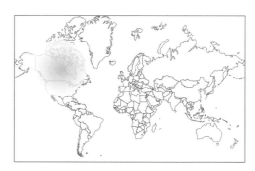

GREEN GLOBES – 165 CERTIFIED PROJECTS
Canada, United States

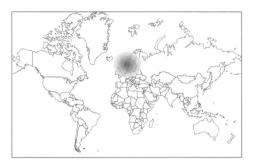

BREEAM – 200 000 CERTIFIED PROJECTS
The Netherlands, Norway, Spain, Sweden,
United Kingdom

MINERGIE – 9000 CERTIFIED PROJECTS
Switzerland

THREE STAR SYSTEM – 12 CERTIFIED PROJECTS
China

Overview of Green Ratings Systems

The term "green-washing" describes the process of overstating a product's or building's sustainability to drive up sales. With all of the information about sustainability and green building practices available, systems have come into place to make sure that developers, architects and contractors are getting it right.

With a goal of shifting the construction industry toward more sustainable practices, a governing agency creates a series of guidelines in consultation with sustainability experts, researchers and industry professionals. These guidelines often include a set of prerequisites that a building must meet before points or credits can accrue. Subjects include energy use and production, water use and conservation, recycling, and materials choices.

One of the early certifications was Energy Star, which was started in 1992 and is run by the US Environmental Protection Agency and the US Department of Energy. It began by certifying products and appliances, before adding new homes certification. To date, over 1 million homes have been certified.

Others, such as the Leadership in Energy and Environmental Design (LEED) rating system, include prerequisites that discourage green field development. Started in 1998 and managed by the nonprofit group United States Green Building Council, LEED assesses sustainability through the design, construction and use of a building. LEED-accredited professionals administer the design and construction submittals, which are verified by an independent third party. The program is also being exported to other countries such as Canada, Brazil and India.

Rapidly developing countries are becoming more cognizant of their building practices. China's Ministry of Housing and Urban Development created the Three Star system in 2006. The first building was certified in 2008.

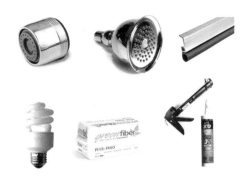

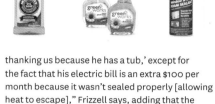

enviRenew

LOCATION New Orleans, Louisiana, USA
DATE 2009–11
END USER 15 neighborhoods,
50 households in each
IMPLEMENTING AGENCY Salvation Army
DESIGN TEAM Ethan Frizzell,
Lindsay Jonker, Liana McGowan,
Alexandra Miller
FUNDER Salvation Army
NUMBER OF UNITS 250
COST PER UNIT $1000 USD
PROGRAM COST $250 000 USD

At first, people were resistant to the "eco stuff." The Salvation Army enviRenew program started giving to select New Orleans residents in 2009, says Lindsay Jonker, enviRenew director. The EcoBaskets full of environmentally friendly household items were meant to help Hurricane Katrina survivors by supplying materials for sustainable, low-cost home modifications and renovations they could do themselves.

Many volunteers aided in the reconstruction of Gulf Coast homes, though some lacked the skills to execute quality work. "We recognized a need to go back into renovated homes with a different set of eyes," explains Captain Ethan Frizzell, The Salvation Army's area commander for New Orleans. "There is this mentality that better than before is good enough. They think, 'You should be

thanking us because he has a tub,' except for the fact that his electric bill is an extra $100 per month because it wasn't sealed properly [allowing heat to escape]," Frizzell says, adding that the goal is to not just change the house, but the culture of the homeowners.

The EcoBasket, a bundle of sustainable products customized to the needs, age and physical abilities of each recipient, is a do-it-yourself way to make a big impact on energy costs and livability. There are three basket configurations for various improvement projects. At a minimum, a basket may include low-flow fixtures, compact fluorescent lights, a solar-powered security light, weather stripping and sealant, and organic cleaning products. Some include cellulose attic insulation and instructions for installing it, and others supply customized solutions by the Louisiana Green Corps, a local green jobs training program for New Orleans youth. The young participants have been helping elderly and handicapped recipients install their items.

Five neighborhoods were selected to receive the baskets from 70 project proposals by New Orleans community groups. One of the recipients was Beryl Ragas. "I didn't know why my house was so cold," Ragas says. "They ended up insulating the doors, in the attic and underneath the sink. It really helped out a lot and my bills dropped by about half." She shared this realization with neighbors and converted some who were initially skeptical.

To date the program has reached 125 New Orleans residents who often hear about it by word of mouth.

TOP
A selection of products included in the EcoBasket.
Photo: enviRenew/The Salvation Army

BOTTOM
Beryl Ragas, recipient of an EcoBasket.
Photo: enviRenew/The Salvation Army

Now House Project

ORIGINAL LOCATION Topham Park neighborhood, Toronto, Canada

DATE 2005–present

END USER 9 households

DESIGN FIRM Work Worth Doing

DESIGN TEAM Gonzalo de Cardenas, Tod Falkowsky, David Fujiwara, Lorraine Guathier, Steve Harjula, Harry Mahler, Heidi Nelson, Alex Quinto

ENGINEER Dave Kalmbach, Patrick Scantlebury (Copperhead Mechanical, Ltd.), Malcolm Stephens

CONTRACTOR Martin Osborne

FUNDERS Canada Mortgage and Housing Competition (2005 Competition); EQuilibrium Sustainable Housing Demonstration Initiative; RBC Royal Bank

COST PER UNIT $50 000 CAD/$50 556 USD

AREA 111 sq m/1200 sq ft

TOP
The siding of Now House 1 was removed for air sealing.
Photo: Steve Harjula/Now House Project

At first glance, this one-and-a-half-story house looks like all the others built after WWII in the Toronto, Canada, neighborhood of Topham Park. However, behind its traditional exterior, Now House produces almost net zero energy, generating nearly as much power as it uses. Often sustainable design focuses on new construction. This project recognizes the importance of upgrading existing housing stock to achieve environmental goals.

Local design studio Work Worth Doing entered Now House idea in the Net Zero Energy Healthy Home competition sponsored by Canada Mortgage and Housing in 2005. "This was really an experiment, nobody else was doing zero energy retrofits," says Lorraine Gauthier, the design team's project manager. "All the other competition winners were building new zero energy houses."

Canada's residential sector represents 17 percent of its energy use and 15 percent of its greenhouse gas emissions, according to a 2010 report by the Office of Energy Efficiency, Natural Resource Canada. Now House takes advantage of the minimal embodied energy required for retrofitting existing housing and avoids the high embodied energy, energy consumption, and emissions associated with the manufacturing and transportation of new materials required for new construction. After the success of the first Now House, the firm completed eight more near-zero energy retrofits around Ontario.

A data-based process of measuring and upgrading is the modus operandi of the project, which starts by studying the baseline performance of a house. The first goal is to reduce the energy load of the house through basic fixes like air sealing and upgrading windows, adding insulation, and installing energy-efficient fixtures, lighting and appliances. Next, the house is reassessed to measure the effectiveness of the upgrades. This data is used to determine the extent of work needed for the HVAC and mechanical systems. Solar electric and hot water systems are installed to reduce the gas and electrical needs as a final step.

The result is a near-net zero House that produces as much energy as it uses. The house is not off-the-grid, but rather the energy it produces is fed back into the power grid. For example, the first Now House uses a grid-tied system that feeds

Now House before it underwent a sustainable renovation. Homeowner had already replaced a traditional shingle roof with a more efficient metal roof.
Photo: Alex Quinto/Now House Project

power into the Ontario power grid. It also falls under a "feed-in" tariff, a utility program in which the power company buys back all power produced by the house at 80 cents per kilowatt-hour while supplying the house with power at approximately 8 cents per kilowatt-hour.

A Now House's success is established by measuring energy consumption meters and comparing pre- and post-retrofit energy bills. This helps document numerous smaller interventions that can be extremely effective in improving sustainability. For example, the fifth Now House received minimal upgrades like air sealing and insulation, new appliances, compact fluorescent lights, and low-flow water fixtures. It went from a Canadian EnerGuide for Houses score of 55 to a score of 74, where 100 equals a net zero House.

The small size of the houses impacts the time it takes to recoup the investment of upgrading through energy savings. "If we doubled the size of the house, which would be more the norm of recent houses, the payback would be a lot faster," Gauthier says. However, renovating larger houses at a better payback rate is not necessarily more efficient because of the materials and energy it takes to complete the renovation.

Work Worth Doing discovered that the cooperation of the homeowner is essential for maximum success. "One family, before the retrofit, used twice as much energy as the other families; and they still are," Gauthier says. "However, we have made an impact on reducing their overall use by 30 percent." Gauthier cautions that this is an evolving process and not a "silver bullet for the answer to all retrofits."

Now House Project is trying to expand its efforts, but its small size makes it difficult to manage projects at a distance. The design team is working to distill what they have learned into a basic system that could be made available online and through a national home retailer, according to Gauthier.

RIGHT
The Now House uses solar energy to heat water.
Image: David Fujiwara/David Fujiwara Architect

BOTTOM LEFT
Workers install insulation to the exterior foundation walls.
Photo: Heidi Nelson/Now House Project

BOTTOM MIDDLE
Spray foam insulation is added to the exterior walls
Photo: Heidi Nelson/Now House Project

BOTTOM RIGHT
Solar thermal panels (on left) provide power for heat. Solar photovoltaic panels (on right) produce electricity that is sold to the local power company.
Photo: Heidi Nelson/Now House Project

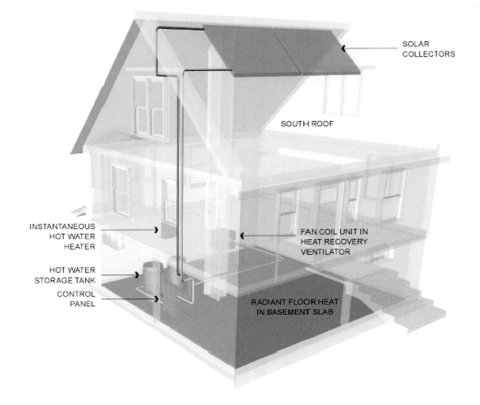

SOLAR COLLECTORS

SOUTH ROOF

FAN COIL UNIT IN HEAT RECOVERY VENTILATOR

INSTANTANEOUS HOT WATER HEATER

HOT WATER STORAGE TANK

CONTROL PANEL

RADIANT FLOOR HEAT IN BASEMENT SLAB

Tour Bois-le-Pretre

LOCATION Paris, France

DATE 2008–11

END USER 100 apartment units

IMPLEMENTING AGENCY Office Publique d'Aménagement et de Construction de Paris and Paris Habitat

DESIGN FIRM Frédéric Druot Architecture

DESIGN TEAM Mario Bonilla, Frédéric Druot, Anne Lacaton, Miho Nagashima, Florian de Pous, David Pradel, Caroline Stahl, Adis Tatarévic, Jean Philippe Vassal

ENGINEERING E.2.I. (cost estimating); Gui Jourdan (acoustics); Inex (systems engineers); VP & Green Engineering (structural); Vulcaneo (fire security consultant)

FUNDER Office Public d'Aménagement et de Construction de Paris

COST € 11.3 million/$15.7 million USD

AREA Expansion from 8900 sq m/95 798 sq ft to 12 460 sq m/134 118 sq ft

NUMBER OF UNITS 96

The concrete facade (before).
Photo: Frédéric Druot Architecture

A rendering of the new glass facade (after).
Photo: Frédéric Druot Architecture

Before and after section drawings of the Tour Bois-le-Pretre.
Image: Frédéric Druot Architecture

The Bois-le-Pretre Tower in the suburbs of Paris, France, is undergoing a metamorphosis. It takes the same basic concept as Now House Project—renovation instead of demolition—and applies it on a larger scale. The 16-story, 96-unit concrete tower, built in 1962 by architect Raymond Lopez, represents the modernist ideal of a high-rise in the park, far removed from the grit of the city.

In 2005, a competition sponsored by Paris's public development and construction department asked entrants to rethink the way low-income and marginalized communities are housed on the city's outskirts. Rather than demolish the structure, which would have wasted the embodied energy of the building and its materials, and needlessly filled a landfill with debris, architects Frédéric Druot, Anne Lacaton, and Jean Philippe Vassal chose to renovate the structure. "The Tour Bois-le-Pretre transformation is first of all an upgrade of comfort, light and space," designer Adis Tatarévic says.

They based their concept on interviews with the residents and previous research on high-rise housing typologies. The simple underlying idea was to expand the size of the apartments while increasing light. The architects also worked to break up the monotonous facade with modern glass balconies. They provide the building with both insulation and added outdoor space. The expansion also introduces more common space and meets accessibility codes.

A phased construction takes a socially conscious approach by allowing residents to remain in their apartments while the renovations are being made. One of the biggest changes was the addition of closed balconies to better climatize the building. Balconies are prefabricated and hoisted into place, cutting down on material waste and installation time. These new balconies can be enclosed during colder months, transforming them into winter greenhouses. Each balcony has a sliding door equipped with thermo curtains made of aluminum, wool and fabric. Aluminum light curtains reflect solar rays and increase ventilation. These features provide a pocket of insulating air that helps regulate temperatures inside the apartments and minimizes the need for heating or cooling.

These features provide up to a 50 percent reduction in energy consumption while expanding the usable floor area of the tower from 8900 square meters (95 798 sq ft) to 12 460 square meters (134 118 sq ft). The transformation is an example of adapting problematic housing typologies to reduce energy impact and improve livability. "A little plastic window is more energy efficient than a big sliding door, but we always prefer the big sliding door because you have to feel good in your house first," Tatarévic says.

TOP RIGHT
The concrete facade was stripped away to allow floor-to-ceiling windows around enclosed balconies.
Photo: Frédéric Druot Architecture

BOTTOM RIGHT
A completed "winter garden" adds light and space to the apartments.
Photo: Frédéric Druot Architecture

Life in 1.5 x 30

LOCATION Dhaka, Bangladesh
DATE 2008
END USER Tea seller and family
DESIGN AGENCY
Architecture for Humanity–Dhaka
DESIGN TEAM BRAC University
students, Zahid Hasan, Kaisar Hossain,
Imrul Kayes, Fardous Habib Khan
ADDITIONAL CONSULTANT
Saiful Haq, Abdun Nime, Mr. Roni
FUNDERS Students of BRAC University;
TRII Landscape Consultant
COST $640 USD
AREA 14 sq m/151 sq ft
OCCUPANCY 2 people

Dhaka, Bangladesh's urban area, is scattered with "grey spaces" that are occupied by micro-enterprises like food and beverage stalls or shops that often double as the owner's home. These blurred gaps between what is owned, controlled or financed by authorities or private developers are often informally claimed by micro-entrepreneurs, who are vital to the country's economy.

OPPOSITE
The 1.5-meter-wide dwelling space is located between an office building and a garage.
Image: Imrul Kayes/Architecture for Humanity-Dhaka

ABOVE LEFT
A 3-D section shows the different levels of the new dwelling.
Photo: Imrul Kayes/Architecture for Humanity-Dhaka

ABOVE RIGHT
The interior of the space before the renovation.
Photo: Imrul Kayes/Architecture for Humanity-Dhaka

According to the Institute of Architects Bangladesh, micro-enterprises are far from trivial, contributing a high percent to the country's gross domestic product. "These occupants are actually helping to restructure and revitalize our cities. They activate the dead spaces and break down boundaries between the public and the private," says Imrul Kayes, a member of Architecture for Humanity's Dhaka chapter.

Project 1.5 x 30 is located in the grey space between two buildings in a neighborhood called Mohakhali. The project, which was undertaken by volunteers with Architecture for Humanity-Dhaka, was conceptualized and funded by architecture students from local BRAC University (founded by the Bangladesh Rural Advancement Committee), and TRII Landscape Consultant. The design wedges a small tea stall between two buildings. The length of the space is 30 feet (9 m) and it spans 1.5 feet (45 cm) at its narrowest and 3.6 feet (108 cm) at its widest.

Imran is the owner of the tea stall. He has lived in Dhaka since age 12, but his family was evicted from their home when the property was taken

over by a large civil engineering studio. A neighbor and owner of the adjacent sweet shop gifted Imran and his father a sliver of his land between the shop and studio for their tea stall, where they also live. Chapter volunteers aimed to transform this dark, gloomy and congested space into a functioning living space and storefront (sometimes referred to as productive housing).

Vibrant colors, natural light, ventilation, and the use of alternative energy sources are key design components of the grey space. It features green plants and rainwater harvesting for a small aquarium. Recycled timber, plywood panels, bamboo mats, corrugated roofing and metal angles were collected from the surrounding area for the project.

The project promotes using overlooked spaces to leverage economic activity and reduce poverty. Beyond improving the living conditions of the family and creating a better functioning storefront, the project also demonstrates the full potential of ad hoc businesses when provided formal spaces from which to operate.

Venezuelan Eco-Cabanas

LOCATION Santa Elena, Venezuela
DATE 2007–8
END USER Peace Villages Foundation volunteers, local workmen
CLIENT Peace Villages Foundation
DESIGNER Kristofer Nonn
FUNDER Peace Villages Foundation
COST PER UNIT $500 USD
NUMBER OF UNITS 2
AREA 16 sq m/170 sq ft
OCCUPANCY 2 people

Many local villagers in Santa Elena, Venezuela, live in hastily constructed shacks that were thrown together during "the invasion," a recent population influx spurred by government-supported mining initiatives. The shacks are little more than tin-covered timber frames sitting directly on the ground. The wooden posts are vulnerable to termites and mold, and the overall structure is susceptible to many problems. Few windows cause inadequate ventilation; loose construction allows snakes, spiders and rodents to enter at will; and the tin roofs shed rain onto the dirt roads, eroding foundations and pathways.

To counter these issues, Manfred Monnighoff, director of the Peace Villages Foundation, decided to use the foundation's Ecological Building Program to construct a healthier, more sustainable alternative to the shoddy abodes. Wisconsin-based designer and builder Kristofer Nonn led the program that spawned the Eco-Cabanas.

The design team's approach focuses on locally available materials rather than radical new ideas. Nonn designed the cabana's foundation piers of precast concrete to prevent rot and termite

TOP
The Wind Catcher Eco-Cabana.
Photo: Kristofer Nonn

BOTTOM
"The invasion," a great population influx in Venezuela, has led to many shanty towns like the one pictured.
Photo: Kristofer Nonn

LEFT
The butterfly roofs collect rainwater.
Photo: Kristofer Nonn

TOP RIGHT
Bottle embedded in the concrete wall bring light to the interior.
Photo: Kristofer Nonn

BOTTOM RIGHT
Tony, a Pemon carpenter from Guayana, cuts boards for the cabanas
Photo: Kristofer Nonn

damage. He integrated shelving into the framing and cladding system and embedded scavenged glass bottles into a concrete wall to let in natural light. The roofs of the two units angle toward each other to channel rainwater into storage barrels, providing a much needed alternative to polluted river water. The structure's wood finish is a mixture of transmission fluid and wax.

Gathering local materials was complicated by the separate laws that govern the use of natural resources for the region's large indigenous population and the highly autonomous national government. Indigenous residents are free to cut and sell wood as they please, but others are required to obtain special permits to prevent large-scale logging and protect the rainforest. One neighbor who started his own cabana had to temporarily stop work due to these restrictions. Nonn circumvented them by having his construction crew, who were of Pemon descent, accompany him into the woods to cut lumber for the cabanas.

Nonn also incorporated some traditional practices like raising the structure on stilts. This method of building was used extensively in pre-Columbian times, but Monnighoff speculates that the stilts fell out of favor because they were considered technologically inferior to Spanish-style stone and concrete foundations.

There was some initial skepticism about Nonn's building methods until he proved the cabanas could withstand Venezuela's drenching rain. Nonn remembers sleeping in a cabana during the first storm after it was built. Several people entered during the night to see if it leaked. Despite many doubts, the drips never came, and interest in the cabanas subsequently spread. Officials are now considering using the Eco-Cabana design to create low-cost, low-impact housing in the Brazilian border town of Pacaraima.

Nonn took it as a compliment when one of the builders joked that he was going to steal the structure. "Tony [a Pemon carpenter] looked at the curved roof one day and said, 'I'll call a couple of my friends and we'll just carry this off home with us,'" Nonn recalls. "I wouldn't doubt that four of them could do it, either."

1OOK House

LOCATION Philadelphia, Pennsylvania, USA
DATE 2008–9
DEVELOPER Postgreen Homes
END USER 10 households
DESIGN FIRM Interface Studio Architects
STRUCTURAL ENGINEER Larsen and Landis
CONTRACTOR Manor Hill Construction
ADDITIONAL CONSULTANTS
MaGrann Associates (LEED)
FUNDING Bank financed
TOTAL UNITS BUILT 10 houses
COST PER UNIT $100 000–$120 000 USD
AREA 107 sq m/ 1150 sq ft

The 100K House is set back between
the 120K House (corner lot) and a
typical Philadelphia row home.
Photo: Sam Oberter/Sam Oberter Photography

An exploded axonometric of the 100K House's sustainable features.
Image: Interface Studio Architects

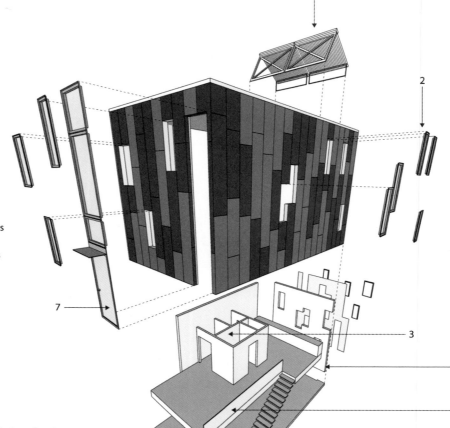

1 Solar hot water panel
2 High performance windows
3 ERV recovery ventilator
4 Structural Insulated Panels (SIPs)
5 Low-VOC coating
6 Radiant floor
7 Insulated steel door

A lot of architects talk about the benefits of mass customization but few are doing it. Prefabricated home building allows buyers to choose customized options from a kit of parts. Most of these homes, with the exception of the mobile home, remain in the domain of wealthy clients and architects seeking to push the boundaries of building delivery methods. Prefab homes are typically more expensive than their traditionally built counterparts of the same size and quality. Postgreen Homes and Interface Studio Architects teamed up to address this challenge with the LEED Platinum–certified 100K House, a single-family prefab house built for $100 000.

Postgreen, a real estate development company started by husband and wife Chad and Courtney

Ludeman, created an online customization tool to make the process of designing a home much like that of configuring a new laptop. Buyers can choose a home model and specify everything from countertops and floors to ceiling fans and appliances. Chief Marketing Officer Nic Darling attributes their large following to social media. "We credit most, if not all of our home sales to social media tools."

The homes are LEED certified, which requires demonstrating leadership in energy and environment designs and involves documenting design and construction decisions from beginning to end with the US Green Building Council. The green consulting firm MaGrann Associates worked with the 100K House team in Philadelphia, Pennsylvania, to verify that the home satisfies the LEED certification checklist. Items on the list include cutting back use of energy, water and gas; reducing construction waste; and using sustainable materials throughout.

Postgreen and Interface Studio Architects started small in the first two years of their collaboration, initially constructing the 100K

> ## "There is one home in particular that we will claim we sold on Twitter."
>
> Nic Darling, Postgreen Homes chief marketing officer

House and then the slightly larger 120K House. Production ramped up and they completed five additional houses in 2010. Three of those houses incorporate solar PV panels and the others were built to the German Passive House standard. The first four houses were built with Structurally Insulated Panels, which are prefab components that were manufactured in a Pittsburgh, Pennsylvania, factory. Their benefits include less material waste, higher wall insulation values, and quick, on-site assembly.

The goal for 2011 was to complete 50 new units. However, they decided to make the shift from prefab to a set of standardized stick-frame construction details. They came to the realization that tract housing was less expensive and

dropped prefab. Their decision was due in part to the availability of low-cost labor created by the recession which began in 2009. "This choice was driven by ease of construction, particularly in an urban environment," Darling says. "Our current strategies get the same or better results with less difficulty." Additionally, the move away from prefab makes it easier for them to expand outside of Philadelphia because they won't have to secure new manufacturers in other areas. "While our wall assemblies and details are unorthodox, they use basic construction techniques which are very familiar to crews all over the country," Darling says. Postgreen Homes is now building the houses themselves through their affiliated company Hybrid Construction.

ABOVE LEFT
HardiePanel vertical siding gives the home its striking appearance.
Photo: Sam Oberter Photography

ABOVE RIGHT
The Ludeman family in the 100K House.
Photo: Sam Oberter Photography

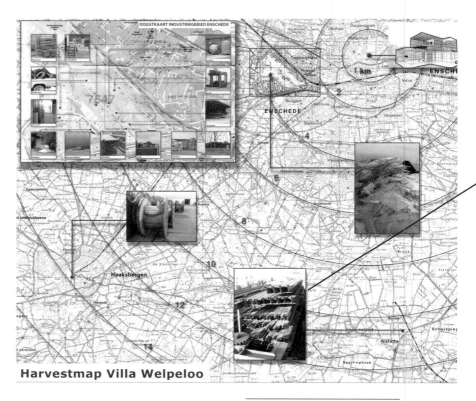

Harvestmap Villa Welpeloo

Superuse Harvest Map

LOCATION Enschede, Netherlands

FEATURED PROJECT Villa Welpeloo

DATE 2006-9

CLIENT Knol and Blans family

DESIGN FIRM 2012Architecten

DESIGN TEAM Jeroen Bergsma, John Bosma, Frank Feder, Jan Jongert, Petra Jutten, Carolien Karamann, Iris de Kievith, Jos de Krieger, Wojtek Witek

CONTRACTOR Den Boer Bouwen en Installeren

COST €900 000/$1.2 million USD

FUNDING Owner-funded

AREA 400 sq m/4306 sq ft

PROGRAM COST €3000-€8000/ $4167-$11 111 USD

WEB RESOURCE www.superuse.org

The 2012Architecten Harvest Map uses Geographic Information System technology to locate and log found materials. It analyzes and catalogues otherwise landfill-bound products in a database that makes them available for projects varying from houses to children's playgrounds. 2012Architecten has taken the gathering instinct into the 21st century with the concept of "superuse."

Superuse is material harvesting on steroids. "It is about how material waste flows can be used in architecture," says Jan Jongert, 2012Architecten principal architect. The firm created Superuse.org, a website devoted to displaying inventive uses of post-consumer and discarded materials.

The Harvest Map project seeks out materials in close proximity to a building site to minimize transportation costs, and Superuse aims to minimize the alteration of those materials to further lower their energy impact. Though much of the materials are used waste such as car tires, they

ABOVE
The Harvest Map tracks recycling opportunities.
Image: 2012Architecten

are exploring pre-consumer waste such as sample materials and new products that cannot be sold. The project also makes use of industrial infrastructure that can be disassembled into new configurations.

Jongert sees no limits to where Superuse can go. "It is a way of thinking that can be applied to any industry," he says. He uses teaching and artwork to test the concept. "We experiment with materials that are more like art or installations, and the knowledge we get we develop more and use in our professional work," Jongert says. In one instance, he built a coffee kiosk from old washing machine doors.

Search techniques range from driving around aimlessly, to studying an area's historical

TOP ROW
These photos show the breakdown of a textile machine into reusable structural steel components.
Photos: 2012Architecten

BOTTOM LEFT
The steel components are bolted together to facilitate reuse should the house be deconstructed.
Photo: 2012Architecten

BOTTOM MIDDLE
Villa Welpeloo during construction.
Photo: 2012Architecten

BOTTOM RIGHT
Completed Villa Welpeloo.
Photo: Allard van der Hoek

"I never feel like I am living in a recycled house."

Ingrid Blans, homeowner

industries, to using satellite imagery to stake out the products. "We use Google Earth because some things are so big and well photographed that you can actually recognize the materials," Jongert says. They've procured items like windmill wings this way.

Superuse requires a lot of flexibility from the architect. "We keep on designing while construction is going on, adapting plans according to the materials that are actually being found and used," Jongert says. Homeowners also need to be patient and flexible. Since the materials are not brand new, there is no warranty guaranteeing their quality.

In The Netherlands, an eco-home called Villa Welpeloo was designed this way. Owners Tjibbe Knol and Ingrid Blans were invested in seeking out recycled materials. "The recycled materials in their house make up 60 percent of the whole," Jongert says. Wooden siding is made from old cable reels from a nearby factory and all of the structural steel was harvested from an old textile factory machine. Because they did not know the steel's specific properties, the engineer suggested they assume it to be the worst quality possible. Although it probably was better than they assumed, since it is secondhand and cheap, using more of it to make up for potential defects was easy.

Diez Casas para Diez Familias (10X10)

LOCATION Guadalupe, Nuevo León, Mexico

IMPLEMENTING AGENCY
School of Architecture at Instituto Technologico y de Estudios Superiores

END USER 10 single family residences (to date)

FEATURED PROJECT Casa Rosenda

DATE 2009–10

PROJECT PARTNER Ball State University College of Architecture and Planning

DESIGN TEAM Pedro Pacheco, Edmundo Palacios, architecture students

ENGINEERS 10x10 team

CONTRACTOR 10x10 team, ATEMPO Diseno y Construccion

FUNDER Private companies in Monterrey and the Instituto Technologico y de Estudios Superiores, Monterrey Campus

UNIT COST 180 000 Mexican pesos/ $14 391 USD

AREA 60 sq m/646 sq ft

OCCUPANCY 6 people

In a spirit similar to the reuse mantra of 2012Architecten, Pedro Pacheco enlisted his students at the School of Architecture at Instituto Technologico y de Estudios Superiores in Monterrey, Mexico, to create designs with found materials. In 1999, Pacheco and Edmundo Palacios founded Diez Casas para Diez Familias, also known as 10x10. Through the university program, students build homes for low-income families in various local areas, helping to improve living conditions by creating homes made with found materials.

"Our architecture department was not doing significant work related to the discipline and I wanted to change that and put into practice what students were learning and really have a social impact," Pacheco explains. Each year, one neighborhood is chosen and students from the university work with 10 families to create 10 designs for a new home. In the end, a single home is chosen for construction. Since the program's inception, 10 homes have been built and 200 designed.

Casa Rosenda, the project completed in 2010, is located in the Nuevo Almaguer neighborhood of Guadalupe, Nuevo León, Mexico, an informal settlement of cramped roofed homes. Maria Rosenda Flores, a maintenance worker at the

ABOVE
Rosenda and family outside their new home, built on the same lot as their original home (pictured opposite).
Photo: Pedro Pacheco/Diez Casas para Diez Familias

> ## "The windows are actually from vending machines. Vending machine glass is triple-pane, which is really good for insulation."
>
> Ernesto Adrian Marroquín Gonzalez, student

university, was living with her two daughters and three grandchildren in a 23-square-meter (250-sq-ft) room before she was selected to receive a house from 10x10.

The students and family were pushed to be innovative and use found materials to build the ultra-modern home. "I estimate that about 40 percent of the materials were recovered reused materials," says Pacheco. "Our goal is to use the recovered materials as is and avoid additional investment in the transformation of the materials into construction materials."

Most of the reused materials were gathered by scrounging around the university. The students found fiberglass panels, originally used as concrete molds for a university construction project. "We saw the potential and we could create walls and floors from the fiberglass molds," architecture student Ernesto Adrian Marroquín Gonzalez recalls. The students also collected discarded wooden planter boxes that were used for the interior stairs and outside deck of the house. "The glass we used for the windows is the most interesting story," Gonzalez says. The house is kept cooler reusing the vending machine glass than it would have been with new windows.

Students and family members participated in the design and execution of the house. "By the end of construction, Rosenda Flores and her daughters knew everything that was going on in the house," Gonzalez says. "If they have any problems with the plumbing or the light fixture, Adriana [Rosenda's 29-year-old daughter] will be able to fix the problem. In my opinion that is a sustainable design—it is not just incorporating reused things, but helping the user own their home."

In addition to the reused materials the 60-square-meter (645-sq-ft) home collects rainwater, uses greywater, and has a passive cooling system. Whereas the previous home was cramped for the family of six, the new home offers adequate space. "My life has changed tremendously. We now have space to live," Flores says.

TOP LEFT
The original house before demolition.
Photo: Abigail Guzman/Diez Casas para Diez Familias

TOP RIGHT
Rocks and recycled concrete used for the foundation.
Photo: Pedro Pacheco/Diez Casas para Diez Familias

BOTTOM LEFT
The house is modular and if needed can be disassembled and moved to a new location.
Photo: Pedro Pacheco/Diez Casas para Diez Familias

BOTTOM RIGHT
The design team used new steel beams to ensure structural integrity.
Photo: Pedro Pacheco/Diez Casas para Diez Familias

10X10 Housing Initiative

FEATURED PROJECT Sandbag Houses
LOCATION Mitchells Plains,
Cape Town, South Africa
DATE 2007–9
IMPLEMENTING PARTNER Design Indaba
10x10 Housing Project
CLIENT Design Indaba/Interactive Africa, Cape
Town
END USER 10 families,
Freedom Park community
FIRST BENEFICIARY Hans Jonker–House
completed in 2008
DESIGN FIRM MMA Architects
DESIGN TEAM Luyanda Mpahlwa,
Uli Mpahlwa, Sushma Patel, Kirsty Ronne
CONTRACT MANAGEMENT
Chinedum Emeruem, Westley Van Wyk
CONTRACTOR
Tech Homes–Schalk Van Der Welt
MATERIAL SUPPLIER
Ecobeams and sandbags:
Mike Trenmere, ECOBUILD Technologies
FUNDER Design Indaba Trust
SPONSORS DesignSpaceAfrica,
PG Bison/Penny Pinchers
CONSULTANTS Henry Herring,
AKI (Structural engineer); Brian Mahachi,
BTKM (Quantity Surveyors)
COST PER UNIT 80 000 South African rand/$10
170 USD
AREA 54 sq m/581 sq ft
OCCUPANCY 5 or 6 people

South Africa's post-apartheid Reconstruction and Development Programme provides brick and concrete mortar houses to people who need them through a program that provides subsidies to private housing developers. The current government subsidy per house is 50 000 South African rand, or $6900 USD. Design Indaba challenged architects to design an alternative to the standard government-funded design with which many people were unhappy. The Cape Town-based [design advocacy] organization organized the 10x10 Housing Project competition. In 2007, they invited 10 teams, each consisting of one international and one South African architect, to design a house for a family in Mitchells Plains township, an informal community 40 kilometers (25 mi) from the heart of Cape Town.

The winning design by MMA Architects employs sandbags as a sustainable building material. Sandbags can be used as affordable and effective insulation and offer added protection from weather. "We've got to find different ways of uplifting the people and one of them is obviously going to have to be sustainable building because you've got millions and millions of people," says Luyanda Mpahlwa, a principal architect at MMA Architects. "You can't use the conventional ways, which use high energy and increase the carbon footprint."

The winning design uses EcoBeams, a product of a South Africa-based company, to frame the house. The vertical beams are made of timber connected with a galvanized metal element. Nylon

The 10x10 houses in Freedom Park,
Mitchell Plains, Cape Town,
South Africa.

Photo: Weiland Gleich/Archigraphy.com

bags filled with sand are stacked within the frame and covered with mesh wire and plaster to form smooth walls. These houses do not need foundations and the sandbags act as the anchoring element to further reduce construction costs.

Sandbags have been used in South Africa but the designers pushed boundaries by using them to build a two-story home. Expanding vertically helps to maximize living space on small plots of land. "We had to be very creative about how we would use sandbag building technology because we were not aware if it had been used before," Mpahlwa says. "We had to get the services of an engineer and he had to be innovative about how to support the top structure." Concrete beams were placed on top of the first-floor walls to ensure structural stability, and a concrete beam acted as a foundational element for the second floor.

Ten homes were built from the design and 10 families are now living in them. Each house has a second-story platform that the occupants can use as a patio or make into an additional room. The homes were all placed close to the road to create the largest backyards possible. "We used architecture as a way of empowering a community that has never had a house before," Mpahlwa says.

OPPOSITE TOP LEFT
The Pillay family, residents of a 10x10 Housing Initiative home, stand in front of their former home.
Photo: Yasser Booley/Design Indaba

OPPOSITE TOP RIGHT
Freedom Park, South Africa (before).
Photo: Yasser Booley/Design Indaba

OPPOSITE MIDDLE LEFT
Community members pack sandbags between the vertical EcoBeams.
Photo: Nadya Glawe/Design Indaba

OPPOSITE MIDDLE RIGHT
Applying plaster scratch coat.
Photo: Nadya Glawe/Design Indaba

OPPOSITE BOTTOM LEFT
Framing the second floor of the house.
Photo: Nadya Glawe/Design Indaba

OPPOSITE BOTTOM RIGHT
Construction of the second floor.
Photo: Nadya Glawe/Design Indaba

The second-floor terrace acts as a carport and can be converted into an additional room.
Photo: Wieland Gleich/Design Indaba

Tassafaronga Village

LOCATION Oakland, California, USA

DATE 2005–12

END USER 550 residents with incomes 0–60 percent of Area Median Income; Project Access

IMPLEMENTING AGENCIES Oakland Housing Authority, Habitat for Humanity East Bay (Kinsell Commons)

DESIGN FIRM David Baker + Partners Architects

STRUCTURAL ENGINEERS OLMM Consulting Engineers

ELECTRICAL FW Associates

MECHANICAL/PLUMBING Guttman + Blaevoet, SJ Engineers

CONTRACTOR Cahill Contractors

DEVELOPMENT CONSULTANT Equity Community Builders

LANDSCAPE ARCHITECT PGA Design

LIGHTING DESIGNER Horton Lees Brogden

CIVIL ENGINEER Sandis

MAJOR FUNDERS State of California MHP Loan State of California Infill Infrastructure Grant; 4 percent Low-Income Housing Tax Credits; 4 percent Tax Exempt Bonds; City of Oakland Redevelopment Loan; Oakland Housing Authority Loans; Citibank Loans; Alameda County Loan; Environmental Protection Agency Brownfield Cleanup Grant; Federal Home Loan Bank of LSF–AHP; Deferred Developer Fee

FINANCIAL PARTNERS Citi Community Capital, National Equity Fund, State of California Housing and Community Development Department Multifamily Housing Program, State of California Housing and Community Development Department Infill Infrastructure Grant Program, City of Oakland Redevelopment Agency, California Debt Limit Allocation Committee, California Tax Credit Allocation Committee, US Department of Housing and Urban Development, US Environmental Protection Agency

CONSTRUCTION COST $232 USD per sq ft

COST PER UNIT $431 000–$439 000 USD

TOTAL DEVELOPMENT COST $75.2 million USD (excluding Kinsell Commons)

SITE AREA 7.91 acres (5.33 buildable acres)

BUILDING AREA 23 960 sq m/257 903 sq ft

NUMBER OF UNITS 157 apartment units; 22 single-family dwellings

Interview:
David Baker + Partners Architects:
David Baker, Daniel Simons
Oakland Housing Authority:
Bridget Galka

Developed by the Oakland Housing Authority, Tassafaronga Village is the first affordable-housing project to achieve a Leadership in Energy and Environmental Design (LEED) Neighborhood Development Gold Certified Plan, as well as LEED for Homes Platinum certification for all dwellings.

The project was developed by the Oakland Housing Authority and designed by San Francisco-based architecture firm David Baker + Partners Architects. The firm is known for combining contemporary design with social responsibility and sustainable practices. To learn how the project came together, we talked about the design process and the benefits of LEED certification with Bridget Galka, senior housing program development manager in the real estate development department of the Oakland Housing Authority, and project manager for Tassafaronga Village, principal David Baker, FAIA LEED AP and project architect, and Daniel Simons, AIA LEED AP.

OPPOSITE TOP & MIDDLE
David Baker (top),
Daniel Simons (bottom).
Photos: Brandon Loper/
David Baker + Partners Architects

OPPOSITE BOTTOM
Bridget Galka, project manager for
Oakland Housing Auhority.
Photo: Wendy Ruiz/Oakland Housing Authority

RIGHT
Children play in front of the
Tassafaronga townhouses. The
townhouses use HardiePlank, as an
alternative to vinyl siding.
Photo: David Baker + Partners Architects

How did the affordable housing industry get started?

DS: For a long time it was housing authorities and HUD (Housing & Urban Development). A lot of the housing done under HUD and the housing authority auspices was good design but it didn't work, mainly because it didn't connect across the breadth of the spectrum, the client, operations, all those things. Then they decided in a quasi-conscious decision that it was not effective and that they should outsource it to nonprofits through tax credits and grants instead of directly funding it. Affordable housing became something that was really great to design because we had really great clients.

How has the affordable housing industry changed?

DS: The first affordable housing project we did, the clients had the notion that they should look ordinary. There are still a lot of affordable housing people that think that affordable housing shouldn't stand out, that it shouldn't be wonderful or an incredible place to live necessarily. They think that building it with low construction costs is the goal. We definitely don't feel like that.
DB: It's more true of other parts of the country, than California where there is a lot of affordable housing bureaucracy and they still treat design like a luxury. Architects have to fight really hard to put a window in a corridor, and somebody at this bureaucracy is saying, "We don't allow windows in corridors because they leak, people break them, and people fight about opening them." They have a whole list of reasons.
DS: We brought the highfalutin notion of design back and kept talking to our clients about it. We had to do it gradually over the years. They were very

resistant in the beginning, but in the last 30 years the housing market has changed for the better. We've been lucky to be a part of it.

How did the Oakland Housing Authority select Daniel Baker + Partners to develop Tassafaronga Village?

BG: We are a public agency so we had a competitive process. We put out a Request For Proposals (RFP). It was published in the newspaper and mailed to all of the architectural firms in the area.

The RFP included a very clear process of evaluation and scoring criteria that included qualifications, past performance, green building strategies, understanding of the project, cost and efficiency, and Section 3 hiring of low-income residents. The scoring criteria and evaluation process was published with the RFP so everyone knew how the proposals would be scored. We received 11 proposals from very qualified firms. We interviewed two firms based on the scoring, and chose David Baker + Partners Architects.

David Baker's proposal played on the industrial edge of the site. The plan hid higher density within a development that looked exciting. We had one criterion that asked applicants to explain their vision for green and sustainable design. Back in 2005, it wasn't yet common for architecture firms to have LEED AP professionals. David Baker's response to that question kicked them up a notch.
DB: We knew the LEED Neighborhood Development Pilot Program was going on. At one point we said, "Hey Bridget, is this going to be green? There is this new thing called LEED Neighborhood Development and we should go after it." Because it was a pilot program it was quite inexpensive. When we figured out the

LEFT
The new site plan includes the adaptive reuse of an existing building and an additional parcel of industrial land. The project integrated into the surrounding neighborhood repairing connections through new streets and pedestrian pathways.
Image: David Baker + Partners Architects

ABOVE
The "severely distressed" public housing project before it was developed.
Image: David Baker + Partners Architects

RIGHT
Kinsell Commons, which was
constructed by Habitat for Humanity,
is linked to the main apartment
building at Tassafaronga by a
"Village Green."
Image: David Baker/David Baker + Partners
Architects

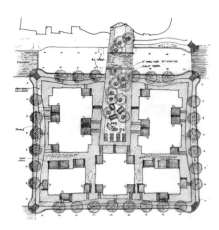

RIGHT
Kinsell Commons, which was
constructed by Habitat for Humanity,
is linked to the main apartment
building at Tassafaronga by a
"Village Green."
Image: David Baker/David Baker + Partners
Architects

FAR RIGHT
Sketch of the courtyard of the main
apartment building at Tassafaronga
Village, which was built over a
parking garage.
Image: David Baker/David Baker + Partners
Architects

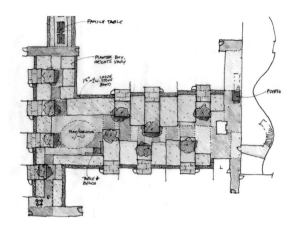

cost, Bridget said, "We'll pay the fees if you manage the process."
We didn't have a third party green consultant, we just did it. So we went
from no certification to LEED–ND Gold and all the homes being LEED for
Homes Platinum.

**These projects require complex financing. Given David Baker + Partners'
experience in affordable housing, do you help your projects find
financing, or tax credits and such, to offset the costs of doing
sustainable design?**
DB: No, never. Usually these projects have 10 or so funders, and the people
who do that have a different talent than we do.
DS: Maybe if we know there is a certain amount of money available for some
sustainable feature, we'll make a suggestion. Alameda County (California,
USA) has grants for sustainable development. If we have a client that is
unfamiliar with them, we'll put them in touch with the right people.

How was Tassafaronga Village financed?
BG: We started the planning process by preparing two HOPE VI grants.
Originally there were 87 public housing units at Tassafaronga that were
deemed to be "severely distressed," which is a requirement to be eligible for
HOPE VI funding. We submitted the first Hope VI application in 2005 and were
unsuccessful. It is a very competitive process and the Oakland Housing
Authority had previously been awarded three large HOPE VI grants in 1998,
1999, and 2000. By the time we submitted the first application for
Tassafaronga the HOPE VI application criteria had been modified to favor
smaller public housing authorities with no HOPE VI grants.

In order to apply for HOPE VI funding you must have a lot of resident and
community meetings to prepare the application. We had five or six meetings in
the community but our application was unsuccessful; so, we tried again the
next year and had another five or six meetings. As a result of the HOPE VI
planning process the vision for the site was taking shape and we were getting
closer to having the site plan we ultimately developed when we submitted our
second HOPE VI application in early 2007.

By participating in the many meetings, the residents got their hopes up
and were generally excited to move away, have all their relocation costs
covered, and maintain the opportunity to move back into a nicer
development. We had invested in creating a viable revitalization strategy
but we didn't get the second HOPE VI grant either. Our Board of
Commissioners had to make the decision to either continue to apply for
HOPE VI grants or try to find another way to finance the revitalization.

The best alternative to HOPE VI was replacing the public housing units with
Section 8 Project–based Vouchers. The Section 8 rental subsidy allows us to
serve the same very low–income households, but with Section 8 you get
enough operating income to pay down debt because the Section 8 Voucher
rent is higher than the public housing unit operating subsidy. We presented
the option of replacing public housing units with the Project–based Section 8
Voucher units as a way to maintain the same level of affordability but tap into
higher rental income that would allow us to obtain a permanent loan. The
board decided to proceed with the Project–based Voucher approach, so, in
fact, there are no public housing units at Tassafaronga now but there are
actually more units for very low–income households.

In addition to the loan on Section 8 rental income, the Oakland Housing
Authority had resources from years of good fiscal management that we
called our reserves. When the authority does these large revitalization
projects, we commit a part of the reserves as gap financing in order to raise
additional funds from other affordable housing sources. We contribute our
own equity to be more competitive. Between the Project–based Vouchers
and our equity, we were able to raise financing from the typical sources,
such as state tax credits, tax–exempt bonds, city of Oakland
redevelopment funds, state of California bond funds and Federal Home
Loan Bank affordable housing program financing. The state of California had
an Infill Infrastructure grant program to pay for the cost associated with
developing infrastructure associated with urban infill housing. We were
awarded money from that program. We also got some money from the
Environmental Protection Agency for brownfield cleanup and we got some
money from Alameda County.

TOP LEFT
Rendering of the proposed Tassafaronga Village development
Image: David Baker + Partners Architects

TOP RIGHT
Rendering of the abandoned pasta factory that was repurposed to hold supportive apartments and a medical clinic.
Image: David Baker + Partners Architects

LEFT
The completed Tassafaronga Village development.
Photo: Brian Rose/David Baker + Partners Architects

OPPOSITE
Chart of Tassafaronga Village's scoring on the LEED for Neighborhood Development Pilot Project Checklist.
Image: Nick Brown/Architecture for Humanity

Can you walk us through the design of Tassafaronga Village?

DB: There were originally 87 units at Tassafaronga on a 5.5-acre site that were all public housing under the Oakland Housing Authority. Now it is 7.5 acres. They added an abandoned industrial site and an abandoned pasta factory, which allowed them to link a school and a library and complete the street grid.

Tassafaronga now has 157 units plus 22 Habitat for Humanity houses. That's a big jump in density, even with the added acres, which is really to the Oakland Housing Authority's credit.

We scrambled to make sure it was not a homogenous project. We had apartment buildings, which is one typology, townhouses, which are another typology, then we renovated the pasta factory with supportive housing, which is a third typology. We also had the Habitat houses. So we worked to integrate the Habitat houses throughout the project.

Oakland Housing Authority split the project into two phases. We did construction drawings for the first phase, then did the second phase. Phase Two was basically the pasta factory renovation. That was a big enough piece to break out, which helped the financing.

How often does the design team talk to the people that will be living in the housing projects that you design?

DB: We never talk to the people that will live in them because nobody has any idea who they actually will be. So, it's impossible to talk to them. Most nonprofit developers don't have good post-occupancy programs either, where they really go and systematically talk to people [about the design]. We've done it quite a bit, informally, and it's totally amazing.

DS: If we do community meetings there may be some residents that might be there, and sometimes the nonprofits will have people review the design.

DB: So when we're designing, we try to channel the residents. We try to make a place where we would like to live. The idea being that we're not too terribly different from other people.

So, what have you learned over the years about designing a building that better serves its residents?

DS: There are dumb things that are easy but a lot of people forget. There are a few spaces in every apartment building that people are going to be in outside

LEED FOR HOMES PROJECT CHECKLIST

PROJECT NAME: Tassafaronga Village, Oakland CA
AWARD GOAL: Platinum

Category	Points Attempted	Points Possible	Description
Innovation and Design Process (ID)	10	11	Preliminary rating, Integrated project team, LEED for Homes credentialed professional on team, Design charrette, Building orientation for solar design, Durability planning, Durability management, Third-party durability management verification, Building reuse, Bay friendly landscape maintenance, Affordable housing, Bicycle parking
Location and Linkages (LL)	10	10	**Tassafaronga was awarded LEED for Neighborhood Development, Gold certification for the following:** Smart location, Proximity to water and wastewater infrastructure, Imperiled species and ecological communities conservation, Wetland and water body conservation, Farmland conservation, Floodplain avoidance, Brownfield redevelopment, High-priority brownfield redevelopment, Preferred location, Reduced automobile dependence, Housing and jobs proximity, School proximity, Steep slope protection, Open community, Compact development, Diversity of uses and housing types, Affordable rental and for-sale housing, Reduced parking footprint, Street network, Access to surrounding vicinity, public spaces and active public spaces, Community outreach and involvement, Construction activity pollution prevention, LEED certified green buildigs, energy efficient buildings, Reduced water use, Building reuse and adaptive reuse, Minimize site disturbance through site design and construction, Stormwater management, Heat island reduction, Recycled content for infrastructure, Construction waste management, Comprehensive waste management, Increased affordability for rental and for-sale housing, Further reduced parking footprint, Increased housing and jobs proximity, Bay friendly landscape maintenance plan, LEED accredited professional
Sustainable Sites (SS)	19	22	Erosion controls during construction, Minimize disturbed area of site, Noninvasive plants, Basic landscape design, Limit conventional turf, Drought tolerant plants, Permeable lot, Permanent erosion controls, Management of run-off from roof, Very high density development
Water Efficiency (WE)	11	15	High-efficiency irrigation system, Third-party inspection, Reduce overall irrigation demand by at least 45%, Very high efficiency fixtures and fittings
Energy and Atmosphere (EA)	18	38	Performance of ENERGY STAR for homes, Exceptional energy performance, Title-24 lighting, Advanced lighting, High-efficiency appliances, Water-efficient clothes washer, Refrigerant charge test, Appropriate HVAC refrigerants
Materials and Resources (MR)	11.5	16	Framing order waste factor limit, Detailed framing documents, Detailed cut list and lumber order, Framing efficiencies, FSC certified tropical wood, Environmentally preferable products, Construction waste management planning, Construction waste reduction
Indoor Environmental Quality (EQ)	11	21	Basic combustion venting measures, Enhanced combustion venting measures, Basic outdoor air ventilation, Third-party performance testing, Basic local exhaust, Enhanced local exhaust, Room-by-room load calculations, Return air flow/room-by-room controls, Third-party performance test/multiple zones, good filters. Indoor containment control during construction, Radon-resistant construction in high-risk areas, No HVAC in garage, Minimize pollutants from garage, Exhaust fan in garage
Awareness and Education (AE)	3	3	Basic operations training, Enhanced training, Public awareness, Education of building manager
Project Totals	93.5	136	Certified Platinum (need 90 - 110 points)

of their own unit. They're going to be doing laundry, getting their mail, walking down the corridor to the front door. These spaces are opportunities. If you don't treat these spaces as afterthoughts, they provide opportunities to meet their neighbor, to sit outside and read a book, or bring some daylight into a corridor.

DB: We're trying to green stairs so that people don't use the elevator as much. If we can [create] a connection to the outdoors, maybe an outdoor barbeque, that's huge. The other thing about affordable housing is that there are more kids. There is a need for more community space. We think a family-oriented kids classroom is a really good idea. People can set up ad hoc childcare. If it's designed to be acoustically separate, kids can have music lessons or play in a punk band.

DS: People think a community room will get used once a month to gather all the residents and give them info. We were talking with the developer of a project we did 10 years ago, and they said the community room is booked both Friday and Saturday three months in advance. Residents hold weddings, quinceañeras—all kinds of things.

When you are designing affordable housing, if you do include a nice mailroom, a nice community room, and a nice lobby, we're only talking about 5 percent of the square footage of the building —and a lot of that isn't good space for a unit because they are odd leftover spaces or next to a mechanical space. So, for your overall budget, if you're adding fancy cabinets to every unit, you are never going to be able to afford it. But if you take a few spaces that are key to the building community and make them more dramatic, you're not going to break your budget.

Do you have much latitude in suggesting new ideas?

DB: We work under the premise of having a lot of ideas. Most recently, with Mercy Housing, they kept saying, "Yes, yes... ," until we got to the chickens. Then they said, "No, no we can't do chickens," which is probably reasonable. We even said, "Just chickens, no roosters!" but they still said no.

Your projects are known for engaging the streetscape well. What are the ways that you work to enhance pedestrian friendliness?

DB: It's really important to make your edges as active as possible. That is easier said than done. Projects have requirements that take up space, like transformer rooms, exits and garage entries. In an urban context it is pretty common to have the entire facade filled. It's really good to look at precedents. For example, when you are designing retail, look at retail that works.

DS: Yeah, you don't have to reinvent the wheel.

DB: But it's hard to copy the wheel, for a lot of people, and it's really hard for architects. There are a couple of areas where it's great, though, a walkup storefront, or a bike rack. You'd be amazed at how few architects locate a bike rack so that you can lock a bike to it.

We also try to create a hierarchy of open space. We have what we call a Feng Shui–compliant entry sequence where you enter into a courtyard from an urban area so that you're not just going through the door into a lobby or to your mailbox.

Permeability is important too. There is a tendency to [design] a doughnut. Massive buildings that are hollow on the inside. They have a very nice courtyard but you can't see the courtyard from the outside.

We include daylight throughout and a lot of open space. It's not actually more expensive. People love it. You don't want to be afraid to think up new ideas, but you don't want to forget the good ideas from the past either. A nice place for people to sit and read their mail with a recycle bin, for example, which is a pretty dumb concept, but it's amazing to pull it off.

How do you manage the costs of LEED/green design?

DS: My standard line, which I think is totally true, is if you want to do the cheapest building possible, then absolutely, green design is a little bit more expensive. If you're doing a nice building anyway, because you're going to be managing it for the next 50 years, then at that level, you have a certain amount of discretionary spending. If you decide to use that discretionary budget on sustainable features, then you shouldn't really be spending any more.

DB: If you just took all the fake bricks off of a project you could make it LEED Platinum. Typically, there are multiple inefficiencies that are hard for the client to pick out. I've gone into projects, and said "Wow, those chairs are $600 USD each…" I guess the client didn't look at that particular invoice."

Do you always pursue LEED? What are the benefits?

DB: We always suggest it. There are some marketing advantages, but I also think it's a really great way to organize the team. It really is a broad-based, comprehensive standard.

DS: A building is an incredibly complicated thing, with millions of moving parts and hundreds of people involved. Keeping track of all the little decisions that you need to make is hard. By bringing some accountability to the process, LEED helps you keep track of those things.

DB: There was some study, where they figured out that if you do random blower door tests, the quality of your insulation goes up substantially because they really don't want to redo it. So the contractors end up saying, "You know, they're going to do one of those goddamn blower tests, so take a little bit more time with it to get it right."

DS: We've done projects that are LEED certifiable, where we did the checklist, and just didn't do the certification process. It's not a bad thing, it's better than nothing, but it's not a LEED certified building. It's like saying, "I took the class, I just didn't take the final."

Is it typical of the client to pay for the registration?

DB: Somebody has to, and that can be a big sticking point. The registration fees are about $80 000. On a $43 million project, $80 000 is not a lot. But on smaller projects, there is a lot you can do with $80 000 to improve the building. So a lot of nonprofits will ask, "Why should I pay for this certification when I can put a stone countertop in each unit for the cost of registration?"

Do you try to use innovative technologies in your projects?

DS: We work in a realm where we're housing a lot of families, so there's only so much innovation involved, because experimentation implies a certain level of failure and you don't want to experiment with the poor, obviously. We want maybe 95 percent of the things we're putting in to be as tried and true as possible. Nonprofits don't have a lot of money and they want their operating costs to be super low. So if we design a super complicated system that has to be tuned every year or two, it won't happen and it will stop working.

DB: The more complicated a system, the more things you have to fix. I'd rather just open a window in the corridor than have a high-tech fan system.

How often do you do value engineering? What do you fight to maintain?

DB: Constantly. We have our primitive strategies. Basically, we lard the roast. So you'll have an outer ring of defenses, and then you'll get stuff you care about more. It varies. We didn't have that solar system in Tassafaronga Village, and it was big, $700 000 or $800 000. Then we had the savings to pay for it, because the economic climate changed.

DS: Construction cost is all subjective. It's not as absolute as you think and sometimes it surprises us. There was one mechanical system that we were thinking about using, that seemed a little bit nicer. It turned out that the nicer one, in this particular instance, from this particular subcontractor, was cheaper. So now our project has a nicer mechanical system in it, but the fact is, on another project, I would have been wrong.

DB: Sometimes people start with the idea Take All The Nice Stuff Out, which is anything nice that they can see, like nice windows. We try to spend more money on windows because that's one of the ways you achieve higher sustainability. They do perform better, and it's not as noisy. For a long time, we had to fight so hard to get anything beyond the worst imaginable technical performance on the windows, and we just got to the point where we had to say "Sorry, we just have good windows."

DS: The contractor is always brought on early, usually in schematic design, or design development. It's much more iterative: they're doing budgets every two or three months. We are able to control the costs better that way than the traditional design, bid, build process.

> ## "We also try to create a hierarchy of open space. We have what we call a Feng Shui-compliant entry sequence where you enter into a courtyard from an urban area so that you're not just going through the door into a lobby or to your mailbox."
>
> David Baker, David Baker + Partners Architects

DB: We've done away with the competitive bid process; we did that a few times, maybe in the '80s and it was always a disaster.

What were some of the design changes you made to the Tassafaronga Village Project?

DB: We struggled with the townhouses in particular because we wanted to do something that was modern but contextual, which is very difficult. There are not that many unit plans but they are pinwheeled. They are rotated and flipped.

There are only three or four unit plans in the whole townhouse scheme and three in the apartment building. It is common to try to minimize the number of different unit plans. First of all, you have code issues, it is an immense amount of work to get units to be efficient and code-compliant. Second, in terms of construction, these buildings need to have a certain amount of repetition or they get too expensive. So we did this Victorian idea that you can have the same unit with a different facade.

The question is, "How do you take a super cheap material and make it more interesting?" For example, we used HardiePlank siding, and we did a fancy detail with a very prosaic material, just a thin piece of sheet metal at the joint. You don't want to join HardiePlank horizontally, so this allows you to use it more efficiently because you don't have any long runs that give you problems with expansion and contraction.

On the pasta factory, [the entry screens] were going to be solar collectors, but the Oakland Housing Authority said, "We want them on the roof because then we can have more of them, and they will be less susceptible to vandalism."

We came up with this idea of doing stormwater management. What triggered that was the LEED-ND goals, so we talked the city of Oakland into letting us bio-filter the street water, which was really hard to do. Stormwater management has become code now. We also included traffic-calming features, and this is not a traffic-calmed area of Oakland. So originally people were just driving over the curbs where we had sidewalk extensions. We had to add bollards. Recently, some truckers decided that driving through this site is a shortcut. So all these gigantic rigs try to go through and get stuck. They put up "Trucks Not Allowed" signs, but they still come.

Have Building Information Modeling (BIM) and Integrated Project Design (IPD) strategies facilitated this process?

DB: Absolutely, contractors are doing it because it gives them a competitive advantage, and we like working with those contractors.

DS: We have a project in schematic design right now, where we're going through a bunch of iterations on the exterior. We gave the contractor a 3D building model and they mapped the materials on it, did take-offs, sent us back color-coded PDFs with a table at the bottom of the sheet of square footages of each one. They're able to say, "This material at this square footage in these locations on the building will cost this much," which allows us to make direct comparisons. That's real value engineering; that kind of analysis of the budget helps you figure out where you get the most bang for your buck.

DB: Right, they take the Revit models, use them with other contractors and put them into NavisWorks and figure out all the crashes. It's really amazing because if you figure out all these discrepancies in your working drawings before you build it, it's a lot easier to fix than out in the field, which is the old way.

Do you ever work with physical models?

DB: We typically build a small-scale site model, usually a presentation and community tool so people understand how it fits in. I don't think physical models are a good way to work, because the labor-flexibility ratio is too high. Personally, I think—and this will sound weird—instead of building a beautiful professional, one-sixteenth-inch model, you should build a room full-scale. They're both about the same cost, and a room is really interesting and useful.

What are the things that can go wrong? Do you have a good example?

DB: We always have problems, nothing is ever perfect. Sometimes I feel like Coyote in the Roadrunner cartoons.

DS: You can design a really fantastic building but if it isn't maintained and the residents hate the management, then it doesn't matter. There is a limit to how much great design can improve the quality of living. We are lucky that a lot of the nonprofits we work with are great. They are really good at managing buildings and making nice places for people to live.

Solar Decathlon

LOCATION Washington, DC, USA
PROJECT TYPE Design-build competition
DATE 2002–present
IMPLEMENTING AGENCY US Department of Energy
FEATURED PROJECT ZEROW House,
Rice University
LOCATION Houston, Texas, USA
DATE 2009–10
DESIGN TEAM 150 students and faculty of
Rice University School of Architecture
PROJECT COORDINATION
David Dewane, Allison Elliott, Nonya Grenader,
North Keeragool, Kathryn Pakenham,
Danny Samuels, Rebecca Sibley
STRUCTURAL ENGINEER Christof Spieler
MECHANICAL ENGINEER Brent Houchens
CONSTRUCTION Boyer Contractors Engineers
Inventors, Chiaramonte Construction Company,
Energy Efficient Insulation, Enphase, Houston Area
Plumbing, IBEW Local Union 716, Joint Apprentice
Committee, Jones Roofing, Marek Brothers
Company, MG Sheet Metal Works, Rice Building
Workshop, Rogers Air Conditioning, Unirac,
Wayne Electric, Inc.

ADDITIONAL CONSULTANTS American Institute of
Architects, Boyer Contractors Engineers Inventors,
Burr Consulting Engineers, Linden, Lonnie
Hoogeboom, IBEW Joint Apprenticeship,
the Plumbers Local Union, Redding
IN-KIND CONTRIBUTIONS A&E Graphics Complex,
Allied Powder Coating, Apricus Solar, Berger Iron
Works, Inc., Carlisle Syn-Tec, Cinco Solar, Daltile,
Green-Zip Partition, IKEA Business, ILOS
Corporation, JC Glass, Kohler, Lighting Unlimited,
MBCI Metal Roof and Wall Systems, RAM
Industries, Simpson Strong Tie, Stahlman Lumber
Company, Standard Renewable Energy,
Weatherization Partners, Ltd.
FUNDERS Rice Design Alliance, Rice Energy and
Environmental Systems Institute, Rice Faculty
Initiatives Grant, Rice University Shell Center for
Sustainability, Rice University School of
Architecture, Rice University School of
Engineering, Susan Vaughan Foundation, various
firms and individuals, US Department of Energy
COST $123 200 USD
AREA 48 sq m/517 sq ft (conditioned); 65 sq m/
700 sq ft (footprint with porches, decks)

On the dark green end of the spectrum, the US Department of Energy Solar Decathlon is a collegiate design–build competition showcasing the latest advances in material science, alternative energy use, and sustainable housing technologies.

Each year, 20 teams from around the world compete to produce the "greenest" home possible. The houses are judged in several categories related to design, comfort and sustainability. In the decade since the biennial competition began, some of the entries have resulted in million-dollar houses. Because there was no spending limit in the past, the Solar Decathlon introduced a new affordability category for the 2011 competition.

The ZEROW House by Rice University won second place in the architecture category in 2009. It was also the least expensive at $123 000, proving a beautiful, well-designed home can be affordable. "It was nice to see the simplicity of the design and the simplicity of the systems stand up to houses with 10 times our budget," says architecture student Rebecca Sibley, who was part of the design team. The University of Louisiana at

TOP LEFT
Current ZEROW House artist–in–residence Steffani Jemison.
Photo: Eric Hester/ZEROW House

TOP RIGHT
The ZEROW House on the National Mall.
Photo: Eric Hester/ZEROW House

BOTTOM
The ZEROW House is based on the row house typology of Houston's Third Ward.
Photo: Eric Hester/ZEROW House

FEATURED PROJECT BeauSoleil Louisiana Solar
Home, University of Louisiana, Lafayette
LOCATION Lafayette, Louisiana, USA
DATE 2008-9
DESIGN TEAM Denisse Castro, Scott Chappuis,
Jeremy Creduer, William Depa, Chris Dufreche,
Catherine Guidry, Greg Jefferson, Gretchen
LaCombe-Vanicor, Chris Leger
STRUCTURAL ENGINEER Desormeaux/Hebert
ELECTRICAL ENGINEER Bob Henry
MECHANICAL ENGINEERS William Depa,
M & E Associates
CONTRACTOR/MANUFACTURER Self-contracted
ADDITIONAL CONSULTANT Edward J. Cazayoux
FUNDERS US Department of Energy;
Lafayette Public Trust
COST $300 000 USD
AREA 74 sq m /800 sq ft (internal);
139 sq m/1500 sq ft (total)

Lafayette's $250 000 BeauSoleil Solar Home was another cost-effective design, and the team is continuing to explore cheaper tactics.

A major criticism of the Solar Decathlon is that the houses are transported to the competition site each year, so although they may have a net zero footprint, the program's energy use conflicts with its green mandate.

In addition, because the homes are fabricated locally and trucked to the competition, it is "more expensive than if it was built just once," says Gretchen LaCombe-Vanicor, a student project manager for BeauSoleil. The process also leads to some structural challenges. The University of Illinois at Urbana-Champaign's Gable House was decapitated for the ride to the jury in Washington, DC, in order to comply with highway height and width restrictions. Reassembling the house took four days.

Team California, a collaboration between California College of the Arts and Santa Clara University, navigated time commitments, the distance between the schools, and varying approaches to problem solving. Their Refract House was the only student-led team. "The architects lean towards imagination and creativity, yet they had to give in to reality, and we, as engineers, had to give in to design and open up our brains to work together to make it a real life project," recalls Dan Ruffoni, a structural engineer from Santa Clara University. "Nobody was paying any attention to us," says Annessa Mattson, a project manager. "Our professors were really hands off, they wanted us to learn by trial and error, and we were our best check on each other." Team California created a house that blended beauty and performance, clinching first place in the Architecture category and second in the Engineering category.

BeauSoleil Home also won the Market Viability and People's Choice contests. "We wanted to design a home that embodies where we live and how

we live," says Geoff Gjertson, the students' faculty advisor. "A lot of Cajun culture is focused around impromptu gatherings where people cook, play music and entertain, and we wanted to facilitate those activities."

In most cases, Solar Decathlon houses are used as educational and research tools after the competition. While some have been sold to private buyers, ZEROW House is unique in that it was donated to a nonprofit. "We took the competition seriously, but we really wanted to find a place for the house, and give it a life after the competition," says Nonya Grenader, a faculty architecture lead. The students suggested making Project Row Houses and are working to design a new model of affordable housing in Houston's Third Ward.

Gable House focused on regional architectural precedents with a simple, iconic gable, reinvigorating the vernacular form with new technology and recycled materials. The siding was reclaimed from a 100-year-old barn and the decking was pulled from a defunct grain elevator. "Farmland is really changing around here," says faculty lead Mark Taylor. "We wanted to have a memory of these vernacular buildings, reusing them for people that are living close to the land, but more forward thinking in terms of energy use." The team also focused on passive building techniques rather than active energy generation. Gable House was the first Solar Decathlon entry to earn PassiveHaus certification, considered the gold standard of sustainable rating systems.

Many of the innovative technologies employed in the Solar Decathlon houses require instructions. ZEROW House resident Steffani Jemison suggested hanging curtains in the light-core for privacy and adding counter space. "I am still discovering new things about the house, there are a lot of thoughtful surprises," Jemison said after five months in the house.

Students said the hands-on nature of the competition was a once-in-a-lifetime learning opportunity. "I feel very well prepared for the professional world," says Scott Chappuis, a student on the BeauSoleil team. "Many of the guys I work with are surprised by how much I know." An added benefit, the students will take what they learned about sustainable design into their professional lives.

OPPOSITE TOP
University of Louisiana Lafayette students guide the BeauSoleil Home onto a trailer for transport to Washington, D.C.
Photo: Philip Gould/BeauSoleil Louisiana Solar Home

OPPOSITE MIDDLE
Student Scott Chappuis installs mechanical louvers.
Photo: Philip Gould/BeauSoleil Louisiana Solar Home

OPPOSITE BOTTOM
Installing the roof of the BeuSoleil Home on the National Mall.
Photo: Philip Gould/BeauSoleil Louisiana Solar Home

TOP RIGHT
The BeauSoleil Home at the 2009 Solar Decathlon in Washington, D.C.
Photo: Catherine Guidry/BeauSoleil Louisiana Solar Home

BOTTOM RIGHT
The BeauSoleil Home has a "transitional porch" that links the large kitchen and generous outdoor decks.
Photo: Philip Gould/BeauSoleil Louisiana Solar Home

Galisteo Basin Preserve

LOCATION Galisteo Basin Preserve, Santa Fe, New Mexico, USA
DEVELOPER Commonweal Conservancy
DATE 2003–23
FINANCING Los Alamos National Bank
CONSERVATION AREA 13 076 acres
TOTAL SITE AREA 13 522 acres
FEATURE PROJECT Milder Residence
DESIGN FIRMS Signer Harris Architects, WoodMetalConcrete
CONTRACTOR Fred and JJ Milder
UNIT COST $2 million USD
UNIT TYPE 4-bedroom house
UNIT AREA 464 sq m/5000 sq ft

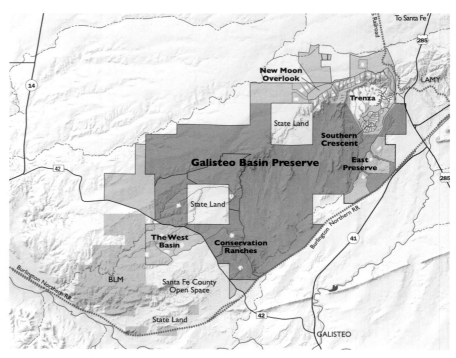

TOP
The Galisteo Basin Preserve mixes private and public conservation land in one development.
Image: Computer Terrain Mapping and Site Workshop/Commonweal Conservancy

BOTTOM LEFT
Map illustration of Commonweal Conservancy's development strategy
Image: Computer Terrain Mapping and Site Workshop/Commonweal Conservancy

BOTTOM RIGHT
The yellow area shows how the Galisteo Basin Preserve could have developed, potentially resulting in sprawl, without a conservation plan.
Image: Computer Terrain Mapping and Site Workshop/Commonweal ConservancyMapping and Site Workshop/Commonweal Conservancy

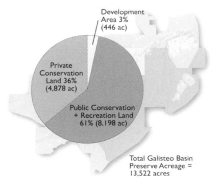

Development Area 3% (446 ac)

Private Conservation Land 36% (4,878 ac)

Public Conservation + Recreation Land 61% (8,198 ac)

Total Galisteo Basin Preserve Acreage = 13,522 acres

LEFT
Completed Milder home.
Photo: Kirk Gittings

ABOVE
A land use chart for the Galisteo Basin Preserve.
Image: Computer Terrain Mapping and Site Workshop/Commonweal Conservancy

The Commonweal Conservancy was founded in 2003 to provide an alternative model for development of open spaces and sensitive landscapes in the American Southwest. Founder Ted Harrison drew on 17 years of experience with the national nonprofit Trust for Public Land to produce stringent guidelines for developing historic ranching lands and protecting the region from unchecked sprawl. Though it seems counterintuitive to protect open space by developing a part of it, Harrison believes sensitive development can do this.

Typically, conservancy groups are at odds with property developers, but in this case, the property developer is the conservancy group. In Galisteo Basin Preserve, the price tag on the new homes funds a land trust that will permanently protect about 90 percent of the 13 522-acre former ranch near Santa Fe, New Mexico. Through Harrison's principle of limited development with deliberate preservation of open space, 965 homes will be built, mainly in Trenza village, but also on a small number of larger "conservation properties."

The ranchland was previously owned by the Thornton family for generations. Commonweal was able to enter into a bargain sale purchase and sales contract over five phased acquisitions that also allowed the family to claim substantial tax savings from the sale of land to a nonprofit. The acquisition also involved the simultaneous purchase and sale of the Milder property in a joint escrow closing, generating necessary operating capital for Commonweal's first six months of existence. This strategy was used for three other lots, allowing the conservancy to establish enough market viability and capital to convince Los Alamos National Bank and other lenders to provide loans for additional land purchases.

Homeowners' contracts enforce strict sustainable building practices so that Trenza village will be a net zero community, according to Harrison. Fred and JJ Milder, who bought the first lot, chose to go off-the-grid with their design. "Once you make one decision and become aware of the waste, how much energy

is being used, and how many materials are unhealthy for you or the environment, it becomes easier and easier to make the next decisions in the right directions," Fred Milder says.

The real estate contract also includes a crucial provision called a "Conservation Easement," which separates the property ownership from the development rights. With the purchase of each home, a section of open space goes to the conservancy for preservation, avoiding potential for future land speculation and parcel divisions.

This new development plan resulted in the Galisteo Basin Conservation District and is guiding the new Sustainable Land Use Development Plan for Santa Fe County. "We had this opportunity to dream big, to fit together all these ambitions, so that even if we only accomplished 70 percent of our ambitions it would still be compelling enough to wake a few people up," Harrison says. The new tax district will use funds from conservation easements, long-term open space leases and fee title interests to preserve the land.

Western Harbour B001 Development

LOCATION Malmö, Sweden

DATE 1998–present

END USER Mixed-income community

IMPLEMENTING AGENCY
City of Malmö Planning Office

DESIGNERS Klas Tham, Hans Olsson,
Ralph Erskine Architect, Moore Ruble Yudell
Architects & Planners, POYRY ARCHITECTURE OY,
Santiago Calatrava, SWECO FFNS Arkitekter AB,
Wingårdh Arkitektkontor AB

DEVELOPERS GROUP
Bengt Nevsten fastigheter, Botrygg, Briggen,
ByggVesta, Derome, Diligentia, Haga Gruppen,
HSB, Ikano Bostad, JM, Midroc, MKB,
NCC, PEAB, Skanska, Stena fastigheter,
Tornahem, Wihlborgs, White

ENVIRONMENTAL STRATEGY MANAGER
Mikael Edelstam

FUNDERS Swedish government through
local investment grants; European Union's
Fifth Framework Programme

DEVELOPMENT COST
SEK 777 million/$121 million USD

AREA 175 hectares/1.75 sq km

POPULATION 4600 residents, 7000 workers
(as of April 2011)

WEB RESOURCE www.Malmö.se/English/
Sustainable-City-Development/PDF-archive

"We had to ask ourselves: where do we want to be in 10 years? That's the direction we should take."

Ilmar Reepalu, Malmö mayor

Photo: Bojana Lukac/City of Malmö Planning Office

Aerial view of Western Harbour. The development seeks to set a new standard for sustainable urban planning.
Photo: Bojana Lukac/City of Malmö Planning Office

Malmö, Sweden, is working on creating a global example for ecologically sustainable urban development by building the "city of tomorrow" (recalling the famous Le Corbusier book of the same name) in a former industrial district. The redevelopment is of note because it created framework within which sustainable development could be encouraged, financed, executed, measured and maintained by the private sector.

B001, the first phase of the city's plan to develop the Western Harbour, is located on a man-made peninsula, 175 hectares (1.75 sq km) in size, that juts into the Baltic Sea. Situated on a former brownfield site, the harbour seeks to achieve 100 percent locally produced renewable energy targets. As of 2010, the redevelopment included 2560 homes, 4330 residents, 290 businesses, a university, and 18 hectares (180 000 sq m) of green space.

The planning process incorporated sustainability goals and measures even before plots were made available for development. Once a land use plan had been established, a Request for Proposals (RFP) was issued to developers. It was issued with two important documents: first, a detailed plan, which served as the master plan for the site; second, the B001 Quality Programme. What New Urbanism was to planning walkable cities, the B001 Quality Programme is to sustainable development. It established a common basic standard and obliged the parties to meet or exceed quality measures. The programme set parameters for everything from material choices, to landscaping, to architectural expression. While not prescriptive, it served as a compact between the city, developers, and future residents, outlining both sustainability targets and the parties responsible for achieving them. Monthly lectures helped define the vision and ensured accountability.

The SEK 777 million ($122 million USD) B001 pilot project was financed by the Swedish government, the European Union, local investment plans and private investors.

Malmö established a target to run all buildings with renewable energy by 2020, and run the entire city with renewable energy by 2030. To achieve that target, the city put the onus on the developer, by requiring energy provision through renewable sources only. It set a target for energy consumption not to exceed 105 kilowatt-hours per square meter. Individual projects were permitted to deviate from this goal, "so long as the average consumption target can be achieved for the B001 site as a whole." Similar targets were set for information technology, greening the urban environment, transit, construction material choices, waste management, water and sewage. To lift the architectural character of the new development, developers were required to work with professional architects, and all architects had to be approved by the city of Malmö.

Electricity is supplied by a 1.5-megawatt wind turbine and 120 square meters (1291 sq ft) of photovoltaic cells. The development's water is heated by 1400 square meters (15 069 sq ft) of solar collectors combined with geothermal heat pumps. Generating 6.3 million kilowatt-hours of energy per year, the wind turbine has the capacity to supply up to 2500 residential units with power. The solar devices produce 5000 kilowatt-hours of energy per year. If the district produces more energy than required, the surplus is sold to the city of Malmö. Conversely, if insufficient, Western Harbour purchases energy from Malmö.

Western Harbour's waste collection system utilizes vacuum chutes to transport garbage and organic waste to a central location. There, the garbage is burned to generate heat and steam, and the organic waste is fermented to produce biogas. Planners modified the peninsula's landscape to create a continuous ridge that directs rainwater to sea while promoting water retention in the soil. Additionally, a network of channels and canals are modeled after natural wetlands to control and naturally purify stormwater.

While B001 has thus far fallen short of its energy targets (it consumes 120 to 200 kilowatt-hours for every square meter of usable floor area annually, 15 to 95 kilowatt-hours above its target), it has provided a successful model for cities to coordinate sustainable development using market-based tools.

In its third phase of development, Western Harbour has grown from a population of 7000 residents in 2008 to more than 12 000 in 2011. The result has been highly enviable with walking paths, restaurants and other amenities. "For the first few years, people refused to move to the district because it was too expensive, too far from the city, but now everyone wants to move here," says Björn Stenbeck, a Western Harbour restaurant owner since 2001.

ABOVE LEFT
To encourage public transit use, there are fewer parking spots than dwellings.
Photo: Top Seangsong/Flickr

ABOVE RIGHT
The Turning Torso, by Santiago Calatrava, anchors the development.
Photo: Ronny Bergström/City of Malmö Planning Office

Commur

Marsupial Bridge & Media Garden

LOCATION Holton Street Viaduct, Milwaukee, Wisconsin, USA

DATE 2005–6

END USER Pedestrians and bicyclists of Brewers Hill, Brady Street and Beerline B neighborhoods

IMPLEMENTING AGENCIES City of Milwaukee, Wisconsin Department of Transportation

DESIGN FIRM La Dallman Architects

ENGINEER Bloom Consultants

ELECTRICAL ENGINEER Powrtek Engineering

LIGHTING DESIGN Noele Stollmack Lighting Design

CONSTRUCTION Lunda Construction

FUNDING Federal Congestion Mitigation and Air Quality Grant Awarded to the city of Milwaukee Department of Public Works; matching funds from the city of Milwaukee

COST $3.35 million USD

LENGTH 195 m/642 ft

WIDTH 3 m/10 ft

Once an unused, unsafe space, the new Urban Plaza under the bridge hosts a Media Garden and is a vibrant neighborhood gathering space.
Photo: La Dallman Architects

171

Once a center of industry for the northern Midwest, Milwaukee, Wisconsin has been dealing with declining investment along its waterfront for decades. Such is the situation for many cities in America's Rust Belt. Milwaukee's urban fabric is cut off from the Milwaukee River by warehouses that sprang up when the region's manufacturing and shipping businesses were more prosperous. Some of the now-blighted interstitial spaces between vacant buildings, infrastructure and transportation right-of-ways in this area are considered dangerous by residents. In 2005, Milwaukee initiated an innovative project to transform one of these spaces: the Holton Street Viaduct, built in 1926. Today it is a focal point for the riverfront's redevelopment.

The historic Brady Street commercial corridor and Beerline B neighborhood sit on either side of the Milwaukee River. In 1993, the Brady Street Business Improvement District followed the guidance of gallery owner Julilly Kohler to make small-scale street improvements to the area. In 1999, it initiated the Crossroads Project to enhance the pedestrian connectivity of Brady Street to nearby neighborhoods and to the riverfront.

After hearing of plans for a standard pedestrian bridge over the river, Kohler conceived of the Marsupial Bridge: a bridge that hung from the hulking Holton Street Viaduct, weaving a pathway through its piers and trusses. The bridge would connect the Brady Street corridor to the Beerline B neighborhood and provide a safe and attractive route across the Milwaukee River. The sidewalks of the Holton Street Viaduct go along a busy four-lane asphalt road. A bus shelter on Brady Street serves as a gateway to the new bridge. La

Dallman Architects developed the master plan, which carved out the under spaces of the southeastern buttresses of the Holton Street Viaduct for a Media Garden where performances and gatherings take place.

The new Urban Plaza introduces light and activity into the degraded, shadowy area under the bridge. "Before it was totally wasted space full of busted bottles and used condoms," says Gaby Kupfer, who worked across the street at the Trocadero Gastrobar. "When it first opened, it literally shed light on those wasted urban spaces." It is used for a variety of purposes from performing arts stage to outdoor movie theater, and is an informal meeting place for cyclists and skateboarders.

Lighting designed by Noele Stollmack helps keep the space safe and alive at night. Low-level

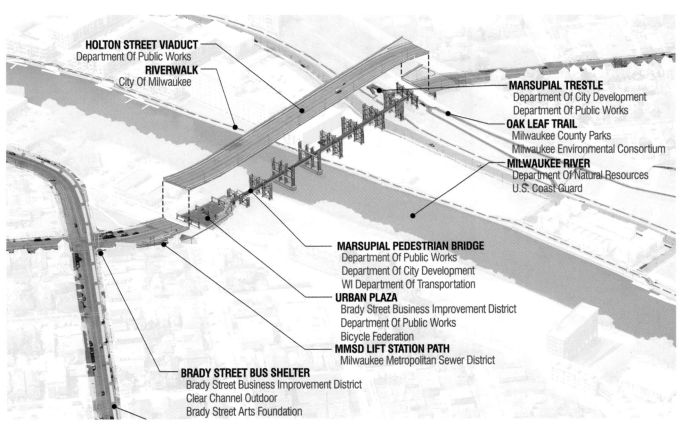

HOLTON STREET VIADUCT
Department Of Public Works

RIVERWALK
City Of Milwaukee

MARSUPIAL TRESTLE
Department Of City Development
Department Of Public Works

OAK LEAF TRAIL
Milwaukee County Parks
Milwaukee Environmental Consortium

MILWAUKEE RIVER
Department Of Natural Resources
U.S. Coast Guard

MARSUPIAL PEDESTRIAN BRIDGE
Department Of Public Works
Department Of City Development
WI Department Of Transportation

URBAN PLAZA
Brady Street Business Improvement District
Department Of Public Works
Bicycle Federation

MMSD LIFT STATION PATH
Milwaukee Metropolitan Sewer District

BRADY STREET BUS SHELTER
Brady Street Business Improvement District
Clear Channel Outdoor
Brady Street Arts Foundation

OPPOSITE
The Marsupial Bridge, a new footbridge, hangs off of the Holton Street Viaduct, which was originally built to carry streetcars.
Photo: Jim Brozek/La Dallman Architects

TOP
The Crossroads Project is a plan to revitalize the Milwaukee River waterfront neighborhoods.
Photo: La Dallman Architects

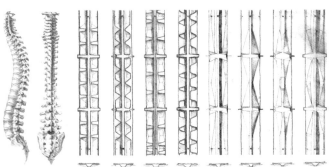

ABOVE
The structure of a spinal cord is the inspiration for the Marsupial Bridge's design.
Photo: La Dallman Architects

RIGHT
The completed "skeletal" construction of the Marsupial Bridge from underneath.
Photo: Jim Brozek/La Dallman Architects

lighting illuminates the surface of the bridge and overhead theatrical framing projectors direct focused beams of light when more illumination is needed, at the same time minimizing light pollution on the river below. The "lumibenches" are a "lensed, gasketed, marine-grade fluorescent fixture placed within the reflective white cavity of the hollow benches," providing dramatic lighting for the performance space.

The revitalized Urban Plaza also features a multimedia art installation called RiverPulse by local artist Ray Chi. Real-time data about the Milwaukee River's temperature, turbidity,

electrical conductivity, dissolved oxygen and water flow directs light animations on a long vertical surface that mimics the play of light along the surface of the water.

The projects have been successful in creating a stronger connection between two sides of Milwaukee. "I really liked that [the designers] recycled the infrastructure of the bridge to reconnect Milwaukee over the river," Kupfer says. "The river was a total industrial wasteland for decades and projects like this are critical to the reformation of urban communities."

Glowing acrylic "lumibenches" keep the urban space safely lit at night and provide seating for visitors.
Photo: La Dallman Architects

Tiuna el Fuerte Cultural Park

LOCATION El Valle, Caracas, Venezuela
DATE 2006–10
END USER 500 at–risk children daily
CLIENT Latent Voices Collective, Tiuna El Fuerte Foundation,
DESIGN FIRM Lab.Pro.Fab
DESIGN TEAM María Alejandra Bausson, Silvia Colmenares, Dis. Sebastián Miranda,
STRUCTURAL ENGINEERS Carlos Bezanquen, Esteban Tenreiro
ELECTRICAL/MECHANICAL Tomas Borras
CONTRACTOR Fab T Workshops
FUNDERS Consejo de Prevencion Social y Seguridad Ciudadana; Funvi; Funda Caracas; Fundacion Infocentro; GOB. Dtto. Capital; Odebrecht; Ministerio del Interior y Justicia; Ministerio de Transporte y Comunicaciones; MOPVI; Pdvsa La Estancia; Proyecto Capsula
COST $3.3 million USD total; $10 000 USD (per unit); $333 USD (per sq m)
PARK AREA 5859 sq m/63 066 sq ft
BUILDING AREA 4118 sq m/44 326 sq ft
TOTAL AREA 9977 sq m/107 392 sq ft

Tiuna is an experimental collective. "We came together in 2005, taking up the rebellious urban arts as arms in a struggle to radically transform the society in which we live," its website states. The self-described "public art activists" provide youth ages 3 to 18 with an alternative to violence by encouraging personal development and expression through graffiti, street art, poetry, video and radio production, film, circus arts, dance, music, and theater at the Tiuna el Fuerte Cultural Park. Tiuna is an alternative public space that "facilitates the interchange, self-expression, formation, recreation, and inclusion of lower-income youth." The collective received financial support from the mayor's office for the first six years of operation, and are now running on

ABOVE
Rather than cleaning graffiti off the repurposed shipping containers, the designers embraced the artwork and made it a feature of the buildings.
Photo: Eduardo Sauce/Lab.Pro.Fab

BELOW
Innovative, reused shipping containers create the structure.
Photo: Lab.Pro.Fab

ABOVE LEFT
A former parking lot, the site is
wedged between two main roads in the
El Valle neighborhood of Caracas.
Photo: Eduardo Sauce/Lab.Pro.Fab

ABOVE RIGHT
The stage is open for all to use,
such as the local dance collective
(pictured)
Photo: Eduardo Sauce/Lab.Pro.Fab

donations, mostly from corporate sponsors.

Tiuna is located in a former parking lot in the El Valle parish in Caracas, Venezuela, a densely populated neighborhood with few parks and one square foot of green space per person. The park borders a highway, the main thoroughfare to western Venezuela, and blocks of low-income apartment buildings. "Tiuna was not conceived as a terrain or lot, but rather an extension of the street," recalls Alejandro Haiek, an architect with Lab.Pro.Fab.

Lab.Pro.Fab started holding community meetings in 2005 to discuss turning the Tiuna project into a living experiment for social activism and engagement. "We try to use at least 40 percent of our time to research experimental projects," Haiek says. "Architects, sociologists, landscape architects and communication experts are involved."

Any organization or person can use the space, but they have to pay for their use by teaching an academic course for the local youth. Latent Voices, an activist group, organized a graffiti art day in a juvenile prison with support from Tiuna. The Laboratory of Urban Arts uses the space to teach youth in three areas: hip-hop, popular and alternative communication, and performing arts and music. Their intensive all-day workshops have been held once a week since 2008, serving approximately 800 youth over the years. Four productions combining singing, dancing, music and street theater are a result of the program.

Tiuna's buildings are built from converted containers and other recycled materials. The modular containers have been transformed into classrooms, offices, laboratories, a skate park, and a permeable theater. Other materials such as cardboard cup holders were used to provide sound insulation in the radio station and recording studios. Community member Lorena Freitez, of the activist group Latent Voices, stresses the importance of reusing the castoff materials. "Our choice of architecture reflects our political beliefs," she says. "We want to create an alternative use or value to those materials and people that have been excluded from the formal discourse of the city." Embraced by the community, the park "meets the aesthetic and symbolic references of the young people that we work with," Freitez says.

The park is now about halfway through its transformation, and the architects are revising their original plans based on community input. Miqueas Figuera, a local musician who uses the recording studio and is a member of the collective, has planted many of the new trees, and advocated for a hostel and tennis courts.

Two of the auditoriums and their supporting classroom and laboratory spaces, each called a nucleus, have been completed and a third is in the works. "Our initial goal was five," Haiek says, "But now three to preserve more green space. At this moment we really want to transform this parking lot into a park."

High Line

LOCATION New York City, New York, USA

DATES 1999–2011

IMPLEMENTING AGENCY City of New York

DESIGN FIRMS Diller Scofidio + Renfro, James Corner Field Operations

PLANTING DESIGNER Piet Oudolf

ENGINEERING Buro Happold

CONTRACTOR KiSKA Construction

ENVIRONMENTAL ENGINEER GRB Services

CIVIL/TRAFFIC ENGINEERING Philip Habib & Associates

STRUCTURAL ENGINEERING/HISTORICAL PRESERVATION Robert Silman Associates

PUBLIC FUNDERS New York City: $112.3 million USD; Friends of the High Line: $44 million USD; Federal government: $20 million USD; State of New York: $400 000 USD

PRIVATE FUNDERS Christy and John Mack Foundation; Philip A. & Lisa Marie Falcone; The Diller–von Furstenberg Family Foundation; Hermine & David Heller; Adam & Brittany Levinson; The Tiffany & Co. Foundation; Pershing Square Foundation; Michael & Sukey Novogratz; Donald Pels & Wendy Keys

PHASE 1 COST $86.2 million USD

PHASE 2 COST $66 million USD

TOTAL COST $152.3 million USD

LENGTH 2.33 km/1.45 mi

PEDESTRIAN TRAFFIC 5000 to 20 000 people daily

New York City's High Line has undergone a dramatic transformation over the last 80 years. It opened in 1934 as a highly celebrated elevated railway for trains carting goods from the city's factories through Chelsea and the meatpacking district. Today, it's a jewel of the city—an artfully landscaped public space with walking paths and greenery.

More than a beautiful park, the High Line is an example of successfully bringing a wide range of stakeholders together around the transformation of a contentious landmark. When the last train departed the High Line carrying a load of frozen turkeys in fall of 1980, train buff and actor Peter Obletz spent every cent he had trying to save it from being demolished. Obletz's vision was to revitalize freight operations and bring passenger trains to the High Line; however, he died in 1996 while the embattled railway's fate was still in limbo and property owners and developers were fighting to tear it down.

Friends of the High Line was formed in 1999 to preserve the railway. It was a long battle of lawsuits, campaigning and fundraising, but construction started in 2006, and the first phase, spanning from Gansevoort Street to West 20th Street, opened in 2009. The second section, from West 20th Street to West 30th Street, opened in the spring of 2011.

In 2005, a competition was held for the redesign of the railway, and the architect and landscape architecture firms of James Corner Field Operations and Diller Scofidio + Renfro won the bid to transform the High Line into a public park. Funded by the grassroots nonprofit organization Friends of the High Line, and the city of New York, as well as by private donors, the project is widely lauded as an overwhelming success.

Inspired by the way indigenous plants had thrived on the abandoned rail, the designers sought to preserve that sense of natural beauty.
Photo: Lisa Switkin/James Corner Field Operations

Saving the High Line

A timeline of stakeholder engagement

1929

The West Side Improvement Project, which includes the High Line, is approved. The project cost $175 million USD in the 1930s.

1950s–'60s

Growth in trucking reduces train use and in 1960 the southernmost portion of the High Line is demolished.

1983

Consolidated Rail Corporation (Conrail) puts the High Line up for sale. Congress passes the National Trails System Act, allowing inoperative rails to be used as recreation space.

1987

The Interstate Commerce Commission (ICC) reverses the sale to Obletz after it is opposed by local and state agencies, Chelsea Property Owners (38 landholders gunning for demolition), and a development company planning to build a highway on the Lower West Side.

1851–1929

Tenth Avenue becomes known as "Death Avenue" because of the number of accidents involving freight trains and street-level traffic. Men on horses, called the "West Side Cowboys," ride before trains waving red flags to improve safety.

1934

Trains begin using the High Line, an elevated railway running south from 34th Street to Gansevoort Street, about 9 meters (30 ft) above New York City's meatpacking district.

1980

The High Line shuts down. After a decade of declining use, the last train hauls away frozen turkeys a few weeks before Thanksgiving.

1984

Conrail files an intent to abandon the High Line when no government agencies come forward to purchase it. Actor and train enthusiast Peter Obletz buys the rail for $10 USD in hopes of revitalizing train operations.

FAR LEFT
Train chugging along on the High Line in 1953.
Photo: James Shaughnessy/courtesy of Friends of the High Line

LEFT
Above view of the High Line during construction of phase two.
Photo: Justine Heilner/James Corner Field Operations

Peter Obletz, in 1972, standing next to his rail counter–diner car under 11th Avenue, bought from Amtrack for $3500 USD.
Photo: Peter A. Richards

High Line champion Peter Obletz dies of cancer on May 4, 1996, at the age of 50.

1996

Robert Hammond and Joshua David meet at a community meeting about its proposed demolition. They decide to start the nonprofit Friends of the High Line to save it.

The pair's first two objectives are to file a lawsuit challenging the demolition order by Chelsea Property Owners and conduct an economic feasibility study for the High Line. They register a free Yahoo e–mail account—a key step in maintaining community support—that today has 10 000 contacts. It will take six years to gather the signatures needed to apply for a Certificate of Interim Trail Use from the federal Surface Transportation Board.

1999

Amanda Burden, Gifford Miller
Photo for Amanda Burden: City of New York
Department of City Planning
Photo for Gifford Miller: Edward Reed/City of New York

1992

The Interstate Commerce Commission commits to declaring the High Line "adversely abandoned" and will approve its demolition if Chelsea Property Owners can ensure costs exceeding $7 million (Conrail's maximum obligation) will be covered.

1997

Through a merger and acquisition of Conrail with CSX Transportation Inc. and Norfolk Southern Railway, ownership of the High Line passes to CSX Transportation Inc.

2000

The fight to stop the High Line from being demolished gets the attention of three key people who will have significant roles in its preservation.

Amanda Burden, then a member of the New York City Planning Commission, then–City Council member Gifford Miller, and well–known photographer Joel Sternfeld all go to bat for the High Line. Sternfeld photographs the High Line for Friends of the High Line's promotional materials.

Chelsea Property Owners ramps up efforts to get funding for the demolition.

LEFT
Friends of the High Line founders Joshua David and Robert Hammond.
Photo: Joel Sternfeld/Luhring Augustine, New York

BELOW
High Line (before).
Photo: Joel Sternfeld/Luhring Augustine, New York

Actor Edward Norton sees Sternfeld's work in *The New Yorker.* He becomes the first of many celebrities to support the High Line.

On December 20, his last day in office, Mayor Rudolph Giuliani signs an agreement with Chelsea property owners, and others, consenting to the abandonment and demolition of the High Line.

Acting on an earlier petition filed a month before by the New York City Council, Manhattan Borough President C. Virginia Fields, six Chelsea residents and Friends of the High Line, a judge issues an injunction halting the demolition on the grounds that related property easements along the route of the viaduct should have been subject to the city's uniform land use review procedure.

Michael Bloomberg, a High Line supporter, is elected mayor of New York City. He appoints Amanda Burden chair of the city's Planning Commission. Gifford Miller is elected speaker of the city council. Miller uses his new post to access funds for the High Line and moves to rezone the area so owners of properties beneath it will be able to sell their air rights, thus raising property values. This plan will be completed in 2005.

Mayor Michael Bloomberg
Photo: City of New York

Fashion designer Diane von Furstenberg hosts a launch party for a design competition by Friends of the High Line. It garners 760 entries from 36 countries. The jury includes designers, city planners and business owners.

Friends of the High Line receives 1500 individual donations even before publishing the winning concept design. On July 22, the city commits $15.75 million in funding for the High Line's conversion to public space.

2001

2003

Edward Norton
Photo: Henry Chan

Casey Jones
Photo: Kelly Kennedy

2002

In February 2002, Friends of the High Line releases Reclaiming the High Line, a comprehensive reuse and planning study, co-sponsored by The Design Trust For Public Space.

The Design Trust for Public Space offers a fellowship to architect Casey Jones to do a planning study for the reuse of the rail line.

Martha Stewart and Edward Norton co-chair a Summer Benefit Party for Friends of the High Line. It will become a regular = high-profile event.

Diane von Furstenberg and Barry Diller
Photo: Melissa Rosenberg, Michele Asselin/InterActiveCorp

LEFT
High Line (before). Real estate values soared after the railway was reopened to the public.
Photo: Joel Sternfeld/
Luhring Augustine, New York

BELOW
Construction workers watch the ground-breaking ceremony of the High Line redevelopment project.
Photo: Edward Reed/
City of New York

RIGHT
Mayor Bloomberg at the Section 2 opening.
Photo: Spencer T. Tucker/
City of New York

James Corner and Lisa Switkin of James Corner Field Operations
Photo: James Corner Field Operations

Liz Diller, Richard Scofidio and Charles Renfro of Diller Scofidio + Renfro
Photos: Abelardo Morell

Rezoning of the West Chelsea neighborhood is completed, enabling new commercial and residential growth.

The High Line gets a Certificate of Interim Trail Use and ownership is transferred to the city of New York. Development for public use can finally begin.

Section 1 of the High Line opens.

2005

2009

2004

Three major announcements help secure the High Line's preservation. New York City increases its funding to over $43 million. The state of New York and Conrail support the city's request to rail-bank the High Line. Landscape architecture firm Field Operations is hired along with design firm Diller Scofidio + Renfro to create the High Line's master plan.

2006

2011

The High Line redevelopment breaks ground on April 10, 2006.

Section 2 of the High Line opens.

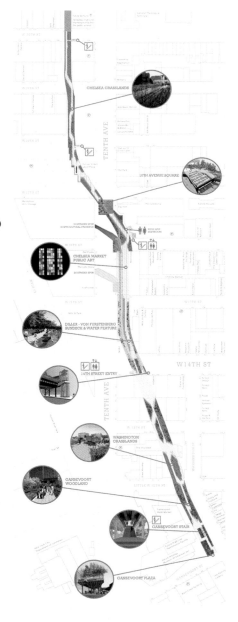

ABOVE
Map of the High Line highlighting features of the park.
Image: Friends of the High Line

Centre pour le Bien–être des Femmes

LOCATION Ouagadougou, Burkina Faso, Africa
DATE 2006–7
END USER 3035 people: general consulation;
1505 people: health education
CLIENT Voix de Femmes, Burkinbé NGO
IMPLEMENTING PARTNER
Associazione Italiana Donne per
lo Sviluppo (AIDOS)
DESIGN FIRM FAREstudio
DESIGN TEAM Giuseppina Forte,
Joao Sobral, Erika Trabucco,
Emanuela Valle
PROJECT ARCHITECT
Riccardo Vannucci, FAREstudio
SITE SUPERVISION Joao Sobral, Erika Trabucco
PROJECT MANAGEMENT Elena Bonometti,
Clara Caldera, Paola Cirillo, AIDOS
Sophie Sedgho (Voix de Femmes)
CONTRACTOR/MANUFACTURER S.art Décor
FUNDERS Democratici di Sinistra Political Party;
European Commission
COST €210 000/$300 531 USD
BUILDING AREA 500 sq m/5382 sq ft
SITE AREA 1600 sq m/17 222 sq ft
OCCUPANCY 60 people

"I Have Rights" is written in five different languages across the vibrant brick red exterior of Centre pour le Bien–être des Femmes et la prévention des mutilations génitales féminines 'Gisèle Kambou' (CBF). The off-the-grid women's health center near Ouagadougou, Burkina Faso, was designed by FAREstudio in partnership with Associazione Italiana Donne per lo Sviluppo (AIDOS), an Italian non-governmental organization committed to supporting women's rights and advocating for women around the world.

The building is the first formal structure in Section 27, a squatter camp outside the capital. "The center has helped to beautify the area," says Alice Bagagnan Ilboudo, 35, a user of the clinic. "The color and how it is constructed means that you know immediately that the building is the center." It stands out for that reason, and because the designers chose attention-grabbing super-graphics to convey the statement. "We could have painted figures or ideograms, but painting something written in all the different languages spoken there meant to show to local people the building's aim to be universal and made for the whole community," says Erika Trabucco, site supervisor from FAREstudio.

"I have rights" is both the local non-governmental organization's slogan and a strong statement. The building shouts it out loud giving a voice to those who have traditionally not had access to, or knowledge of, their legal and human rights. The center provides medical, legal, educational and psychological services for more than 4500 clients annually. It functions as a community center where meetings, health classes and weddings are held for men and women.

The climate, funding and political constraints in Burkina Faso caused lead architect Riccardo Vannucci to design a self-sufficient structure. "Politicians and government might pledge to support the building but I could not trust them and thus designed the building to be off-the-grid

J'ai des droits

OPPOSITE TOP
A girl rides her bike past the center, constructed of sundried, locally made bricks.
Photo: Cariddi Nardulli/FAREstudio

OPPOSITE BOTTOM
In 2010, 1065 boys and 41 men attended classes on sexual and reproductive health at the center.
Photo: Sheila McKinnon/FAREstudio

ABOVE
Women and children standing outside the center. The clients range in average age from 25 to 35 years old.
Photo: Sheila McKinnon/FAREstudio

and function without government support," he says. Energy is generated by the rooftop photovoltaic panels (PV), and with the exception of the medical rooms that need a generator to filter the air, it requires no additional electricity. The building is lifted above the ground to avoid dust, large barrels collect rainwater for the garden, and the roof is detached from the walls for passive cooling.

Alima Konate, the center's director, says that the PV panels produce enough energy for the center, but dust and heat are issues in summer. It is taboo for women to seek help in this area and the center offers a necessary level of privacy, according to AIDOS Project Manager Paola Cirillo. "For gynecological diseases we were ashamed to go and get help. Now we go to the

center for awareness sessions," Ilboudo, a client, says.

One of the most common legal issues women request assistance with is marriage protection. The center organizes legally recognized weddings to help ensure women will be provided for if a marriage fails. "This is not just something nice but something important from the legal point-of-view," Cirillo says. "Women usually only have a traditional wedding. This means that if the relationship ends they are left with nothing; no child support or alimony." Spurred by the success of the center, the government has started to contribute funding for additional infrastructure to the area. A maternity center was completed in December 2010.

SOS Children's Villages Lavezzorio Community Center

LOCATION Chicago, Illinois, USA
DATE 2004–8
END USER 425 foster care children and community members
CLIENT SOS Children's Villages Illinois
DESIGN FIRM Studio Gang Architects
STRUCTURAL ENGINEERING Thornton Tomasetti
ELECTRICAL/MECHANICAL ENGINEERING CCJM Engineers Ltd
CONTRACTOR Bovis Lend Lease
ADDITIONAL CONSULTANTS
Charter Sills (Lighting);
Cini–Little International (Food Service);
Site Design Group (Landscape)
FUNDERS City of Chicago
(Safe Homes for Kids
and New Homes for Chicago programs);
Illinois Housing Development Authority
Donation Tax Credits Fund and Illinois
Affordable Housing Trust Fund;
materials donations (various)
COST $3.5 million USD
AREA 1486 sq m/16 000 sq ft

SOS Children's Villages International was founded after WWII to help reconnect orphaned siblings. Of the roughly 518 000 foster youth in the United States, three out of four are separated from their siblings, according to the organization. Each village is a cluster of individual homes that share some common facilities while allowing children to live in a dwelling with their biological siblings under the care of a trained foster parent. The children's villages are intended to give their young residents a greater sense of stability and community.

Today, there are 518 children's villages and 392 SOS youth facilities worldwide. In 2004, the group began building the first SOS village in a major urban area, Chicago's Auburn–Gresham neighborhood. The community center provides crucial office and therapy spaces that neighbors requested when they were questioned during the early planning stages for the children's village. "We asked the community what they needed and they said, 'We don't need another set of

A small-scale test of the differing concrete concept featured on the exterior of the building.
Photo: Studio Gang Architects

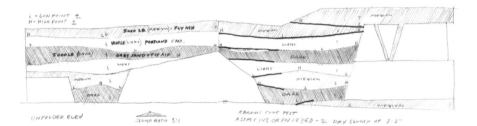

ABOVE
A sketch details the layering of different concrete mixes in the main wall of the community center.
Image: Studio Gang Architects

RIGHT
The concrete wall during construction.
Photo: Scott MacDonald/Hedrich Blessing

basketball courts, we want a learning center and a family education center where we can strengthen and build families together with the community,'" SOS Illinois Director Tim McCormick says.

The community center acts as a gateway to the SOS Children's Village, a community of 16 homes, with an average of five children in each, interspersed in a community located nine miles from downtown Chicago.

The organization hired Studio Gang to design the community center. One of the challenges was to create a design that flowed from one space to another while permitting staff to maintain visual contact with the youth, according to architect Jeanne Gang. "You need to provide spaces that are welcoming and feel safe, but that's not always a big open space," Gang says. For example, the recreation room can be sealed by doors, but windows in the doors allow adults to observe and monitor safe play. The computer lab's open plan provides the same effect while creating a vital space for the neighborhood.

The client and architects often relied on donated materials and services to see the project through to completion. This complicated the design process. Contractor Bovis Lend Lease contributed by donating excess building materials that were left over from other sites. The firm created a spreadsheet of materials to track donations by what they wanted, what they might get, and what they had been promised. They also evaluated how those donations and shifts would affect the design. "They were happy to get anything, but we still had our standards and did a lot more analysis on them. There was a lot of compromise and collaboration," Project Manager Beth Kalin says.

The materials that were eventually donated influenced the look and feel of the finished product. Originally, the firm anticipated a donation of bricks that would clad the exterior. That never happened and they improvised by integrating various concrete mixes from different sources, resulting in a wavy concrete exterior. "We did small mock-ups, then did a full-scale trial with the

concrete in the elevator shaft," Kalin says. At the final hour, a manufacturer offered to donate all the concrete, but the firm decided to stick with the pattern concept anyway. "We were still pretty nervous when they did the big wall," Kalin recalls.

"The first impression I had of the building was that it was a concrete jungle gym," says Child and Family Services Coordinator Rochelle Ingram. "One of the things that drew me [to the building] was that it looked so out of the ordinary for the Auburn–Gresham area," she says. "The community center is noticeable, eco-friendly, child-friendly, and it looks inviting." Ingram enjoys working in the building where the youngsters love to race up the stairs and slide down the banisters.

Youth who use the facility embrace it. "People that try to keep themselves academically involved sometimes don't have access to the knowledge they need or a computer," says Tevaughn Seay, a teen who frequents the center. "So they have to find it in a book, and in this neighborhood, not too many homes have books."

The Lavezzorio Community Center is the gateway into the SOS Illinois Children's Village.
Photo: Steve Hall/Hedrich Blessing

187

Interior of the prefabricated
retractable classroom in the Karail
slum of Dhaka, Bangladesh, designed
by Architecture for Humanity–Dhaka
for the Jaago Foundation in 2011,
a charitable foundation providing
free education.
Photo: Imrul Kayes/
Architecture for Humanity–Dhaka

Children who were taught in classrooms with daylight scored as much as

20%

higher on standardized tests in math

26%

higher in reading than other students in the same school district with less light

The Role of Emerging Energy-Efficient Technology in Promoting Workplace Productivity and Health: Final Report / 2002 research project report by Heschong Mahone Group, conducted with 9000 students in California, Washington and Colorado.

In 2004, the average cost of a classroom was

$108

USD per square meter in Asia

$119

USD per square meter in Africa

while the average cost of a classroom in the US was

$1 367

per square meter.

"Operations Evaluation Department Report," World Bank, 2004. (www.worldbank.org/oed/education/documents/education_primary_determinants_paper.pdf)

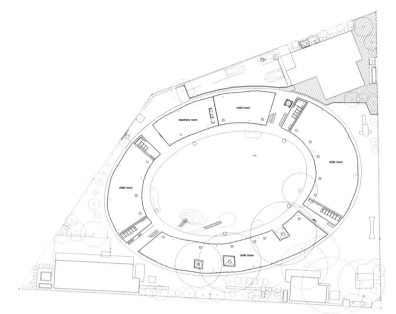

Fuji Kindergarten

LOCATION Tachikawa, Tokyo, Japan

DATE 2005–7

END USER 600 students

CLIENT Fuji Kindergarten

DESIGN FIRM Tezuka Architects

DESIGN TEAM Takaharu Tezuka, Yui Tezuka

ART DIRECTOR Kashiwa Sato

STRUCTURAL Masahiro Ikeda Co.

CONTRACTOR Takenaka Corporation

ADDITIONAL CONSULTANTS Masahide Kakudate Lighting Architect & Associates

FUNDERS Self-funded

COST 450 million Japanese yen /$5.8 million USD

OUTER CIRCUMFERENCE 183 m/600 ft

INNER CIRCUMFERENCE 108 m/334 ft

HEIGHT 2.1 m/7 ft

When tasked with building a kindergarten in the Tokyo suburb of Tachikawa, architect Takaharu Tezuka asked himself, "What do kindergarteners do?" The answer: they run in circles.

In 2007, Tezuka and his wife and partner Yui teamed up with art director Kashiwa Sato of the casual apparel company Uniqlo to develop Fuji Kindergarten's innovative circular learning space. Today, Fuji Kindergarten is one of the largest kindergartens in Japan. Owner and Director Sekiichi Kato asked the team to come up with a concept for a school with a teaching and learning arena that would provide endless possibilities for its nearly 600 students.

The building is a distorted oval shape with wood decking on the roof that doubles the play area of the kindergarten and adds a vertical dimension that encourages exploration. The building accommodated three zelkova trees that are original to the property. Each classroom has a rope safety net leading up to the roof where a huge slide takes them back to the courtyard if they don't feel like using the stairs. The classrooms are separated by modular wooden storage blocks and feature

ABOVE
Site and first-floor plan.
Image: Tezuka Architects

OPPOSITE TOP
An aerial view of the oval wooden roof deck shows students playing.
Photo: Tezuka Architects

OPPOSITE BOTTOM
Adjustable walls can be completely removed to create a learning environment without physical boundaries.
Photo: Tezuka Architects

movable glass walls that can be opened on hot days. "We aim for Fuji to be an example of change for education and hope to set the standard for the future," Kato says. "We want children to not only learn from their teachers but from the trees, stones and earth that surrounds them. From that knowledge they learn that they are part of the environment and need to take responsibility for it."

"This kindergarten is all about creating games," Tezuka says. With fewer toys, children are pushed to be creative about play. "There has been extensive research conducted after this kindergarten was opened and studies show that students at Fuji [Kindergarten] make up 12 games a day to play instead of the usual six. Much of that [change] is attributed to the accessibility the students have to a variety of open spaces," Tezuka says.

Under Sato's art direction, the uniforms were redesigned to stimulate the school's unique atmosphere. "I changed the logo and designed the uniforms to reflect the freedom of Fuji [Kindergarten]," Sato says. The children wear brightly colored T-shirts with "Help Me Do It Myself" written on them.

TOP
An old zelkova tree rises through the center of a classroom.
Photo: Tezuka Architects

BOTTOM
Students sport casual, brightly colored uniforms.
Photo: Tezuka Architects

Kindergarteners sit safely behind a protective fence on the inner edge of the school's oval roof.
Photo: Tezuka Architects

When tasked with building a kindergarten in the Tokyo suburb of Tachikawa, architect Takaharu Tezuka asked himself,

"What do kindergarteners do?"
The answer: they run in circles.

Green
School
Bali

LOCATION Sibang Kaja Village,
Bali, Indonesia
DATE 2005–7
END USER 160 students
CLIENT Yayasan Kul–Kul
(Green School managing nonprofit)
DESIGN FIRM Area Designs (site plan);
PT Bambu (structures)
DESIGN TEAM Effan Adhiwira,
Miya Buxton, Hanno Burtscher,
Phillip Beck, Stephanie Gunawan,
Erin Johnson, I Nyoman Kerta,
Cheong Yew Kuan, Aldo Landwehr,
Yulianto Maliang, I Kendra Spanton,
Gusti Ngurah Putra Wiarsa,
Heru Wijayanto
STRUCTURAL ENGINEERS
Universitas Gadjah
Mada civil engineering faculty
CONTRACTOR PT Bambu
BAMBOO CONSULTANT Joerg Stamm
FUNDERS John and Cynthia Hardy
COST $3.12 million USD
AREA 7785 sq m/83 800 sq ft

The Heart of School building
is the largest bamboo building
on campus.
Photo: Nyoman Widiantaval/
Green School Bali

The Kul-Kul Bridge was one of Green School Bali's first structures.
Photo: Nyoman Widiantaval/Green School Bali

The Green School in Bali, Indonesia, stretches the traditional use of bamboo in innovative and experimental ways, demonstrating the untapped architectural possibilities of this strong and versatile building material. The school structure is also an advertisement for the unorthodox teaching methods it shelters. "Changing the physicality not only gets people to imagine something different, it allows people to manifest things to be different," says co-founder John Hardy.

John and Cynthia Hardy moved to Bali in the mid-1970s. Then, after watching *An Inconvenient Truth*, which John jokes "ruined his life," the couple decided to start a school that taught an educational curriculum combining traditional and scientific subjects with a green studies program. The subjects include carbon footprint analysis, water studies and organic farming.

The facilities are interspersed over an area of 8 hectares (80 000 sq m), immersed in a tropical setting of lush vegetation. The master plan was designed by Cheong Yew Kuan, founding architect at Singapore-based Area Designs. Beyond the main building, the campus includes an auditorium, sports field, gymnasium, libraries, ponds, vegetable gardens and walkways. The Kul-Kul Bridge—a bamboo suspension bridge that covers a 20-meter (66 ft) span—links the two sides of the campus over the Ayung River. The river is used by community members to go to and from rice fields, temples, work and school.

Bamboo stems are selected by individually testing each stem's density on-site. "Bamboo just grows everywhere, in people's backyards and river valleys, you don't have to give it much," says Elora Hardy. "And if you only harvest the mature stems, about 25 percent of a clump, it will grow indefinitely."

The buildings are 95 percent bamboo, which is treated with Borax salt to repel bugs and termites. *Petung* bamboo is lashed together to form vertical structural members and long-span arches. The columns are tied to the concrete point foundations by threading the foundation rebar through river rocks and into bamboo. The river rock lifts the rebar far enough off the ground to prevent the bamboo from getting wet. Lightweight *tali* bamboo is used for secondary structural elements, such as rafters, and fixed with bamboo pins. The roofs are constructed out of *alang alang*—traditional Balinese grass strip tiles, with large overhangs to protect the structure from excessive sun and moisture. Walls are constructed using traditional Balinese mud building techniques.

The company PT Bambu constructed the buildings, with engineering services provided by Professor Ir. Morisco, who leads the structural engineering laboratory in the department of civil and environmental engineering at Universitas Gadjah Mada, in Yogyakarta, Indonesia. His colleagues Ashar Saputra and Inggar Irawati also participated. The design team produced detailed construction models that the engineers transformed into a computer model to test for axial, wind and earthquake loads.

The physical models also became the basis for the construction. "All of the drawings we do are for our own planning, for the client, the building department and the engineers to look at," said Hardy. "But the people who do the buildings only refer to the model." The construction crews started with the smaller, simpler buildings, like faculty housing, and worked up to the larger high-profile buildings.

The main building on the campus, called the Heart of School, is a three-story structure containing three interconnected spirals, for a total of 2000 square meters (22 222 sq ft) of floor space. It is 20 meters (66.7 ft) high and the main bamboo poles are 18 meters (60 ft) tall and 25 centimeters in diameter. To build this structure, PT Bambu used more than 2600 bamboo poles and 10 000 strips of *alang alang*.

TOP RIGHT
Open-air classrooms allow students to learn from nature.
Photo: Nyoman Widiantaval/Green School Bali

MIDDLE RIGHT
The Mepantigan structure houses performing arts programs such as drama and music.
Photo: Nyoman Widiantaval/Green School Bali

BOTTOM RIGHT
Classes are held in a bamboo yurt when the weather is bad.
Photo: Nyoman Widiantaval/Green School Bali

Olifantsvlei Primary School

LOCATION Kliptown, Johannesburg, South Africa
DATE 2006
END USER 80 students
CLIENT Olifantsvlei Primary School
DESIGN AGENCY Institute of Experimental
Architecture ./Studio3 at the
University of Innsbruck
DESIGN TEAM Astrid Dahmen, Volker Giencke,
Walter Prenner, students
ENGINEERING Nowy & Zorn
FUNDERS Province South-Tirol, Shanduka
Foundation, Tirol and Vorarlberg
COST €90 000/$125 000 USD
BUILDING AREA 150 sq m/1615 sq ft
SITE AREA 12 000 sq m/129 167 sq ft

The Congress of South African Trade Unions recently declared that South Africa's schools are in crisis, calling them "dumping grounds for children" and "bleak, uninspiring places, where violence and abuse are rife." This may have been the case at Olifantsvlei Primary School near Johannesburg, South Africa, before it was reinvented by a group of architecture students. The 80-student preschool invites students to engage in their education through a jungle gym-like construction. While playgrounds alone won't transform the country's education system, the Olifantsvlei preschool makes a dramatic break from the typical design of schools constructed under South Africa's apartheid era by associating learning with fun. The goal is to break the cycle of poor public education in South Africa.

The preschool, completed in 2006, was designed and built by architecture students from the Institute of Experimental Architecture ./Studio3 at the University of Innsbruck in Austria. The architecture students, led by assistant

professor Astrid Dahmen, collaborated with the preschool's teachers.

"The community was very open about the design but they wanted the design to enable a new learning style," Dahmen says. "They did not want the teacher to be in front of the students teaching, but with the students learning together."

The facility consists of two classrooms, an outdoor play area, a kitchen and restrooms. An expansive roof structure was donated by the manufacturer Hoesch Bausysteme because of a production flaw. It unifies the campus and shades

OPPOSITE TOP
Two classrooms are housed under a steel canopy.
Photo: Verena Rauch/./Studio3

OPPOSITE BOTTOM
Students play in the shade between classrooms.
Photo: ./Studio3

TOP RIGHT
The school building is integrated with the play area.
Photo: ./Studio 3

BOTTOM RIGHT
The double roof helps cool down the school.
Image: ./Studio3

the area between the two classrooms. "The students use the shaded area for break as well as learning," Dahmen says. "In this way the area works as a third outdoor classroom."

Constructed from wrinkled tin sheeting, the roof is designed with striking angles that make the school stand out against the backdrop of the city. Students can scamper up the pitch to play on the vivid green, yellow, cyan and hot pink wooden trapezoids and rectangles inserted in the tin slope. The tin roof absorbs most of the solar heat and the deep roof angles direct channels of air throughout the space. The body of the school is made of exposed steel frame and plywood.

"I visit the school often and the structure is still really beautiful and so enjoyed by the children," says Donné Nicol, executive director of the Shanduka Foundation, which funded the project. Since the construction of the Olifantsvlei Primary School, the foundation has continued to support the school and funded the addition of more classrooms, a library, science lab, and a sports court.

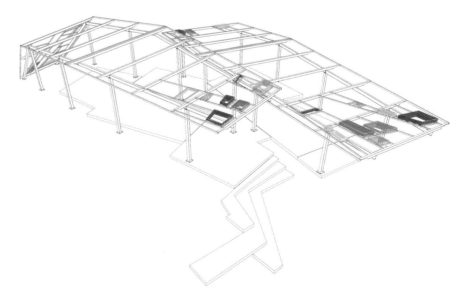

The Bridge School connects the banks of a small river. The round building in the background is a tulou, a 400-year-old fortress.
Photo: Li Xiaodong/ Li Xiaodong Atelier

Bridge School

LOCATION Xiashi village,
Pinghe County, Fujian Province, China
DATE 2008–9
END USER 1200 Xiashi Village residents,
including 35–40 students
who attend the school
CLIENT Xiashi Village
DESIGN FIRM Li Xiaodong Atelier
CONSTRUCTION DRAWINGS
Hedao Architecture Design
PROJECT TEAM Wang Chuan,
Chen Jiansheng, Nie Junqui, Liu Mengjia,
Liang Qiong, Li Xiaodong, Li Ye
CONTRACTOR Zhangzhou Steel
and the people of Xiashi Village
FUNDERS 50 percent government;
40 percent private;
10 percent Li Xiaodong (ongoing costs
funded by local government)
COST $95 000 USD
BUILDING AREA 240 sq m/2583 sq ft
SITE AREA 1550 sq m/16 684 sq ft

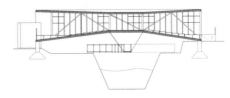

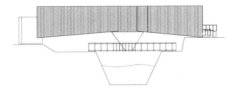

ABOVE
Two section diagrams of the Bridge School's rooms.
Image: Li Xiaodong/ Li Xiaodong Atelier

TOP RIGHT
Long timber slats create shade while allowing views from the bridge.
Photo: Li Xiaodong/ Li Xiaodong Atelier

BELOW
Aerial drawing of the Bridge School.
Image: Li Xiaodong/Li Xiaodong Atelier

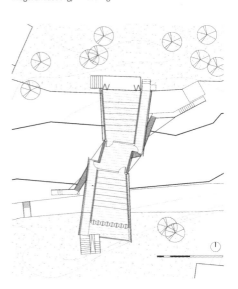

"The whole idea is to find an architectural solution to sustain the old community."

Li Xiaodong, architect

The Bridge School at Pinghe in Fujian, China, is both a school and a link between places and times. In an effort to connect an old way of life with the future of the community, architect Li Xiaodong designed a school on a bridge over a small river that runs through the rural Xiashi Village. The village is also home to two *tulous* (traditional Hakka fortresses), one on either side of the river. These 400-year-old enclosed earthen structures provided defense against rivals hundreds of years ago and were a communal living space for villagers until the 1950s. The school's unusual location was chosen to encourage appreciation of these ancient structures.

The project was managed by Chen Jiansheng, a former village resident who grew up in one of the tulous. It took about a year of exploration before laying down a plan for the school. "We found that the area's most ancient culture was in collapse," Jiansheng says. "But in the last 20 years, because there's no one living in them and because of a lack of protection and preservation, more than 80 percent of them have collapsed."

In designing the school, architect Xiaodong wanted to incorporate a connection between the new community space and the historical communal lifestyle tied to the deteriorating fortresses. Xiaodong realized that a bridge would be the perfect structure to physically and metaphorically bring the past and the present together. "The idea is to integrate the new with the old, not copy the old in form," Xiaodong says. "The intention of a new form which is in contrast to the old is to 'pinch' the consciousness of the old community through defamiliarization, thus to rejuvenate the old." The Bridge School brings people together from both sides of the river,

much the same way tulous united people through communal living for hundreds of years.

Arranging to transport construction materials into rural Xiashi was challenging. The bridge's frame is lightweight steel that rests securely on concrete piers. Thin timber slats let in a golden light through the walls. The wedge-shaped classrooms taper toward the bridge's center and also function as a theater and play structure. A walkway suspended beneath the school is an easy way to cross from one side of Xiashi to the other.

Since construction was completed in 2009, 40 children from both banks learned to read and write inside the bridge. The students range in age from 7 to 9. Xiaodong has noted a distinct change in the community. "This change is not just due to the project itself but also the wide publicity of the project," he says.

ABOVE
Stepped seating replaces chairs in the classrooms.
Photo: Li Xiaodong/ Li Xiaodong Atelier

LEFT
The revolving doors allow the space to shift for different occasions.
Photo: Li Xiaodong/ Li Xiaodong Atelier

> ## "Now we are saying that your children are so valuable that we are giving them a fantastic building."
>
> Monica McGeever, head teacher

Hazelwood School

LOCATION Glasgow, Scotland
DATE 2003–7
END USER 54 students with
multiple sensory impairments
IMPLEMENTING AGENCY Glasgow City Council
DESIGN FIRM Alan Dunlop Architect Limited
DESIGN TEAM Maggie Barlow,
Gordon Brown, Alan Dunlop, Fergal Feeney,
Gordon Murray, Stacey Phillips
ENGINEER Buro Happold
LANDSCAPE ARCHITECT
City Design Co-Operative
QUANTITY SURVEYORS Thomas and Adamson
CONTRACTOR/MANUFACTURER
Sir Robert McAlpine
FUNDER Glasgow City Council
COST £6.8 million/$10.9 million USD
AREA 2666 sq m/28 697 sq ft

The new Hazelwood School for Children and Young People with Sensory Impairment is the only educational institution in Glasgow, Scotland, of its kind. Students may be blind and deaf, or they could be physically handicapped and struggle with a learning disability. "Our children are probably the most disabled children in Glasgow," says Monica McGeever, the school's head teacher. "When they were being schooled in [two] run-down buildings, that didn't send a great message in terms of the value we put on children with disabilities." In 2003, the Glasgow City Council decided to build a single school for young people with multiple sensory impairments. It was finally completed in 2007.

In the United Kingdom, school procurement is done through a public–private partnership. Construction companies bid to build schools and the local governments pay for them over time.

Rather than select the cheapest option, as is often the case under this system, the Glasgow City Council decided to hold a design competition for a school that would accommodate children with special needs.

Architect Alan Dunlop was selected out of the six local architects invited to participate and launched a challenging 18-month community-focused design development period. He wanted to explain to students who were blind and deaf the design of the school and made models of cardboard for them to feel. The design charrettes with teachers, parents, therapists and doctors were a key way for Dunlop to learn about the struggles disabled youth face on a daily basis. "When the clinicians took me through the range of problems that each child can have it was overwhelming," Dunlop says. "In many ways I had

LEFT
The school's design accommodates the site's existing trees.
Photo: Keith Hunter

OPPOSITE
A textured "trail rail" helps guide students through the tactile environment.
Photo: Andrew Lee

to put aside everything I had learned as an architect and in architecture school."

These discoveries informed every aspect of the school's design. The team developed a strategy that focused on using highly tactile materials to promote sensory navigation so that different spaces are defined by gravel, grass, woodchips and floor markings. The ceiling heights in classrooms differ to create distinct acoustical environments. A slate wall strategically positioned to absorb warmth from the sun delineates classroom levels.

The transitions between spaces facilitate "trailing," which is when a visually impaired person runs their hand along a wall or handrail. The locker wall in the main corridor is faced with cork that helps these students find their way around. In the old building there were thick red handrails on the walls that gave the school "an institutional feel," Dunlop says. "Depending on the angle of the wall related to the entrance of the classrooms they know exactly where they are."

The thoughtful design of the main trailing wall also facilitates sensitizing students to closer contact. "There is one young man who had great difficulty moving independently around his previous school," McGeever recalls. "When he came to Hazelwood, within a matter of weeks he was moving around the school, almost with no support whatsoever."

TOP RIGHT
Non-toxic interior finishes were used because of the student body's heightened sensitivity.
Photo: Andrew Lee

RIGHT
The building's low profile minimizes its impact on the site and surrounding neighborhood. It weaves through trees that were on the site before it was built.
Photo: Andrew Lee

ABOVE
Students dine in the cafeteria. The design emphasizes daylight.
Photo: Andrew Lee

RIGHT
A site plan of the school shows its curved shape.
Image: Alan Dunlop Architects

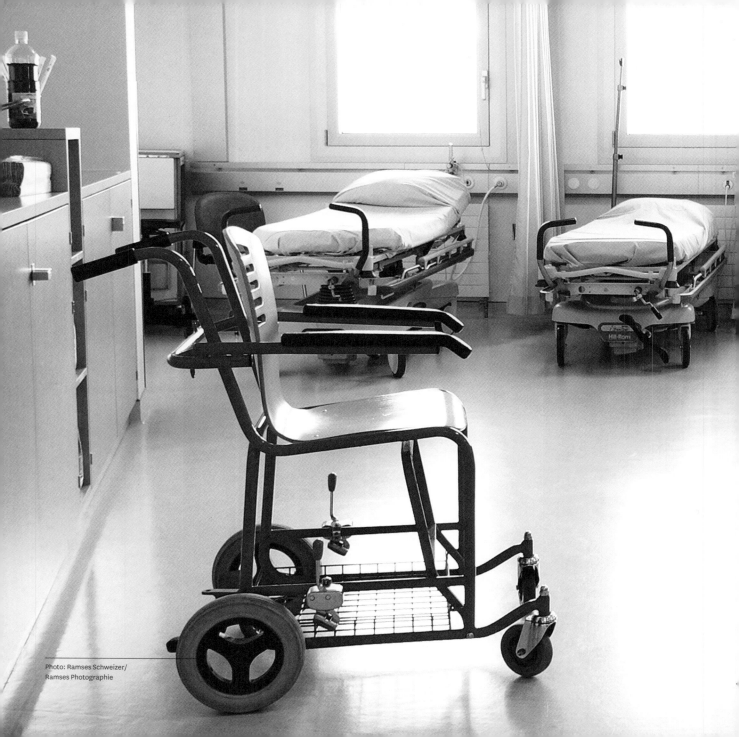

In 2007, the country with the lowest Healthy Life Expectancy (HALE) was

Sierra Leone, at **35 years of age**

the country with the highest Healthy Life Expectancy was

Japan, at **76 years of age**

Healthy Life Expectancy (HALE) at Birth (years), WHO Data, World Health Organization.

In developing economies 1 in 12 persons 60 or older lives alone

In more developed regions 1 in 4 persons over 60 lives alone

World Population Ageing 2009. Population Division, Department of Economic and Social Affairs, United Nations. 2002: New York.

In 1950, **8** % of the world's population was over 60 years old

In 2000, that percentage grew to **10** % and is expected to grow to **21** % by the year 2050

World Population Ageing 2009. Population Division, Department of Economic and Social Affairs, United Nations. 2002: New York.

The number of Americans 60 and over is expected to grow to

92.2 million by 2030

112 million people by 2050

The current number of nursing homes in the US is 16 000.

"Projections of the Population by Age and Sex for the United States 2010 to 2050," Population Division, U.S. Census Bureau, 2008. And "2004 National Nursing Survey: Facilities" Center for Disease Control and Prevention/National Center for Health Statistics www.cdc.gov/nchs/fastats/nursingh.htm

Maggie's Cancer Caring Centres

LOCATIONS United Kingdom;
Hong Kong, China; Barcelona, Spain
DATE 1994–present
END USER Cancer patients and their families
CLIENT Maggie's Cancer Caring Centres
FUNDER Maggie's Cancer Caring Centres
DESIGN FIRM Frank Gehry (Dundee),
Neil Gillespie (Lanarkshire), Zaha Hadid (Fife),
Rem Koolhaas (Glasgow), Kisho Kurokawa
(South West Wales), Richard Murphy
(Edinburgh), David Page (Highlands),
Richard Rogers (London), and
Chris Wilkinson (Oxford)

The physical experience of cancer is terrible, and unfortunately many patients and their families also are left with little recourse when it comes to understanding and coping with the psychological and emotional challenges of the illness.

Maggie's Cancer Caring Centres are built around the world as an alternative space where cancer patients and their families can receive counseling for the hardships of cancer within the context of a welcoming, supportive environment. There are 10 locations in the United Kingdom; one in Hong Kong, China; and six more are in the planning stages in the UK and Barcelona, Spain. The architecture, serene landscaping, and welcoming atmosphere provide a comfortable setting that stands in contrast to the institutional experience in which most cancer patients and their families find themselves immersed.

Maggie Keswick Jencks and her husband Charles Jencks began the Cancer Caring Centre project in 1994, after Maggie was diagnosed with cancer. As Charles says in *The Architecture of Hope*, a book about the project, "A Maggie's Centre is meant to be welcoming, domestic, warm, skittish, personal, small-scaled and centered around a kitchen or a place to make coffee and tea."

FEATURE PROJECT Maggie's Dundee
LOCATION Dundee, Scotland, UK
DATE 2003
DESIGN FIRMS
Gehry Partners, James F Stephen Architects
STRUCTURAL ENGINEER ARUP Scotland
LANDSCAPE DESIGN Arabella Lennox-Boyd
CONTRACTOR HBG Construction?
COST £1.3 million/$2.1 million USD
AREA 225 sq m/2422 sq ft
OCCUPANCY 150 people

Patients stretch their arms on the grassy lawn of Maggie's Dundee.
Photo: Christopher Simon Sykes/
Maggie's Cancer Caring Centres

FEATURED PROJECT Maggie's London
LOCATION London, UK
DATE 2001–8
DESIGN FIRM Rogers Stirk Harbour + Partners
STRUCTURAL ENGINEER Arup
CONTRACTOR ROK
ADDITIONAL CONSULTANTS Vin Goodwin
(access consultant); Warrington Fire
(fire consultant)
COST £2 million/$3.2 million USD
AREA 370 sq m/3983 sq ft
OCCUPANCY 200 people

The role of client was one that Charles was unfamiliar with, despite being a preeminent architectural critic. However, his industry knowledge allowed him to draw on years of connections to the world's best architects who deployed their talents in the service of creating uplifting environments. Unlike most projects, the brief for a Maggie's Centre is fairly open-ended but is guided by a simple principle: good design can make a difference in the lives of cancer patients.

"My kids, who are 10 and 12, have found it an easy place to visit and to understand what's happening to Dad and lots of other people," says Bruce Tasker, a patient at the Dundee, Scotland Center, designed by Frank Gehry. "They're not troubled by the fact that it's a cancer caring centre, whereas in the hospital ward they'd be intimidated by the formality, unfamiliarity and sterility."

The locations are built around a central kitchen as a gathering space, much like a home. "The concept of visitors gathering around the kitchen table is very much alive," says Jim Carr, a patient at Maggie's in Fife, Wales, designed by Zaha Hadid. "It is there that people share their stories, hopes and fears . . . and food. This is a strangely intimate experience."

Creating a connection to nature is also an important part of the Dundee Centre, which is

fashioned after Brochs, the stone circular dwellings dotting Scotland's highlands. The low-lying center in Dundee incorporates a two-story tower that overlooks a garden labyrinth of rocks along an immaculately trimmed lawn, offering a sweeping view across the Tay Estuary.

"The [tower's] ship deck on the south side is my favorite place to pass time, think, worry, feel good, feel bad, lose myself," says Tasker. "It's intimately connected to the building and keeps me in touch with people inside as it's overlooked by the large kitchen and social area windows." Tasker adds that it makes him feel like he is flying high above the trees and "on top of the world."

In contrast to the Dundee Centre's pastoral setting, the London Centre, designed by Rogers Stirk Harbour + Partners, sits in the hustle and bustle of Charing Cross. As a nod to Maggie Jencks' interest in Eastern gardening (she wrote the book *Chinese Gardens*), the design team, which included landscape architect Dan Pearson, aimed to create an intimate connection between the indoor and outdoor space. "The relationship of inside to outside is what contributes to extraordinary sense of place," says Ivan Harbour, a partner with Rogers Stirk Harbour + Partners.

Friends Center at Angkor Hospital for Children

LOCATION Siem Reap, Cambodia
DATE 2006–8
PROJECT TYPE Visitors center and offices
CLIENT Angkor Hospital for Children
DESIGN FIRM Cook + Fox Architects
STRUCTURAL ENGINEER Severud Associates
ELECTRICAL/MECHANICAL ENGINEER
Dagher Engineering
SUSTAINABILITY CONSULTANT
Ryan Maliszewski, Furuyama Yasuyuki
CONTRACTOR Villa Parc Engineering
FUNDER
Sterling Stamos Capital Management
COST $250 000 USD
AREA 342 sq m/3681 sq ft

Severe poverty has threatened the health of Cambodian children throughout the country's tumultuous history. The stunning child mortality rate is mainly due to preventable ailments like bacterial pneumonia and diarrhea. Photographer Kenro Izu founded Friends Without A Border in 1996, inspired to improve children's health after traveling there. Three years later, the organization opened Angkor Hospital for Children in Siem Reap, Cambodia. The Center for Friends Without a Border, featured here, was completed in 2008 and sits on the hospital's grounds.

The center provides a separate space for visitors to learn about the hospital without compromising patient privacy. "The center is very open and you can see through the building to the hospital so you feel like you're a part of the complex without being in it," says Basil Stamos, a physician and partner for Sterling Stamos Capital Managment, which funded the building. It also provides office space for Friends Without a Border and hosts art exhibits, health classes and training sessions.

New York–based Cook + Fox Architects designed the sustainable building. (Lead architect Rick Cook first adopted children from Cambodia in 2002.) "When they are older and know about their country's situation they will want to know how we helped," he says. The center is inspired by sacred building techniques of the Khmer people (Cambodia's largest ethnic group). The nine structural bays are laid out in a square grid, recalling the axial symmetry of nearby temples. The canted roof drains to a pool and rainwater cistern. "The Angkor Wat temples have very

The Friends Center is located at Angkor Hospital for Children in Siem Reap, Cambodia.
Photo: Cook + Fox Architects

The podium base of the building creates a place for visitors to sit.
Photo:Cameron Sinclair/
Architecture for Humanity

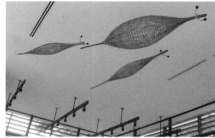

help us be kind to the environment

Rainwater is collected in this pond, which overflows into an underground cistern. The water from the cistern is filtered and used in and around the Friends Center. Our bio-diesel capable generator supplies a portion of our electricity. Our bio-fuel is produced by recycled cooking oil for cheaper and cleaner fuel. [...] building was designed pro bono by Cook+Fox Architects. [...] Stamos Capital Management to raise funds for Ange[...] [...]stackable.

LEFT COLUMN
Sustainably harvested bamboo
louvers on the exterior cladding satisfy
aesthetic and environmental needs.
Photo: Cameron Sinclair/
Architecture for Humanity

MIDDLE COLUMN
A rainwater collection pond in
the central atrium demonstrates
resourceful water storage.
Photo: Cameron Sinclair/
Architecture for Humanity

RIGHT COLUMN
Compostable toilets are a virtually
water-free way to dispose of waste and
empty into a composting unit outside.
Photo: Cameron Sinclair/
Architecture for Humanity

Sustainable Strategies Diagram

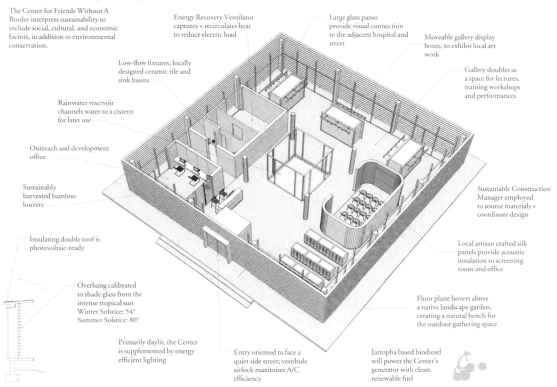

The Center for Friends Without A Border interprets sustainability to include social, cultural, and economic factors, in addition to environmental conservation.

Energy Recovery Ventilator captures + recirculates heat to reduce electric load

Large glass panes provide visual connection to the adjacent hospital and street

Moveable gallery display boxes, to exhibit local art work

Low-flow fixtures, locally designed ceramic tile and sink basins

Gallery doubles as a space for lectures, training workshops and performances

Rainwater reservoir channels water to a cistern for later use

Outreach and development office

Sustainable Construction Manager employed to source materials + coordinate design

Sustainably harvested bamboo louvers

Local artisan crafted silk panels provide acoustic insulation to screening room and office

Insulating double roof is photovoltaic-ready

Floor plane hovers above a native landscape garden, creating a natural bench for the outdoor gathering space

Overhang calibrated to shade glass from the intense tropical sun
Winter Solstice: 54°
Summer Solstice: 80°

Primarily daylit, the Center is supplemented by energy efficient lighting

Entry oriented to face a quiet side street; vestibule airlock maximizes A/C efficiency

Jatropha based biodiesel will power the Center's generator with clean, renewable fuel

COMMUNITY : HEALTH

advanced hydrological engineering," Cook says. "This simple gesture, making the rainwater collection a central feature of the building, connects the present to a cultural tradition."

Sterling Stamos hired Ryan Maliszewski to research sustainable strategies for the center. "The biggest challenge was trying to mediate the global modern efforts toward sustainability with the Khmer culture and construction practices," Maliszewski says. He coordinated between Cook + Fox and the local contractors. This eased the communication problems between the designers and builders. Shading slats around the exterior were originally meant to be made of koki wood, which has historically been used to build boats, but the political and cultural ramifications of its harvesting during the Khmer Rouge era has made it difficult to procure. After exhausting all other

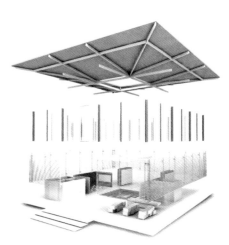

options, Maliszewski was forced to order bamboo fiberboard from southern China. "It was sort of a win-lose because we were trying to source local but [this example] typified some of the barriers we hit," he says. "If we wanted to make this work we had to look outside of the 250-mile radius." Although koki wood is culturally valuable, the finished product uses a more sustainable material.

TOP
Illustration of sustainable design strategies used in the Friends Center.
Image: Cook + Fox Architects

BOTTOM
Exploded axonometric drawing of the building components.
Image: Cook + Fox Architects

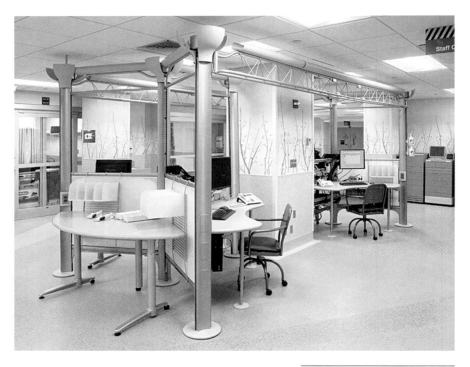

Pebble Project

LOCATION USA, Canada,
United Kingdom, Netherlands
DATE 2000–present
IMPLEMENTING AGENCY
The Center for Health Design
CLIENTS Health care providers and
research institutions
MAJOR FUNDERS Fees from 37 members
COST OF MEMBERSHIP $10 000–$30 000 USD
PROGRAM COST $500 000 USD annually
FEATURED PROJECT ER One,
Washington Hospital Center
LOCATION Washington, DC, USA
PROJECT PHASE In development
DESIGN FIRM Huelat Parimucha
Healing Design
FUNDER
Washington Hospital Center Foundation
COST $100 million USD

The Center for Health Design is an organization that promotes the use of evidence-based design in health care environments. Members share knowledge gained through a universal research methodology. The organization's Pebble Project evaluates the design of health care facilities and shares those findings with the health community. Its aim is to produce a ripple effect throughout the health care industry much like a pebble thrown into a pond.

Participating hospitals conduct baseline research as they build or renovate facilities. The Pebble Project team measures the success of the design implementation. Oftentimes small design details can have a significant impact on health outcomes and Pebble Project partners run the gamut in terms of purpose and innovation.

Project ER One in Washington, DC, investigates infection control in emergency settings using a full-scale simulation and training laboratory and 10-bed hospital addition at Washington Hospital Center. The design team from Huelat Parimucha Healing Design used creative materials and

Typically, nursing stations are situated at either end of a hospital corridor. At ER One, in Washington, DC, nursing stations are strategically placed in the center to improve responsiveness.
Photo: Joseph Patrick Parimucha/
Huelat Parimucha Healing Design

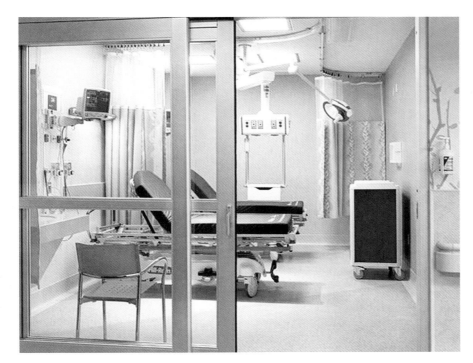

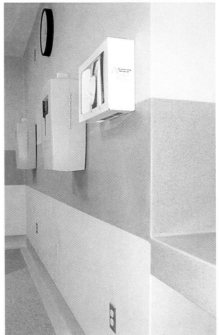

features such as Corian walls and integrated sinks, seamlessly connected rubber flooring, and silver ion-embedded antimicrobial paint. Fractal patterns on the simulation room's floor highlight a path to hand-washing stations and a pale blue "touch strip" four feet up the wall highlights the area of the wall most commonly contaminated by handprints from doctors and patients. In a critical emergency situation when a team might only have 30 seconds between patients, disinfecting the blue "touch strip" will keep the focus on taking the most effective preventive measures.

The Clinical Cancer Center at Froedtert & The Medical College of Wisconsin is studying a "hub" model designed by OWP/P Architects. With this approach, an interdisciplinary care team circles around the patient, as opposed to the patient traveling to multiple locations for various types of appointments. The cancer center aims to decrease the time needed to undergo a course of treatment by up to 40 percent through improved coordination of care.

At Laguna Honda Hospital and Rehabilitation Center, in San Francisco, design firms Anshen + Allen and Stantec Architecture worked with Laguna Honda Joint Venture Architects to provide wheelchair-accessible raised planting beds, making it possible for more of the center's residents to garden. Textured pavers underfoot help them to find their way.

Ann & Robert H. Lurie Children's Hospital of Chicago is one of the most ambitious vertical-plan hospitals in the world. During planning, a youth advisory board met regularly with the design teams from Zimmer Gunsul Frasca Architects, Solomon Cordwell Buenz, and Anderson Mikos Architects. They offered input on details from shelving near the sinks, to a bathroom door designed like a barn door. Hospital spokeswoman Mary Kate Daly says she's heard good and bad feedback from the young patients. One liked that it was easy to enter the bathroom while hooked up to an IV, while another rejected an idea for a space to play veterinarian in because they only wanted to think about healthy animals.

ABOVE LEFT
A blue stripe shows where hands are most likely to touch, and contaminate, a wall in ER One, in Washington, DC.
Photo: Joseph Patrick Parimucha/ Huelat Parimucha Healing Design

ABOVE RIGHT
Patient rooms in Project ER One are designed to accomodate a sudden influx of patients during a crisis.
Photo: Joseph Patrick Parimucha/ Huelat Parimucha Healing Design

NO RUNNING
SHOVING

Since 2005, schools in Broward County, Florida, have "No Running" signs posted in their playgrounds.
Photo: Tom Woodward/Flickr
Graphic : alix ogilvie/ Architecture for Humanity

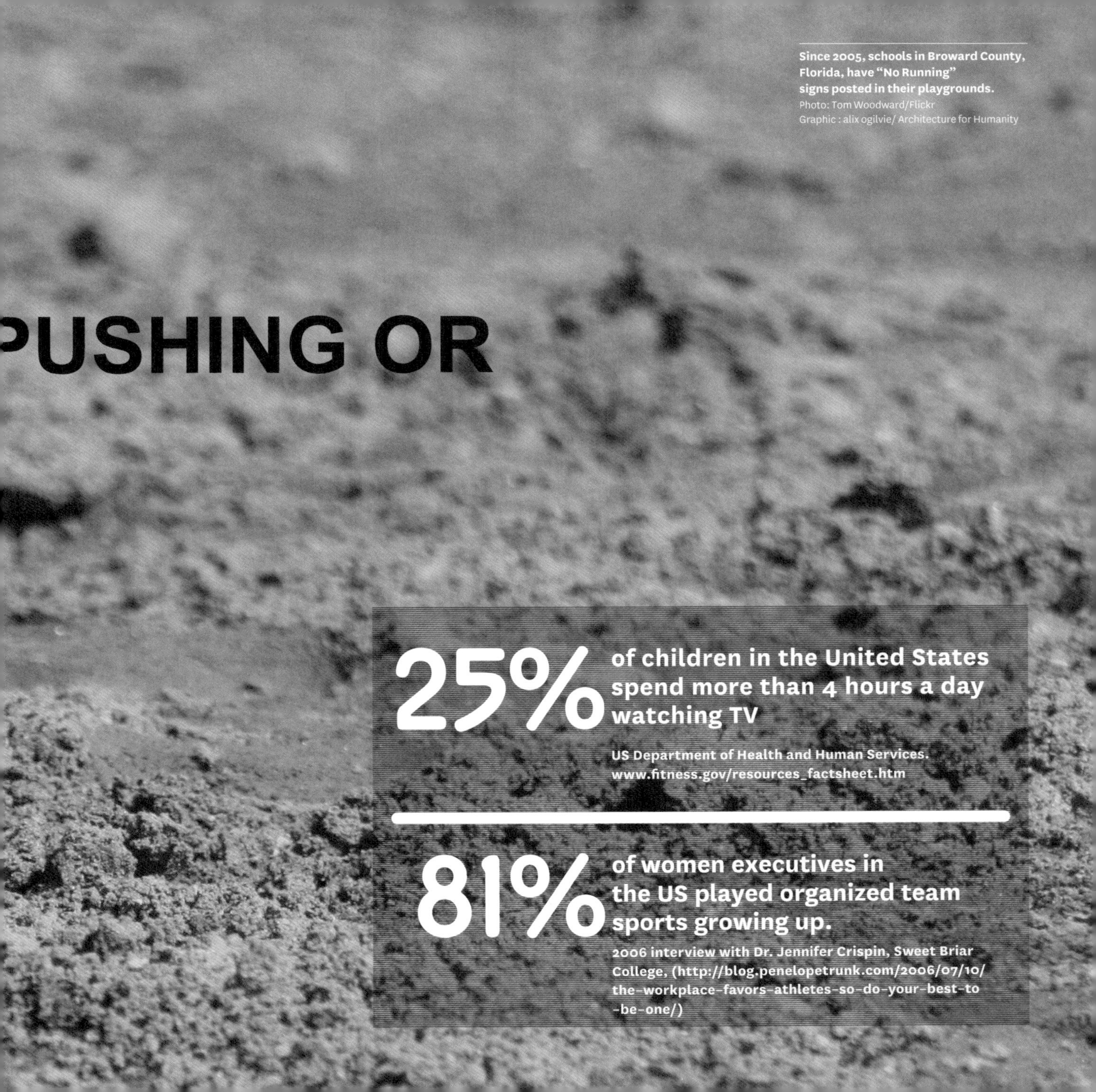

PUSHING OR

25% of children in the United States spend more than 4 hours a day watching TV

US Department of Health and Human Services. www.fitness.gov/resources_factsheet.htm

---

81% of women executives in the US played organized team sports growing up.

2006 interview with Dr. Jennifer Crispin, Sweet Briar College, (http://blog.penelopetrunk.com/2006/07/10/the-workplace-favors-athletes-so-do-your-best-to-be-one/)

Mahiga Hope High School Rainwater Court

LOCATION Mahiga, Nyeri District, Central Province, Kenya
DATE 2009–10
END USER 1500 residents of Mahiga
CLIENT St. Joseph Mahiga Primary and Secondary School
IMPLEMENTING AGENCY Architecture for Humanity
PROJECT MANAGERS Greg Elsner, Michael Jones
DESIGN FIRM Dick Clark Architecture
CONTRACTORS Boslika Building Contractors (general contractor), Chaga Electricals (mechanical contractor), Gumbi & Associates, Samuel Maina Ndlrague (water tank contractor)
ENVIRONMENTAL CONSULTANT Mazingira & Engineering Consultants
FUNDERS Architecture for Humanity; Willie and Annie Nelson; Nike; Nobelity Project
COST $84 150 USD
AREA 451 sq m/4850 sq ft
WATER STORAGE 30 000 liters/7925 gal

It started with a tree. Joseph Mutongu, a local conservationist, wanted to introduce a tree growing program at the school his son attended. The Mahiga Hope School is located in a dusty rural village in the Aberdare Mountain Range in central Kenya. Most families are subsistence farmers and at the time were in the midst of a four-year drought. The school needed water to allow the tree to grow, but more importantly to provide some clean drinking water to its students. Joseph took it upon himself to find a way to make it happen.

There were three options: to rely on the municipal waterline, which worked two weeks of the year; to drill an expensive bore well; or to develop an off-grid rainwater catchment system. A chance encounter with Turk and Christy Pipkin of the Nobelity Project created the opportunity for

the third option. In 2008, Joseph, Turk and the school installed a simple gutter system on one of the school's wooden structures. Rainwater was collected in a small tank and purified with an ultraviolet system. For a few thousand dollars, the school suddenly had access to a small supply of water. The team then had a bolder idea, to provide water for every student all the way to the end of high school.

For a rural school, access to water is the key for focused learning. Children don't have to walk miles to collect unsafe water, school lunches can use clean water for cooking and for drinking, and safe access to sanitation prevents disease and ensures teenage girls stay in school. The idea was born of tackling two uniquely different issues, the desire of the children to have access to sports and the need for safe drinking water. Turk and Christy

worked with Dick Clark Architects to develop a concept for a rainwater court and entered into the Gamechangers design challenge run by Architecture for Humanity and Nike. As one of the winners of the competition, the school was awarded financing, construction management and a one-year design fellow who would live and work in Mahiga.

Greg Elsner arrived in Mahiga with a task to design and build a multi-purpose basketball court that would collect up to 30 000 liters of water, with a budget on par with a simple borehole well. Partnering with local architects Multiplex Systems, Elsner and the team utilized local hand-cut stone (*Mahiga* means "stone"), a steel structure that mirrors traditional Kenyan art, and a two-panel metal roof to build the 436 sq m (4850 sq ft) structure. Going beyond a court, the architects

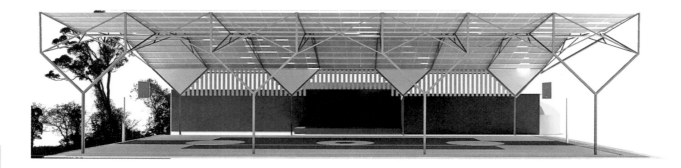

designed a small stage that could be used for community meetings, movie nights and weddings.

Like many institutional projects, this was more than a structure; it became a community catalyst. In less than 18 months student test scores jumped from the lowest to the highest in a district of 600 schools; enrollment in the high school tripled; the school had electricity for the first time; it installed a computer lab and a library and a two-story high school was built. Mahiga went from a derelict rural school to a model education campus.

When the court finally opened it had not rained in over three months. Over 1000 community members stood in the midday sun under a cluster of umbrellas to see the first basketball game played on the new court. As halftime approached, dark brooding clouds rolled across the skyline and by the time of the last shot the heavens opened up. Most building openings are dampened by a downpour, but in the case of the Mahiga rainwater court, it was the best way possible to celebrate. Joseph collected the first bowl of clean water to nourish a tree still growing in a corner of the schoolyard.

TOP
Schematic perspective of the court.
Image: Greg Elsner/
Architecture for Humanity

ABOVE
Students pose outside Mahiga Hope High School. The rainwater court supplies the school with water.
Photo: Turk Pipkin/Nobelity Project

LEFT
Foreman Robert Mwangi of Boslika Building Contractors smiles as heavy rains roll in.
Photo: Greg Elsner/Architecture for Humanity

TOP LEFT
Staking out the site for the
rainwater court.
Photo: Greg Elsner/Architecture for Humanity

SECOND FROM TOP LEFT
Setting the foundation for the
rainwater court.
Photo: Greg Elsner/Architecture for Humanity

THIRD FROM TOP LEFT
Raising the first of eight columns.
Photo: Greg Elsner/Architecture for Humanity

FOURTH FROM TOP LEFT
Underside of completed rain–
collecting roof.
Photo: Greg Elsner/Architecture for Humanity

FIFTH FROM TOP LEFT
Wire cage framing for the water cistern
with a capacity of 15 000 gallons.
Photo: Greg Elsner/Architecture for Humanity

BOTTOM LEFT
The water cistern, and everything
related to water on the court, is
painted yellow.
Photo: Greg Elsner/Architecture for Humanity

RIGHT
Setting up a basketball hoop.
Photo: Greg Elsner/Architecture for Humanity

"We finished it right when the rains came.
Keep in mind it had not rained in the
previous three months."

Greg Elsner, Architecture for Humanity design fellow

Skateistan

PROJECT NAME Skateistan Skate Park
LOCATION Kabul, Afghanistan
DATE 2007–present
END USER 360 students weekly
CLIENT Skateistan, Director Oliver Percovich
DESIGN FIRMS Convic Design, IOU Ramps
ENGINEER
Afghan National Olympic Committee;
Afghanyar Construction Company Ltd;
Engineer Moheen; Engineer Reza
BUILDING CONSTRUCTION ACCC
SKATE PARK CONSTRUCTION
Andreas Schützenberger, IOU Ramps
FUNDERS Embassy of Denmark;
Embassy of Norway; Embassy of Germany;
Nike; Architecture for Humanity;
Skateistan Denmark, Germany, Poland
and USA; various individuals
COST $617 303 USD
AREA 1800 sq m/19 375 sq ft

It is hard enough to get cities to implement permanent skate facilities—to do it in a place ravaged by destruction caused by civil wars and foreign invasions is a pretty radical idea. In June 2009, a coalition of local and international skateboarders came together to break ground in Kabul, Afghanistan, on the Skateistan Skate Park. Today, hundreds of local kids hit the ramps and half-pipes at this safe haven each week.

The project grew out of informal skateboarding sessions at an abandoned fountain in Kabul's Mekroyan district. In 2007, Australian skaters Oliver Percovich and Sharna Nolan were joined by a number of local kids from the area. The group soon turned into a posse of young skaters and "Ollie" decided to form Skateistan, the country's first coed skateboarding school.

As skateboarding is one of the few noncombat sports in Afghanistan, the team soon discovered that it was attractive to both girls and boys. However, local customs prohibited girls over 12 from skating in public. Percovich decided to tackle this head-on by building an indoor skate park, and to their surprise, the country's largest indoor sports facility.

With land donated by the Afghan National Olympic Committee and assistance from various

ABOVE
Murza Mohammadi performs a rock-n-roll to "fakie" on the mini ramp.
Photo: Jacob Simkin/Skateistan

BELOW
Fazila Shirindl skating the ramps. Part of Skateistan's mission is to empower girls.
Photo: Jacob Simkin/Skateistan

government, corporate and private donors, the dream slowly became a reality. A local construction company built the Quonset hut–inspired structure for a reduced rate. Australian skate park builders Convic Design was enlisted to work on an outdoor park and IOU Ramps from Germany agreed to build the ramps. Like many on the construction team, Andreas "Schutzi" Schützenberger, founder and director of IOU Ramps, was a little concerned at first.

Construction was no easy task. Tools and materials had to be shipped in from overseas, electricity would go out for long periods of time, and eye protection for local welders was little more than basic sunglasses. Once the heavy lifting was done the team added a little flavor to the park. A local volunteer was talking to a waiter at a nearby restaurant and heard about a man outside of town who had a few old Russian rockets in his backyard. "I always try to bring a little magic into the park and I thought a rocket would be unbelievable to put in," Schutzi says. Within 24 hours, Skateistan had its signature ramp, the rocket wall.

While the complex is surrounded by fences with sniper screens and guards to protect the youth inside, the turmoil outside is forgotten as Pashtun youth share their boards with Tajiks and Hazaras. The center includes classrooms for after-school programs and access to computer training. For an hour in the park, kids spend an hour in the classroom.

TOP RIGHT
The building has few openings to protect the youth from gunfire.
Photo: Jacob Simkin/Skateistan

MIDDLE RIGHT
Local skaters Wahila Mahmodi (L) and Fazila Shirindl (R).
Photo: Rhianon Bader/Skateistan

BOTTOM RIGHT
Go Skateboarding Day in Kabul, a sign of peace.
Photo: Jacob Simkin/Skateistan

BOTTOM FAR RIGHT
Noorzai Ibrahimi jumps a ramp.
Photo: Rhianon Bader/Skateistan

Gimnasio Vertical

PROJECT NAME Gimnasio Vertical

PROJECT LOCATION
Chacao, Caracas, Venezuela

DATE 2001–4

END USER 15 000 users monthly

IMPLEMENTING AGENCY
Municipality of Chacao, Caracas, Venezuela

DESIGN FIRM Urban–Think Tank

DESIGN TEAM Alfredo Brillembourg,
Marielly Casanova, Eduardo Kairuz,
Hubert Klumpner, Francisco Martin,
Jose Antonio Nuñez, Mateo Pinto,
Matias Pinto, Ricardo Toro

STRUCTURAL ENGINEER Andres Steiner

SUSTAINABILITY ENGINEER Battle McCarthy

CONSULTANTS
Thomas Auer–Transsolar (sustainability),
Felix Caraballo (community outreach),
Freddy Ferro (electrical services),
Intégral Ruedi Baur & Associés (graphic design),
Roberto Nino (sanitary services),
Jose Miguel Perez (sport coordinator),
Miquel Sureda (fire protection),
Luis Torres (construction management)

FUNDER City of Caracas, Venezuela

COST € 750 000/$1 million USD

AREA 47 899 sq m/515 581 sq ft

Designated recreation spaces are limited in
Venezuela, where over half the population lives
in dense, urban areas. The Gimnasio Vertical
(Vertical Gym) was conceived by international
architecture firm Urban–Think Tank, which has
an office in Caracas, Venezuela. The gym was
designed as a solution to the area's need for
more sports facilities. To address the lack of
available land in the city, Urban–Think Tank
designed a multi-level, multi-purpose gym
with the same sized footprint as a soccer field.
"Instead of outward mobilization, we need
to move upward," says architect Alfredo
Brillembourg, one of the co-founders of
Urban–Think Tank.

The first Vertical Gym was built in the
municipality of Chacao, in Caracas, and has four
floors of multi-purpose space. The first floor
consists of a basketball court and dance studio;
the second has a weight lifting area, running
track, and rock-climbing wall; and the top floor
is an open-air soccer facility with covered
spectator stands. All of the areas can be used at

ABOVE
**Chess and karate tournaments take
place simultaneously on separate
floors.**
Photo: Urban–Think Tank

BELOW
**Exterior view of the the gym. It blends
into the urban landscape of Caracas.**
Photo: Urban–Think Tank

the same time, maximizing the occupancy of the building. "With 15 000 users each month and a reduction of crime of nearly 30 percent, I think this first gym has been very successful," Brillembourg says.

All 35 gym users polled in a recent Urban–Think Tank survey say they use the facility at least twice a week, half of them going three or more times per week. Before the gym opened, 25 percent of those polled say they did not participate in sports. Maria Betania Mortiz Reneron, 16, says she goes multiple times a week to "stay physically fit." Jonathan Quinonez, 15, likes to play indoor soccer at the

Vertical Gym because it is a healthy, drug–free activity.

Chacao Mayor Leopoldo Lopez appreciates that it involves the recovery of public spaces and their transformation into facilities that promote sports. The Vertical Gym complies with international standards for disabled sports venues and often hosts community events. Every week, thousands of people use the gym, which is also intended to help curb the growing number of Venezuelan youth caught in gang violence. "Now the vision is to build 100 Vertical Gyms for Caracas," he says. The vertical model inspired plans for three more gyms

in Venezuela, one in Amman, Jordan, and one in New York City.

Urban–Think Tank is designing a Vertical Gym tool kit for modularity so a flexible number of floors with different purposes can be customized, depending on need. The gym's steel structure was welded on site; however, future gyms will use prefabricated bolted steel that can be assembled and disassembled for possible relocation or reuse. "We want the Vertical Gym to be able to organically grow and add facilities such as swimming pools, parking structures, social centers, agricultural centers, and marketplaces," Brillembourg says.

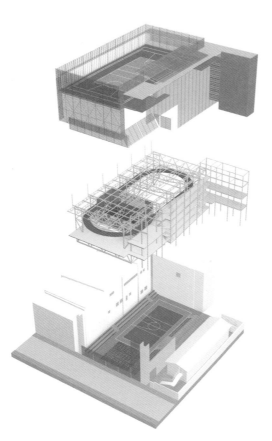

RIGHT
Axiomatic exploded view of the multi–story Vertical Gym.
Image: Urban–Think Tank

FAR RIGHT TOP
Children play on the outoor rooftop field.
Photo: Urban–Think Tank

FAR RIGHT MIDDLE
The indoor track circles the weight room, shown below.
Photo: Urban–Think Tank

FAR RIGHT BOTTOM
The large basketball court includes spectator seating and can be used for other sports or community events.
Photo: Urban–Think Tank

In 2008

11800

worldwide terrorist attacks against civilians resulted in

54000

deaths

40%

of total attacks occurred in the Middle East

FBI Report on Terrorism

In the United States, attendance at religious institutions increased by

25%

in the two months after 9/11.

"How America's Faith Has Changed Since 9/11," The Barna Group, 2001. www.barna.org/barna-update/article/5-barna-update/63-how-americas-faith-has-changed-since-9-11?q=september

The interior of the small chapel. People visit mostly to pray.
Photo: Joao Caeiro, Fulvio Capurso

Chapel of San Isidro Labrador

LOCATION San Bartolo Coyotepec, Oaxaca, Mexico

DATE 2010

END USER 40 visitors per week

PROJECT SPONSOR
Mayordomo Benito Guzmán Canseco

DESIGN TEAM Luis Cabral, João Caeiro, Fulvio Capurso

FUNDERS
Mayordomos Benito Guzmán
Canseco and Don Julio; V
arious donated labor and supplies

COST $1500 USD

AREA 15 sq m/161 sq ft (covered area)

SITE 80 sq m/861 sq ft
(surrounding stone-paved area)

More than one-third of the earth's population lives or works in structures made from earth. However, western building techniques are considered better in many parts of the world where raw materials were traditionally used. This is the case in the town of San Bartolo Coyotepec, in central Oaxaca, Mexico. For 4000 years the area's natives used earth as a structural building block, but today this method is often considered a mark of poverty. The design team behind the community's small Chapel of San Isidro Labrador sought to undo this stigma and tap into Mexican history by using the region's indigenous building materials.

The chapel is made of large red bricks of compacted earth. Architects João Caeiro and Fulvio Capurso wanted to show that this traditional practice could lead to a contemporary space, and teach community members how to do it themselves. They met with local officials to conceptualize the project, and the land and materials were donated. "The media makes our people think that the best thing is to build with industrialized materials," explains then-Mayordomo Benito Guzmán Canseco, the elected community member responsible for the chapel and current president of the Council of Oaxaca.

An educational model for efficient, structurally-sound rammed earth building techniques, the chapel was built with the help of 200 community members. It is constructed of tamped earth bricks, made from a mixture of two types of earth and a small amount of cement that is molded in a wood box form. "The walls were treated with nopal cactus juice," Caeiro says. "This is a technique used since ancient times; the juice contains a natural binding agent which acts as a sealant and is effective in waterproofing the mud clay walls." The chapel entrance is framed by a lattice of reeds woven through lightweight metal that serves as a modern homage to the region's traditional fences. Local artists contributed seven black ceramic t iles embedded into the north plaza wall that highlight the history of the town from pre-Hispanic Zapotec culture.

A covered rectangle with one completely open wall and a cross-shaped window in the rear, the chapel is surrounded by a stone-paved open area. It is a gathering space for the annual celebration of San Isidro, patron saint of the farmers. Making the chapel's construction a community-based project has helped the people of San Bartolo Coyotepec regain an appreciation for the earth-building technique. Four hundred people came to the opening ceremony and about 40 people visit the chapel every week.

A side view of San Isidro Chapel. Walls create visual barriers from the road.
Photo: Joao Caeiro, Fulvio Capurso

La Ruta del Peregrino

LOCATION Jalisco, Mexico

DATE 2008–10

END USER 2 million people who make the annual pilgrimage on the trail from Ameca to Talpa de Allende, Mexico

CLIENT Secretaría de Turismo and Secretaría de Desarrollo Urbano, Gobierno del Estado de Jalisco

DESIGN FIRMS Ai Wei Wei (Fake Design), China; Christ & Gantenbein, Switzerland; Dellekamp Arquitectos + Periférica, México; ELEMENTAL, Chile; Godoylab, Mexico; HHF Architects, Switzerland; Rozana Montiel, Mexico; Luis Aldrete, Estanzuela + Atenguillo, Mexico; Taller TOA, Mexico; Tatiana Bilbao Architects, Mexico

ENGINEER Fernando Castillo Díaz, Armando Montejano

FUNDERS Gobierno del Estado de Jalisco, Secretaría de Turismo and Secretaría de Desarrollo Urbano

COST PER SITE
1.3–7.7 million Mexican pesos/
$103 941–$615 655 USD

NUMBER OF SITES 9

TOTAL PROGRAM COST
$38.6 million Mexican pesos/$3.1 million USD

Ermita de San Rafael, designed by Dellekamp Arquitectos + Periférica, looks weightless as it rests on the uneven terrain near Jalisco, Mexico.
Photo: Iwan Baan

Two million devout Mexicans make the Ruta del Peregrino pilgrimage in the southwest state of Jalisco every year during the holy week leading up to Easter. The trek of 117 kilometers (73 mi) to visit the Rosario Virgin begins in the town of Ameca and ends in the town of Talpa de Allende. For years the pilgrims lacked water, food and shelter along the route, but due to the increasing number of people making the pilgrimage, the Mexican Ministry of Tourism sponsored a team of international architects to design not only shelter and water installations, but also religious and vista sites along the route. All nine sites are complete. These locations make the journey safer and add permanence to the old tradition. The improvement attracts tourists to the area throughout the year, boosting the local economy.

Each architectural site was designed to work in harmony with the environment and heighten site-specific experiences of the pilgrimage. The Mirador Espiazo Del Diablo lookout point, designed by the Chile-based firm ELEMENTAL, stands at the tallest point of the trek at 1800 meters (6000 ft) above sea level. The hike to the point is the most challenging part of the trek and this site provides a resting spot. Pilgrims enter this square rock vista point through an angled tunnel, cantilevered over a mountain slope to frame the valley below. "With the new sites, the truth is that it is a very nice experience and your faith grows," says pilgrim Antonio Bolanios. "Through the pilgrimage you are grateful and realize the Virgin will always be with you."

Derek Dellekamp, of Dellekamp Arquitectos + Periférica, was moved by the initial interaction people had with Void Temple, a large stone ring that rests in a wooded area. "I say it was very powerful. People were very excited about it as well as very surprised," he recalls. "It is our hope that every year the sites will be more a part of the story and narrative of the pilgrimage and continue to evolve."

TOP LEFT
Ermita En La Falda Del Cerro Del Obispo designed by Ai Wei Wei | Fake Design juts out over a valley.
Photo: Iwan Baan

MIDDLE LEFT
A circular staircase leads to the top of Mirador Los Guayabos by HHF Architects.
Photo: Gabriel Guadian/Architecture for Humanity-Guadalajara

BOTTOM LEFT
Although not pictured here, this site, along with a few of the others, has since been marred by graffiti.
Photo: Iwan Baan

OPPOSITE TOP
Monumento a La Gratitud by Dellekamp Arquitectos + Periférica is the first site on the trail.
Photo: Iwan Baan

OPPOSITE MIDDLE
A typical shelter where pilgrims sleep on the journey.
Photo: Gabriel Guadian/Architecture for Humanity-Guadalajara

OPPOSITE BOTTOM
Albergue by Luis Aldret, of Estanzuela + Atenguillo, is a beautiful place for pilgrims to sleep in during their trek.
Photo: Iwan Baan

Luis Aldrete, of Estanzuela + Atenguillo, designed shelter structures affording adequate shelter for people to rest and rejuvenate for a few hours or all night. "Both the shelters and the service areas were designed to be copied and repeated," Dellekamp says. "The sense is that these can be placed in sites in future years and reproduced in order to give better services to the pilgrims."

The various designs have brought pride as well as income to the small adjoining towns. "After the placing of these pieces, communities committed to protect the area, so that is something that we believe is very powerful," Dellekamp says, adding that the places have become part of the town's fabric. Tourists are now visiting the sites all through the year, which benefits the local town. "The narrative of the pilgrim is just gaining strength and these sites are adding to the story of the pilgrimage," he says.

Anti-Memorial to Heroin Overdose Victims

LOCATION St Kilda, Victoria, Australia
DATE 2002
END USER
General public, Needle Exchange,
The Prostitute Collective, Salvation Army
CLIENT Needle Exchange,
The City of Port Phillip, The Melbourne Festival
DESIGNER SueAnne Ware
RESEARCH ASSISTANTS
Adrian Drew, Yvette Romanin
INSTALLATION Blake Farmar-Bowers,
Matt York, Harley Blacklaw
FUNDING The Melbourne Festival
COST $30 000 (Australian)/$31 749 USD
AREA 10 km/6.2 mi

Most memorials stand tall to commemorate fallen heroes and past events, but in 2002, in Melbourne, Australia, the Anti-Memorial to Heroin Overdose Victims occupied the streets and sidewalks of the St Kilda neighborhood, its tough aesthetic illustrating the hard-scrabble existence of the people it remembered.

The installation was designed by SueAnne Ware, a professor of landscape architecture at the Royal Melbourne Institute of Technology. She and her collaborators filled planters with red poppies. They stenciled spray-painted quotes from drug users and mourning family members on the sidewalks, and attached resin memory plaques to the flower boxes with the cherished mementos of overdose victims. The installation linked three streets in the St Kilda neighborhood to confront distinct social groups and classes: the drug users and outreach organizations of Grey Street; consumers and business people in the Fitzroy Street commercial district; and families and tourists strolling the Lower Esplanade along the beach.

"What we see in the public realm is art that you can't touch," Ware says. "We wanted a sense of vulnerability; we placed the plaques low to the ground so people had to bend down and really engage with them."

TOP
Red poppies commemorate heroin deaths.
Photo: SueAnne Ware

BOTTOM
The anti-memorials lined the depicted route in the St Kilda suburb of Melbourne.
Image: SueAnne Ware

"Eventually people started walking over it, which is what we wanted. We never intended to create a cemetery in the middle of the sidewalk."

SueAnne Ware, landscape architect

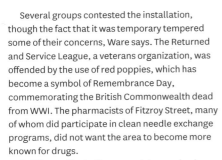

Several groups contested the installation, though the fact that it was temporary tempered some of their concerns, Ware says. The Returned and Service League, a veterans organization, was offended by the use of red poppies, which has become a symbol of Remembrance Day, commemorating the British Commonwealth dead from WWI. The pharmacists of Fitzroy Street, many of whom did participate in clean needle exchange programs, did not want the area to become more known for drugs.

Public reaction to the memorial was mixed. "One client [of a treatment center] came up to me while we were putting in the installation, and he said, 'We don't need art, we need rehab,'" Ware remembers. Someone even scrolled "Wish you were heroin" next to the installation in chalk.

During the first week the anti-memorial also had an unintended effect on pedestrians. "People treated the text as if it were a grave; they wouldn't walk on top of it," Ware says. "Eventually people started walking over it, which is what we wanted. We never intended to create a cemetery in the middle of the sidewalk."

Other members of the community were grateful for the memorial, and were especially appreciative of the tone. It redefined those who had died as people instead of anonymous statistics. "People left flowers and wrote us e-mails thanking us for remembering those that they loved and missed," Ware recalls. "Many of the family members and other IV drug users were incredibly grateful to see their loved ones recognized with dignity and not shame."

TOP LEFT
A pedestrian crouches to view one of the flower box memorial plaques.
Photo: SueAnne Ware

TOP RIGHT
Closeup of stenciled text.
Photo: SueAnne Ware

BOTTOM
Closeup of Resin Memorial Plaque that holds mementos of the deceased.
Photo: SueAnne Ware

Estadio Nacional, Memoria Nacional

LOCATION Santiago, Chile

DATE 2002–10

IMPLEMENTING AGENCY
Ministry of Public Works

DESIGN AGENCY Regional Metropolitano
de Ex–Presas y Presos Políticos

DESIGN TEAM Mark Boelter,
Alexandra Buzhynska, Marcel Coloma,
Carlos Duran, Claudio Guerra,
Wally Kuntsman, Zachary McKiernan

FUNDING Chilean government; various

COST $2000 USD and material donations

OCCUPANCY 47 000 people

For 58 days in the autumn of 1973, Chile's National Stadium served as a holding place for political prisoners who were tortured and sometimes executed. Following the military coup that overthrew the democratically elected government of Salvador Allende, General Augusto Pinochet and his junta detained Chilean nationals and foreigners, priests and students, and men and women in the stadium. Estimates of the number of individuals incarcerated on stadium grounds from September to November of 1973 range from 7000, as reported by the Red Cross, to often-cited figures of between 20 000 and 40 000 people.

Left untouched after a multi-million-dollar stadium renovation completed in 2010, Escotilla 8 is a potent memorial in situ. Narrow planks rest on worn concrete posts and uneven flooring. These wooden bleachers, a vestige of the 1973 stadium structure, stand in stark contrast to the homogenous, and pristinely-aligned industrial seating throughout the rest of the renovated structure.

The memorial exposes a national scar. It is part of a larger effort to redress the wrongs of a violent and troubled period in Chile's history that began at the turn of the century as the people began to reflect more openly on the Pinochet era. In 2003, Chile's National Stadium was declared a national monument and some parts of the stadium, such as Camarín 3, a dressing room where prisoners in 1973 found themselves isolated and hidden from the outside world, were assigned a special protection status. Following these designations, the Regional Metropolitano de Ex–Presas y Presos Políticos made plans for Estadio Nacional, Memoria Nacional. This stadium memorial project includes murals, a memorial wall, plaques, sculptures, exhibits, a museum, the preservation of writings inscribed on stadium walls by prisoners, and the Avenida de la Memoria, an axial allée that is both a memorial walk and a ceremonial entrance to the stadium.

For many, the mere sight of the wooden benches—an island of weathered grey in a sea of

TOP
**The Escotilla 8 Memorial features
original benches as an in situ
memorial.**
Photo: Mark Boelter

bright crimson—stirs a rush of memories and emotions. For those unfamiliar with the events that transpired in the stadium during that period, Escotilla 8 engages them visually, provoking questions about what led to that point in history.

Despite official approval of the entire memorial plan in 2010, only Escotilla 8 and several commemorative pedestals have been built thus far. Questions of how to convey the traumas of the coup and Pinochet years and integrate those memories into the present are highly contested and controversial in Chile. Opposing views on the value of public remembrances, particularly those that recall atrocities and violations of human rights, have impeded the construction and funding of the remaining phases of Estadio Nacional, Memoria Nacional.

ABOVE
Photographs of the Stadium as a detention center in the 1970s.
Photo: Mark Boelter

TOP RIGHT
Candles placed outside the Escotilla 8 Memorial at Chile's National Stadium.
Photo: Mark Boelter

BOTTOM RIGHT
A temporary installation on the Stadium's gates remembers the missing.
Photo: Mark Boelter

Basic
Services
Material

Emergency Water Bladder

LOCATION Various
DATE 1990–present
DESIGNER Structure-Flex
MANUFACTURER Structure-Flex
END USER
60–3300 people per day at minimum
Sphere standards of
15 liters per person, per day
CAPACITY
1000–50 000 liters/264–13 208 gal
FEATURED AGENCY Oxfam

Water bladders are an efficient, life-saving method of distributing and storing potable water in emergency situations. Produced by Structure-Flex and distributed by Oxfam, an international aid agency, the bladders first arrived in Haiti after the devastating earthquake that struck near the capital of Port-au-Prince in January 2010. Oxfam has been using the water bladders for over 20 years. Resembling huge yellow pillows, they are in high demand in Haitian communities. In the wake of the magnitude 7.0 earthquake, half a million people are dependent on such systems for water.

Oxfam implemented the water bladders in Delmas 48, a refugee camp located in Port-au-Prince that is situated on what used to be a golf course. Shortly after the earthquake it became a makeshift home to an estimated 50 000 people per night. The demand for water was so high that Oxfam had to implement five water bladders as well as semi-permanent storage tanks.

The bladder has a filler cap and tap, and is made of thermoplastic coated polyester. This material can last for years, and the only maintenance necessary is patching the bladder should it spring a leak. Though the design may be simple, water bladders have the potential to save millions of lives through their deployment.

They are easy to ship and set up with the help of community members. It takes just one Oxfam worker to install a tap stand, which functions as a faucet. Oxfam strives to provide camps with the Sphere Humanitarian Charter and Minimum Standards in Humanitarian Response of 15 liters of water per person, per day. Under the Sphere standard, a 10 000-liter bladder can provide water for 700 people a day.

Kenny Rae helped set up Oxfam's water sanitation program in Port-au-Prince. "People always emphasized to us that water is the most important necessity. It was 95°F and people hadn't had clean water for days, and then we suddenly arrived," Rae recalls. "We not only provided clean drinking water, but set up separate men's and women's areas where they could bathe. They were so thankful."

The main drawback is that the tanks have to be shipped from the United Kingdom, which is a costly delay during an emergency. They are also dependent on water delivery from trucks, which can be interrupted by fuel shortages, traffic or washed-out roads. Haitian water truck drivers are doing the best they can to serve their communities and keep the bladders full.

ABOVE
Men filling up an empty water bladder.
Photo: Jane Beesley/Oxfam

BELOW
A boy helps fill a water bladder in Haiti following the 2010 earthquake.
Photo: Jane Beesley/Oxfam

Rainwater HOG

LOCATION Australia, USA

DATE 2004

DESIGN TEAM Sally and Simon Dominguez

CAPACITY 180 liters (Australia)/51 gallons (USA)

AREA 500 mm x 220 mm x 1800 mm (Australia)/
20 in x 9.5 in x 71 in (USA)

COST PER UNIT $297 USD per HOG

FEATURED PROJECT
McKinley Elementary School
Rainwater HOG Installation

DATE 2010

END USER 350 students, 20 teachers

CLIENT McKinley Elementary School,
Rebuilding Together San Francisco

PROJECT MANAGER Kat Sawyer (Tap the Sky),
San Francisco Green Schoolyard Alliance

INSTALLER Rogers Remodel

INSTALLATION 7 Rainwater HOGs

FUNDERS
Community Challenge Grant-Urban Watershed,
part of the San Francisco Public Utilities
Commission; Rainwater HOG

COST $5000 USD (installation not included)

Rainwater tanks are the primary source of water in many parts of the world. However, today almost 60 percent of the world's population lives in cities. While a clean water supply is an escalating global challenge, traditional rain barrels have been abandoned because they're too big and bulky to fit in a crowded urban environment. As a solution to this, Rainwater HOGs can be integrated with both timber or steel frame construction, and the tanks can be mounted on a wall, stored underneath the structure, or even buried underground.

The Rainwater HOG was designed by San Francisco Bay Area-based Australian architect Sally Dominguez. She saw the need for a low-profile, space-efficient, modular rainwater catchment holder that slides in tight corners, underneath decks and patios, and alongside walls. At 20 inches wide, its slender design allows the HOG to fit between US standard 24-inch floor joists. A filled HOG has twice the R-value [thermal resistance] of concrete. The system is designed to be modular, so tanks can be hooked together to increase storage volume, and manufactured using

ABOVE
The green containers are Rainwater HOGs installed at the Green House Project in Studio City, California.
Photo: Rainwater HOG

food-grade virgin polyethylene to prevent contaminating the water supply.

More than 2500 units have been installed in residences, businesses and schools globally. The largest installation of HOGs thus far is located in Nundah State School, in Queensland, Australia. It consists of 114 individual tanks that hold up to 5814 gallons of water. One school in Madagascar is installing several HOGs as benches to store emergency water. One school in Madagascar is installing several HOGs as benches to store emergency water, and several HOGs travel to the Burning Man festival in the Nevada desert each year. "My long-term goal for this project is that it could be sold for $50 at IKEA and this technology would be available for everyone," Dominguez says.

ABOVE LEFT
HOGs ready for installation at McKinley Elementary School.
Photo: Kat Sawyer

ABOVE MIDDLE
Down spout connected to Rainwater HOGs.
Photo: Kat Sawyer

ABOVE RIGHT
A boardwalk covers the Rainwater HOG at McKinley Elementary School.
Photo: Courtney Beyer/
Architecture for Humanity

BELOW
About 5670 gallons of rainwater has been harvested and cycled through the system since installation.
Photo: Courtney Beyer/
Architecture for Humanity

The San Francisco Green Schoolyard Alliance and funding from the Community Challenge Grant helps schools in San Francisco install water catchment systems. Each HOG retails for $297 and four were donated. The installation was donated by Jamie Rogers of Rogers Remodel. For McKinley Elementary School, space was a limiting factor for a water catchment system. Kat Sawyer, project manager for San Francisco Green Schoolyard Alliance's Tap the Sky, a program that works to coordinate installation of water catchment systems in schools, knew that the HOG would be a perfect solution for McKinley. "It is a very low-profile system and the HOGs 'go away' visually," Sawyer says. The seven installed HOGs, with a holding capacity of 350 gallons, fit perfectly behind a classroom and water the school's native garden.

A boardwalk built over the system is now a new play area for the students. "It is all about how much room a school can give up on the playground. It was the design details of the HOGs that made a water catchment system possible for this school," Sawyer says.

Sundolier

PRODUCT Sundolier
MANUFACTURER Sunflower Corporation
COST Starting at $15 000 USD
NUMBER OF INSTALLATIONS 10 (to date)
FEATURED PROJECT Science Technology
Engineering and Math Facility
LOCATION Denver, Colorado, USA
CLIENT Cherry Creek School District
ARCHITECT Hutton Architecture Studio
FUNDING Bond measure

TOP
**Sun Harvester on the roof of
Southern Hills Middle School in
Boulder, Colorado**
Photo: Peter Novak/Sundolier

The Sundolier, a cross between a skylight and a low-grade telescope, is a high-tech, active natural daylight system. Resembling a chandelier, it is about the size of a small car. Manufactured by the Sunflower Corporation at a starting cost of $15000, it can be used to illuminate up to 743 square meters (8000 sq ft) of multi-story space, from education facilities, to factories, to military bases. By harnessing natural daylight, the company claims the Sundolier can eliminate up to 40 percent of a building's energy use, according to Sunshine Corporation CEO Peter Novak. A conventional light chimney channels light from a skylight through reflective ductwork into an interior space. The Sundolier's flower-like "petals" capture a greater amount of daylight, concentrating and dispersing it more effectively over a larger area.

The Sundolier is built from a series of 2-D mirrors. It uses five levels of optics to redirect daylight through a rooftop opening. It can span multiple stories and emits a soft, no-glare light that can be reflected off of ceilings and walls, and be directed for spotlighting.

The Cherry Creek School District in Denver, Colorado, has installed the Sundolier. The district incorporated the technology into a new facility intended to raise student performance in science and technology. The new Science, Technology,

Engineering and Math facility serves students from an existing high school, middle school and five elementary schools within a 2.4-kilometer (1.5-mi) radius. All of the schools have historically performed below national and state testing averages. Design firm Hutton Architecture Studio seized the opportunity to build a sustainable building that would fully integrate the sustainable design methods into the teaching curriculum.

The school installed the Sundolier in the facility's main lobby. Students use the Sundolier to learn about light tables, Fresnel lenses, reflectors, and filters. For example, students in the school's health science classes observe the Sundolier as it tracks the sun's azimuth and altitude, and students study elements of daylight as they relate to health and wellness. Other classes and workshops focus on the effects of UV light, how the body stores vitamins, and various aspects of the physics of light.

Novak believes that policy changes on the national and state level through tax credits and energy-saving incentives could prompt a shift in the way people value daylight. "What we're pushing for in the 'daylighting' industry is a recognition of daylighting as a renewable resource," Novak says.

> "The energy industry has created good tools for supporting energy production, but the energy-efficiency world needs to catch up. If I cancel a watt, that has a bigger impact than if I generate one."
>
> Peter Novak, Sunflower Corporation CEO

TOP
Diagram shows how a Sundolier projects sunlight into interior spaces.
Image: Peter Novak/Sundolier

BOTTOM LEFT
A Boulder, Colorado, classroom is lit with a Sundolier.
Photo: Peter Novak/Sundolier

BOTTOM RIGHT
In Colorado, a Longmont High School classroom is lit by a Sundolier.
Photo: Peter Novak/Sundolier

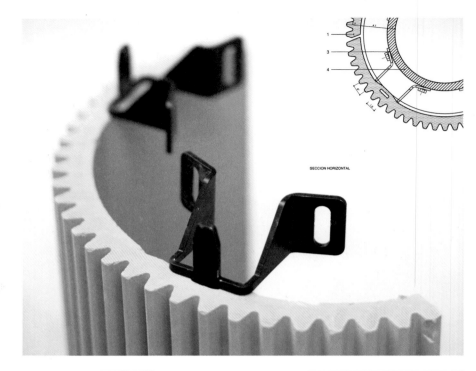

SECCION HORIZONTAL

Ceramic Pillars

FEATURED PROJECT
Spanish Pavilion for Expo Zaragoza 2008
LOCATION Zaragoza, Spain
DATE 2005–8
CLIENT Sociedad Estatal para
Exposiciones Internacionales
DESIGN FIRM Mangado y Asociados SL
DESIGN TEAM Cristina Chu, José Mª Gastaldo,
Richard Král'ovič, Francisco Mangado,
César Martín Gómez, Hugo Mónica
STRUCTURAL ENGINEERS
Jesús Jiménez Cañas, Alberto López
ELECTRICAL/MECHANICAL ENGINEERS
Iturralde y Sagüés Ingenieros
CONTRACTOR Constructora San José
LIGHTING Architectural Lighting Solutions
ADDITIONAL CONSULTANTS
Cener–Ciemat
(bioclimatic design specialists),
Decorative–Cumella
FUNDER Client funded
COST € 18.5 million/$25.7 million USD
AREA 8000 sq m/86 111 sq ft

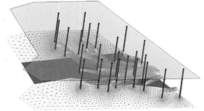

PERCORSO DELL'ARIA EMMESSA DAGLI SGM
PATH OF AIR PROPELLED THROUGH SMG

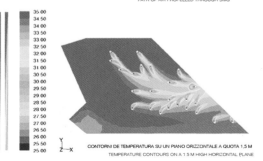

CONTORNI DI TEMPERATURA SU UN PIANO ORIZZONTALE A QUOTA 1.5 M
TEMPERATURE CONTOURS ON A 1.5 M HIGH HORIZONTAL PLANE

ABOVE
Detail of a ceramic pillar.
Photo: Pedro Pegenaute

TOP CORNER
**Diagram of the space
between the ceramic pillar
and column that allows
cool air to pass through.**
Image: Mangado y Asociados SL

LEFT MIDDLE
**Diagram of air circulation
through the pillar.**
Image: Mangado y Asociados SL

LEFT BOTTOM
**Temperature gradient
demonstrating thermal cooling
properties of the ceramic pillars
throughout the structure.**
Image: Mangado y Asociados SL

OPPOSITE
**Pillars sit in a pool of
water and from the water
to cool the building.**
Photo: Pedro Pegenaute

The Spanish Pavilion built for Expo Zaragoza 2008 not only looks like a forest of trees, it acts like one too. Each pillar was designed with a vertical metallic hollow core, clad with modular ceramic elements that serve as devices for passive cooling and ventilation. "Similar to a tree, the ceramic elements absorb water from the shallow pond, then water evaporates as the clay gets warmer over the day, cooling down the air temperature," explains lead architect Francisco Mangado. "This is a very simple idea, inspired by the natural environment, which also combines well the use of ceramic, a traditional technique in my country."

The manufacturing process of the clay extrusions was uncomplicated, using modest materials from traditional Spanish architecture such as terra cotta to create a contemporary building. Energy use was minimized in all stages of the building lifespan, from the material manufacturing, to the construction process, to the building's operation.

"The whole project had to pass an audit conducted by the rules of the European Economic Community in order to achieve a maximum environmental health standard," says Mangado, adding that the flow of water through the ceramic columns at night decreased the daily running time of the air conditioner by four hours and noticeably lowered the temperature.

In addition, recycled materials such as glass, wood shavings, cork and rubber, combined with dry construction methods, contributed to the project's low embodied energy. Renewable energy systems such as solar collectors, photovoltaic panels and water accumulators for rainwater harvesting were integrated on the roof.

The international expo allowed the public to view unique building techniques. Rather than being demolished or dismantled, as often happens to exhibition buildings, the pavilion is being readapted into a facility for climate change research where visitors will be able to experience the results of sustainable construction methods.

> **"The most familiar materials are capable of anything if pushed and trusted by the architect."**
>
> Francisco Mangado, architect

Ecological Concrete Additives

Concrete is the most commonly used building material worldwide. In recent years, manufacturers have been working to create products that enhance the performance of concrete in a number of ways. Often these products take the form of additives. Typically found in powdered or liquid form, concrete additives are included during the mixing process to achieve various effects. Additives are not new. They have been around for generations; however, new formulas are focused on making concrete more sensitive to environmental and ecological concerns. Here are a few examples.

EcoCreto

PRODUCT NAME EcoCreto
LOCATION Projects in Italy, Mexico, Sweden and the United States
DATE 1996–present
MANUFACTURER ECOCRETO
PRODUCT DESIGN
Nestor de Buen, Jaime Grau
MATERIAL USE Concrete paving
COST PER UNIT
$151.20 USD per cubic meter/
$115.50 USD per cubic yard of
additive to concrete

Experimenting with different concrete mixtures for paving panels, chemist Jaime Grau stumbled upon a formula that made water-permeable concrete, but discarded it because it leaked. What appeared as a flaw to Grau, architect Nestor de Buen recognized as an opportunity when he spotted the sample tile in the scientist's lab. When de Buen learned of the pervious paver he realized it was the solution to a longstanding design problem: how to make pavement that drains like soil.

Concrete is made from aggregate (sand, gravel or other fill) mixed with water and cement. To create a porous concrete, large grains of gravel three-eighths of an inch round are used

---

TOP
A hillside in Mexico City, where regular concrete has contributed to depleted aquifers.
Photo: Marina Micheli/Flickr

Pervious concrete often eliminates the need for costly stormwater drainage systems and detention ponds.
Photo: Nestor de Buen

Estadio Omnilife in Guadalajara, Mexico, is paved with EcoCreto to help with drainage.
Photo: Nestor de Buen

instead of sand and mixed with cementious or fly ash. Called pervious concrete, the technique has been in use for many years. However, it is difficult to mix. Too much water and the aggregate gathers at the bottom, too little and it doesn't bond correctly—so it can only be installed by specialists. "Additives like EcoCreto reduce the skill needed by installers and the mixture plant," explains Michael Bledsoe, president of Pervious Concrete, based in the state of Washington, USA. "Concrete paving needs to hold together for decades with cars and trucks passing over it, and it has to drain well. These additives increase the chance that an inexperienced crew can install it successfully."

Grau and de Buen named their product EcoCreto and later sold the technology. It is one of a number of new chemical compounds introduced in recent years that slow the hydration process. The concrete does not need to be covered to prevent water from evaporating and it allows for a greater tolerance in a range of temperature conditions.

Mixing cement and additives with large grains of gravel rather than sand, a typical concrete ingredient, allows water to pass through EcoCreto

pavers at a rate of 4 inches per minute (240 in per hour). Water will still drain through at 4 inches per minute, if up to 40 percent of the voids in the concrete are compromised. Although it can become clogged with dirt and debris over time, pressure washing restores the concrete's effectiveness.

EcoCreto is applied like asphalt, laid over a sub-base of stones and a geo-textile fabric. Wire and rebar are not recommended, as the water coming through the cement will cause them to rust. Even though it's porous, the cement is relatively strong. A 4-inch section can support 3000 pounds per square inch (psi) within 24 hours, and 5000 psi within 28 days. Freezing temperatures do not compromise its effectiveness, according to Dr. Robert Roseen, of the University of New Hampshire Stormwater Center, which found that a porous concrete parking lot on campus functions equally well in all seasons.

Added benefits of the water–permeable concrete include cooling paved areas and cleaning drained water. Air pockets in EcoCreto retain less heat than asphalt or conventional concrete, which can make a city's temperature 8 degrees warmer than surrounding open space. And the large grains

that allow water to percolate through EcoCreto also filter pollution particulates.

Pervious pavement offers hope for urban areas facing water crises. Mexico City, for instance, receives nearly 30 inches of rain per year, usually in heavy bursts during the summer. The risk of flooding has led the city to create a series of canals and drains that divert the water out of the city and directly to sea. Consequently, the aquifers under Mexico City are not being replenished and the water table is dropping by as much as 1 meter per year in some parts of the city. This is making it harder to extract water from the 450 wells that supply 70 percent of the city's water, according to Mexico City water officials. The depletion of the city's extensive aquifers makes the soil shift and sink, causing numerous foundational problems for the city's roads, sidewalks and buildings, which can tilt and rise in unpredictable and dangerous ways.

As more people become familiar with best practices around stormwater management, pervious concrete holds promise. Ironically, a product once considered a mistake could now become an important tool in the push for greater sustainability.

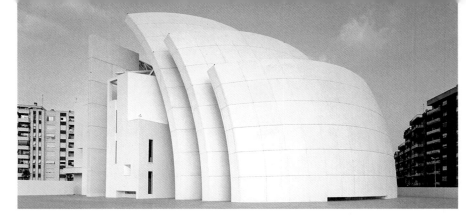

Smog–Eating Concrete

PRODUCT TX Active
MANUFACTURER Italcementi
DATE 1996–present
MATERIAL USE
Exterior concrete facades and surfaces
FEATURED PROJECT
Church Dio Padre Misericordioso
(Jubilee Church)
LOCATION Rome, Italy
CLIENT The Vatican
ARCHITECT
Richard Meier & Partners Architects
CONCRETE FABRICATOR Italcementi
APPLICATION Building facade
COST $1.35 USD/kg

TOP
Finished church. First project to be constructed using TX Active.
Photo: Richard Meier & Partners Architects

MIDDLE
Graphic showing how sun activates the TX active cement which soaks in pollutants from the air.
Credit: ESSOC Italcementi Group

BOTTOM
Concrete panels set in direct sunlight, perfect for TX Active to work.
Photo: Richard Meier & Partners Architects

Finally, concrete is being produced to trap and neutralize pollution. While designing Rome's modern Dives of Misericordia (Jubilee Church), American architect Richard Meier asked Italian cement giant Italcementi to produce a cement that would stay clean and white. The company developed a "smog–eating" cement product called TX Active. It is one of a number of photocatalytic cement products that have entered the market. The product is made from cement infused with titanium dioxide, which is normally used to maintain the brightness of white paints. The chemical is self–cleaning, and can trap and neutralize air pollutants.

Sunlight activates titanium dioxide, which accelerates a natural process that oxidizes chemicals that come in contact with the cement. TX Active and its competitors purport to cut down pollutants exhausted by motor vehicles, and industrial processes such as nitrogen oxides, sulfur oxides, and volatile organic compounds.

The product does not work indoors unless there is sufficient daylight, as it relies on a photocatalytic process, and it is 30 to 40 percent more expensive than conventional cements. However, a thin layer of photocatalytic concrete applied over regular cement is enough to oxidize ambient pollutants, explains Enrico Borgarello, Italcementi's head of research and development.

He claims that if cement products such as TX Active covered 15 percent of Milan's surface area, it would reduce air pollutants by half. While repaving Milan with the product would be costly at $1.35 per kilogram, manufacturers hope the increased construction costs will be recouped through lower maintenance costs.
Please note: *Architecture for Humanity neither endorses nor makes any warranties or claims regarding the uses and performance of specific products mentioned in this profile. The information is provided solely for reference.*

Manufacturers are also looking at ways to make concrete more durable. Hycrete Technologies has developed an admixture, extending the life of concrete by waterproofing it and reducing corrosion. This is important for uses such as rainwater collection tanks, which are often buried underground and are expensive to replace, as well as other infrastructure uses where cracking can reduce the life of concrete.

Concrete is porous, absorbent, and breaks down from pollutants. Typical concrete waterproofing methods include applying membranes or sheet-applied bentonite to the surface of the concrete, which adds an extra step and prevents it from being recyclable.

Like EcoCreto, Hycrete is an additive that makes installation easier and less error prone. It works by sealing byproduct hydrocarbon in the capillaries that is created when the Hycrete mixes with concrete. In addition, the company claims it bonds concrete to the steel rebar reinforcement forming a protective layer that prevents corrosion. According to the company's website, "Hycrete admixtures remain an integral part of the concrete matrix for the life of the structure. The molecule doesn't break down. It won't leach out." The company goes on to say that no reapplication is needed, and contextualizes Hycrete as a "green" concrete that will not be replaced frequently.

BELOW LEFT
Illustration of Hycrete admixture filling in cracks in concrete to prevent water absorbtion.
Image: Hycrete, Inc.

TOP RIGHT
Drops of water on the surface of Hycrete show its waterproof properties.
Image: Hycrete, Inc.

BOTTOM RIGHT
A completed greywater cistern for Yorktown High School is made with Hycrete.
Photo: Perkins Eastman|EE&K

Waterproof Concrete

PRODUCT NAME Hycrete
MANUFACTURER Hycrete, Inc.
MATERIAL USE
Waterproof concrete for infrastructure
COST $3-$7 USD/sq ft
FEATURED PROJECT Yorktown High School
LOCATION Arlington, Virginia, USA
DATE 2010
CLIENT Arlington Public Schools
GENERAL CONTRACTOR Hess Construction
DESIGNER Perkins Eastman | EE&K
CIVIL ENGINEER ADTEK Engineers, Inc.
CONCRETE CONTRACTOR
Canyon Concrete Contracting
CONCRETE MIX Superior Concrete
FUNDER Arlington Public Schools
APPLICATION 240 000-gal/
90 850-liter concrete cistern

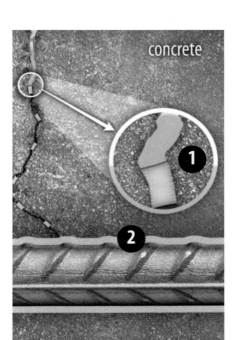

Papercrete

FEATURED PROJECT Da Mor Lee School
LOCATION Pingtung County, Taiwan
DATE 2009
END USER John Lamorie, Shelly Wu,
50 students
CLIENT Da Mor Lee School
DESIGN TEAM/CONTRACTOR
John Lamorie, Shelly Wu
FUNDER Self-funded
COST $248 000 New Taiwan dollars/
$8512 USD
AREA 75 sq m/807 sq ft

John Lamorie is one of the only foreigners in rural Pingtung County, Taiwan, where large gravel companies and family betel nut farms occupy most of the land. Locals were understandably curious when, in 2009, he began building a small home and English school out of recycled newspaper. "Before we were even finished, we had people coming up, trying to poke holes in the blocks, saying, 'Is this really paper?'" he recalls.

A former professional building inspector, Lamorie was well qualified to tackle the trial-and-error aspects of building with papercrete, a mixture of paper, water and concrete used in ways similar to adobe. Papercrete has been around since at least the 1920s but is not widely used. Though labor-intensive, it recycles waste material, has excellent insulating properties, and is inexpensive and strong. With reinforcing and waterproofing, it is ideal for tropical southern Taiwan.

Lamorie and his Taiwanese wife, Shelly Wu, a yoga instructor and fellow English teacher, designed the building themselves and recruited their students to collect over 1400 kilograms (3086 lb) of paper. "We have a reward system for the school, little tokens that students can redeem at a local shop, so we just extended that, " Lamorie says. "We got paper every couple days, nicely bundled and weighed."

Lamorie made 1300 papercrete blocks to form the walls, plus additional batches for mortar and plaster. He fabricated a papercrete mixer to combine the water, newspaper and cement, out of a lawnmower blade and a 500-liter plastic water tank. A pickup truck bed was the base for the trailer. Lamorie welded the lawnmower blade inside the tank to the driveshaft of his car, so as he drove down along local roads, the trailer he was towing mixed the papercrete.

When combined, the papercrete was poured into rectangular molds 15 x 15 x 40 centimeters in size. Boric acid and borax are added to the mixture to make it fire resistant. The bricks were moved after 24 hours, then dried for several weeks to several months, depending on the weather.

The papercrete blocks were easy to stack within the building's post-and-beam structure and could be cut to fit with only a handsaw. Concrete nails and reinforcing steel bars were inserted into the blocks for typhoon and earthquake resistance.

TOP
Completed Da Mor Lee School made from more than 1300 papercrete bricks.
Photo: John Lamorie

OPPOSITE
Series of photos show the entire process from brick making to building.
Photos: John Lamorie

Plastiki rPET

LOCATION Pacific Ocean
PROJECT TYPE Plastiki Expedition
DATE 2010
SPONSORING ORGANIZATION MYOO
PROJECT COORDINATOR
Matthew Grey, MYOO
NAVAL ARCHITECT Andrew Dovell
DESIGN TEAM
Nathaniel Corum, Jason Iftakhar,
Michael Jones, Michael Pawlyn,
Greg Pronko, Mike O'Reilly
ADDITIONAL SUPPORT
Andy Fox, Architecture for Humanity;
Ashley Biggin, University of Southern California
School of Architecture
LENGTH OF VESSEL 18 m/60 ft
OCCUPANCY 6 people

"I want to say one word to you. Just one word . . . plastics." So goes one of the most memorable lines from the iconic film *The Graduate*. That was 1967. Today, the limitless potential of plastic has come at an environmental cost that has led many to question the material's widespread use and benefits. Plastic waste is perhaps the most visible drawback, and has created a large and looming problem. The North Pacific Gyre, a swath of circular currents twice the size of Texas, has trapped a large amount of plastic, which ultraviolet rays degrade into microscopic particles. A 2001 study by oceanographer Charles Moore, published in the Marine Pollution Bulletin, reported an average of 334 271 pieces of plastic per square kilometer of ocean.

David de Rothschild, founder of the environmental organization MYOO, formerly Adventure Ecology, was inspired by a United Nations Environment Program report outlining the threat to our oceans, and Thor Heyerdahl's pioneering Kon-Tiki expedition of 1947. He decided to draw attention to the problem by building the Plastiki, a 60-foot-long catamaran made of reclaimed soda bottles that instantly became a plastic waste pin-up when it set sail from San Francisco,

TOP
The Plastiki prototype sits in San Francisco Bay, in 2009. The design was improved for better handling turbulent ocean waters.
Photo: Nathaniel Corum/
Architecture for Humanity

BOTTOM
Interior of the Plastiki's cabin, outer shell designed by volunteers with Architecture for Humanity.
Photo: Nathaniel Corum/
Architecture for Humanity

California to Sydney, Australia, in March 2010. On a mission to reevaluate plastic waste as a resource, the Plastiki spent four months at sea sending a "message in a bottle" to the watching world. "Waste is fundamentally a design issue and plastic is not the enemy," de Rothschild says. "We need to redefine our understanding and use of the material."

He journeyed 8000 nautical miles to report on the health of the world's oceans, in particular the colossal amount of plastic waste floating out of sight. The concept of this ambitious project was to construct the entire vessel out of recycled polyethylene terephthalate (PET) bottles. MYOO approached the design team behind the product development and incubation company, Level 2 Industries, to experiment with the material. After research and testing, they decided to fill the catamaran's two pontoons with 12 500 2-liter plastic bottles filled with carbon dioxide to make them more rigid.

The cabin acts as a self-sustaining home for the six-person crew, providing shelter from the unforgiving heat and tropical storms of the Pacific Ocean. The design team employed principles of "biomimicry" design, looking to nature for solutions.

A specially developed technology incorporating recycled PET (rPET) was used to engineer the superstructure of the boat. Recycled plastic fibers replace the commonly used unrecyclable fiberglass or costly carbon fiber. The two masts, measuring 12 and 18 meters (40 and 60 ft) tall, are made from reclaimed aluminum irrigation pipes and the sails are handmade from recycled PET cloth. The bonding agent is recycled and also biodegradable—it is made from sugarcane and cashew nut husks. Following the success of Plastiki, MYOO has entered into a joint venture to market recycled PET under the name Seretex for a variety of uses, from sporting goods to disaster relief shelters.

TOP LEFT
Production of recycled polyethylene terephthalate (rPET) sheets used to build the Plastiki.
Photo: Luca Babini

TOP RIGHT
The rPET sheets are cut and sanded into pieces that make the Plastiki's hull.
Photo: Luca Babini

BOTTOM LEFT
This large panel of rPET forms the bottom of one of the pontoons.
Photo: Luca Babini

BOTTOM RIGHT
The Plastiki is the world's only fully recyclable boat.
Photo: Nathaniel Corum/Architecture for Humanity

Politics, Policy & Planning

$12 billion
spent on graffiti
removal in
the US in 2002

Center for Problem-Oriented Policing

$40 million:
budget for the
Arts in Education
account at the
US Department of
Education in 2012

US Department of Education, FY2012 President's Budget

One of nine graffiti pieces by the renowned street artist Banksy on Israel's West Bank barrier.
Photo: Marco Di Lauro/Getty Images

المبادرة الوطنية الفلسطينية

Favela Painting Project

LOCATION Vila Cruzeiro,
Rio de Janeiro, Brazil
DATE 2005–present
END USER 34 houses and
nearby favela residents
IMPLEMENTING AGENCY
Soldados Nunca Mais Program of
the Ibiss Foundation
DESIGN FIRM Haas&Hahn
ARTISTS
Jeroen Koolhaas, Dre Urhahn, and
young men living in the Rio Favelas
FUNDER
Grants, donations, sponsorships
COST $200 000 USD
AREA 150 sq m/1615 sq ft (Boy with Kite);
2000 sq m/21 528 sq ft (Rio Cruzeiro);
7000 sq m/75 347 sq ft (Praça Cantão)

Colorful painted rays decorate the exteriors of 34 houses in the hillside slum Praça Cantão in the center of Rio de Janeiro, Brazil. Artists Jeroen Koolhaas and Dre Urhahn (Haas&Haan) enlisted locals to help create the artwork spanning 7000 square meters.
Photo: Haas&Hahn

BARBEARIA
ZE DO CARMO

About 827 million people live in slums worldwide. Yet investments focused on water sanitation and infrastructure do little to mark a visual change in the community. With minimum expenditure in comparison to mainstream interventions, street artists are reimagining informal settlements from Kenya to Brazil.

In 2006, after filming a documentary for MTV in Rio de Janeiro and São Paolo, Brazil, Dutch painters Jeroen Koolhaas and Dre Urhahn were inspired to start the Favela Painting Project through their new organization, Haas&Hahn. They created murals in two poor areas to help beautify the landscape. "All the hills are covered with slums and the slums are used as the scapegoats to all the problems of Brazil," Urhahn says. "We wanted to make a visual intervention, so that just by looking at the favelas you get a completely different perspective and you are forced to change your thinking." As of 2010, three large-scale painting projects had been completed.

The program hires and trains young men from the community to paint in the favelas, providing an alternative direction for the most likely

Faces of Favelas

LOCATION Kibera, Kenya; Morro da Providência, Rio de Janeiro, Brazil
DATES 2003–present
ARTIST JR
FEATURED PROJECTS 28 Millimeters: Women Are Heroes; The Wrinkles of the City; Face2Face
FUNDER Self-funded

demographic to join gangs. "Everybody asks me if I made that painting," said Vitor Luis da Silva, 15, while playing basketball on a court next to the mural *Boy with Kite*, spanning 150 square meters (1614 sq ft). "Thanks to God, yes. I learned a lot by doing it. If I wasn't involved in these projects, I think I would be in the drug gang, maybe even shooting," he said.

After the first mural, people took note and thousands poured into the favelas for the 2008 Rio Cruzeiroo opening ceremony to see the Japanese-style painted concrete river of fish swimming 2000 square meters (21 527 sq ft) down the hillside. In addition to tourists visiting the favelas to view the art, the employment opportunities for the young men who worked on the project are expanding.

Residents of the area have a new perception of their neighborhood, especially the 34 houses painted in colorful stripes for the O Morro project. "We wanted to find a way for these people to have a sense of pride about their neighborhood and to show the outside world that they feel good about themselves. By putting a small film of paint on the whole surface of the favela we thought that we

would be able to bridge this gap," Koolhaas says. Haas&Hahn hope to expand the project, bringing color to the strong-spirited community as it strives to overcome crime and violence.

JR, a photographer from Paris, is similarly bringing art to slums. In 2006, JR went to Clichy Montfermeil, a low-income area of Paris, and took portraits of community members. He then pasted them in the bourgeois areas of Paris to draw attention to the conflicts among them.

Motivated by an ambitious mission "to post art all over the world," JR travels to embattled areas and uses renegade art to amplify the issues. His projects focus on women as heroes, among other themes. "I want to celebrate the strength and courage of women who live in places where they are targets in wartime and are discriminated against in times of peace," he says.

LEFT
Women Are Heroes project,
Morro da Providência,
Rio de Janeiro, Brazil, 2008.
Photo: jr-art.net

ABOVE
Women Are Heroes Project,
Kibera Slum, Nairobi, Kenya, 2009.
Photo: jr-art.net

L.A.S.E.R. Tag

LOCATION Worldwide

DATE 2005–present

PARTICIPANTS
11 Graphiti Research Lab chapters in Amsterdam, Australia, Brazil, Canada, Colorado, Houston, Kyoto, Luxembourg, Mexico, Utah, Vienna

DESIGN COLLABORATIVE
Graffiti Research Lab

PRODUCT DESIGN
James Powderly, Evan Roth

COLLABORATORS
Mike Baca, Eyebeam OpenLab, Free Art and Technology (F.A.T. Lab), Steve Lambert, Todd Polenberg, Theo Watson, Jamie Wilkinson, Bennet Williamson

FUNDERS
EyeBeam Art & Technology Center; self-financed

COST $200–$1500 USD

Laser Tagger: Rotterdam, Netherlands, 2007
Photo: Evan Roth, James Powderly, Theo Watson/Graffiti Research Lab

270

Graffiti has long been an artistic form of expression for the masses to vent their political frustrations and personal longings. Graffiti Research Lab is inventing innovative applications that fuse off-the-shelf technology with a sense of daring and humor. "It was never about us [the members] putting stuff up," says founder Evan Roth. "Graffiti Research Lab is about making tools for people we thought were underrepresented in the city. A lot of the time that meant graffiti writers, but it also includes activists and people who just want to have fun."

The L.A.S.E.R. Tag system requires equipment but is accessible for an enterprising young activist. The open-source code (available at Theo Watson's blog) feeds into a laptop attached to a projector and camera, controlled by a 60-megawatt laser, described on the website as "super illegal and very dangerous." When moving the laser pointer on the designated surface, the camera tracks its position, recording the movements and beaming them back onto the building via the projector.

The result is graffiti without the permanent markings that enrage city officials and property owners. "The press is more willing to report on a project because that act of vandalism has been removed," says Roth. "But removing the destructive aspect was never the point for James and I." The L.A.S.E.R. Tag system also minimizes the danger to graffiti writers: they are much less likely to be arrested and they can make a big statement without trespassing, and climbing dangerous structures like billboards and silos. The system, which takes time and multiple people, turns graffiti into performance art on the scale of a 10-story building.

Within the graffiti community, there are various opinions on this new tool. Some feel that not leaving a mark makes the project a toy, but there is another side that says bigger is better. "You can see this debate going on inside [a graffiti artist's] head," says Roth. "They are thinking, 'On the one hand, this is impermanent, but on the other, I just wrote my name five stories tall in five seconds.'"

A precursor to L.A.S.E.R. Tag in Washington Square Park, New York City. The system evolved through trial and error.
Photo: Evan Roth/writing by HELL

Cool Biz/
Warm Biz

LOCATION Japan
DATE 2005–present
IMPLEMENTING AGENCY Ministry of the
Environment of Japan

Cool has a new meaning for suit-wearing Japanese businessmen. Traditional work clothes include formal attire and darker suits, even during hot, humid summers. However, under pressure to curb greenhouse gas emissions, theJapanese goverment initiated a policy that put the environment before fashion.

In 2005, Yuriko Koike, Japan's environment minister, was tasked with reducing the nation's emissions by 6 percent to meet 1990 Kyoto Protocol targets. She teamed up with former Prime Minister Junichiro Koizumi and encouraged men to stop wearing suits in the summer—to be cool and casual, so that office buildings could ease up on air-conditioning.

To kick off Cool Biz, top government officials led by example and went to work without jackets and ties. The recommended setting for air conditioners in government and office buildings was increased to 28°C (82°F). The program, which continues today, is voluntary and no penalties are assessed if the guidelines are not followed.

Cool Biz is not without its tradeoffs. Some people feel the temperatures are being kept too high in office buildings. According to research by Shinichi Tanabe, a professor of architecture and environmental engineering at Tokyo's Waseda University, each additional degree above 25°C (77°F)cuts worker productivity by 1.9 percent.

The program was a success in meeting some environmental goals, and roughly 30 000 organizations are participating today. The program inspired a counterpart, Warm Biz, that encourages people to layer up in the winter.

Japanese Prime Minister Junichiro Koizumi sports a casual summer shirt in observance of the country's Cool Biz campaign.
Photo: STR/AFP/Getty Images

Greywater Action

LOCATION Bay Area, California, USA
DATE 1999-present
IMPACT 100 home upgrades and training for 20-25 participants per workshop
DESIGN TEAM Laura Allen, Christina Bertea, Tara Hui, Andrea Lara, Cleo Woelfle-Erskine
FUNDERS Fees from service and contract jobs funded by municipal water districts; California Green Jobs Program; Various grants
COST PER UPGRADE $200-$3000 USD
BOOK *Dam Nation: Dispatches from the Water Underground*

TOP
Workshop participants learn how to build a greywater system one day in 2008.
Photos: Laura Allen/Greywater Action

RIGHT
Diagram of tubing that can be configured to transport water from the washing machine to the garden.
Image: John Russell/WaterSprout

Greywater Action began as a grassroots solution for high water consumption. In 1999, founders Laura Allen and Cleo Woelfle-Erskine started a garden behind their housing cooperative. They were shocked when the water bill arrived and decided to build a low-tech greywater reuse system in the backyard. Not only did it lower their bill, it eased the demand on California's diminishing water tables.

The Oakland-based organization uses advocacy and education to help spread the word about reusing water. The group is run by six core members, including several female plumbers. Greywater can be reused from sinks, showers or washing machines as long as it has not come in contact with human waste. While the water may

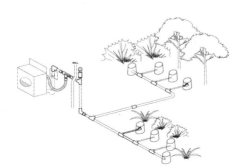

contain traces of dirt, if homeowners switch to eco-friendly detergents and soaps it is a safe irrigation source for yards and gardens. The water can also be used for secondary purposes like flushing the toilet. "Building a greywater reuse system is a way to personally engage in a positive way with the larger, environmentally damaging water infrastructure that typically serves our communities," says Allen, who is also a primary school teacher and incorporates greywater use into her curriculum.

For 11 years, Greywater Action built a series of prototypes and observed how they worked over time. Until 2009, California made much of greywater reuse illegal. However, the group, along with others, lobbied to change the state's policy.

Today, the organization teaches community workshops about building do-it-yourself greywater catchment and distribution systems. "It's fun to see your laundry water grow a bountiful backyard oasis," Allen says.

They designed two main types of greywater reuse systems. The first system routes greywater directly from a washing machine's pressurized drain hose into the garden. In California, this system can be legally constructed without a permit. The second system, which requires a permit, collects water from sinks, tubs and showers.

In 1800

30%
of the world's population lived in urban areas

In 1900

14%
lived in urban areas

In 2008

50%
of the global population lived in urban areas

Most population growth is concentrated in the world's poorest countries.

Population Reference Bureau www.prb.org/

Woman and child in Netaji Nagar, South West Delhi, India.
Photo: Jon Rainbow/Society for the Promotion of Area Resource Centers

In–Situ Slum Rehabilitation

LOCATION Yerawada slum, Pune, India

DATE 2008–11

TARGET 750 dwellings

IMPLEMENTING AGENCIES
National Slum Dwellers Federation,
The Society for the Promotion of
Area Resource Centres

DESIGN FIRMS
Prasanna Desai Architects (building design
and construction); Urban Nouveau
(community plan and concept design)

COMMUNITY CONSULTING TEAM
Filipe Balestra, Rafael Balestra,
Guilherme de Bivar, Carolina Cantante,
Sara Göransson, Mahila Milan,
Urban Nouveau, Martinho Pitta,
Remy Turquin, SPARC

CONTRACTOR
SPARC Samudaya Nirman Sahayak

MAJOR FUNDER
National Urban Renewal Program

COST €4500/$6250 USD

AREA 25 sq m/269 sq ft per dwelling

UNITS 156 completed

When people refer to slum upgrading, most
community members hear "slum removal." Rather
than making improvements to the dwellings already
present, often the current residents are relocated
and their homes are demolished in favor of new
constructs. While the formal nature and scale of
this approach might have a certain appeal, it comes
at the cost of damaging the social fabric of the
community and the financial capital already
invested in the slum. "The tendency is to look at the
slums as an infected part of the city," says Filipe
Balestra of Urban Nouveau, who contributed to the
initial concept design and community participation
phases of the In–Situ Slum Rehabilitation. The
project is run by the Indian non–governmental
organization Society for the Promotion of Area
Resource Centres (SPARC).

In 2008, SPARC asked Urban Nouveau, run by
Balestra and Sara Göransson, to design a housing

50 meter

TOP
Aerial Collage of the
Yerawada Slum, Pune, India
Image: Urban Nouveau

ABOVE
Mother Teresa Nagar Acupuncture
Map of Mother Teresa Nagar, an
informal urban area in Pune, India.
Photo: Urban Nouveau

rehabilitation concept for seven eligible slums in Yerawada, located in Pune, India. The plan upgraded individual houses, preserving the existing household footprints and settlement layout, and keeping intact important social and economic networks. The main principle was to upgrade dwellings made from scrap materials and build formal, permanent concrete structures in their place.

In 2009, Urban Nouveau held an exhaustive series of community consultations in each settlement, using sketches and models to open a dialogue about what kinds of designs were needed and how the benefits of the scheme could best reach the community. In this way, the designers began to understand the needs of the community and were able to formulate design concepts that were innovative and yet still answerable to the individual needs of each household.

Prasanna Desai Architects continued the dialogue first started by Urban Nouveau to formulate a final set of design typologies, making alterations to those designs as needed during the process of demolishing the *kuccha* (tin–roof houses) and constructing the new *pucca* (concrete houses). The firm also aggregated houses into larger apartment blocs using interlocking units. SPARC Samudaya Nirman Sahayak, the contracting arm of SPARC, and the Pune Mahila Milan, a group of women's collectives that manage credit and savings activities, as well as construction of toilets in their communities, managed the construction of the houses themselves.

The architect's site office was centrally located in the Yerawada slum, next to the Mahila Milan office. The office's open-door policy encouraged residents to check on the design and construction progress of their units. "There is a lot of community participation," says Carrie Baptist, of SPARC. "People are not afraid to go into [Prasanna Desai's and Mahila Milan's] office to talk things through. Everything is posted on the walls so the whole process is super transparent."

The Indian government financed all the construction projects under the National Urban Renewal Mission, allocating 300 000 rupees ($6535 USD) per dwelling. SPARC required families to commit 10 percent of the cost of construction from their own funds as a cash contribution. After

the community consultations, the initial design proposal consisted of two house typologies for the units based on survey plans. However, as the project developed, it became evident that many alterations to the designs were necessary to fit each household's individual needs. The dimensions of each plot often changed after demolition. A site's dimensions could only be accurately measured after the existing house was demolished. Consequently, each house has essentially been customized with the participation of the household.

TOP
Completed houses in Sheela Salva, Pune, India.
Photo: John Rainbow/ Society for the Promotion of Area Resource Centers

BOTTOM
Urban Nouveau led many meetings with the community to discuss the design.
Photos: Urban Nouveau

Leadership Live: An excerpt from *Brick City* with Mayor Cory Booker

FEATURED PROJECT Brick City
PROJECT TYPE TV show
LOCATION Newark, New Jersey, USA
DATE 2009–11
PRODUCTION STUDIO Benjamin Productions
DIRECTORS Mark Benjamin, Marc Levin
EXECUTIVE PRODUCER Mark Benjamin,
Marc Levin, Forest Whitaker
PRODUCERS Sarah Barnett, Michael Klein,
Evan Shapiro, Sundance Channel
MAIN CHARACTERS Brooke Barnett, attorney;
Cory Booker, Newark, New Jersey mayor;
Creep, youth counselor; Jayda, founder of
Strong Women; Garry McCarthy, police
director of Newark; Deshaun "Jiwe" Morris,
author; Michelle Thomas, director of
federal grants for The Ferguson Group

When Mayor Cory Booker took office in Newark, New Jersey, in July 2006 it was a city plagued with high crime, high unemployment and low investment. His three predecessors had all been indicted on criminal charges, with many of their aides serving jail time for corruption. However, rather than painting a glossy picture of what he hoped his city could become, the Mayor laid the city's challenges—and his administration's ambitious goals—bare for all to see.

Through social networking (the Mayor has nearly 50 000 Facebook fans and over a million Twitter followers), a TV show and a grueling schedule of public appearances, he channeled media as a tool for social engagement and open government. Residents, and anyone who cared to tune in (we watched season one avidly), could follow his progress as he battled internal politics, faced budget showdowns and fought for a "murder–free March." His relentless communication enabled him to connect with and motivate residents of Newark.

Mayor Booker has been known to respond to tweets in the wee hours of the night—especially if they come from Newark residents. Some interpret his surprise appearances as publicity stunts. (In 2009, in response to a Twitter post asking him to send city workers to shovel snow, the Mayor showed up in person to do it himself.) For residents, however, he offered unprecedented access to the halls of power. By allowing cameras to follow him, he demystified the inner workings of city government. Not only could citizens get front row seats to Brick City's transformation— they could participate in it themselves.

Currently in his second term, Mayor Booker's efforts also drew investment and confidence in

Logo for the *Brick City* television series
on the Sundance Channel.
Image: The Sundance Channel

Mayor Cory Booker with Virginia Jones
in front of Brick Towers before it was
demolished, April 2009.
Photo: Jennifer Brown/The Star-Ledger

the city's regeneration. A relentless focus on crime reduction decreased the city's overall crime rate by between 10 and 15 percent annually during his administration. On April 1, 2010, the city of Newark experienced its first homicide-free month in more than 40 years. Despite the financial crisis of 2009 (Prudential, an international financial services firm, is head-quartered in Newark) the city weathered the economic downturn. "This year alone, over 25 development projects will break ground, representing over 2 million square feet of new or renovated space and over $700 million in total development. An estimated 2500 on-site construction jobs and 2500 permanent jobs will result from the construction activity that begins in 2011. We are building our first new downtown hotel, Courtyard by Marriott, in nearly 40 years, and our first new office tower, Panasonic, in nearly 20 years," Booker posted on Quora in 2011. Understandably, the Mayor did not have time to participate in an interview with us. However, we're still friends—on Facebook at least. Instead we've highlighted a few excerpts from seasons one and two of the documentary, Brick City, executive produced by Forest Whitaker, and directed by Marc Levine and Mark Benjamin. Shot in the style of a reality show, Brick City offers a revealing account of not only Mayor Cory Booker's life, but the lives of the residents of Newark—from gang members to the attorneys fighting for them. Just to keep it real, we've interspersed a few of the Mayor's tweets. Enjoy the show.

Show opening: It is just before dawn, street lights still flickering, as Mayor Cory Booker jogs past closed shops on a quiet street. The soundtrack's beat matches the rhythm of his stride, quickening as images of Newark's violent past and present flash onscreen—cut to press conference.

Mayor Booker: Sixty years ago Newark was on the front page of *Harper's* magazine as the most livable city in America. I think the future of the city of Newark in economic development, the future for the city of Newark in public safety and the future of the city of Newark for our children is incredible. This idea that we're Brick City, that we're tough just like bricks, strong, resilient, hard. And when we come together, frankly there's nothing we can't build in this city. So what I'm fighting hard is to put the real face on Newark, I want the headline at the end of this year to read, you know, "Newark is Number One in the Nation for Violent Crime Reduction." Where we are now, I want to end the year on that. So people start thinking this is a safer city to come to.

In this scene we are introduced to some of the characters that the show follows: Bishop Mark Beckwith opens the Newark Interfaith Coalition Violence Awareness Seminar and the full gamut of community members are present. From Garry McCarthy, the white, fish-out-of-water, police director of Newark to Jayda, a multiple offender, mom and Blood gang member.

Bishop Beckwith: We have been working together for the past several months to make a witness and a commitment to this city to reduce violence, to offer hope. We have come together, we have come together and we remain together with the goal to put the brakes on violence in the city.
Choir sings: I'm going to let it, I'm going to let it shine.
McCarthy: Some would say that I've got a pretty tough job, being a police director here in Newark. Being a crazy white guy from the Bronx. I grew up in a place with gangs, guns, and drugs. The Mayor asked me to reform a police agency, and we're doing that. I'm just proud to be here, proud to be a part of it and I thank you all.
Jayda: Good Evening. My name is Jayda. Hey. I am a member of MOB Piru. Better yet Bloods. I was about maybe 13, 14 when I joined the Bloods. There's a lot of things over the 10 years that I have done that I'm not proud of. I've seen the jails. I've seen the institutions. I've lived through, you know, the rapes, through the "banging," as we call it. But I can't just leave it alone. I can't just turn my back on it and act like it never existed just because now I have a 4-year-old son and now I see myself like maybe one day I can be somebody's wife. You know I am somebody's mother already. So what I do is every Wednesday I go and I counsel young ladies at a school, ninth graders. I am in a relationship with a Crip now. I'm Blood and he's Crip (laughs). I never thought that I would even kick it with a Crip much less sleep with one every night and I do. I know that

it's not that serious and this is what I try to teach my ladies. We don't have to bang just to prove a point. I don't even know what the point is.

Mayor Cory Booker shooting hoops at the Midnight Basketball game, part of the Little Bricks Housing Project. Mayor Cory Booker aims to teach sports for social change but still won't let the kids school him on the court.

Kids: Cory Booker!
Boy: Are you ready to get trashed in basketball?
Mayor Booker: What are you saying I'm going to get crushed in basketball? Three nothing.
Man in black: Right there, take 'em.
Off screen crowd members: Play defense, play defense. Game time.

Budget meeting at city hall with Mayor Cory Booker, and business administrator Michelle Thomas. The two will continue to debate budget cuts throughout the series. The cost of safety is hotly debated.

Mayor Booker: The heat on us is that budget nightmare we're in, but it's going to get worse so my panic frankly is getting us to the point where we can be, you know, so-called debt-free by 2000 and...
Michelle Thomas: 14.
Mayor Booker: Um, whatever, 2012, please.
Michelle Thomas: We're going to have to develop some creative solutions. You know the police department for example we are not going to have enough money for overtime. They have already started creating excuses for budget overruns for this year.
Mayor Booker: Say the summer for some reason gets really hot with crime and we have to make some tough decisions. You know an extra hundred thousand dollars for police overtime in order to meet growing demand. So my question is how do you handle something like that?

Former gang member Jayda's story continues to unfold as she struggles to start her nonprofit, 9 Strong Women, to prevent teens from joining gangs and finds herself pregnant. The father is a member of a rival gang, facing criminal charges from a past crime.

Mayor Cory Booker meets with elementary school students in June 2009.
Photo: Anthony Alvarez/
Anthony Alvarez Photography

Jayda: The program that I really wanted you guys to be a part of is called 9 Strong Women. It's not nine of y'all yet, it's 1 2 3 4 5 6 7. Ladies is gonna have to do...Y'all gonna have to do something, you feel me? Like you know how in gangs, to get brought home, you bang bang, you fight. Everybody know, you know, that's what I did with Piru, but we've got to switch it around because we're ladies. But I think that everybody should try to maintain like at least a B average. 3.5, that's a grade point average, right? GPA 3.5? And even if it's not possible, that's what I want us to strive for.
Nydia Parker: (laughing) It's hard...
Jayda: You've got to be serious about this. You feel

ABOVE

Mayor Cory Booker tries to block a shot while playing basketball with youth at Go Newark HoopFest in March 2011.

Photo: Anthony Alvarez/Anthony Alvarez Photography

LEFT

Mayor Cory Booker greets community members at Go Newark HoopFest, March 2011.

Photo: Anthony Alvarez/Anthony Alvarez Photography

me? If I didn't think you were gonna be serious I wouldn't have ask you to come. Don't put your lives at risk just to have friends; it's not worth it.

Jayda meets Mayor Cory Booker at his monthly open house office hours at city hall. She is surprised that he knows about her and anxiously explains her nonprofit idea.

Mayor Booker: I know all about you.
Jayda: Okay, excellent.
Mayor Booker: I've been talking about you behind your back quite a lot.
Jayda: Really?
Mayor Booker: Yes.
Jayda: Um, I actually started a program, 9 Strong Women. They understand that they are...
Mayor Booker: So slow down for a second... so what's the mission of the organization? Like trying to empower women? Is that...?
Jayda: Oh, trying to...
Mayor Booker: What's the mission? Like what's the...
Jayda: The mission, I know personally a lot of ladies that have been murdered, um you know on the streets of Newark, recently, um, we're under attack. You know, we're under attack and, I think that there's not a lot of focus on just the ladies. I mean I'm glad that there is for the males because we need strong men, you know, but we need strong women as well.
Mayor Booker: Okay, so a few things. First of all how do you think I can help because I've got some ideas as well.
Jayda: I just need your guidance.
Mayor Booker: When you come to the end of all the light you know, and you're about to step in the darkness, one of two things is going to happen and this is the definition of faith to me, you're going to find solid ground underneath you when you step or God will send you people who will teach you how to fly. So you've got a story to tell, you've got energy and spirit that I think can do things that other people can't do. You are who you are for a reason. So my thing now is how can we better empower you to unleash that.
Jayda: Thanks a lot.
Mayor Booker: God bless you. God bless you.
Jayda: Likewise.

CoryBooker Cory Booker
Thanks. A little light can cast out a lot of darkness RT @BRJonez: Whenever I need the positive I read your tweets. Don't let Haters deter
31 Jul

CoryBooker Cory Booker
RT @NJ_Planning: Tomorrow is the groundbreaking ceremony 4 the Newark Farmers Market. Fresh food & JOBS! Great for Nwk http://goo.gl/jRszz
22 hours ago ☆ Favorite ⟲ Retweet ↩ Reply

End of first season: Jayda receives a start-up grant for 9 Strong Women. The year 2007 ended with 67 murders, a 32 percent decrease from the prior year. Newark ranks among the nation's leaders in murder reduction.

In season two, the city's budget and public safety meeting saga continues. Mayor Cory Booker meets with Michelle Thomas again in his office. They debate budget cuts—including layoffs that could impact the Mayor's crime reduction strategy.

Michelle Thomas: So, here's my, um, 'cause I thought about that a lot. The average police officer, um, fully loaded, costs you $100 000. So...
Mayor Booker: So that means, for every 10 police officers, that's a million dollars. That's huge.
Michelle Thomas: Huge. Public safety is the most expensive endeavor that this city undertakes. So something is askew. We're not living in a police state. Other municipalities have laid-off firefighters. Other municipalities have laid-off police officers. You have to do something.
Mayor Booker: How can we get another ten million out?
Michelle Thomas: You can't do it without touching police and fire.

Mayor Booker: And so my question is: How much can we get to before we touch police and fire? Michelle, my point is: If it stinks, kill it. If it jiggles, cut it and then after that's done then we gotta go into the bone and the muscle.

Mayor Cory Booker visiting construction sites where Newark residents are building affordable housing. Booker is also gathering ideas for the remodel of his own house, which he just bought in downtown Newark.

Stefan Pryor (deputy mayor for economic development in the city of Newark): There's been a big push to ensure local and minority participation on these work sites. Sixty-seven units and 20 percent affordable and about a third of the workers are from Newark. All of your objectives: green, affordable and Newark workers.
Mayor Booker: I want to hear one thing: Where do you guys live?
Workers (in unison): Newark, New Jersey
Mayor Booker: That's what I like to hear. Brick City in the house. So you're making us look good everyday? I've actually just bought a house around the corner. I'm going to start gutting it out and building it. So maybe I need to come out here and watch you guys. Take notes.

Transition Network

ORIGINAL LOCATION Totnes, United Kingdom
DATE 2006–present
REACH 839 initiatives in 31 countries
CONCEPT Naresh Giangrande, Rob Hopkins
MAJOR FUNDERS Albert van den Bergh
Charitable Trust ; Ashden Trust;
Calouste Gulbenkian Foundation;
Esmee Fairbairn Foundation;
Funding Network; Marmot Charitable Trust;
Polden–Puckham Charitable Foundation;
Tanner Trust; Tudor Trust

ABOVE
**Transition Town residents hold up
an enlarged "Lewes Pound," one of
several local currencies.**
Photo: Mike Grenville

The earth's oil supply dries up, world climates spin out of control, and the human race struggles for survival. It sounds like the perfect plot for an apocalyptic blockbuster, but some scientists say it will really happen. Rob Hopkins, a British instructor of ecological design and co-founder of the Transition Initiative movement, believes some of these things could happen. In preparation, Hopkins developed a 12-step program to transition the rural English town of Totnes from oil dependency to "self-resilience."

With a population of 8000 people, Totnes is the first town to embrace the Transition Movement and "brace itself to withstand the shocks that will come as oil grows astronomically expensive, climate change intensifies, and maybe sooner than we think, industrial society frays or collapses entirely," Hopkins says, cheerfully explaining a theory known as peak oil.

A modern day Buckminster Fuller, Hopkins shares the late inventor of the buckyball's knack for tinkering, but has a strong social policy streak. The idea for the Transition Initiative started with a question: What happens if we look at peak oil

through permaculture design principles? Permaculture, according to its co-originator David Holmgreen, is a design system for human settlements and agricultural systems based on three ethics—caring for the earth, caring for people, and fair sharing of resources. It aims to mimic the natural environment to create sustainable communities that are less dependent on fossil fuel and the global economy.

The Transition Movement is a large-scale social experiment aiming to build local resilience, essentially making a community more self-sustainable in transportation, agriculture, energy production and water use. The framework of Totnes provided a platform for innovative ideas, projects, and businesses to be recognized and imitated. The Transition Network website lists all cities, towns and villages in the Transition

Network on a map with contact details for people who want to get involved. If there are none nearby, the site offers a handbook for starting a Transition Town, as well as books about local resiliency, food, money and sustainable homes.

There are 12 steps to creating a Transition Town: setting up a steering committee that plans its own demise; creating awareness; laying foundations through networking; organizing a "Great Unleashing," or launch party; forming working groups to focus on areas such as food and waste; using existing open space; developing visible and practical manifestations of the project; facilitating the reskilling of the local community; building bridges with local governments; honoring elders; allowing the projects to grow organically; and finally, creating an energy descent plan.

An Energy Descent Action Plan moves a community from oil dependency to sustainable energy use and production. The community-owned Totnes Renewable Energy Society is planning two new energy production facilities, a wind farm with two 2.5-megawatt wind turbines

that will power 2500 homes, and an anaerobic digestion plant (biodigester) that burns methane and carbon dioxide created from bacteria-treated waste.

Totnes also created a unique local currency that holds the same value as a British pound to bolster its economy by keeping more money within the community. Fifty local businesses have agreed to accept the new currency.

"We first saw Transition [Towns] as an environmental initiative, but we increasingly think of it as a cultural initiative," Hopkins says. "It's about how you shift culture to a place that is prepared for economic contraction and oil shocks, and seeing it as an opportunity and not a disaster."

The result is an organization that guides the community, allowing individuals to create their own solutions, rather than having an outsider telling them what to do. This means that no two Transition Towns are the same. "It has been hard to measure the impact of an initiative in its entirety," Hopkins explains. "But here in Totnes we just did Transition Streets, which is about

street-by-street behavior change." The Transition Streets project brought together 60 groups made up of six to eight households that met seven times to figure out ways to reduce their energy and water use. Every household reduced its carbon by about 1.5 tons and saved £700 ($1136 USD) per year, according to Hopkins, who says an added benefit of the Transition Town model is getting to know neighbors and community members better.

THE TRANSITION HANDBOOK
From oil dependency to local resilience

Rob Hopkins
Founder of the Transition movement

"If your town is not yet a Transition Town, here is the guidance for making it one. We have little time, and much to accomplish." — Richard Heinberg, author of *Peak Everything*

Green Light for Midtown

LOCATION New York City, New York, USA

DATE 2009–present

CLIENT City of New York

END USER New York City residents
and tourists; 70 000 bus riders
through Midtown

IMPLEMENTING AGENCY
New York City Department of Transportation

DESIGN
Department of Transportation New York

FUNDER City of New York

COST $1.5 million USD

WEB RESOURCE
www.nyc.gov/html/dot/downloads/pdf/
broadway_report_final2010_web2.pdf

Times Square, the iconic plaza of New York City, was suffering from its own popularity. Thousands of tourists, commuters and New Yorkers were clogging the sidewalks and slowing down traffic. This congestive "ped-lock" was even driving business away. In the 2003 Times Square Office Worker's Survey, 68 percent of the respondents listed congestion as the number-one reason they would want to work somewhere else. It was also a major public safety issue. From 2002 to 2004, there were 91 vehicle–pedestrian collisions, and 192 vehicle collisions at the intersection of Broadway and West 7th Avenue. On August 7, 2010, the day's pedestrian count at the same intersection reached 163 215 people.

So in 2009, the New York City Department of Transportation embraced a drastic move, completely closing five blocks of Broadway between 42nd Street and 47th Street to vehicular traffic. Sixty thousand square feet (5400 sq m) of street space was transformed into public plazas.

Now those wishing to linger can stand in the plazas, leaving the sidewalks free for walking. Tables and chairs offer a place to rest and take in the bustling view, enjoy the sights, or escape the office cubicle. The plazas have led to 35 percent less crash-related injuries to pedestrians and reduced the number of people walking in the street by 80 percent. This was a common occurrence due to sidewalk space constraints. Traffic times have improved by 4 percent, a boon for a city where every minute counts.

It may seem counterintuitive that narrowing a street would ease congestion; however, a body of research shows the opposite is true. The design is based on a theory by Dietrich Braess.

In 2010, in response to broad support for the plazas from New York City residents and Times Square workers, Mayor Michael Bloomberg made the plazas permanent. The city is now planning a redesign of the plazas with Norwegian firm Snohetta to incorporate event infrastructure such as television and cable hookups, security features, and dedicated public performance space.

The theory behind the road closures comes from Braess' Paradox, first put forth by Dietrich Braess in 1968. This mathematical formula states that adding extra capacity to a network, such as a street grid, can reduce overall performance, which Braess proved through a simple experiment: when he added a fifth street to a four-street network, all the vehicles took longer to get through. The reason being, when you add a new avenue to a crowded street grid, the drivers rush to the new street, creating a new traffic jam on that street and those that feed into it. The flipside of the equation is that you can improve traffic flow by reducing capacity.

Dr. Joel E. Cohen, a mathematician at Rockefeller University in New York, and Dr. Frank P. Kelly, of the University of Cambridge in England, published a more detailed statistical

Broadway Plaza

48th–49th Streets Transitway
- Sidewalks remain at same width.
- Dual roadway with landscaped center median.
- Buses routed on eastern roadway.
- Taxi and service vehicles use western roadway.
- Bus stop on center median.
- Trees, information kiosks.

47th–48th Streets Plaza C
- Right-of-way for emergency access and service vehicles.
- Trees, lights, sculpture and information kiosks.

46th–47th Streets Plaza B
- Times Square Theater and Information Center (TKTS, Tourist and Transit Information; Military).
- Outdoor stage for programmed entertainment.
- Special branding area and lay-by for buses.
- Father Duffy monument.
- Trees, banners, kiosks.

45th–46th Streets Plaza A
- Adjacent to proposed Times Square Hotel (Enclosed sidewalk cafe, escalators to retail areas).
- Special branding area and lay-by for taxis (Taxi information and dispatch operations).
- George M. Cohan monument.

Figure 2
Broadway Plaza Site Plan
11-53

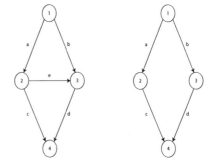

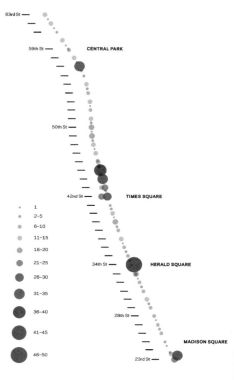

63rd St —
59th St — CENTRAL PARK
50th St —
42nd St — TIMES SQUARE
34th St — HERALD SQUARE
28th St —
MADISON SQUARE
23rd St —

- • 1
- • 2–5
- ● 6–10
- ● 11–15
- ● 16–20
- ● 21–25
- ● 26–30
- ● 31–35
- ● 36–40
- ● 41–45
- ● 46–50

TOP LEFT
Diagram of the pedestrian injuries along Broadway that identified locations for the new plazas.
image: New York City Department of Transportation
Illustration: Pure+Applied

TOP MIDDLE AND RIGHT
Before and after images of Broadway below Columbus Circle.
Photos: New York City Department of Transportation

model that used queuing theory, which describes traffic jams in terms of vehicles lining up on the streets. This more sophisticated version of Braess' original experiment confirmed the original findings, with support from elements of game theory, which states that when everyone acts selfishly (by trying to find the quickest detour or route through a traffic jam), everybody suffers.

One of the major examples occurred in Seoul, South Korea, when mayor Lee Myung Bak decided to daylight the Cheonggyecheon River in 2003. To create the new 1000-acre park, Bak had to tear down the highway that had covered it up. Contrary to predictions,

traffic improved throughout the city as people took advantage of the newly revamped bus systems and alternative routes.

The New York Department of Transportation drew on these theories and experiments to take away some of the options that drivers had to choose from. Much of Broadway's traffic was diverted to 7th Avenue, which still continues through the heart of Times Square unimpeded, often with longer green light times; five bus lanes were also redirected to 7th Avenue. This led to a 13 percent increase in bus travel times on 6th Avenue and a 50 percent decrease in wait times for southbound buses on 6th Avenue and 7th Avenue.

Walking School Bus

LOCATION Over 40 countries
DATE 1994–present
END USER 15 000 primary and
middle school students
ADVOCATE David Engwicht
(Creative Communications)
FUNDER
Federal–Aid Highway Program (US)

**Westvale Trailblazers take the
walking school bus in Waterloo,
Ontario, Canada.**
Photo: Green Communities Canada

According to the US Centers for Disease Control
and Prevention, over half of the students in the
United States walked to school in 1969. Today,
that number is less than 13 percent, and in one
notable case, a Utah mother was arrested for
allowing her child to walk to school alone. With
this cultural change has come a rise in obesity,
asthma and other health concerns.

The Walking School Bus is a return to the
simple idea of walking to school. It addresses
many of today's most vexing challenges, while
simultaneously instilling lifelong healthy habits in
school–age children.

In the early 1990s, Australian David Engwicht
was disappointed in the government's response
to traffic issues and published *Towards an
Eco-City: Calming the Traffic*. In this book he
proposed the idea of a "walking school bus," a
group of students walking to school under the
supervision of at least one adult. His message
struck a chord and the first Walking School Bus
debuted in Brisbane, Australia. Now thousands of
students walk to school with the program. As of
2007, in Auckland, New Zealand, 100 schools had
Walking School Buses in operation with 4000
students participating.

**Students walk to Rockbridge School
through a state park in Columbia,
Missouri, USA.**
Photo: PedNet Coalition Inc.

A walking school bus takes students on an
organized walk to school. It works just like a
school bus route without the bus. Students join
the Walking School Bus at defined meeting points
along a route. In Columbia, Missouri, the PedNet
Coalition oversees one of the largest Walking
School Bus programs in the United States, with
11 elementary schools participating. In addition to
parent volunteers, the program recruits students
from the nearby University of Missouri to help
supervise the routes. "Not only do the kids get
exercise before school, they form trusting, strong
bonds with the college students that are there
everyday to talk with the students," says Amy
Lewis, a physical education teacher. Lewis
coordinates three routes for about 40 students.

Jenn Sonnenberg is the mother of a third grade
boy who takes the Walking School Bus to school.
"His teachers say that he gets the wiggles out and
can sit down and focus," she says.

99%

of total Internet subscriptions in June 2009 were accessed using mobile phones

UN Conference on Trade and Development: Information Economy Report 2010

There was a

480%

increase in global Internet use from 2000 to 2011

Internet World Stats www.internetworldstats.com/stats.htm

Of the

119 million

internet users in Africa

31 million

used Facebook in 2010

In 2000 there were only

4.5 million

total internet users in Africa

Internet World Stats www.internetworldstats.com/stats.htm

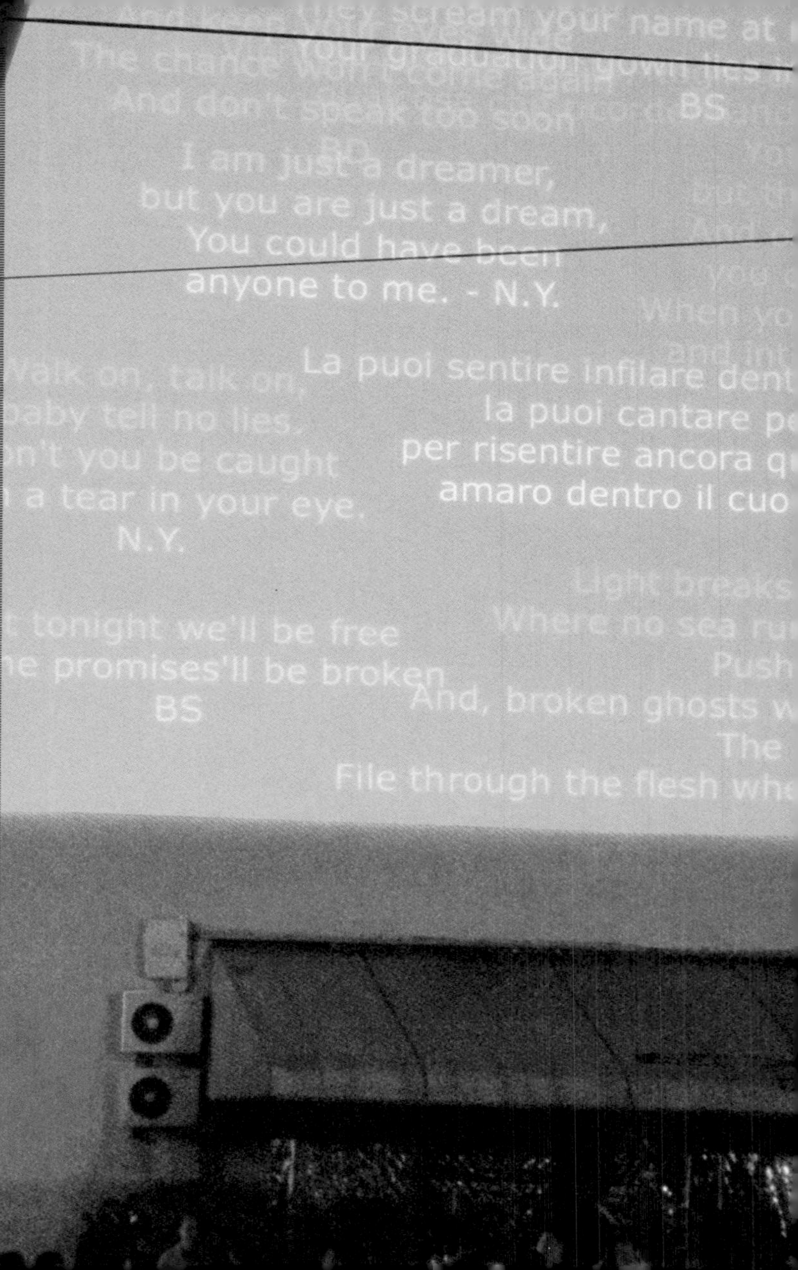

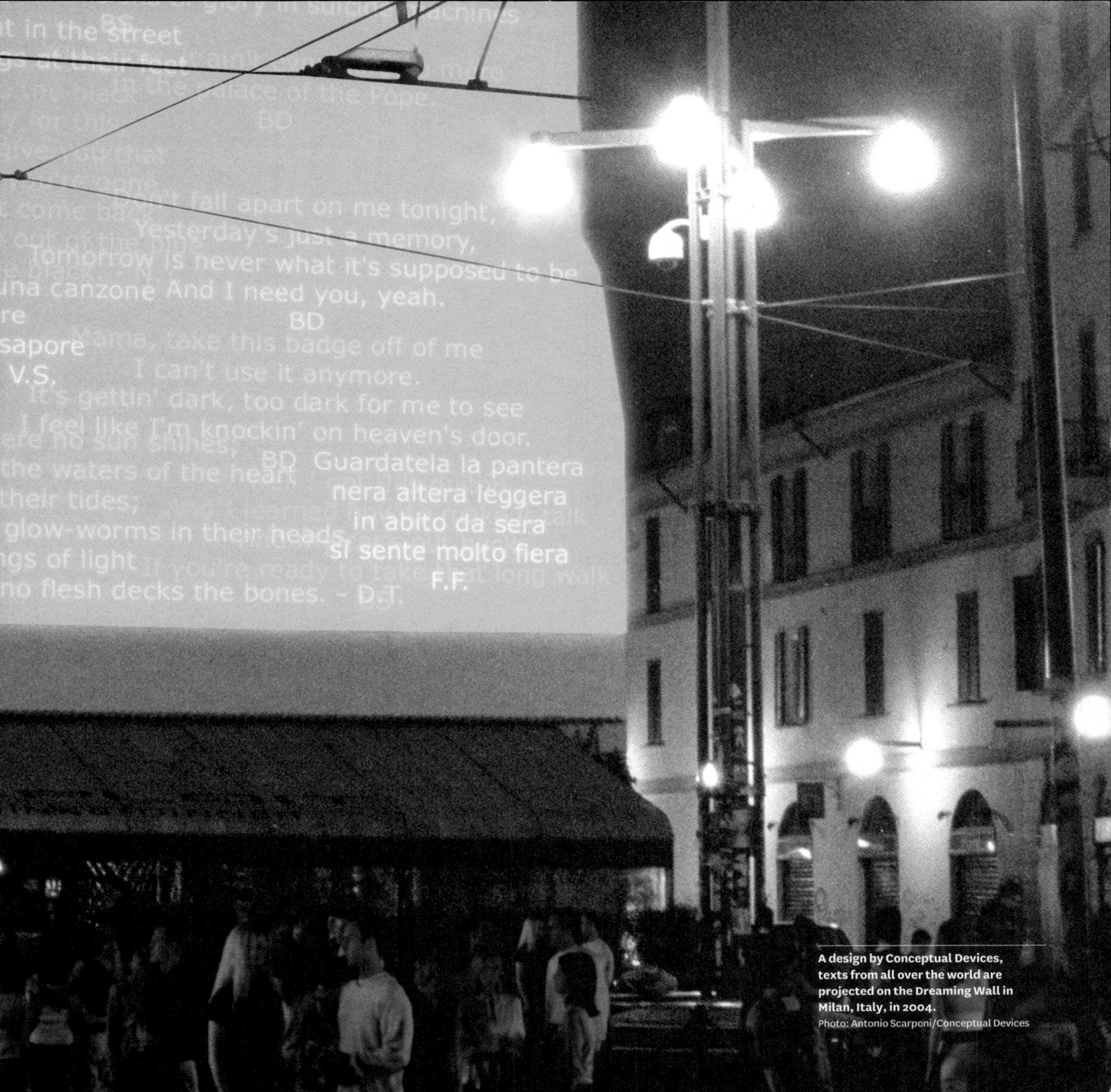

A design by Conceptual Devices, texts from all over the world are projected on the Dreaming Wall in Milan, Italy, in 2004.
Photo: Antonio Scarponi/Conceptual Devices

Let's Do It!
2008

LOCATION Estonia
PLANNING 2007–8
DATE May 3, 2008
IMPLEMENTING AGENCIES
227 local governments in Estonia
PROGRAM DESIGN
Kadri Allikmäe, Henri Laupmaa,
Rainer Nõlvak, Toomas Trapido
PROJECT PARTNERS Ahti Heinla,
Agni Kaldma, Tatjana Lavrova,
Anneli Ohvril, Jüri–Ott Salm,
Birgit Tolmann, Eva Truuverk, Tiina Urm
FUNDER Ministry of the Environment
SUPPORTERS Eesti Energia; Elion;
Estonian Army; Estonian Energy;
Estonian Environmental Inspection;
Estonian Fund For Nature; Estonian Map Centre,
Ltd.; EMT; Estonian National Broadcasting
Company; Environmental Investment Centre;
State Forest Management Centre; Hansabank;
Nokia; Nutiteq (over 500 partners)
COST €500 000/$694 450 USD

In the summer of 2007, Toomas Trapido, a member of the Estonian parliament, sat down with Rainer Nõlvak, an information technology entrepreneur and then–chairman of the Estonian Fund for Nature, to discuss collaborating on environmental projects. [Trapido's first slide] laid out a plan to clean up the numerous illegal dumping sites around the country over several years. Nõlvak immediately supported the idea, and suggested they organize a country-wide cleanup in a single day.

Over the course of the next few months, as they added important partners such as the Estonian National Broadcasting Company, the State Forest Management Centre, and the Ministry of the Environment, to name a few, the concept started to become a reality. "Garbage in forests, seashores and other public spaces touches lots of people deeply," explained Trapido, emphasizing that it is also "a problem that everybody can help solve." To support the cleanup, waste management companies agreed to waive all fees except for transportation expenses. Additionally, 80 percent of the trash haul was diverted for recycling.

Before they could start picking up trash, however, they first had to locate it. Over 700 volunteers mapped 10 656 sites using global positioning system (GPS) enabled cell phones donated by Nokia. The sites were uploaded to a Google Earth–based program written by Ahti Heinla, a founder of Skype. Uploading photos was considered, but decided against because it could be difficult, expensive and unreliable. And besides, said Heinla, "mapping using mobile phones is the easiest method to use."

Mapping was key to generating public support. As Tiina Urm, now a member of the international Let's Do It! team, explains it, the problem was that nobody knew how bad the illegal dumping really was. The GPS software "made it possible to put the garbage on the map," Urm says. "That was the first time people could see the face of the problem."

To ensure that the sites would get cleaned up, the Let's Do It! team sought the support of each one of the 227 local governments in Estonia. Only seven did not participate, and they subsequently executed their own public cleanup days due to public pressure.

TOP LEFT
Screenshot of map from the Let's Do It! website.
Image: www.Letsdoitworld.org

TOP RIGHT
Volunteers participate in the Let's Do It! 2008 cleanup in Estonia.
Photo: Tonis Valing/Let's Do It! World

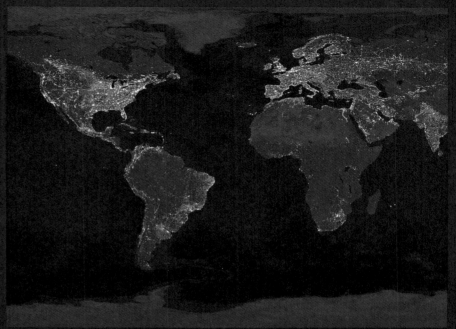

Light Pollution

ADVOCATE International Dark–Sky Association
LOCATION Worldwide
DATE 1988–present
FOUNDERS Dr. David L. Crawford, Dr. Tim Hunter
FUNDERS Membership dues; Gildea Foundation Grant; National Science Foundation Grants; Pauley Foundation Grant; Southwest Parks and Monuments Association Grant

Throughout the ages, mankind has been concerned with keeping the darkness at bay, using fire, lamps, and now, electrical lights. But in the last century, a reversed trend has emerged to bring back the night sky. Simply put, darkness is vanishing in the face of pervasive, and often unnecessary lighting. Several organizations—scientific and otherwise—have started programs to combat the spread of light pollution.

The International Dark–Sky Association is the oldest organization dedicated to reducing light pollution. Founded in 1988, it strives to turn down the lights on excessive energy use. Their initiatives range from education and advocacy, to industry specifications. The organization works with local governments to establish lighting ordinances and enforcement in places such as Hawaii, New Hampshire and Italy.

Why is light pollution a problem? Apart from the environmental drawbacks of increased energy use due to inefficient and misdirected lighting, and the decreased visibility of the stars at prime astrological viewing sites, light pollution also has a number of adverse biological effects on humans and wildlife. *Environmental Health Perspectives*, a monthly, peer-reviewed journal published by the National Institute of Environmental Health Services and dedicated to the effect of the physical environment on human health, featured a study linking disruption of circadian rhythms, insomnia, depression, cancer and cardiovascular disease with excess light. The American Medical Association adopted a resolution in 2009 that supported the reduction of light pollution.

In addition, many types of wildlife, particularly those that are nocturnal, are also severely affected. The effects include vulnerability to predators as well as disruption in mating cycles and migration patterns.

Earth's lights glow from space. North America and Europe are clear light pollution culprits.
Photo: Visible Earth/NASA

Crowd-Sourced Mapping

Ken Banks refers to himself as a mobile anthropologist. "I can't possibly understand everyone's problems, so it's hard for me to fix them. But what I can do is use my IT skills to support communication for people that can fix problems," he says. Banks is on the frontline of a movement that is using technology to identify and map community needs by crowd sourcing information that can be responded to by authorities and individuals.

Whether mapping violence in inner cities, preventing health emergencies, or responding to disaster situations, the idea has proven extremely helpful. Together, these technologies are opening the door to to a new approach to urban planning. Call it crowd-sourced urban planning.

In 2005, Banks created FrontlineSMS, responding to a request by the park services in Mozambique and South Africa for tools to facilitate better communication. "I found at the time that most of the tech communication tools were too complicated or relied on the Internet," Banks recalls. "Based on the experience I had working with NGOs across Southern Africa, I knew most did not have the funds for a tech-IT director, or the luxury of access to the Internet." Thus, Banks wrote open source software for an intuitive system that could be universally used. "After

14 000 downloads I think we can safely say that the software has been useful," he says.

One user of FrontlineSMS is Ushahidi, a geographic information system mapping software with a name that means "testimony" in Swahili. It was born in response to the 2008 post-election violence in Kenya. Ory Okolloh, one of Ushahidi's founders and an avid blogger, noticed a disconnect between what individuals were blogging and what the mainstream news and government were reporting of the violence. The mapping visualization platform was developed to allow feeds from different sources such as text messages, Twitter, and YouTube to be organized and mapped in real time, giving community members up-to-date, reliable information on potential hotspots.

"We are not just crowd sourcing," says Patrick Meier, director of crisis mapping and new media at Ushahidi. "Individuals are contributing but are also receiving valuable information." Ushahidi uses FrontlineSMS software to upload incoming text messages onto their maps. Users can tailor information to their area of interest. "For example, if you programmed a specific map using Ushahidi, anything that gets mapped sends you an automated text message. We hope this helps people make more informed decisions."

Similarly, other community-based mapping initiatives are allowing citizens to better understand and communicate their needs. Kibera, Kenya, one of the largest slums in Africa, was a blank spot on most maps until November 2009 when young Kiberans created the first free and open digital map of their own community using OpenStreetMap. "Kibera being such a well-known place locally and internationally, yet not represented on the map. Simply, it deserved to be on the map." With icons, the map denotes important locations such as water sources, hospitals and places of worship. Map Kibera decided to push mapping further and launched Voice of Kibera, using the Ushahidi platform, as a citizen reporting resource. Residents as well as media sources report information about events by text message. They can be anything from cleanup day locations to the fixing of drainage systems. These reports are then geographically visualized on the Kibera map.

Medic Mobile, a technology health organization, has found another application for the FrontlineSMS technology and Ushahidi. After the devastating 2010 earthquake in Haiti, Medic Mobile, with a dozen other tech-mobile companies, made it possible for people to text to online crowdsourcing platforms with their requests for help.

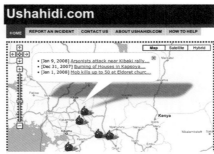

FrontlineSMS

LOCATION Various
DATE 2005–present
CLIENT Various
FUNDER Various
END USER 14,000+ downloads
COST $1 million USD
FOUNDER Ken Banks
TEAM Alex Anderson, Sarah George,
Laura Walker Hudson, Ryan Jones,
Sean McDonald, Amy O'Donnell,
Florence Scialom
WEB RESOURCE
www.frontlinesms.com

Ushahidi

LOCATION Kenya; all over
DATE 2008–present
CLIENT Various
FUNDER Various
END USER
Communities around the world
TEAM Henry Addo, Caleb Bell,
Heather Ford, Jon Gosier,
Matthew Griffiths, Brian Herbert,
Erik Hersman, Emmanuel Kala,
Linda Kamau, David Kobia,
Ory Okolloh, Ahmed Maawy,
Ory Okolloh, Patrick Meier,
Charl van Niekerk, Juliana Rotich,
Limo Taboi
COST $900 000 USD
WEB RESOURCE
www.ushahidi.com

OpenStreetMap

LOCATION Global
DATES 2004–present
END USER Various
FUNDER
Open Street Map Foundation
through membership fees
and donations
COST $81 000 USD
FOUNDER Steve Coast
WEB RESOURCE
www.openstreetmap.org

TOP LEFT
**A training session in Namaingo District,
Uganda. FrontlineSMS is free to use.**
Photo: Loyce Kyogabirwe/FrontlineSMS

TOP MIDDLE
**Ushahidi uses community-based
mapping to share crime reports
and other key information.**
Image: Ushahidi

TOP RIGHT
**First ever map of the Kenyan
slum Kibera made using the
OpenStreetMap platform.**
Image: Map Kibera Trust

Of all US households, in 2009

2.3 million

or 2.2 % live more than a mile from a supermarket and do not have access to a vehicle

Economic Research Service Report Summary, USDA – 2009 www. ers.usda.gov/Publications/AP/AP036/AP036_reportsummary.pdf

In 2007, fast food restaurants spent

$294 million

on marketing messages aimed at children

The Healthy Eating Guide www.thehealthyeatingguide.com/ healthyeatingstatistics.html#bookmark2

An empty shopping cart abandoned in Chicago, Illinois, a city where researchers have identified areas that lack access to healthy food.
Photo: Mike Innocenzi / flickr

Worldwide approximately

1.6 billion
people over age 15 are overweight

and at least

400 million
adults are obese

WHO projects that by 2015,

2.3 billion
adults will be overweight

and more than

700 million
will be obese

World Health Organization www.who.int/mediacentre/ factsheets/fs311/en/index.html

Food Deserts

PLANNING APPROACH Food Deserts
CONCEPT AUTHOR Mari Gallagher
LOCATION Chicago, Illinois, USA
DATE 2006–present
FEATURED PROJECT Fresh Moves Mobile Market
IMPLEMENTING AGENCY Food Desert Action
PROJECT MEMBERS
Steven Casey, Sheelah Muhammad,
Jeffrey Pinzino, Khalilah Worley
DESIGN AGENCY
Architecture for Humanity–Chicago
DESIGN TEAM
Joseph Altshuler, Marissa Brown,
Lee Bouchard, Laura Bowe,
Katherine Darnstadt, John Joyce,
Tom Hagerty, Tina Kress, Thomas Kubik,
Laurel Lipkin, Geoff Malia, Meghann Maves,
Myriam Migrditchian, Lety Murray,
Peter Ogbac, Stephanie Pifko, Mig Rod,
Daniel Rollet, Dena Wangberg,
Will Wingfield
MAIN FUNDER Boeing;
Chicago Transportation Authority;
ChiWest ResourceNet; GreenBuild;
JP Morgan Chase; Polk Brothers;
UIC Urban Health Program partner

TOP AND BOTTOM
These maps of Chicago, Illinois,
indicating lack of access to healthy
food, and published by Mari Gallagher,
helped coin the term "food desert."
Images: Mari Gallagher Research & Consulting

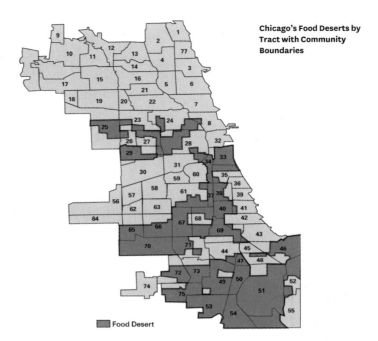

Chicago's Food Deserts by Tract with Community Boundaries

■ Food Desert

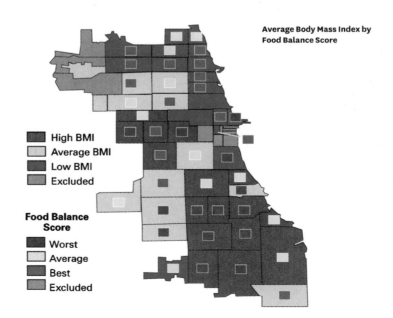

Average Body Mass Index by Food Balance Score

■ High BMI
□ Average BMI
■ Low BMI
■ Excluded

Food Balance Score

■ Worst
□ Average
■ Best
■ Excluded

In July of 2006, researcher and consultant Mari Gallagher published a groundbreaking report, *Examining the Impact of Food Deserts on Public Health in Chicago*, in which she coined the term "food desert." A food desert does not describe an area without food, but rather, an area with a severe imbalance of fringe food such as fast food restaurants and convenience stores as opposed to mainstream grocery stores that sell fresh produce, fruit, dairy and meat. This often results in significant health issues for the underserved population. The report also overlays statistics on Chicago's racial demographics and income, and though food deserts often correlate with low-income, minority neighborhoods, this is not always the case.

Publicity surrounding the report has led to several different approaches to the problem around the country. The effects were even felt in the White House. The US Department of Agriculture released an online "Food Desert Locator" on its website as part of First Lady Michelle Obama's Let's Move! Campaign against childhood obesity.

Community activists Steven Casey, Sheelah Muhammad, and Jeff Pinzino worked together to find their own solution and founded Food Desert Action. Their research revealed that opening individual markets would not address the widespread need quickly or efficiently. Inspired by observations of food deliveries while on a vacation in Jamaica, Casey proposed the idea of a mobile market. In Jamaica, vendors brought meats one day, dairy another, and the idea of driving fresh foods directly to customers back home took root. By eliminating bricks and mortar, the team realized they could inexpensively reach many communities. The mobile markets could also become much more than a purveyor of food.

TOP
Fresh Moves mobile produce market bus was designed by Architecture for Humanity–Chicago with Food Desert Action to sell produce.
Photo: Katherine Darnstadt/Architecture for Humanity–Chicago

BOTTOM
Interior of the Fresh Moves mobile produce market bus.
Photo: Katherine Darnstatdt

Smarter Lunch Rooms

LOCATION Ithaca, New York, USA
CONSULTING AGENCY
Cornell Food and Brand Lab
DATE 2007–present
END USER 30 000 students
CLIENT Plattsburgh High School;
1500 other schools
RESEARCH LEADS
David Just, Brian Wansink
ADDITIONAL SUPPORT
Sandra Cuellar (school relations coordinator),
Elaine Hill (analyst), Lisa Mancino (researcher),
Collin Payne (researcher),
Mitsuru Shimizu (analyst),
Laura Smith (operations manager)
FUNDER US Department of Agricutlure
COST $34 USD per school

Self-proclaimed "stealth health" leader Brian Wansink describes the Smarter Lunch Rooms initiative as "choice architecture." Through seemingly insignificant design changes, the initiative "leads a person to take an apple instead of taking a cookie, all the while letting them think that their own volition led them to do so," says Wansink, a professor at Cornell University in the Food and Brand Lab.

In 2006, Wansink published *Mindless Eating*. The book, stemming from 20 years of research, made revealing correlations between food consumption and food marketing and placement. It concludes that packages and containers, labels and lights, colors and shapes, distractions and distances—in short, design—influence people's eating choices in restaurants, supermarkets, and even at home, more than they realize.

When he took a leave of absence from Cornell to serve as executive director of the US Department of Agriculture's Center for Nutrition Policy and Promotion in 2006, Wansink applied the same product placement methodology that companies use to sell unhealthy choices to selling healthier options in school lunchrooms. The lunchroom redesign focuses on rearranging, relocating and renaming foods with the aim of directing students to healthier choices. Changes vary from locating the vegetables to the front of the buffet line, to hiding the chocolate milk behind the skim milk, and placing ice cream in the freezer with opaque covered lids. "It has to be a low-cost, no-cost change, and no change can cost more than $50," Wansink says. "If it costs more than $50, we go back to the drawing board."

CASH KIDS EAT HEALTHIER!

High school students using debit cards eat 143% more calories at lunch.

THE PROBLEM WITH GOING TRAYLESS:

Trayless students eat 21% less salad, but no less ice cream.

Most of these changes have proven to raise sales by 20 percent, but two stand out for Wansink. The first is to change the location of whole fruit. "Simply taking whole fruit, which is typically served in a stainless steel pan and usually behind a sneeze shield, and put it in a nice bowl in a well-lit area where it's easy for people to grab, creates an amazing increase in sales," he says. Four of the five New York pilot program schools saw more than a 100 percent increase in whole fruit sales in the first semester of implementation. The last school added a spotlight to the fruit bowl and had a 186 percent increase, which even Wansink thought was "just crazy." The second most effective design move is to rename the vegetables. "By simply calling corn, creamy corn, country corn, or even Karen's korn, veggie sales increased by 27 percent."

Plattsburgh High School in upstate New York was one of the first schools to implement cafeteria changes as part of the Healthy People 2020 Project pilot program. In December 2009, the school bought 175 fruits per month from distributors, based on demand. By March, after the changes were made, the school purchased 1067 whole fruits per month to meet the increased demand.

In addition to schools, Wansink is working with corporate lunchrooms and the US military to recreate environments that promote healthy choices. Since the program started in 2007, about 1500 schools in the United States have incorporated healthy lunchrooms.

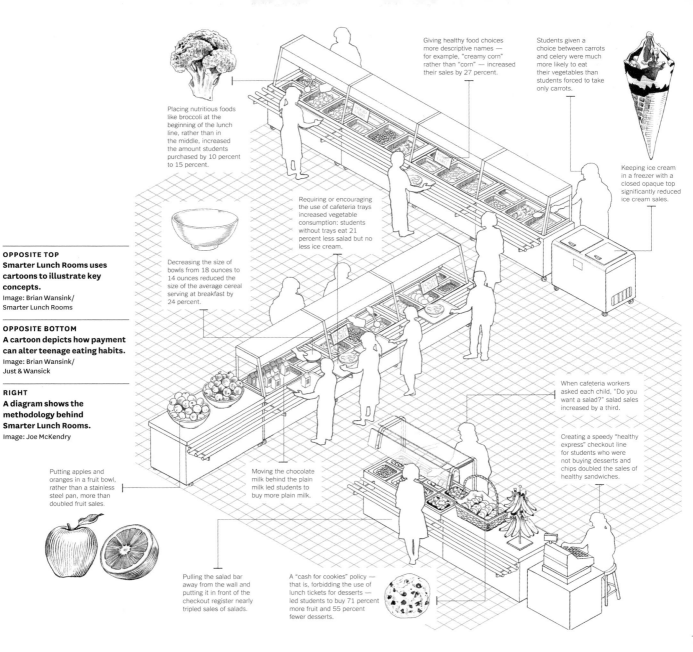

Giving healthy food choices more descriptive names — for example, "creamy corn" rather than "corn" — increased their sales by 27 percent.

Students given a choice between carrots and celery were much more likely to eat their vegetables than students forced to take only carrots.

Placing nutritious foods like broccoli at the beginning of the lunch line, rather than in the middle, increased the amount students purchased by 10 percent to 15 percent.

Keeping ice cream in a freezer with a closed opaque top significantly reduced ice cream sales.

Requiring or encouraging the use of cafeteria trays increased vegetable consumption: students without trays eat 21 percent less salad but no less ice cream.

Decreasing the size of bowls from 18 ounces to 14 ounces reduced the size of the average cereal serving at breakfast by 24 percent.

OPPOSITE TOP
Smarter Lunch Rooms uses cartoons to illustrate key concepts.
Image: Brian Wansink/ Smarter Lunch Rooms

OPPOSITE BOTTOM
A cartoon depicts how payment can alter teenage eating habits.
Image: Brian Wansink/ Just & Wansick

RIGHT
A diagram shows the methodology behind Smarter Lunch Rooms.
Image: Joe McKendry

When cafeteria workers asked each child, "Do you want a salad?" salad sales increased by a third.

Creating a speedy "healthy express" checkout line for students who were not buying desserts and chips doubled the sales of healthy sandwiches.

Putting apples and oranges in a fruit bowl, rather than a stainless steel pan, more than doubled fruit sales.

Moving the chocolate milk behind the plain milk led students to buy more plain milk.

Pulling the salad bar away from the wall and putting it in front of the checkout register nearly tripled sales of salads.

A "cash for cookies" policy — that is, forbidding the use of lunch tickets for desserts — led students to buy 71 percent more fruit and 55 percent fewer desserts.

Cary Fowler collects seeds. "Most people don't think about this, but our agricultural crops are on the frontlines of climate change and will be the first to be affected," says Fowler, executive director of the Global Diversity Crop Trust. "What we are conserving for the future are options." The seeds collected contain precious genetic variation that might otherwise be lost. They are being preserved in the Svalbard Global Seed Vault, located in arctic Norway. Although there are over 1000 seed banks in the world, this seed vault, close to

Svalbard Global Seed Vault

LOCATION Svalsatveien, Longyearbyen, Svalbard, Norway
DATE 2006–8
IMPLEMENTING AGENCIES
The Global Crop Diversity Trust;
Government of Norway;
Nordic Genetic Resource Center (NordGen)
PROPERTY MANAGER
Statsbygg, on behalf of the
Norwegian government
DESIGN FIRM Barlindhaug Consult AS
DESIGN TEAM Trond A. Hansen,
Louis Lunde, Peter W. Søderman
STRUCTURAL ENGINEER
Barlindhaug Consult AS
GEOTECHNICAL ENGINEER
Sverre Barlindhaug, Multiconsult AS
CONTRACTOR Leonhard Nilsen & Sønner
FUNDERS The Royal Norwegian Ministry
of Agriculture and Food;
The Royal Norwegian Ministry
of Environment;
The Royal Norwegian Ministry
of Foreign Affairs
COST $9 million USD
CAPACITY 4.5 million seeds,
samples of 500 seeds each

the North Pole and lodged in a permafrost mountain, is the ultimate lair for preservation.

Barlindhaug Consult AS won the bid because of its previous work in Svalbard and understanding of the unique and harsh building conditions. "It is a combination of mining construction and building construction because the portal building is actually a building, but everything from the portal building into the vaults is like a mine," says lead architect Peter Søderman. "It is strange for an architect to design a building that is not supposed to have any inhabitants except seeds and is not supposed to be a place that you visit."

The sleek architecture portal building (the only visible part of the facility) protrudes from the snowy hostile environment and is adorned with a jewel lighting art installation that glows at night and reflects the sun in the day. "It is a very picturesque facade but it is also a practical thing," Søderman says. "[The wedge shape] divides the stone masses and snow on the slope, so that rocks and snow roll down on either side of the entrance." The design team worked with geologists and engineers to understand the geology of the mountain, which directed their construction and design decisions. A 100-meter (328-ft) steel tube protrudes from the portal entrance through the different geological layers and connects to the main three cave-like chamber vaults, each with the capacity to store 1.5 million different seed samples.

The team faced many challenges constructing a building that could hold up to the low temperatures necessary to preserve seeds. Limited building materials and sub-zero temperatures also made the construction process difficult.

OPPOSITE
Artist Dyveke Sanne's glass mosaic adorns the entrance.
Photo: Mari Tefre/Global Crop Diversity Trust

TOP LEFT
Women preparing seed packets to ship to the Seed Vault in Ibadan, Nigeria at the International Institute of Tropical Agriculture.
Photo: International Institute of Tropical Agriculture/Global Crop Diversity Trust

ABOVE LEFT
Shelves inside the Seed Vault store seeds from around the world.
Photo: Mari Tefre/Global Crop Diversity Trust

TOP RIGHT
International Rice Research Institute employees preparing packets in Los Baños, Laguna, Philippines.
Photo: International Rice Research Institute/Global Crop Diversity Trust

ABOVE RIGHT
Global Crop Diversity Trust Executive Director Cary Fowler holds seed containers in the vault.
Photo: Kalie Koponen/Global Crop Diversity Trust

BELOW
Rendering of interior and exterior of the Seed Vault.
Image: Global Crop Diversity Trust

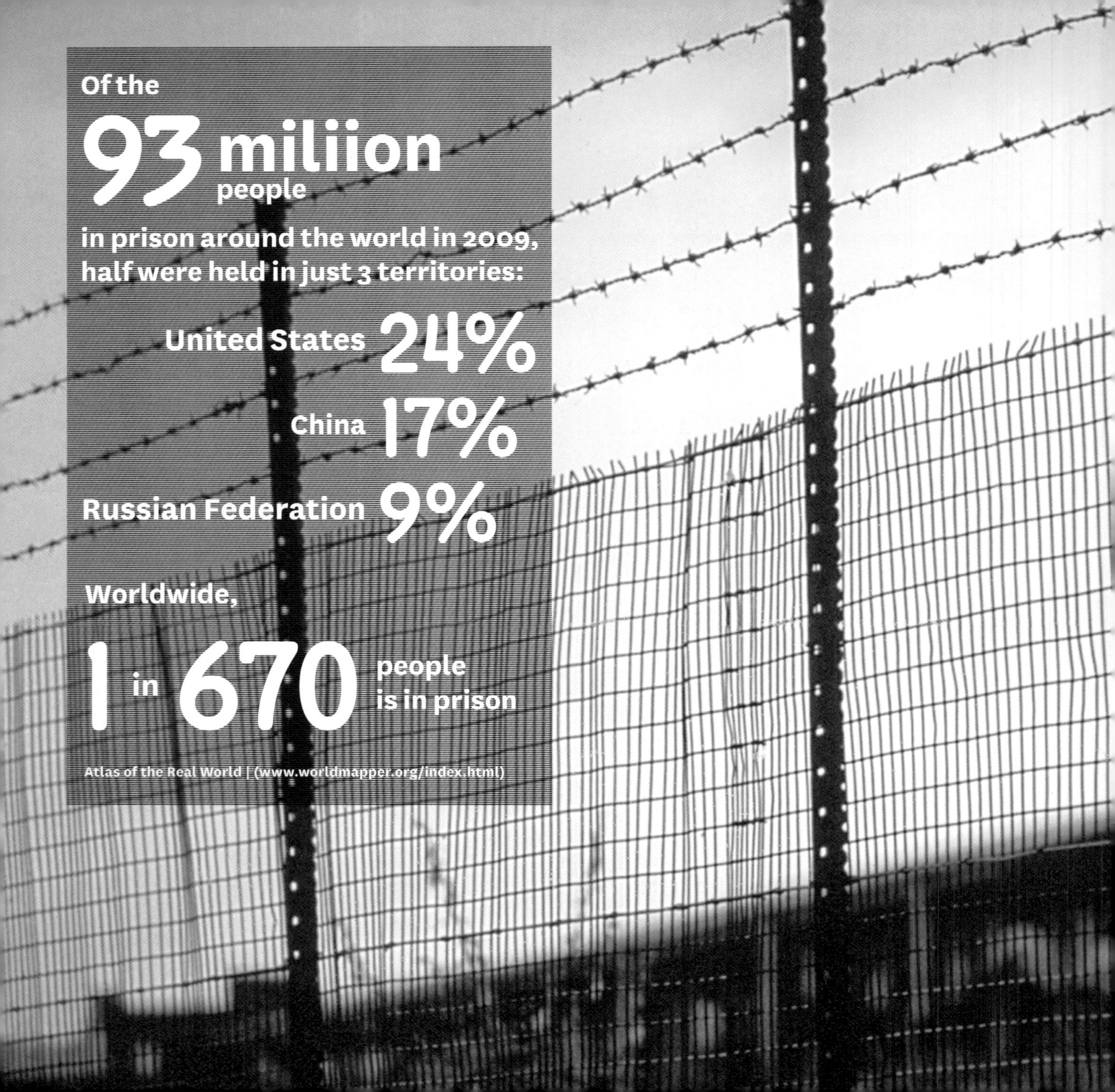
Of the
93 miliion
people
in prison around the world in 2009,
half were held in just 3 territories:
United States 24%
China 17%
Russian Federation 9%
Worldwide,
1 in 670 people
is in prison
Atlas of the Real World | (www.worldmapper.org/index.html)

Example of barbed wire fencing in South Africa, in 2002. Most public space in Africa is walled or fenced for fear of crime.
Photo: Asia Wright/Architecture for Humanity

Violence Prevention Through Urban Upgrading

LOCATION Khayelitsha, Cape Town, South Africa

DATE 2006–14

END USER Approximately 200 000 people in four neighborhoods of between 25 000 and 50 000 residents each

IMPLEMENTING AGENCY City of Cape Town, Kreditanstalt für Wiederaufbau (German Development Bank)

PLANNING AHT Group, SUN Development PTY

ASSOCIATED FIRMS ARG Design, Charlotte Chamberlain & Nicola Irving Architects, Jonker & Barnes Architects, Macroplan Townplanners, Masimanyane Community Participation, Partners for Impact, Naylor & Van Schalkvwyk, Talani Quantity Surveyors, Tarna Klitzner Landscape Architects

ADDITIONAL CONSULTANTS Masimanyane Management Consultancy

FUNDERS City of Cape Town; German Development Bank; provincial and national South African funding; private sector funding

PROGRAM COST 400 million South African rand/ $55.6 million USD

Youth participate in an HIV/AIDS prevention program taking place at the Football for Hope Center in the Khayelitsha township, one of several interventions designed to reduce violence and instill a sense of community pride.
Photo: Mark Warren and Unathi Mkonto/ Architecture for Humanity

Khayelitsha, a township of Cape Town, South Africa, was established in 1985 during the apartheid era. It has experienced some of the highest crime rates in the Western Cape. In 2003, the area reported 358 murders, 588 sexual crimes and more than 3000 incidents of violent assault, according to the Crime Information Management Centre of the South African Police Services. At night, it was unsafe to return from work, and the township, which has few paved roads or formal structures, was difficult to patrol.

Recognizing that the many factors leading to the area's high crime rate were often interlinked, the city of Cape Town, German Federal Ministry for Economic Development, South African Treasury and Khayelitsha Development Forum called for the creation of a neighborhood-wide strategy. An initial baseline survey identified the top three crimes, which were murder, rape and robbery. However, rather than using traditional urban planning methods and tools, the team mapped data using a geographic information system (GIS) to identify areas prone to crime and develop social and architectural interventions.

The result was a $57 million, five-year pilot program called Violence Prevention through Urban Upgrading. The program's commonsense approach resulted in a 33 percent reduction in murder in 2009 in Harare, the first area where it was implemented, with almost no incidents of murder reported in public spaces. Public perceptions have changed as well, with 48 percent of people surveyed in 2011 reporting they felt safety was improving compared to only 21 percent in 2007 when the program began.

Specifically, the program focuses on reducing crime by identifying where crime takes place and making small, but targeted interventions at the spots where crime is most likely to happen (referred to by VPUU as "Hot Spots"). These interventions may be as small as removing vegetation that predators could use as cover or as large as a community center and park.

Interventions (referred to as "Active Boxes" by VPUU to connote the concept of activating a public space) are strategically located so that pedestrians are always in view in high crime areas. "The Active Boxes are a good illustration of how an integration of built, social and place management interventions can transform perceived dangerous spaces into positive and owned spaces," explains Michael Krause, director of Sustainable Urban Neighborhoods Development, the implementing partner of VPUU.

The program sets strict standards for architects designing interventions and designs are reviewed by a community board. "The buildings don't have hideaway corners or nooks where people can hide and observe as you

Murder
House breakings
Gangsterism
Rape
Abuse
Domestic violence
Stabbings
Youth related violence
Robbery
Hijackings
Motor vehicle accidents

CRIME MAPPING
VPUU starts by mapping specific neighborhoods marked by high perceptions of crime in the township. Each area has a population of about 50 000 people. In each of these targeted neighborhoods, which VPUU calls "Safe Node Areas," the community is engaged to track crime and make crime maps. Crime incidents are recorded by neighborhood patrols and through monthly household surveys. Information tracked includes the location of the crime, the type of crime, and type of victim. Information is tracked using GIS and used to create crime maps.
Image: SUN Development

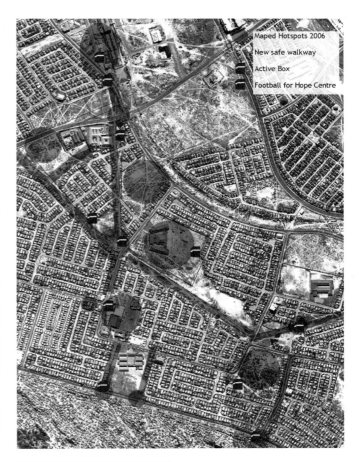

"HOT SPOT" MAPPING

The locations where the highest incidents of crime occur are referred to as Hot Spots. Hot Spots identify areas where one or more interventions are needed. VPUU maps crime frequency rates and overlays information such as frequently used routes within the neighborhood to identify Hot Spot zones.

Image: SUN Development

"ACTIVE BOX" LOCATIONS

VPUU then works to identify opportunities for investment in the targeted neighborhoods. Investments are located along frequently used routes and high-crime areas in the Hot Spot zones. Projects may be libraries, schools, businesses, pedestrian pathways or sports facilities. Projects (referred to as "Active Boxes") are specifically designed to offer eyes on the street, improve lighting and remove "blind spots" that can lead to crime. Wherever possible, facilities are required to include a second-story, 24-hour surveillance watchtower with 360-degree visibility.

Image: SUN Development

approach the building," says Cedric Daniels, manager of urban design for the city of Cape Town. "This follows the very basic principle that if a criminal knows he is being observed, can be identified and can get caught for a crime, he is less likely to perform a criminal act."

In addition to changes in the built environment, investments are made in social programs such as neighborhood policing and rape prevention in the same areas.

One of the projects that illustrates VPUU's holistic approach is the new Ncomu Road Urban Park. At one corner of the park is the Ncomu Road Urban community building designed by the firm ARG Design. Anchoring the opposite corner is the new Football for Hope Centre, also designed by ARG Design with Architecture for Humanity. Operated by Grassroots Soccer, the Football for Hope Centre and adjacent football pitches offer sports and youth leadership training as well as HIV/AIDS education.

The park's buildings are not enclosed by fences or gates as is typical in South Africa. Instead, they engage with the street. "This is intended to invite residents to freely use the variety of spaces, to interact and engage with the programs being offered," says Verena Grips, a project designer for both centers. At night, a caretaker guards the new park from a second-story flat with 360-degree sightlines, offering an "eyes on the street" view and creating a place where residents can seek help if they feel threatened. The park also includes a playground for young children and is navigated by well-lit, paved pedestrian pathways. Throughout the area, similar "Active Boxes" have been built or are planned to ensure safe passage for residents

To date, there are a total of 10 completed projects that aim to reduce crime in seven crime Hot Spots. VPUU's success in Harare helped it secure funding until 2014, and the city plans to expand the program throughout the township.

TOP
Road in the Khayelitsha suburb of Harare that backs up to the Ncomu Road Urban Park. Pictures taken in October 2008 before upgrading.
Photo:Oana Stanescu/Architecture for Humanity

BOTTOM
The Ncomu Road Urban community building, complete with second-story watchtower and windows for 360-degree observation after upgrading.
Photo: Architecture for Humanity

OPPOSITE
After the introduction of the Violence Pre- vention through Urban Upgrading program, which includes sports training and facilities, incidents of violent crime fell sharply in the Harare Precinct.
Photo: SUN Development

In 2005 there were

219
murders

893
violent assaults

In 2009 there were

124
murders

554
violent assaults

Source: Crime Information
Management,
South African Police

Red Hook Community Justice Center

LOCATION Brooklyn, New York, USA

DATE 1994–2000

END USER Community members
in a catchment area of 200 000 people

CLIENT New York Unified Court System

IMPLEMENTING PARTNER
Center for Court Innovation

DESIGN FIRM Alta Indelman, architect

ENGINEERING B. Thayer Associates,
Jack Green Associates, James Wiesenfeld
& Associates

LIGHTING DESIGN
Domingo Gonzales Associates

CONTRACTOR York Hunter

CONSULTANTS
Davis Brody Bond Architects,
City of New York, State of New York, US
Department of Justice

COST $5.47 million USD

AREA 1 858 sq m/20 000 sq ft

The United States leads the world in the number of people incarcerated. During the 1990s a movement began to address the issues that lead to high recidivism rates. Community court is an effort to reform the courtroom from the inside out. The Center for Court Innovation, a public-private partnership was in New York City in 1993 to serve as the research and development arm of the city's court system and pilot demonstration projects. Its research showed that a large number of the people who failed to appear in court were charged with minor offenses, clogging courtroom dockets and resulting in more serious consequences for the accused. In part, this was because the court date was often several weeks after the time of arrest and the courtroom would often be in another part of the city that was difficult for them to reach. To address this problem, the center established community courts where defendants are held for trial, appear before a judge, and, if convicted, serve their sentence all from a community justice center located in the same neighborhood as their arrest.

The Community Court model was first piloted in four neighborhoods with high rates of nonviolent crime in the New York area. At a Community Court, defendants are held in a holding cell on-site while they await trial rather than being transferred to the city's jail. They come before the judge within 24 hours. A single judge handles cases that would ordinarily go to three different courts: criminal, civil and family. By handling minor crimes, delinquency matters and landlord-tenant disputes in one place, the judge is able to try offenders in the context of the community.

If convicted, they immediately serve their sentence before being released. This is unlike a traditional court, where defendants are scheduled to serve their sentences at a later date at a different location.

Community service projects are aimed at paying back the community where the crime was committed. The projects usually consist of cleanup or physical labor. For some offenders who need extra supervision, rooms are set up within the court (right next to the desk of the community service coordinators) where they can complete community service hours inside. Part of the sentence may also include social services. Access to city agencies, job training and substance abuse treatment programs are all located on-site.

Swift sentencing "sends the message to offenders that crime has consequences and that they will be held accountable for their actions," says Greg Berman, the director of the Center for Court Innovation. "Downtown, I only have jail or out. Here, I have a number of different tools to use to get to people's problems so that they don't come in front of me again," explains Judge Alex Calabrese, of Brooklyn's Red Hook Community Justice Center. Max Johnson, a former offender who has appeared before judges at both Red Hook and traditional courts, says he appreciates the Community Court model. "The difference between Red Hook and other courts is when you go to regular courts you just see a lawyer and they talk about the case. There is no concern about the real problems of the person."

This innovative approach to justice required re-engineering the physical layout of the courthouse as well. To assist designers in rethinking the architectural blueprint of the traditional courthouse for new Community Courts, the Center for Court Innovation created a set of design criteria.

The look and feel of the Community Courthouse is less institutional and more friendly. Some common changes to the standard court layout include: Community Courts have a street presence, invite citizens to walk in if they need services; they have spaces set aside for community meetings, mediation and classes;

glass panels replace holding cell bars; and someone is stationed at the front to assist visitors. These features, among others, make the look and feel less institutional and more friendly.

One of the key components is office spaces that house social workers and liaisons across a range of social services providers and city agencies, including social workers, job-training coordinators, social counselors, drug and mental health coordinators and community service coordinators.

At the Red Hook Community Court in Brooklyn, pictured here, the open-air office allows these agencies, which are typically housed in different locations, to work within arm's reach of each other, making support for cases quick and effective.

Beyond the conventional court business, Community Court may also house programs addressing a specific community issue or needs of a target population. A popular Red Hook program is the youth court, run entirely by specially trained teenagers. The youth court handles low-level cases referred by either the police or the court. The idea is simple: to use peer pressure as a positive force to get troubled teens back on track. The youth court's meeting room at Red Hook Justice Center is directly across the hall from the holding rooms of offenders, offering a real perspective on the consequence of crime.

The results of the Community Courts have been overwhelmingly successful. For example, the police precinct local to the Red Hook Justice Center is now the safest in Brooklyn. An independent survey of defendants sponsored by a grant from the US Department of Justice revealed that 86 percent felt their case was handled fairly by the Community Court. The report concluded that "by offering a wider range of non-custodial sentences (including social and community services), Red Hook Community Justice Center is offering a more transparent and collaborative atmosphere for defendants, all of which may heighten defendant perceptions of fairness."

Design Pak for Community Courts

Community Courts seek to rethink how courts do business. A Community Court should strive to communicate this mission in ever facet of its design. All elements of the court should reflect a sense of respect for the judicial process and for all those who participate in it. Design Pak offers a set of fresh design ideas in an effort to spark new conversations about courthouse design.

THE FOLLOWING PAGES OUTLINE FIVE BASIC CONCEPTS:

- Community Courts are accessible
- Community Courts are more than courtrooms
- Community Courts share information
- Community Courts show respect
- Community courts get the word out

COMMUNITY COURTS ARE ACCESSIBLE – DESIGN CAN MAKE THE COURT WELCOMING

- Makes courtroom proceedings visible and audible to all; a smaller courtroom can often encourage greater intimacy.
- Recognize the importance of street presences – a prominent neighborhood location and visible signage send the message that the court welcomes citizen participation.
- Place prominent and uniform direction signs in public spaces.
- Let visitors know who the judge is – post his/her name at the entrance of the courtroom.

COMMUNITY COURTS ARE MORE THAN COURTROOMS – NEW PARTNERS CAN HELP THE COURT SOLVE NEIGHBORHOOD PROBLEMS

- The court should be a resource for the entire community – set aside space for community meetings, mediation, and evening classes; use glass doors to communicate a sense of openness.
- Seize the moment of arrest by locating counselors, job trainers and educators on-site, under one roof; an open office plan will enhance communication.
- Some offenders sentenced to community service may benefit from the extra supervision that comes with being on-site.
- Set up a health clinic to address public health issues like tuberculosis and sexually transmitted diseases that affect individuals as well as the community.

COMMUNITY COURTS SHARE INFORMATION – EASY ACCESS TO INFORMATION CAN IMPROVE THE DELIVERY OF SERVICES

- Place the daily court calendar where it can be seen by both the public and defendants.

- Provide the public with information about health care, job training and how to negotiate the court system.
- Station someone at the entrance of the court to assist visitors.
- Advertise on-site social services with large, bilingual posters.
- Use technology to link the courtroom to social services and community services sites, ensuring that shared information is accurate and up-to-date.

COMMUNITY COURTS SHOW RESPECT – ALL AREAS CAN EXHIBIT RESPECT FOR THE JUDICIAL PROCESS

- Keep lawyering out of the hallways – create a private and accessible area for defendants to meet with their attorneys.
- By making holding cells dignified – including a pay phone, sink, and mirror, and privacy partition for the toilet – the court can positively influence the behavior of the defendants.
- Use secure glass panels instead of bars to improve visibility for guards and habitability for defendants.
- Sentence offenders to community service work crews that keep the courthouse spotless.
- Advertise 'success stories' – defendants who have succeeded in treatment or who have been placed in jobs.

COMMUNITY COURTS GET THE WORD OUT – LET THE COMMUNITY KNOW ABOUT THE COURT'S WORK

- Create a name for the court that reflects its roots in the community; use logo consistently, on everything from stationary to banners to community service uniforms.
- Develop visible community service projects that 'pay back' the neighborhood.
- Create vehicles for the public to learn what's going on – websites, newsletters, videos, etc.
- Post "before" and "after" photos of the community service projects – tree plantings, graffiti removal, etc.

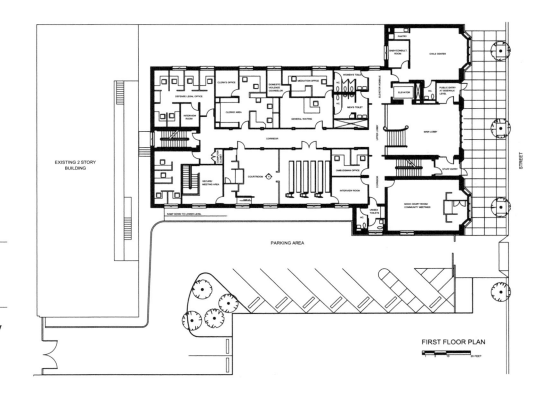

SECOND FLOOR PLAN

LOWER FLOOR PLAN

FIRST FLOOR PLAN

EXISTING 2 STORY
BUILDING

PARKING AREA

STREET

OPPOSITE
**Excerpt from design guideline
created by the Center for Court
Innovation in 1997.**
Courtesy of Center for Court Innovation

TOP, RIGHT
**Floor plan of the Red Hook Community
Justice Center, an example of how
courts adapt space for community
engagement.**
Image: Alta Indelman

Trau Kod Dam

LOCATION Siem Reap, Cambodia
DATES 2007–8
END USER 9000 residents
in the Balang Commune
IMPLEMENTING PARTNER
Human Translation
PROJECT MANAGER
Tobias Rose-Stockwell
ENGINEERING
Engineers Without Borders–USA
New York Professional Chapter
DESIGN TEAM Matthew Bussman,
William Cao, Jason Chan, Bryse Gaboury,
Maria Jarnia, Jessica Miller, Tim Weiss,
Ryan Woodward
GENERAL CONTRACTOR
BQC Construction, Kong Chanda
ADDITIONAL CONSULTANTS
Steve Forbes, Sukh Gurung
FUNDER Private donors
COST $260 000 USD
LENGTH OF DAM 20 m/66 ft

Water shapes a community. In many cases it defines it. The Trau Kod Dam at the Balang Commune reservoir is no different. It was first built in the Angkor Period and has had a long and storied history.

In the 1970s it entered a very dark period. Thousands of Cambodians were put to work by the Khmer Rouge to expand the dam as part of an agricultural reform movement. Then in the '80s and '90s this land became one of the last battlegrounds in the final days of the reign of the Khmer Rouge. The embankment was destroyed and land mines scattered the area. From 1998 the reservoir was unusable.

In 2004, Tobias Rose-Stockwell, then a 24-year-old traveler, arrived in Balang on the back of a motorbike with friend Tracey Rolls. They were greeted by community leaders and local monks who shared the story of the dam and the plight of nearly 9000 people suffering from malnutrition as farmers. They were left with dry reservoirs and canals that could only yield one rice crop a year. Rose-Stockwell, naive to the journey ahead, committed to help restore this century-old local resource. Thus was the birth of Human Translation,

the community-focused development organization that saw the project through.

When he learned of the land mines, Rose-Stockwell convinced the Cambodian Mine Action Center to clear the land. Then he enlisted Engineers Without Borders–New York to help engineer and project manage the construction. EWB–USA member Steve Forbes came to see the project and Rose-Stockwell recalls him exclaiming 'I don't think you realize how big this is, Tobias. It's big,' This would be the organization's biggest dam project to date.

The project consisted of building a water gate as well as repairing and strengthening the earthen embankment, which expanded the reservoir. There was a 20-meter (65-ft) gap in the earthen embankment. The broad concrete water gate is closed during the monsoon season to capture water in the 50-hectare (123-acre) reservoir and is raised during the dry season to irrigate rice fields.

Bryse Gaboury, Matt Bussman and Maria Jarina from Engineers Without Borders worked on the embankment reconstruction and hired BQC Construction to oversee the construction of the dam. On a local level, Human Translation hired translators and engineering coordinator Ong Chanda to train and work with 200 community members for the construction and repair of the reservoir and water gate.

Four years into the project, and realizing this was a huge undertaking, Rose-Stockwell went to try to raise additional funds back home. Like many project ambassadors, he had spent countless months applying for grants and funding, scraping together around $30 000. At an auction in Northern California, the rest of the funds needed, $90 000, were raised in three minutes after a furious round of bidding. The project jolted into overdrive and soon the dam was complete.

The ecosystem of change created ripples way beyond the local community. Dormant canals came to life, public health initiatives were launched, school building began and sustainable rice production was suddenly feasible. Bryse Gaboury summed up the secondary benefits, "The innovation was not in the design; the innovation was how this dam changed people's lives."

OPPOSITE TOP
Monks stand atop Trau Kod Dam during construction.
Photo: Bouny Te

OPPOSITE MIDDLE
Side view of dam under construction.
Photo: Bouny Te

OPPOSITE BOTTOM
Aerial shot of the completed Trau Kod Dam.
Photo: Human Translation

TOP
A ceremony by the Ministry of Agriculture, Forestry and Fisheries to reintroduce fish into the reservoir.
Photo: Bryse Gaboury/Engineers without Borders–New York

RIGHT
Several hundred fish being released into the reservoir.
Photo: Bryse Gaboury/Engineers without Borders–New York

"Our most beautiful buildings must be in our poorest areas."

Sergio Fajardo, mayor of Medellín, Colombia, from 2003 to 2007

Proyecto Urbano Integral

LOCATION Medellín, Colombia
DATE 2004–9
AFFECTED POPULATION 170 000 inhabitants
IMPLEMENTING AGENCY
Empresa de Desarrollo Urbano de Medellín (Economic Development of Medellín)
PROGRAM MANAGEMENT Carlos Alberto Montoya Correa, Carlos Mario Rodríguez Osorio, Alejandro Echeverri Restrepo
DESIGN TEAM Luis Fernando Arango Arboleda, Eliana Idárraga Castaño, Carmen Elisa Hurtado Figueroa, Andrés Benítez Giraldo, Esteban Henao, Héctor Javier Cruz Londoño, John Octavio Ortiz Lopera, Mauricio Iván Mendoza Martinez, Ana Milena Vergara Monsalve, Oscar Montoya, Francesco Maria Orsini, Diego Armando Pino Pino, Claudia Juliana Portillo Rubio, Carlos David Montoya Valencia, Oscar Mauricio Santana Vélez, Isabel Arcos Zuluaga
ADDITIONAL AGENCIES
Programa de Paz y Reconciliación (Peace and Reconciliation Program)
FUNDER City of Medellín
PROGRAM COST $365 million USD
AREA 158 hectares/390 acres

Starting in the 1960s, political instability led to the rise of paramilitary groups and armed conflict throughout Colombia. As groups such as Revolutionary Armed Forces of Colombia rose to power, violence forced Colombia's rural poor from their land. The flight from the countryside into the urban area led to the rise of informal settlements and street crime. Para-military groups and gangs controlled the hillside slums of Medellín. Throughout much of the 1980s and 1990s Medellín was considered the capital of the cocaine trade. (In 1987, *Forbes* magazine estimated that 80 percent of the global cocaine market was controlled by the Medellín Cartel.)

In 1999, then President Andres Pastrana proposed "Plan Colombia." With aid from the United States and other countries, Plan Colombia called for the investment of $7.5 billion USD over the course of the next decade in sweeping reforms aimed at ending the drug trade. While the bulk of these funds were directed toward demilitarization and counternarcotics, Plan Colombia also made way for significant investment—more than $1.3 billion in the United States alone for social infrastructure and programs. These programs worked to disarm paramilitary groups. The national government signed an accord with the paramilitary and narco-traffic groups, and began a long-term commitment to reintegrate ex-combatants into the social fabric of the nation. On the heels of these investments, Medellín's transformation began.

In 2003, Sergio Fajardo, a mathematician and the son of an architect, was elected mayor of Medellín. "We spent all our time saying how our society should be, but the politicians are the ones who make all the decisions in society. So, with a group of friends, we said we are going to have to get into politics." Fajardo ran on a platform of social renewal and articulated a plan for reducing violence and revitalizing the city. When he was elected in 2003, he began implementing the plan: "We had a formula to solve the problem. We have

to start reducing violence, but whenever we reduce violence we immediately have to come back with social interventions. And we brought in architecture," Fajardo explained in a television interview.

"We would go to the poorest neighborhoods and build the most beautiful buildings. So suddenly in the places where there was no hope we were building the most incredible spaces—but all were related to opportunities. " During his administration, the city invested 47 percent of its budget in schools, libraries, cultural centers, public spaces, job training centers and transit. These investments were tied to slum upgrading programs and social programs to reintegrate ex-combatants.

FEATURED PROJECT Metrocable
LOCATION Zona Nororiental de Medellín, Colombia
DATE 2003–4
BENEFICIARIES 170 000 residents in the Zona Nororiental
PROJECT ARCHITECTS María Bustamante, Edison Escobar Osorno
PROJECT ENGINEERS Sergio Acosta, Adriana Arcila, Jorge Ramos
CONSTRUCTION TEAM U.T. Telecabinas Medellín (Pomagalski, ConConcreto, y Termotecnica Coindustrials)
FUNDERS City of Medellín; Metro Medellín
COST $25 million USD
AREA 2072 m/6797 ft
OCCUPANCY 93 cabins

ABOVE
**Medellín's Metrocable scales
the hillside city.**
Photo: Empresa de Desarrollo Urbano/
Alcaldía de Medellín

FAR LEFT
**Near the Santo Domingo area
before improvements were made.**
Photo: Empresa de Desarrollo Urbano/
Alcaldía de Medellín

LEFT
**Paved pathways replace steep
dirt pathways.**
Photo: Empresa de Desarrollo Urbano/
Alcaldía de Medellín

Parque Mirador Niños is located at the base of a Metrocable station. The park hosts community festivals and performance events.

Photo: Diana Moreno/Empresa de Desarrollo Urbano Alcaldía de Medellín

Map showing corridor of project locations.

Image: Empresa de Desarrollo Urbano Alcaldía de Medellín.

The Parque Biblioteca España, designed by Colombian architect Giancarlo Mazzanti, enhances education opportunities for the Santo Domingo barrio youth.

Photo: Empresa de Desarrollo Urbano Alcadia de Medellin

A health center was one of the many community projects built to improve the city.

Photo: Michael Grote/Architecture for Humanity

Terraced pathways reinforce steep inclines around the Metrocable.

Photo: Michael Grote/Architecture for Humanity

Children's park in Santo Domingo provides a safe place fo r youth to play.

Photo: Empresa de Desarrollo Urbano Alcaldía de Medellín

The Line K Metrocable station was completed in 2006 and helps connect the barrios to downtown.

Photo: Diana Moreno/Empresa de Desarrollo Urbano Alcaldía de Medellín.

The Cedzco are business centers that offer workshops and business advice.

Photo: Michael Grote/Architecture for Humanity

Ex-combatants who participated in jobs training in tandem with development.
Photo Credit: Michael Grote/
Architecture for Humanity

Kids play in one of several new parks intended to create peace through the creation of public space.
Photo: Empresa de Desarrollo Urbano
Alcaldía de Medellín

Proyecto Urbano Integral not only focused on building safe transportation systems, education hubs and business development facilities, but also focused those investments in place, ensuring that new libraries were located near transit hubs and bridging barrios separated by creeks and deep ravines.

"We use architecture in a very simple way to change the mind of the people and the barrios," said Alejandro Echeverri Restrepo, then the city's director of urban projects for the mayor's office of Medellin.

The first Proyecto Urbano Integral revitalization area was Communa Noroiental in the Santo Domingo—one of the city's poorest and most violent neighborhoods. It is home to 11 neighborhoods of 170 000 residents, most living in informal dwellings along the steep hillsides to the north of the city center. Perhaps the most attention-getting project is the city's Metrocable transit system. To connect the informal barrios to the subway and the formal city in the valley below, the city built a public gondola that scales the steep hillside. Running the length of the gondola

is a series of public parks, job training centers and schools. At the top, purposely situated next to the metro station, the city built Parque Biblioteca España (now one of five library parks in Medellin). Designed by architect Giancarlo Mazzanti, it resembles three massive, etched black boulders and is visible throughout the city. Completed in 2007, at a cost of $4 million USD, it marked the first formal civic structure in the informal settlement.

"Violence has terrible consequences all over, one of those is that violence splits society into smaller groups. So instead of becoming citizens, we are fearful of other people in the city, we are restricted. So what we did was we created new public spaces which are going to come together. Together these public spaces and new transit helped to create links between barrios and the city, providing greater access to jobs, services and opportunity.

Medellin, the center of Colombia's textile industry, funded the upgrades through a mix of national funding and new taxes. In 2002 the city had expanded the scope of an existing local economic development corporation, charged

with upgrading public spaces, and renamed it Empresa de Desarrollo. As an autonomous agency, it had broad latitude to partner across sectors and across agencies allowing it to direct and thread funding from different city budgets. This was a key element to the success of the city's urban upgrading initiatives. To date, the city has invested 424 billion Colombian pesos ($212 million USD) in tandem with another $360 million USD in annual spending on education.

By 2007, the city's murder rate had fallen to 26 murders per 100 000 inhabitants. While the changes have not ended violence altogether (after a downward trend, the city's murder rate spiked again in 2009, more than doubling to 170 per population of 100 000), they have brought a sea change in the social landscape of the city. Today, the Empresa des Desarrollo has more than 180 projects underway. In each barrio a community manager helps to coordinate and integrate the projects with social initiatives and goals, such as job training for ex-combatants. Tourism has increased, along with property values—and property taxes.

A 46-meter bridge connects the Granizal and Santo Domingo neighborhoods.
Photo: Empresa de Desarrollo Urbano Alcaldía de Medellín

Project Updates

Some of the projects we featured in *Design Like You Give a Damn: Architectural Responses to Humanitarian Crises* (2006) have expanded or changed since the book was published. Architecture for Humanity checked in to find out what's been going on, what worked, and what didn't, since we left off. Here's what we found out (with page number references from the original text).

Design Like You Give a Damn

Since 2006, *Design Like You Give a Damn: Architectural Responses to Humanitarian Crises* has had seven printings, sold more than 30 000 copies, and ranked among the publisher's top architecture books. We've spotted it all over the world. Universities and architecture schools use it as part of their teaching curriculums, and we use it to train our staff and volunteers. "A copy of *Design Like You Give a Damn* will take you a long way when you don't have access to your design firm's library or the Internet," says Kate Stohr, co-founder of Architecture for Humanity. Leading up to its spring 2012 release, the highly anticipated second book in the series gained a following on Twitter under the handle @DLYGAD.

Appirampattu Ville Center

Logan Amont only had a few hours to admire his finished building before leaving the community of Appirampattu in 2003. When he returned with his wife in 2009, Amont discovered that the library in earthen-walled Appirampattu Village Center (see page 200) was repurposed as a living space for a man and child. Amont made some improvements while back in India. He replaced the deteriorated bamboo stage with a solid, concrete structure and hooked up electricity for lighting and fans. The doors were replaced and the slope of the roof adjusted for better water drainage. Today, the roof features a blue and white ceramic tile mosaic, inspired by the paintings on the exterior walls of the village homes.

Gando Primary School

Since completion of the Gando Primary School (see page 250) in Burkina Faso, designer Diébédo Francis Kéré has added an addition and the school now serves more than 900 students. "The ceiling of the extension building is a vault with slits for light and ventilation. Cavities have been integrated in the vault where the enclosed air works as a buffer to reduce overheating inside the classrooms," Kéré says. The government was pleased with the outcome of Gando Primary School and a formal program was created for Kéré to design schools in the Gando style throughout Burkina Faso. He has completed a housing complex for six teachers and their families and plans are moving ahead for a community library and women's center.

Hopi Nation Elder Home

Red Feather Development Group is continuing to create housing for Native Americans and reduce overcrowding in communities since the success of the Hopi Nation Elder Home (see page 150), which was built in Hotevilla, Arizona, using strawbales as bricks. The method has been further refined and similar homes have been built for Northern Cheyenne and Ojibwa tribes. Indigenous Community Enterprises, which serves Navajo, had the development group create a series of dwellings on scattered sites in Mexico and Northern Arizona for Navajo elders. A two-bedroom home can be built for under $50 000. Wherever possible, the homes utilize passive and active solar panels for off-the-grid locations, and each new design is more sustainable than the last.

Pallet House

The Pallet House (see page 114) was inspired by the possibility of housing 84 percent of the world's refugees with just one year's supply of American shipping pallets. Over the past 10 years, it has evolved from a purely transitional structure into a potentially permanent dwelling. I-Beam continues to improve the design, making each prototype more structurally sound while experimenting with different material combinations such as corrugated plastic and metal for exterior sheathing, as well as stone, mud, earth, wood and Styrofoam insulation to fill the wall cavities. I-Beam launched an effort to send the houses to Haiti after the 2010 earthquake, but was unsuccessful in getting them into the country.

PlayPump

PlayPump (see page 282), the spinning roundabout designed to pump water as children play on it, has not been the success designer Ronnie Stuver hoped for. The idea behind PlayPump was to create a fun way for children (who are often a village's primary water collectors) to gather water. However it was received negatively in some cultures where women are responsible for water gathering because it is difficult for older women to use. Additionally, some devices went into disrepair for extended periods in communities with no access to maintenance people. Although there was negative press on the PlayPump, its manufacturer is working to improve the design so it performs better.

Quinta Monroy Housing Project

The ELEMENTAL Housing Initiative at Pontificia Universidad Católica de Chile debuted the Quinta Monroy Housing Project (see page 164) in 2003 by successfully resettling 93 families on the same land they were living on for 30 years. An incremental building method allowed for higher quality construction where it counted, created support for organized growth, and ultimately turned public housing into an asset that had the potential to appreciate in value over time instead of becoming a diminishing governmental burden. This same incremental building method resurfaces in their Monterrey Housing project in Santa Cantaria, Mexico, and elsewhere.

Super Adobe/ Nader Khalili

Nader Khalili died in 2008, three years after Architecture for Humanity interviewed the Iranian born architect about Super Adobe (see page 104) for the first edition of *Design Like You Give a Damn*. At first a theoretical design for humans living on the moon, the method of filling plastic bags with lunar dust and affixing them to each other with velcro is, to date, still on display at the California Institute of Earth Art and Architecture (Cal-Earth), which he founded 20 years ago and his family continues to run. Much in the same way that he provided shelter for Iraqi refugees at the Baninajar Refugee Camp with Super Adobe, the Cal-Earth team has responded to the earthquake in Haiti with Haiti One, an alternative for tent camps.

Resources

In writing this book, we were aided by a number of helpful sources. Below you'll find a selection of these resources, from financing guides to development models, that we found most useful.

ABT ASSOCIATES, INC. AND AMY JONES & ASSOCIATES FOR THE DEPARTMENT OF HOUSING AND URBAN DEVELOPMENT AND THE FEDERAL EMERGENCY MANAGEMENT AGENCY
Developing a More Viable Disaster Housing Unit: A Case Study of the Mississippi Alternative Housing Program
February 2, 2009

AGA KHAN AWARDS FOR ARCHITECTURE
www.akdn.org/architecture

MICHELLE ALLSOPP, ADAM WALTERS, DAVID SANTILLO, AND PAUL JOHNSTON
Plastic Debris in the World's Oceans
Greenpeace, Amsterdam.
www.greenpeace.org/international/en/publications/reports/plastic_ocean_report

ANDERSON ANDERSON ARCHITECTURE
Prefab Prototypes: Site-Specific Designs for Offsite Construction
Princeton Architectural Press, New York: 2006

ELLIS ANDERSON
Under Surge, Under Siege: The Odyssey of Bay St. Louis and Katrina
Jackson, MS: University Press of Mississippi, 2010

PAUL ANDREAS AND PETER CACHOLA SCHMAL, EDS.
Takaharu + Yui Tezuka: Nostalgic Future/Erinnerte Zukunft, Berlin: Jovis, 2009

ARCHITECTURE FOR HUMANITY
Rebuilding After Disaster: The Biloxi Model Home Program
Architecture for Humanity, 2011

ATLANTIC WIND CONNECTION
www.atlanticwindconnection.com

ERIC D. BEINHOCKER
The Origin Of Wealth
Boston, Massachusetts: Harvard Business School Press, 2007

GREG BERMAN
Red Hook Diary Planning a Community Court,
Center for Court Innovation, New York: 1998
www.courtinnovation.org

MATTHEW BISHOP AND MICHAEL GREEN
Philanthrocapitalism
New York: Bloomsbury Press, 2009

CORY BOOKER TWITTER: @CORYBOOKER

BUILDING GREENER CITIES
New York: Strategy+Business, 2010

JOHN CARY AND PUBLIC ARCHITECTURE
The Power of Pro Bono 40 Stories of Design for the Public Good by Architects and Their Clients
Metropolis Books, Los Angeles: 2010

THE CENTER FOR HEALTH DESIGN
Pebble Project, Concorde, California:
www.healthdesign.org/pebble

COMMONWEAL CONSERVANCY
Galisteo Basin Preserve Southern Crescent Community Development Standards
Santa Fe, New Mexico: 2006

CRADLE TO CRADLE
www.mcdonough.com/cradle_to_cradle.htm

CURRY STONE DESIGN PRIZE
currystonedesignprize.com

THE DESIGN WORKSHOP 2006
39571 InfoWash DeLisle, MS
School of Constructed Environments Parsons
The New School for Design, New York: 2008.

DESIGN FOR THE OTHER 90%
New York, NY: Cooper-Hewitt Museum, 2007

DESIGN INDABA
www.designindaba.com

DESIGN TRUST FOR PUBLIC SPACE
Reclaiming the High Line
www.designtrust.org/publications/publication_01highline_book.html

ENERGY EXPERTS
The Role of the Emerging Energy-Efficient Technology in Promoting Workplace Productivity and Health, Final Report,
www.osti.gov/bridge/servlets/purl/795973-2JTndp/native/795973.PDF, 2002

JOHN FEINBLATT, GREG BERMAN, MICHELE SVIRIDOFF
Neighborhood Justice Lessons From The Midtown Community Court,
Center for Court Innovation, New York: 1998
www.courtinnovation.org

THOMAS FAROLE AND GOKHAN AKINCI
Special Economic Zones Progress, Emerging Challenges, and Future Directions
Washington D.C.: World Bank, 2011

KRISTIN FEIREISS
Architecture in Times of Need: Make It Right—Rebuilding New Orleans' Lower Ninth Ward
Prestel USA, New York: 2009

LUKAS FEIREISS
Testify! The Consequences of Architecture
NAi Publishers, Rotterdamn: 2011

DANIEL FISHER
The World's Best Companies. Finding Opportunities In Megacities Around The Globe
New York: Forbes, 2011

CHARLES FISHMAN
A Sea of Dollars
San Francisco: Fast Company, April 2011

RICHARD FLORIDA
The Rise of the Creative Class
Richard Florida, New York: Basic Books, 2002

FRIENDS OF THE HIGH LINE
www.thehighline.org

> **"It makes you feel hopeful. It's like going to a cathedral. [It] makes your spirit soar."**
>
> Martha Murphy, community member who helped build the DeLisle Community Center after Hurricane Katrina, pp. 116–17.

FRONTLINESMS \O/,
www.frontlinesms.com

MARI GALLAGHER RESEARCH & CONSULTING GROUP
Examining the Impact of Food Deserts on Public Health in Chicago
Chicago: 2006
www.marigallagher.com/projects/4/

GLOBAL TARGETS
Local Ingenuity
The Economist, September 2010

GOOD MAGAZINE
Fall Down Go Boom,
www.good.is/post/fall_down_go_boom/, 2008

GREYWATER ACTION
greywateraction.org

HABITAT FOR HUMANITY AND ARCHITECTURE FOR HUMANITY
Transitional to What? Open Architecture Network,
www.openarchitecturenetwork.org/projects/
transitional_to_what

KATHERINE HITE
Chile's National Stadium As Monument, As Memorial,
ReVista Harvard Review of Latin America, Spring 2004,
Cambridge: 2004.
www.drclas.harvard.edu/revista/articles/view/704

ROB HOPKINS
The Transition Handbook
London: Green Books

IMAGINE INSPIRATIONAL SCHOOL DESIGN
www.imagineschooldesign.org

JEFFREY INABA AND C-LAB
World of Giving
Baden, Switzerland: Lars Muller Publishers, 2010

INTERNATIONAL DARK-SKY ASSOCIATION
Practical Guides 1–3
www.darksky.org/resources

INTERNATIONAL FEDERATION OF RED CROSS AND RED CRESCENT SOCIETIES
World Disaster Report
www.ifrc.org/Global/Publications/disasters/WDR/
WDR2010-full.pdf, 2011

JANE JACOBS
The Death and Life of Great American Cities
New York: Modern Library Edition, 1993

MAGGIE KESWICK JENCKS
A View From The Front Line
Maggie Keswick and Charles Jencks
London: 1995
www.maggiescentres.org/about/our_publications.org

PROJECT: DELISLE COMMUNITY CENTER
When residents of DeLisle, Mississippi had nowhere to gather after Hurricane Katrina wrecked the Gulf Coast, SHoP Architects and students from Parsons Design Workshop built them a two-building community space (pictured) that was a pillar of hope for many people who lost their homes.
Photo: Ivan Chabra/Parsons Design Workshop

ABHAS K. JHA
Safer homes, Stronger Communities—A Handbook for Reconstructing after Natural Disasters
Washington D.C.: The World Bank, 2010

ANDRES LEPIK
Small Scale, Big Change: New Architectures of Social Engagement
New York, NY: Museum of Modern Art, 2010

LET'S DO IT! WORLD
Project "Let's Do It 2008",
http://openarchitecturenetwork.org/node/7659/oanattachments

STEVEN D. LEVITT AND STEPHEN J. DUBNER
Super Freakonomics—Global Cooling, Patriotic Prostitutes and Why Suicide Bombers Should Buy Life Insurance
New York: HarperCollins, 2009

HILARY LEWIS AND ROMÁN VIÑOLY
Think New York: A Ground Zero Diary
Victoria, Australia: Images Publishing, 2006

LIVING ON EARTH
Water Permeable Concrete
air date August 4, 2006
www.loe.org/shows/segments.html?programID=06-P13-00031&segmentID=1

LOUISIANA LEGISLATIVE AUDITOR
Alternative Housing Pilot Program: Katrina Cottages
Baton Rouge, Louisiana: March 4 2009

MAGGIE'S CANCER CARING CENTRES
Maggie's Architectural Brief
www.maggiescentres.org/maggies//maggiescentres/home/about/our_publications.html

CARA MCCARTY ET AL.
Why Design Now?:National Design Triennial
New York, NY: Cooper-Hewitt Museum, 2011

MELVIN L. OLIVER AND THOMAS M. SHAPIRO
Black Wealth/ White Wealth,
New York: Routledge, 1997

NEW YORK CITY DEPARTMENT OF TRANSPORTATION
Green Light For Midtown Evaluation Report
January 2010.
www.home2.nyc.gov/html/dot/downloads/pdf/broadway_report_final2010_web.pdf

NEW YORK CITY DOT
The New York City Street Design Manual
www.nyc.gov.html.about.streetdesignmanual.shtml

OPEN ARCHITECTURE NETWORK
http://openarchitecturenetwork.org

OPENSTREETMAP
www.openstreetmap.org

OXFAM
www.oxfam.org

POSTGREEN HOMES
http://postgreen.com/projects/100khouse

JAMES RUSSELL
Rebuilding After Katrina: Can New Orleans and the Gulf Coast Face the Hard Questions?
Architectural Record, June 2006

THE SCOTTISH GOVERNMENT
Hazelwood ASN School Case Study
www.scotland.gov.uk/Resource/Doc/920/0066326.pdf

DAN SENOR AND SAUL SINGER
Start-Up Nation
New York: Twelve, 2009

SECOND ANNUAL DISASTER HOUSING SUMMIT REPORT
Regional Catastrophic Planning Team, July 2011

SHE: SUSTAINABLE HEALTH ENTERPRISES
www.sheinnovates.com

SHELTER CENTER
Collective Center Guidelines
www.sheltercentre.org/library/collective-centre-guidelines-1

SMALL ARCHITECTURE, BIG LANDSCAPES
Terre Haute, IN: Sheldon Swope Art Museum, 2010

SMARTER LUNCHROOMS
www.smarterlunchrooms.org

THE SPHERE PROJECT
The Humanitarian Charter and Minimum Standards in Humanitarian Responses
Northampton: Belmont Press Ltd, 2011

LINA STERGIOU, ED.
AAO: Against All Odds Project
Greece: Papasotiriou Publishing, 2011

JOE STERNFELD
Walking The High Line
Steidl/Pace/McGill Gallery, New York: 2002

STUDIO GANG ARCHITECTS
Reveal
New York, NY: Princeton Architectural Press, 2011

SUPERUSE
Where Recycling Meets Design
http://superuse.org

SUSTAINABLE CITY DEVELOPMENT
Malmo Sweden
www.malmo.se/sustainablecity

ALEXANDER TARRANT
Evan Roth
Juxtapoz Art & Culture, October 10, 2010.

TEN THINGS YOU SHOULD KNOW ABOUT WATER
Traverse City, Michigan: Circle of Blue, July 2009
www.circleofblue.org/waternews/2009/world/infographic-ten-things-you-should-know-about-water

TREEHUGGER DESIGN AND ARCHITECTURE
www.treehugger.com/design_architecture

UN CONFERENCE ON TRADE AND DEVELOPMENT
Information Economy Report 2010
www.unctad.org/Templates/Page.asp?intItemID=3594&lang=1

UNITED NATIONS HUMAN SETTLEMENT PROGRAM (UN_HABITAT)
Cities In A Globalizing World
Malta: Guttenberg Press, 2001

UNITED STATES ENVIRONMENTAL PROTECTION AGENCY
Municipal Solid Waste in the United States 2007 Facts and Figures
www.epa.gov/osw/nonhaz/municipal/msw99.htm

US DEPARTMENT OF ENERGY SOLAR DECATHLON
www.solardecathlon.gov

US DEPARTMENT OF HEALTH AND HUMAN SERVICES
Kids Walk-to-School A Guide to Promote Walking to School
www.cdc.gov/nccdphp/dnpa/kidswalk/resources.htm

US GREEN BUILDING COUNCIL
www.usgbc.org

USHAHIDI
www.ushahidi.com

WHAT IF NEW YORK CITY...
www.whatifnyc.net

WORLD MAPPER
www.worldmapper.org

"This experience really taught us the importance of being humble and to respect the potential and value of local traditions and culture."

Andreas Gjertsen, architect of the *Soe Ker Tie Hias* (Butterfly Houses) project, pp. 80–83

PROJECT: TYIN TEGNESTUE
Refugee Karen children in Noh Bo, Thailand play cards in a butterfly house, a shelter with swings and play areas that was specially designed for their orphanage.
Photo: Pasi Aalto/TYIN Tegnestue

"The school is designed to enable every student to find their niche and be included."

Takaharu Tezuka, architect

PROJECT: FUJI KINDERGARTEN
Little girls play in Fuji Kindergarten, a doughnut-shaped school in Tokyo, Japan with a circular interior and roof deck. The creative design seeks to inspire uniqueness.
Photo: Katsuhisa Kida/Fototeca Ltd.

Contributors

Design is important to every aspect of our lives. It informs the places in which we live, work, learn, heal and gather. We engage all stakeholders in the design process. We believe our clients are designers in their own right. We thank all of the contributors who share this belief and made this book possible—especially our community of partners and clients.

Kate Stohr is the co-founder and managing director of Architecture for Humanity. She has been instrumental in coordinating design services and raising more than $15 million in capital for design-centered community development.

In her role at Architecture for Humanity she has led a number of the organization's community development and reconstruction programs including: Football for Hope, Hurricane Katrina Reconstruction Programs, 2010 Haiti Earthquake Reconstruction, Open Architecture Network, and the acquisition of Worldchanging.

Prior to joining Architecture for Humanity she was a journalist and producer. She is the recipient of *Wired* magazine's 2006 Rave Award for Architecture and was awarded the Royal Society of Arts Bicentenary Medal in 2009. She serves as an adviser to the Clinton Global Initiative.

Together with co-founder, Cameron Sinclair, she accepted the 2008 Cooper-Hewitt Smithsonian National Design Patron Award in honor of the work of Architecture for Humanity, its chapters, volunteers and design fellows.
Twitter @katestohr

Cameron Sinclair is the co-founder and Chief Eternal Optimist (CEO) of Architecture for Humanity, which builds architecture and design solutions to humanitarian crises, and provides pro-bono design and construction services to communities in need. Over the past 12 years, the organization has worked in 44 countries and has over 70 independent citywide chapters. Projects include schools, health clinics, affordable housing as well as long-term sustainable reconstruction, and community development.

As a strong believer in "cultural diplomacy," Sinclair has been working on a series of projects to rethink cultural and civic institutions within the social fabric.

He is a frequent teacher and visiting professor, and he holds an honorary doctorate from the University of Westminster. He is a recipient of the TED prize and a Young Global Leader of the World Economic Forum prize. In 2008, Sinclair and co-founder Kate Stohr received a National Design Award in honor of the work of Architecture for Humanity, its chapters, volunteers and design fellows. In 2011, he was made a Senior Fellow of the Design Futures Council and took an advisory role at USAID with a focus on reforming international aid.

Sinclair and Stohr launched the Open Architecture Network, the world's first open-source community dedicated to improving living conditions through innovative and sustainable design. In 2011, this network merged with Worldchanging to become a central destination for collaborative solutions to change the world.
Twitter @casinclair

Courtney Beyer hails from Los Altos Hills, California and received a BA in social anthropology with honors from the University of Michigan. At Architecture for Humanity she researched and wrote *Design Like You Give a Damn [2]* and assisted with the annual Curry Stone Design Prize competition. She is pursuing a career in human-centered design research and human factors. **Twitter @Csbeyer**

Nick Brown was born and raised in the hot suburban sprawl of Dallas, Texas before moving to Boston, and then San Francisco. A writer on *Design Like You Give a Damn [2]*, he holds a BA in architecture studies from Boston University and a master's of architecture from California College of the Arts. Brown's design interests center around urban housing, affordable housing and green architecture. He updates his blog regularly. **www.nickbrownarch.com/ strugglingarchitecture**

Satu Jackson, LEED AP, joined Architecture for Humanity in 2008. As a program manager, Jackson has overseen school construction programs in Hyderabad, India and Uganda, and curated the Open Architecture Challenge, the annual Curry Stone Design Prize and *Design Like You Give a Damn [2]*. Previously, Jackson worked for Gensler, Los Angeles as well as Access Consulting Pc, a structural engineering firm. Jackson holds a master's in architecture from Montana State University and is pursuing licensure as an architect. She served as a volunteer on the first edition of *Design Like You Give A Damn*. She is fluent in French, German and Spanish.

Jacqueline John is a freelance creative director residing in San Francisco. She has worked as a photo editor for *Bon Appétit* and *Sunset Magazine* and led creative and integrated marketing vision for multiple brands under the Williams-Sonoma umbrella. She studied photography at Santa Barbara's Brooks Institute and was the photo editor on *Design Like You Give a Damn [2]*.

Elizabeth Pfeffer is an independent journalist based in San Francisco who has covered topics ranging from prostitution and human trafficking to depleting social services in low-income communites for local and national publications. An experienced writer, editor and producer, she edited and copy edited *Design Like You Give a Damn [2]*. She has traveled extensively in Latin America and the Middle East. She studied journalism at San Francisco State University and would love to collaborate on another architecture or design project in the future. **Twitter @Liz_SF**

Pure+Applied designs and produces smart, visually-engaging, and accessible work. Rather than apply a style, we develop an approach based on the content and context of the material and by assessing the needs of our client. P+A is committed to working on projects that enrich communities, for example: contributing to the NYC DOT pedestrian plaza project Green Light for Midtown, designing the exhibitions: *Big & Green: Toward Sustainable Architecture in the 21st Century* and *Growing & Greening: PlaNYC and the Future of the City,* and the books: *Street Design Manual* (NYC DOT), *Urban Bikeway Design Guide* (NACTO) and—of course—*Design Like You Give a Damn* 1 & 2. Pure+Applied was founded by Paul Carlos and Urshula Barbour in January 2002, and owes inspiration and gratitude to many, especially Peter Cooper—A Mechanic of New York. **www.pureandapplied.com**

"This project has shown that the community is an important partner in development."

Neema Mgana,
African Regional Youth Initiative founder
Ipuli Rural Center for Excellence

PROJECT:
IPULI RURAL CENTER OF EXCELLENCE
Prior to construction of the medical
training center, women in this
rural community of Tanzania had no
access to maternal health care.
Photo: Cameron Sinclair/
Architecture for Humanity

"We try to channel the needs of the residents. We try to make a place within the constraints where we would like to live. The idea being that we're not too terribly different than other people."

David Baker,
David Baker + Partners Architects, architect of
Tassafaronga Village project, pp. 150–57

PROJECT: TASSAFARONGA VILLAGE
Habitat for Humanity volunteers
helped build Tassafaronga Village,
a LEED Platinum-certified housing
development in Oakland, California.
Photo: Andrew Goldsworthy

Additional Contributors:

Pasi Aalto, Laura Allen, Alissa Anderson, Elmer (Even) Atienza, Jocelyn Augustino, Emile Abinal, Sara Abu-Hejleh, Anthony Alvarez, Sarah Alvarez, Sinketh Arun, Luca Babini, Rhianon Bader, Rachel Bailey, Carrie Baptist, Kyle Barrett, Jane Beesley, Courtney Behan, Amanda Bensel, Ronny Bergstrom, Caitlin Beyer, Renee Bissell, Michael Bledsoe, Mark Boelter, Rebecca Book, Yasser Booley, Mallory Botsford, Jeffrey K. Bounds, Amber Bowen, Clarissa Brendler, Michael Bricker, Peter Brooks, Jim Brozek, Michael Christopher Brown, Nestor de Buen, Gabriela Bueno, Jennifer van den Bussche, Reese Campbell, Krista Canellakis, Elisabeth Carr, Ivan Chabra, Sarah Chan, Renee Charland, Billie Cohen, Elizabeth Cohn-Martin, Dale Conour, Nathaniel Corum, Jessica Cunningham, Marianne Cusato, Rowena Davis, Rebecca Dean, Arianna Deane, Pavitra Dholakia, Molly Dilworth, Bob Dinetz, Michelina Docimo, Celsa Dockstader, Bridget Dodd, Killian Doherty, Sally Dominguez, Meghan Dorrian, Eric Douville, Yes Duffy, Beth Eby, Jeremy Edmiston, Greg Elsner, Terry Erickson, Sara Faith Alterman, Tim Fallis, Kristina Farber, Sormeh Farhangazad, Elizabeth Felicelia, David Fujiwara, Guadian Gabriel, Jobelle Gacuya, Alejandra Galicia, Nicole Garcia, Kirk Gittings, Magen Gladden, Nadya Glawe, Weiland Gleich, Nadia Gobova, Juan Pablo Gomez, Roland Gonzalez, Kelly Gregory, Heidi Grothus, Steve Hall, Elora Hardy, John Hardy, Steve Harjula, Michele Hauser, Alec Hawley, Jared Heming, Andy Hill, Carlene Ho, Allard van der Hoek, Marnie Hogue, Kurt Hoerbst, Mike Innocenzi, Katie Irvin, Wil Jacobs, Matt Jaffe, Matthew Jelen, Karilyn Johanesen, Heather Johnson, Michael Jones, Thomas Jones, Lindsay Jonker, Eric K. Noji, Beth Kalin, Jeremy Karas, Vasilios Katsavrias, Imrul Kayes, Steve Kelley, John Kim, Susan Kim, Henry Kitchen, Julily Kohler, Eric Kostegan, Eric Krawczyk, Phil Kresge, Joel Kucer, Anisha Kumra, Gabrielle Kupfer, Seong Kwon, Becky Lam, Andrew Lee, Parker Lee, Susan Bok Yeong Lee, Rachel Levin, Debra Levin, David J. Lewis, Wenlin Li, Aaron Lim, Federica Lisa, Jonathan Lo, Kenneth Logan, Rafael Longoria, Michelle Luk, Belinda Luscombe, Andrew Ma, Rebecca Macklis, Stephanie Mar, Ben Marks, Zsofia Marton, Melody Mason, Reiko Matsuo, Sarah McAleer, Vikky McArthur, Jim McCluskey, Scott McDonald, Erinn McGurn, Shelia McKinnon, Kara Medow, Nicole Melas, Unathi Mkonto, Anne Moon, Jonathan Morrow, Sumita Mukherjee, Ana Munoz, Freeman Murray, Joseph Mutongu, Sandhya Naidu Janardhan, Cariddi Narduli, Federico Negro, Heidi Nelson, Michelle Nelson, Nicholas Nelson, Kimberly Newcomer, Iheanyi Ngumez, Sam Oberter, Kelsey Ochs, Alix Ogilivie, Katie Okamoto, Haelim Paek, Michael Paganetti, Joesph Patrick Parimucha, Shamoon Patwari, Michael Pawlyn, David Perkes, Stephanie Peterka, Abby Peterson, Brian Phillips, Stacey Phillips, Hannah Poole, Allison Price, Prithula Prosun, Maria Prudlow, Alex Quinto, Marina Ravicini, Dafyd Rawlings, Darren Ray, Edward Reed, Erin Reichert, Michael Richey, Rob Riethmiller, Jeronimo Roldan, Jacqueline Rossiter, Sarah Rowden, Taylor Royle, Wendy Ruiz, John Russell, Roohi Saeed, Loree Sandler, Eduardo Sauce, Kat Sawyer, Jessica Scanlon, Andreas "Schutzi" Schutzenberger, Barry Schwartz, Leslie Schwartz, Top Seangsong, Matt Severson, Rupal Shah, Masoomeh Sharifi Soofiani, Jake Simkin, Kevin Short, David Smolker, Jason Spellings, Angela Starita, Anders Steinvall, Margaret Gould Stewart, Kay Strasser, Anke Stubner, Cynthia Su, Sagarika Sundaram, Zac Taylor, Bounty Te, Laura Tepper, Erin Terry, Carolyn Thomas, Maria Toner, Jessie Towell, Beau Trincia, Ati Tsai, Y. Tsai, Wyanne Tsang, Mackenzie Tucker, Greg Upwall, Tiina Urm, Karen Vanderbilt, Robert Verrijt, Karen Wang, Mark Warren, Molly Watson, Christine Welland, Nori Whisenand, Carin Whitney, Nyoman Widiantara, Jeff Williams, Jessica Williams, Maria Williford, Carrie Wisler, Sarah Wong, Bo Wongkalasin, Asia Wright, Georgia Wright, Yasuhito Yokobori, Tansu Yucel Bozdogan, Stephanie Yung, Adi Zuckerman

> "I love cooking and now I have a kitchen to actually cook in. I make cakes and tortillas to sell in the market on the weekend."

Rosenda Flores, recipient of a sustainable home from the Diez Casas para Diez Familias project, pp. 70–71

PROJECT: DIEZ CASAS PARA DIEZ FAMILIAS
Rosenda Flores and granddaughter stand in the kitchen of her new home, which is mostly made of recycled materials.
Photo: Pedro Pacheco

Acknowledgments

Kate Stohr and Cameron Sinclair

We wish to offer our sincere and heartfelt thanks to all those who graciously contributed to this book. In particular, we would like to thank the National Endowment for the Arts for its support and Architecture for Humanity's own Community Builders, without whose generosity this publication would not have been possible.

To the many contributors and photographers who documented these works, we're inspired and indebted to you in equal measure. We thank you for taking the time to share your knowledge and your dedication—and to answer all those emails we sent your way.

This book was truly a collaboration. Many people lent their time and their talents to the effort. To our team of book researchers, designers, editors and volunteers, thank you. We'd especially like to thank Courtney Beyer, Nick Brown, Satu Jackson, Jacqueline John and Elizabeth Pfeffer. This truly is "the closest to done we've ever been."

We'd also like to thank our friends at Pure+Applied who designed another beautiful book. Thank you for letting us invade yet again. Thanks also to the team at Abrams for their support. We look forward to many more publications together. Finally, we'd like to thank the staff of Architecture for Humanity, whose work each day—no matter the time zone—exemplifies the power of design to build change from the ground up. This book is dedicated to our clients: the passionate, the dogged and determined, the openhearted and the survivors.

We apologize for any errors we may have committed, whether of omission or commission. They were unintentional. We did our best to provide accurate attributions for each project based on the information made available to us. We have also made every attempt to identify accurately the sources and authors of all renderings, sketches and photographs. We recognize that these projects are the result of the dedicated work of many and apologize if we have not given credit where credit is due.

Our aim was to incorporate a broad array of projects from diverse regions, but there are many equally deserving projects we did not have room to include. And, there are no doubt hundreds more that we have yet to discover. We invite you to share them with us.